IT'S A DOG'S LIFE, SNOOPY

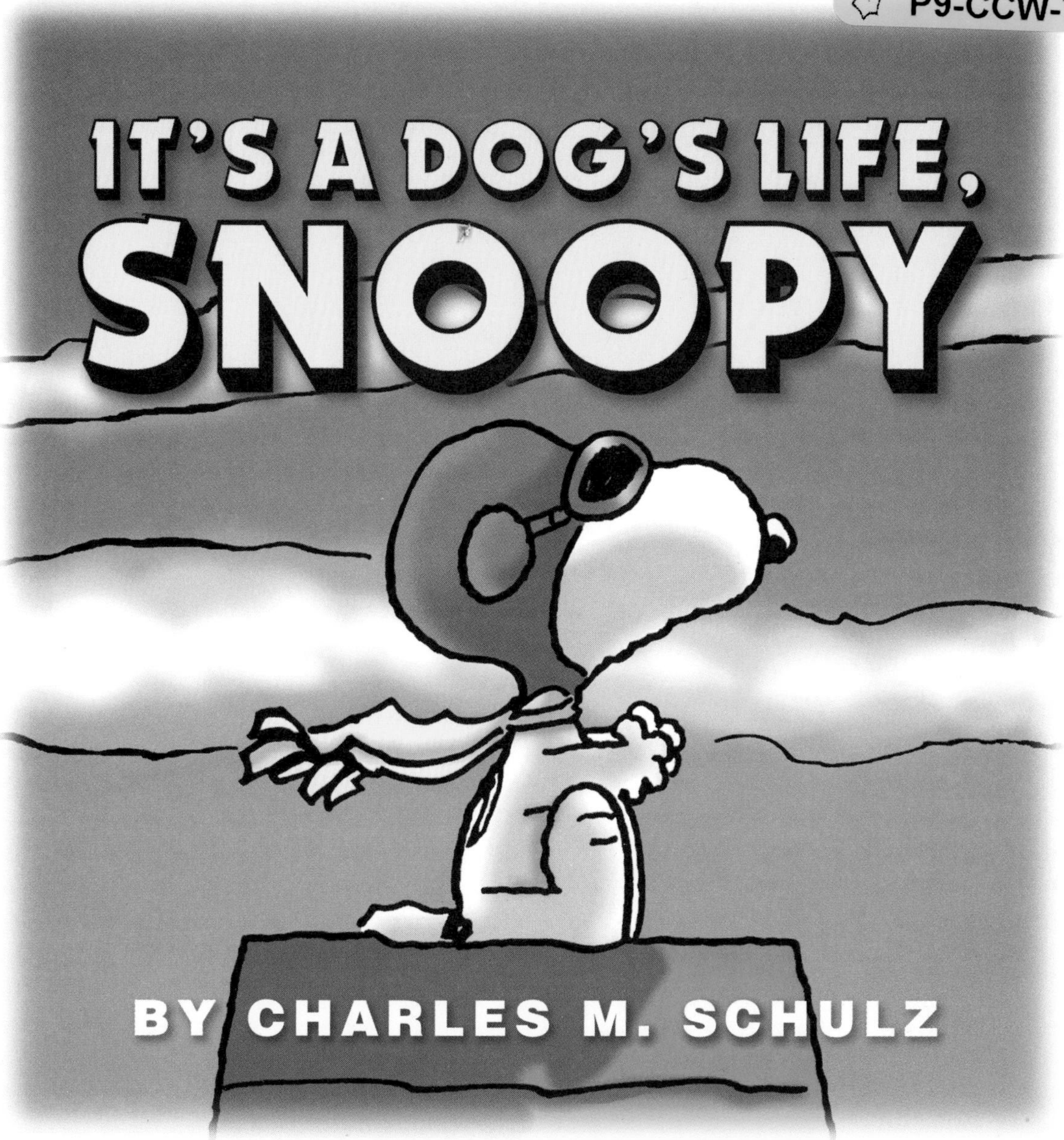

BY CHARLES M. SCHULZ

Ballantine Books * New York

A Ballantine Book
Published by The Ballantine Publishing Group
 Published in the United States by The Ballantine Publishing Group, a division of Random House, Inc., New York, and simultaneously in Canada by Random House of Canada Limited, Toronto. The comic strips in this book were originally published in newspapers worldwide.

Ballantine and colophon are registered trademarks of Random House, Inc.

www.randomhouse.com/BB/
www.snoopy.com

Library of Congress Catalog Card Number: 00-109178

Cover design by Paige Braddock, Charles M. Schulz Creative Associates

ISBN 0-345-44269-5

Manufactured in the United States of America

First Edition: April 2001

10 9 8 7 6 5 4 3

It's a Dog's Life,
SNOOPY

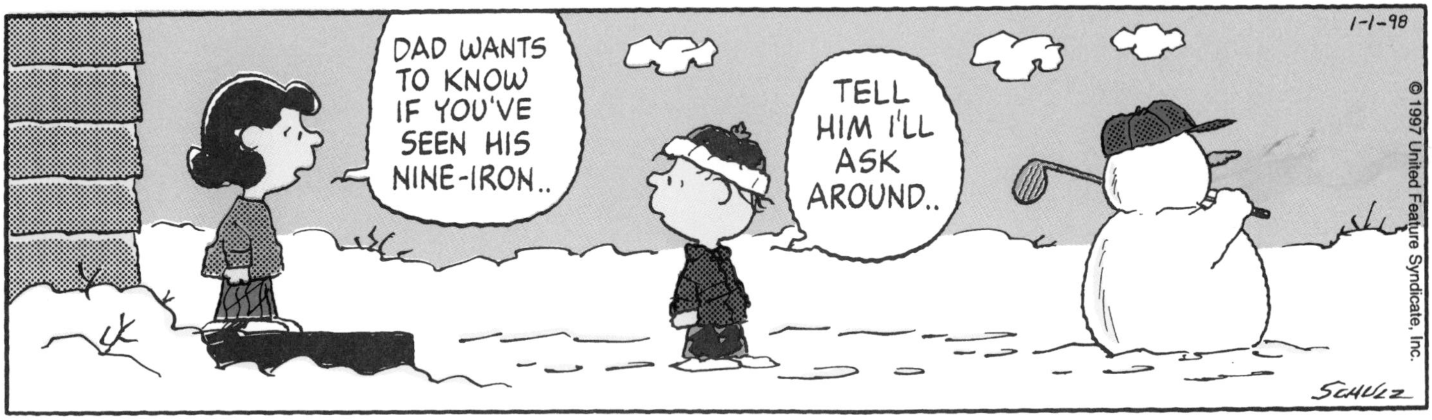
1-1-98
DAD WANTS TO KNOW IF YOU'VE SEEN HIS NINE-IRON..
TELL HIM I'LL ASK AROUND..
© 1997 United Feature Syndicate, Inc.
SCHULZ

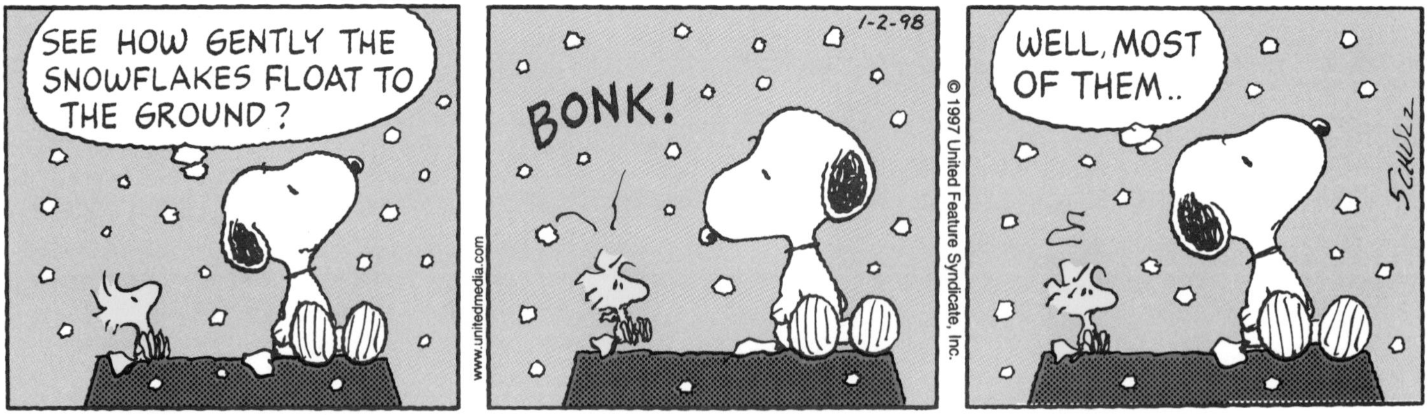
SEE HOW GENTLY THE SNOWFLAKES FLOAT TO THE GROUND?
www.unitedmedia.com
1-2-98
BONK!
© 1997 United Feature Syndicate, Inc.
WELL, MOST OF THEM..
SCHULZ

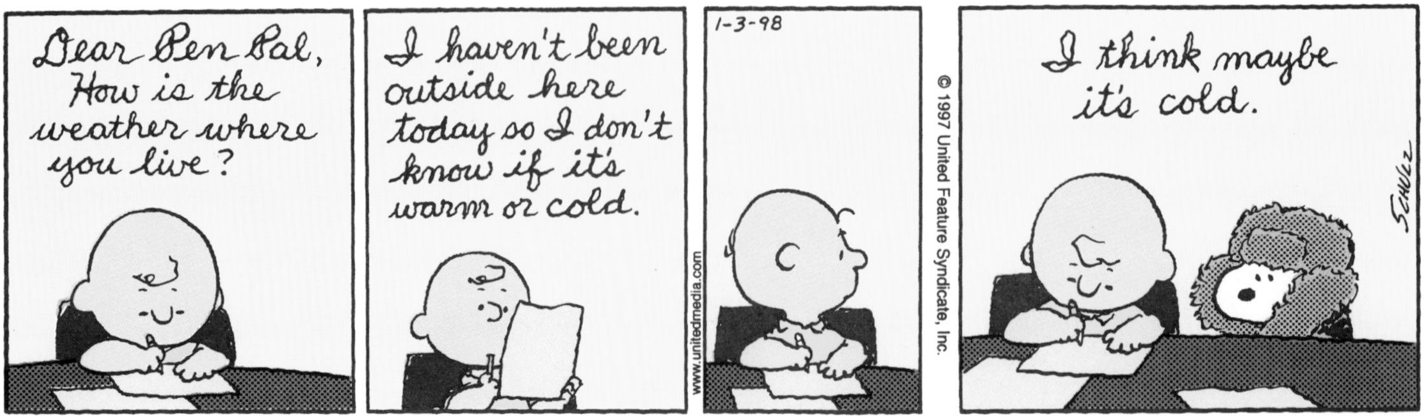
Dear Pen Pal,
How is the weather where you live?
I haven't been outside here today so I don't know if it's warm or cold.
www.unitedmedia.com
1-3-98
© 1997 United Feature Syndicate, Inc.
I think maybe it's cold.
SCHULZ

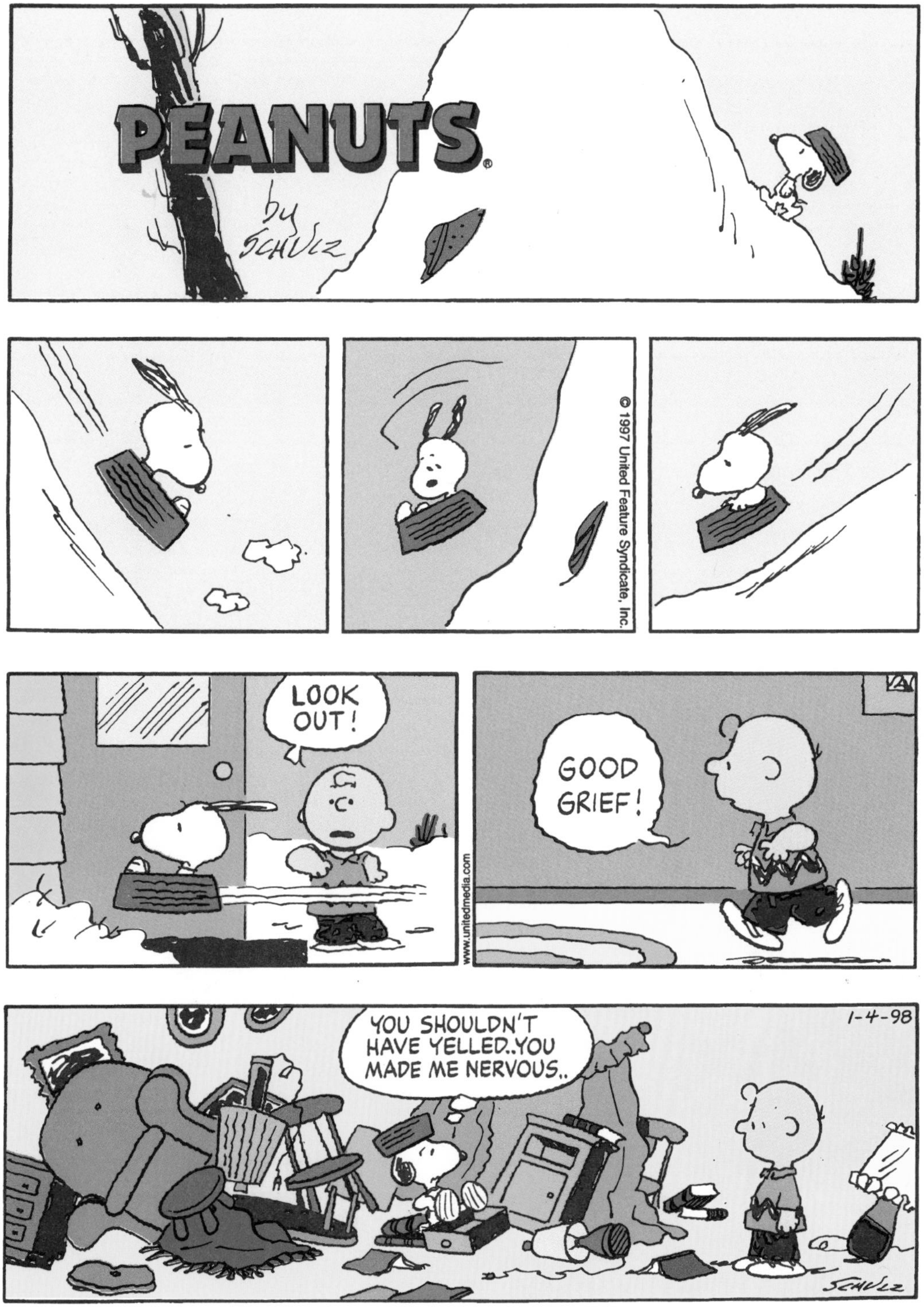
PEANUTS®
by SCHULZ
© 1997 United Feature Syndicate, Inc.
LOOK OUT!
www.unitedmedia.com
GOOD GRIEF!
1-4-98
YOU SHOULDN'T HAVE YELLED..YOU MADE ME NERVOUS..
SCHULZ

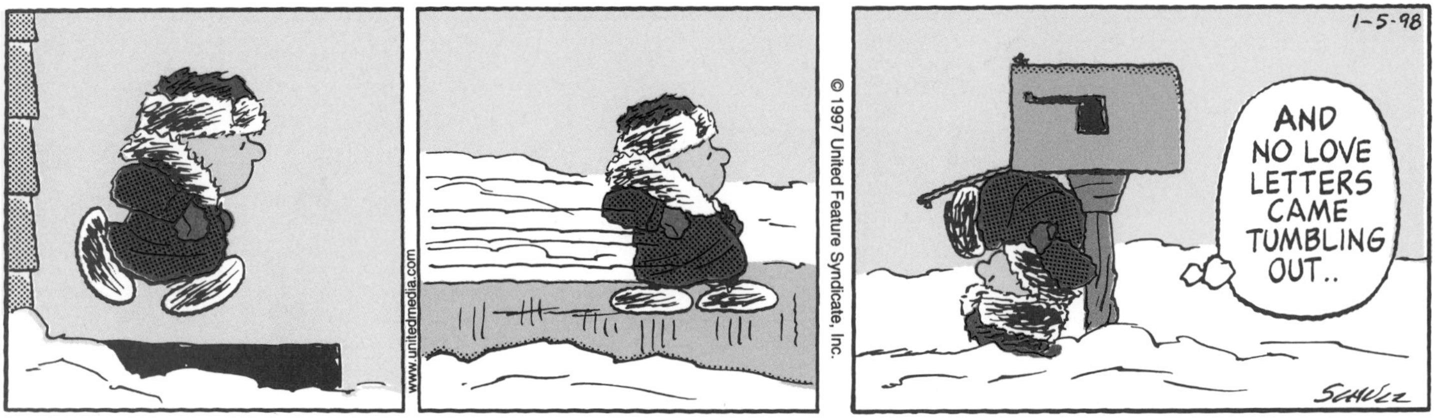
www.unitedmedia.com
© 1997 United Feature Syndicate, Inc.
1-5-98
AND NO LOVE LETTERS CAME TUMBLING OUT..
SCHULZ

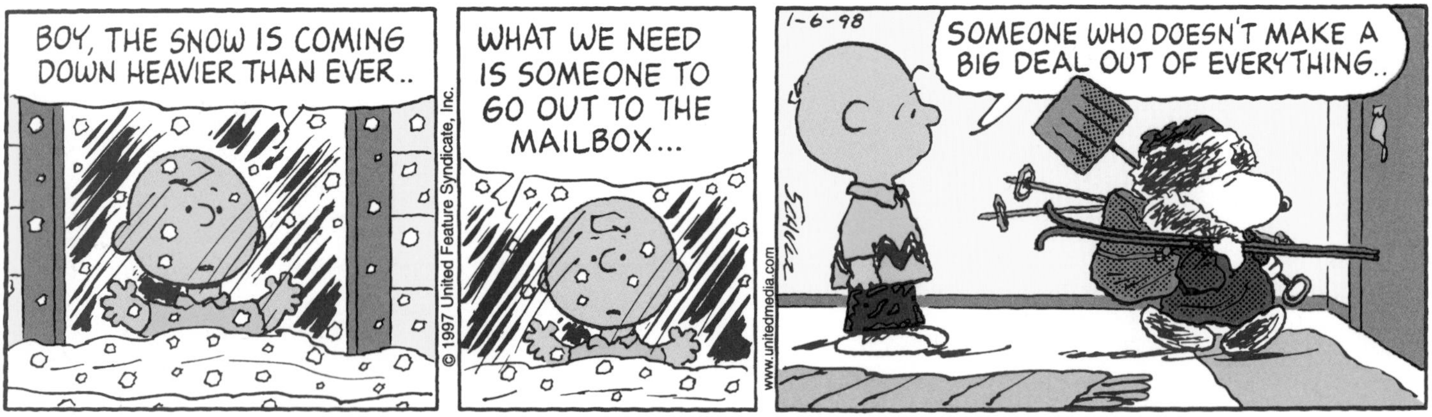
BOY, THE SNOW IS COMING DOWN HEAVIER THAN EVER..
© 1997 United Feature Syndicate, Inc.
WHAT WE NEED IS SOMEONE TO GO OUT TO THE MAILBOX...
www.unitedmedia.com
1-6-98
SCHULZ
SOMEONE WHO DOESN'T MAKE A BIG DEAL OUT OF EVERYTHING..

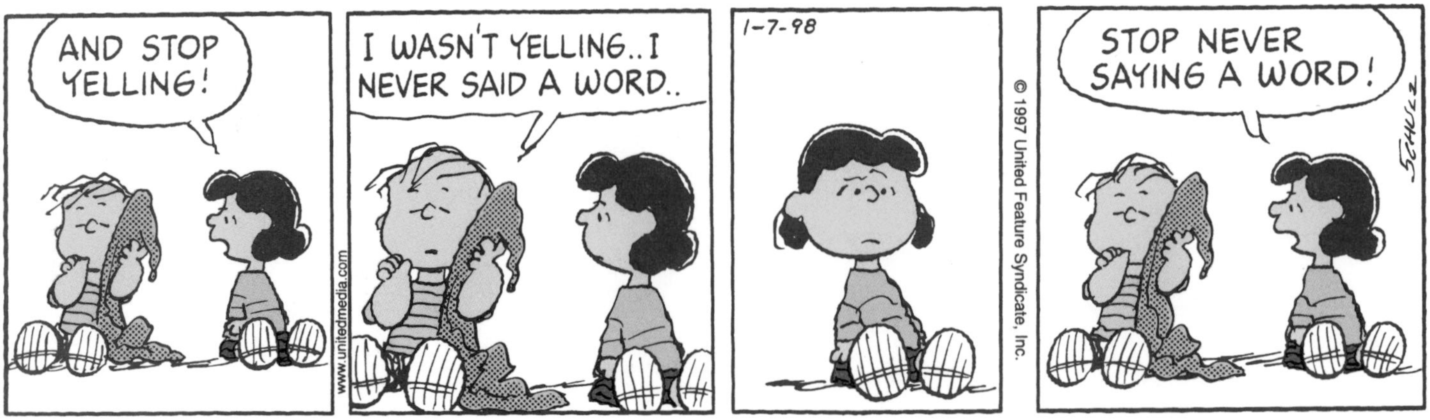
AND STOP YELLING!
www.unitedmedia.com
I WASN'T YELLING..I NEVER SAID A WORD..
1-7-98
© 1997 United Feature Syndicate, Inc.
STOP NEVER SAYING A WORD!
SCHULZ

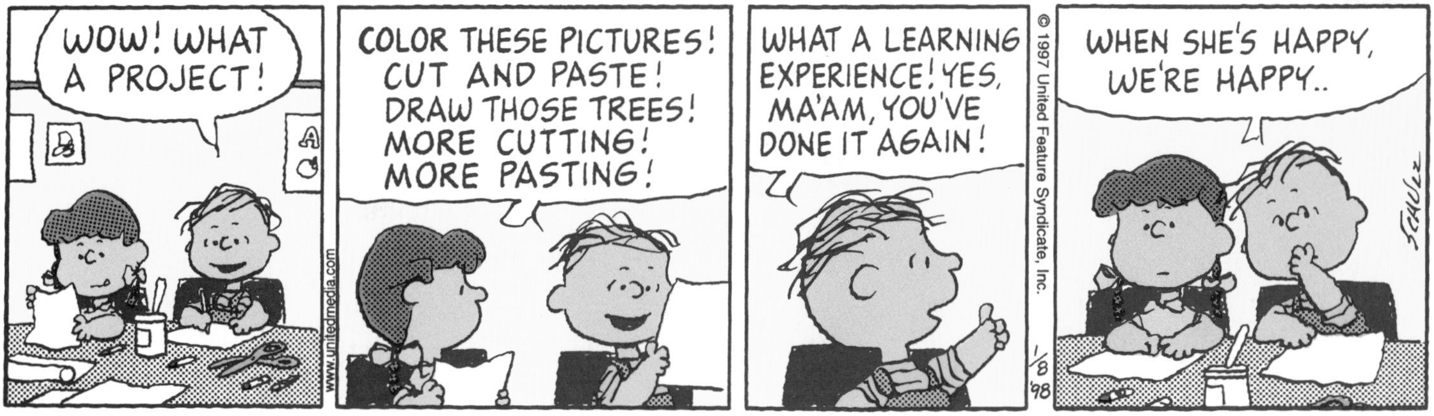
WOW! WHAT A PROJECT!
COLOR THESE PICTURES! CUT AND PASTE! DRAW THOSE TREES! MORE CUTTING! MORE PASTING!
WHAT A LEARNING EXPERIENCE! YES, MA'AM, YOU'VE DONE IT AGAIN!
WHEN SHE'S HAPPY, WE'RE HAPPY..
www.unitedmedia.com
© 1997 United Feature Syndicate, Inc.
1/8/98
SCHULZ

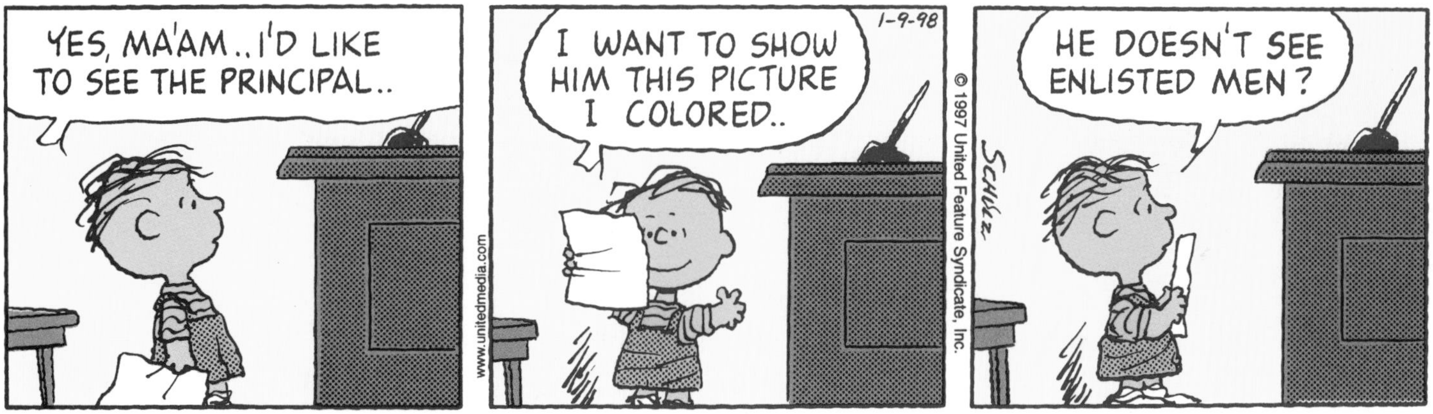
YES, MA'AM.. I'D LIKE TO SEE THE PRINCIPAL..
I WANT TO SHOW HIM THIS PICTURE I COLORED..
HE DOESN'T SEE ENLISTED MEN?
1-9-98
www.unitedmedia.com
© 1997 United Feature Syndicate, Inc.
SCHULZ

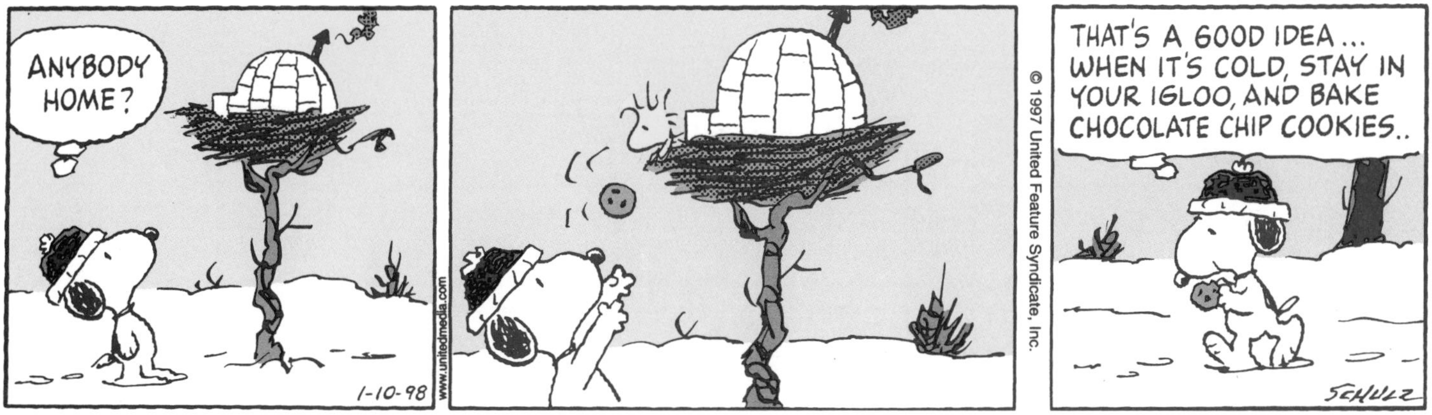
ANYBODY HOME?
THAT'S A GOOD IDEA ... WHEN IT'S COLD, STAY IN YOUR IGLOO, AND BAKE CHOCOLATE CHIP COOKIES..
1-10-98
www.unitedmedia.com
© 1997 United Feature Syndicate, Inc.
SCHULZ

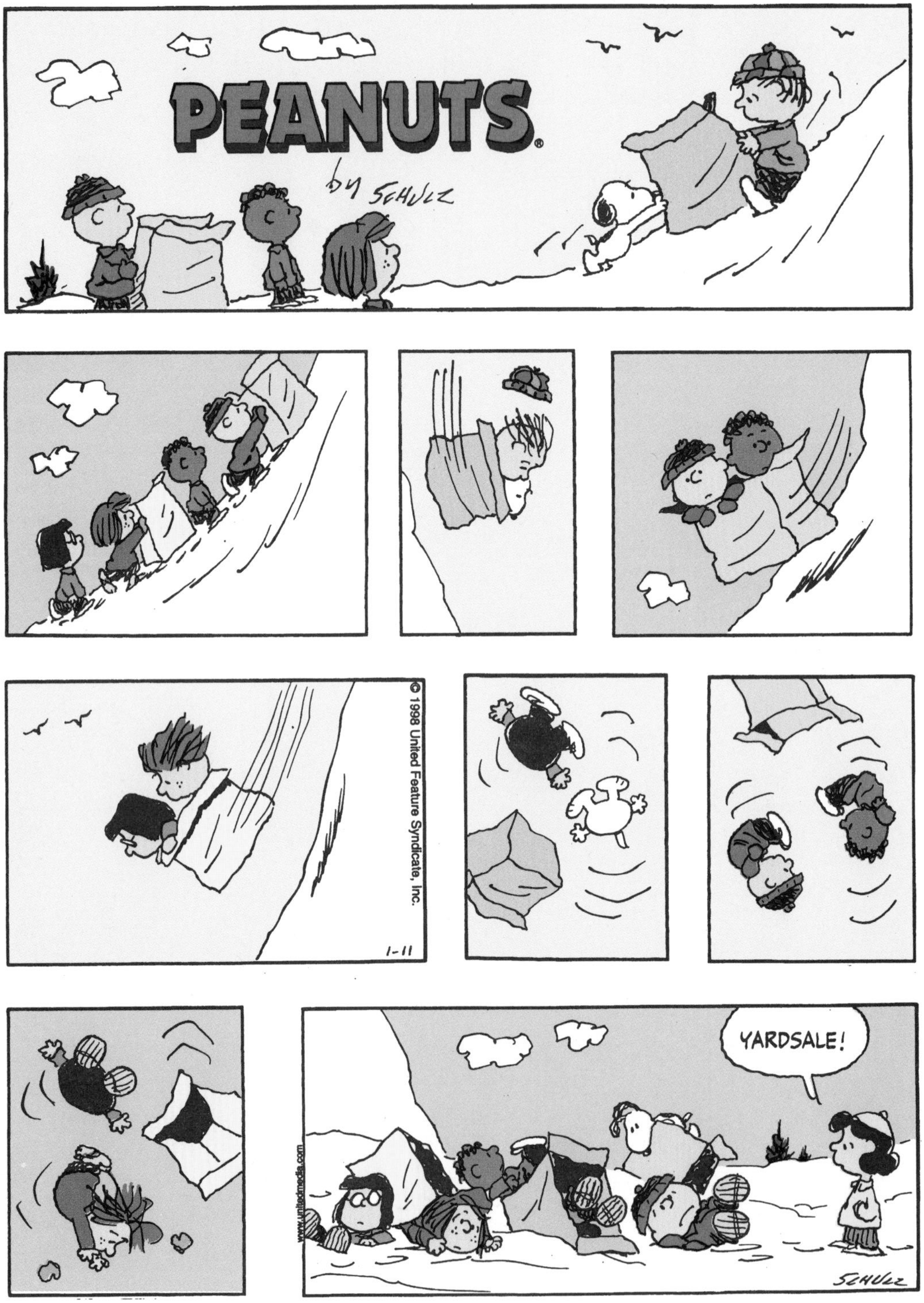
PEANUTS
by SCHULZ
© 1998 United Feature Syndicate, Inc.
1-11
www.unitedmedia.com
YARDSALE!
SCHULZ

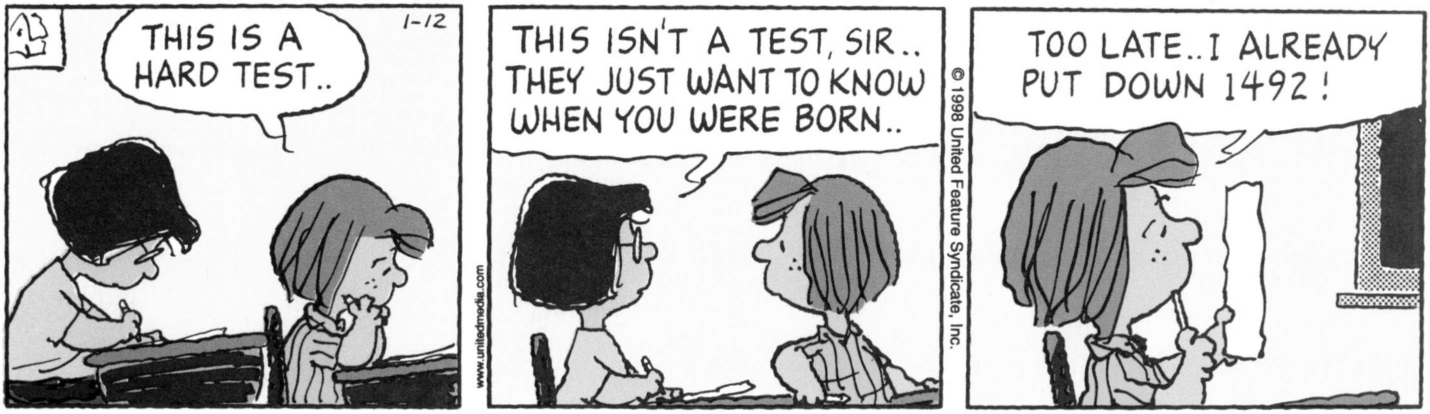
1-12
THIS IS A HARD TEST..
THIS ISN'T A TEST, SIR.. THEY JUST WANT TO KNOW WHEN YOU WERE BORN..
TOO LATE.. I ALREADY PUT DOWN 1492!
www.unitedmedia.com
© 1998 United Feature Syndicate, Inc.

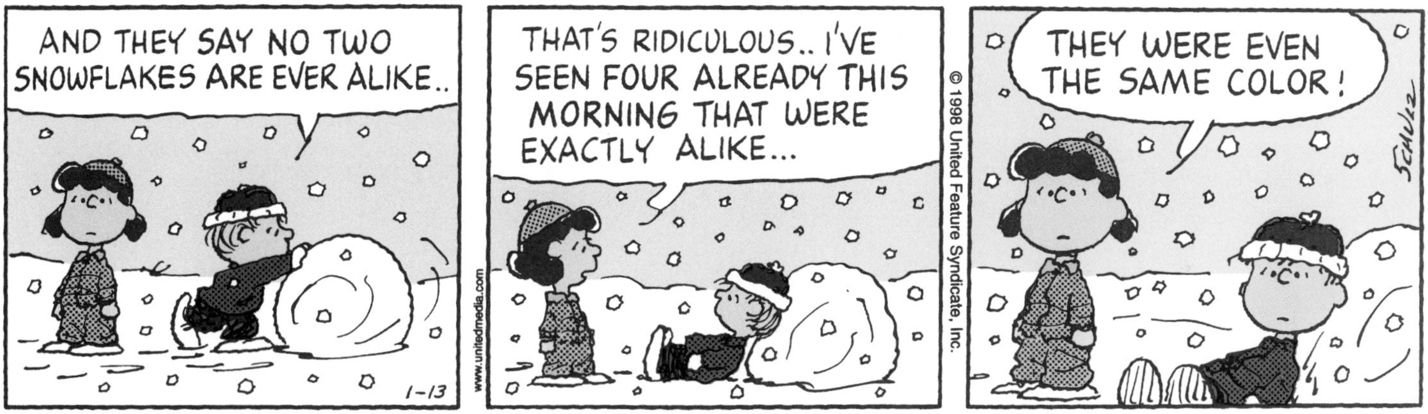
AND THEY SAY NO TWO SNOWFLAKES ARE EVER ALIKE..
1-13
THAT'S RIDICULOUS.. I'VE SEEN FOUR ALREADY THIS MORNING THAT WERE EXACTLY ALIKE...
THEY WERE EVEN THE SAME COLOR!
SCHULZ
www.unitedmedia.com
© 1998 United Feature Syndicate, Inc.

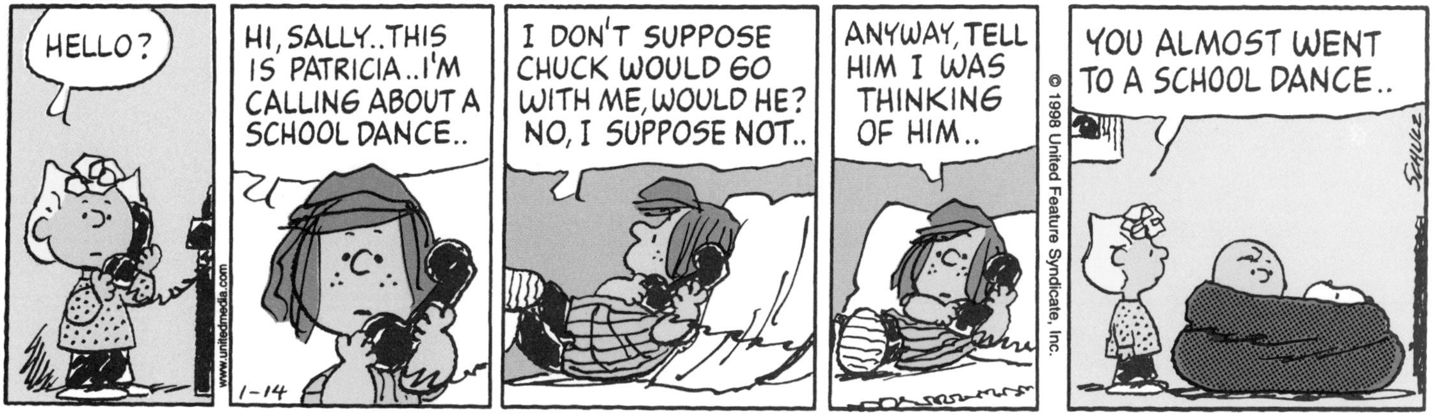
HELLO?
HI, SALLY.. THIS IS PATRICIA.. I'M CALLING ABOUT A SCHOOL DANCE..
1-14
I DON'T SUPPOSE CHUCK WOULD GO WITH ME, WOULD HE? NO, I SUPPOSE NOT..
ANYWAY, TELL HIM I WAS THINKING OF HIM..
YOU ALMOST WENT TO A SCHOOL DANCE..
SCHULZ
www.unitedmedia.com
© 1998 United Feature Syndicate, Inc.

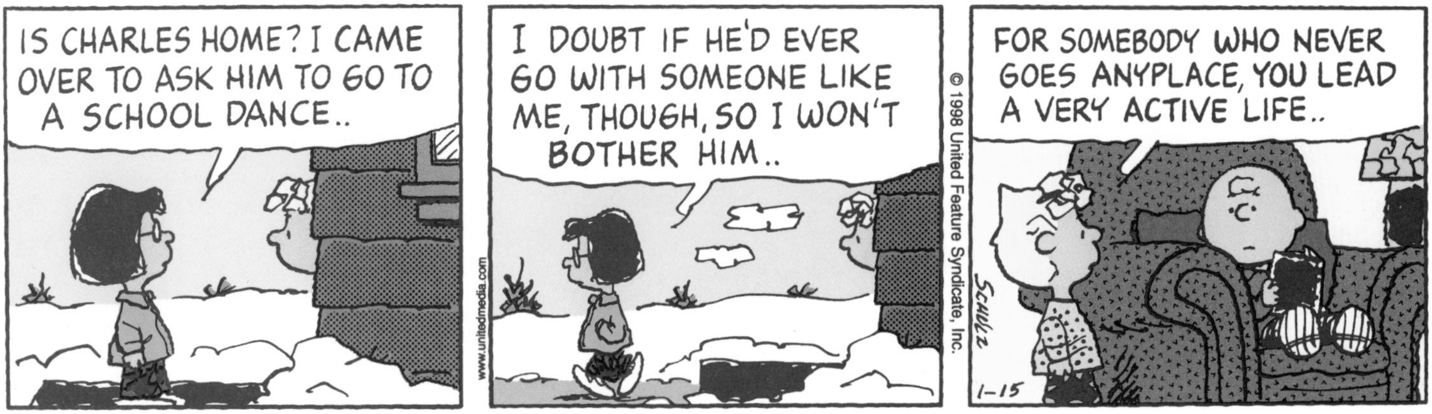
IS CHARLES HOME? I CAME OVER TO ASK HIM TO GO TO A SCHOOL DANCE..
www.unitedmedia.com
I DOUBT IF HE'D EVER GO WITH SOMEONE LIKE ME, THOUGH, SO I WON'T BOTHER HIM..
© 1998 United Feature Syndicate, Inc.
FOR SOMEBODY WHO NEVER GOES ANYPLACE, YOU LEAD A VERY ACTIVE LIFE..
SCHULZ
1-15

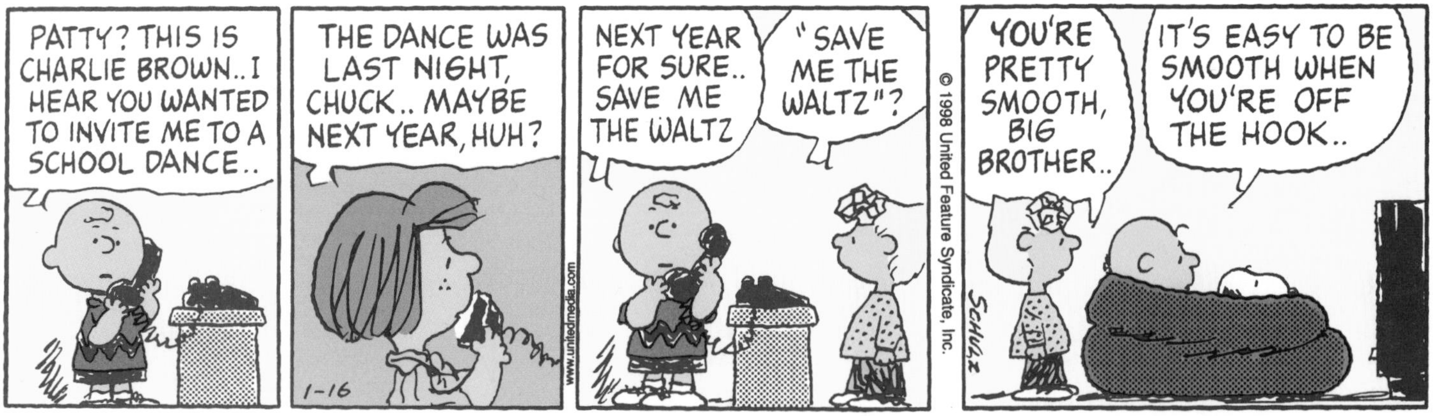
PATTY? THIS IS CHARLIE BROWN.. I HEAR YOU WANTED TO INVITE ME TO A SCHOOL DANCE..
THE DANCE WAS LAST NIGHT, CHUCK.. MAYBE NEXT YEAR, HUH?
1-16
www.unitedmedia.com
NEXT YEAR FOR SURE.. SAVE ME THE WALTZ
"SAVE ME THE WALTZ"?
© 1998 United Feature Syndicate, Inc.
YOU'RE PRETTY SMOOTH, BIG BROTHER..
IT'S EASY TO BE SMOOTH WHEN YOU'RE OFF THE HOOK..
SCHULZ

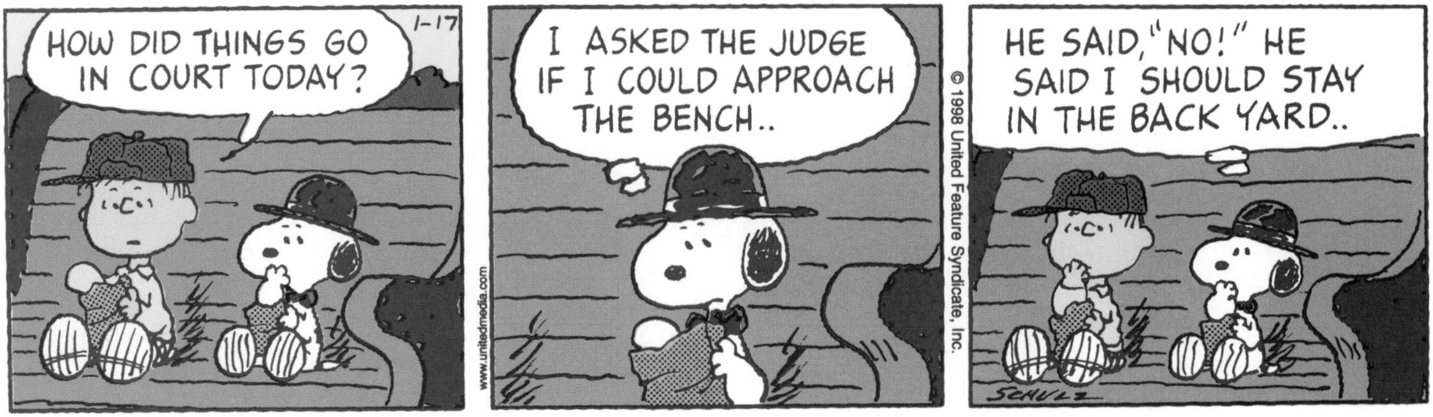
HOW DID THINGS GO IN COURT TODAY?
1-17
www.unitedmedia.com
I ASKED THE JUDGE IF I COULD APPROACH THE BENCH..
© 1998 United Feature Syndicate, Inc.
HE SAID, "NO!" HE SAID I SHOULD STAY IN THE BACK YARD..
SCHULZ

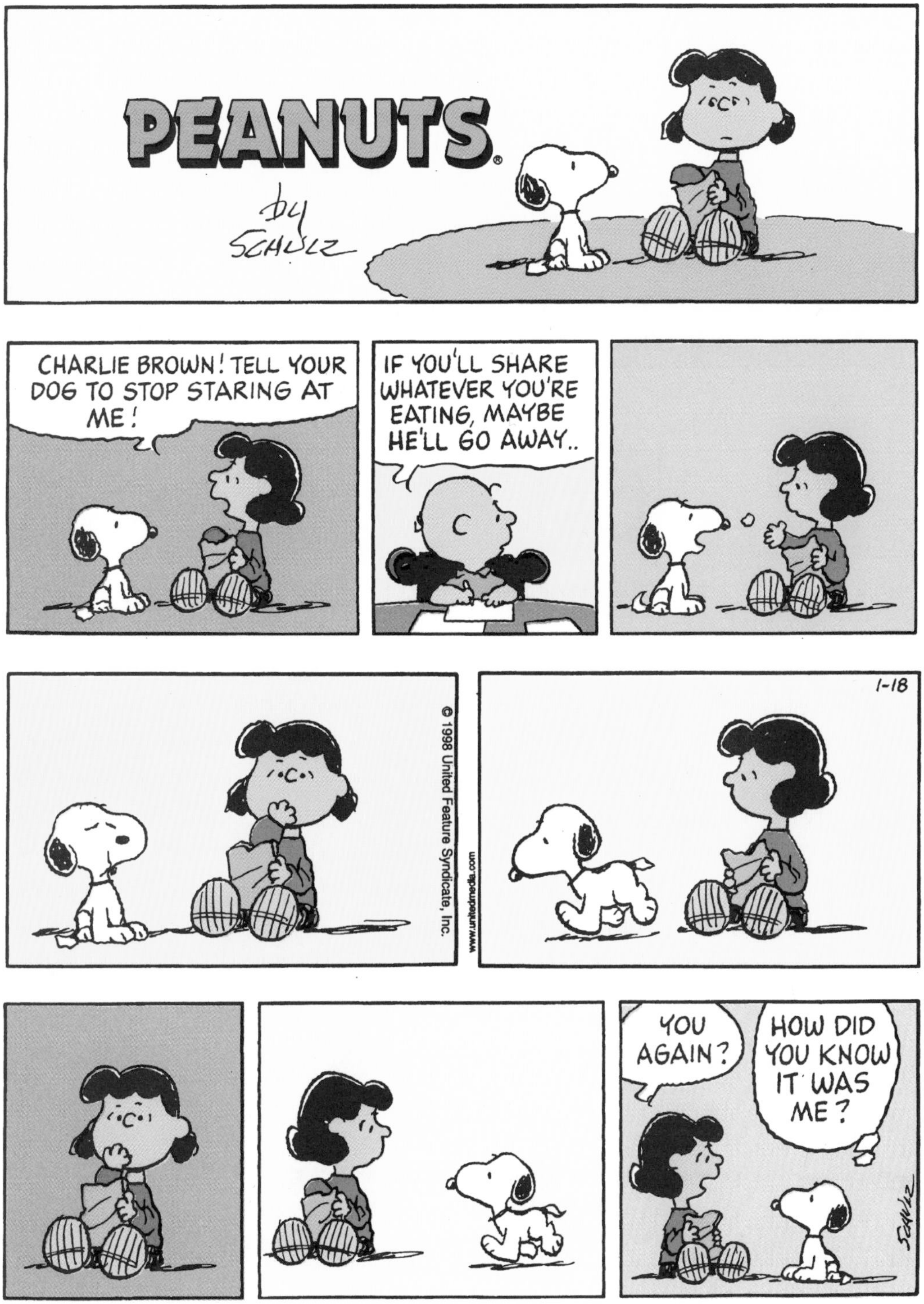
PEANUTS®
by SCHULZ
CHARLIE BROWN! TELL YOUR DOG TO STOP STARING AT ME!
IF YOU'LL SHARE WHATEVER YOU'RE EATING, MAYBE HE'LL GO AWAY..
© 1998 United Feature Syndicate, Inc.
www.unitedmedia.com
1-18
YOU AGAIN?
HOW DID YOU KNOW IT WAS ME?
SCHULZ

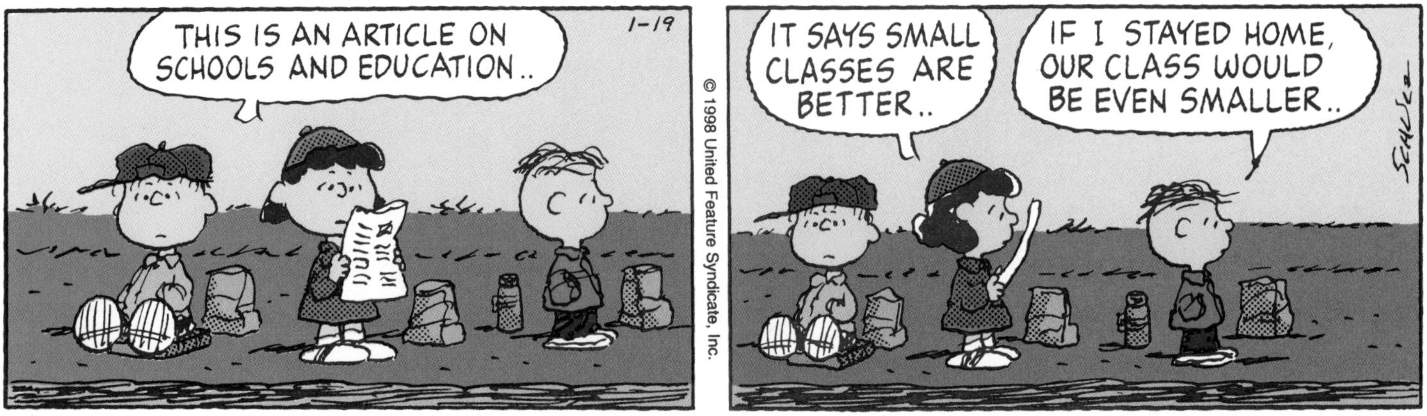
1-19
THIS IS AN ARTICLE ON SCHOOLS AND EDUCATION..
IT SAYS SMALL CLASSES ARE BETTER..
IF I STAYED HOME, OUR CLASS WOULD BE EVEN SMALLER..
SCHULZ
© 1998 United Feature Syndicate, Inc.

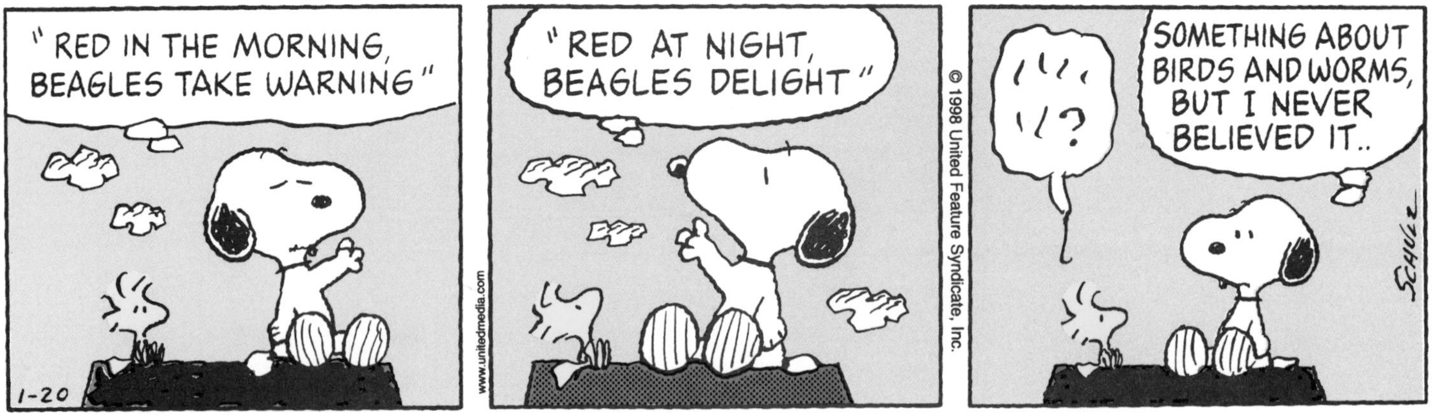
"RED IN THE MORNING, BEAGLES TAKE WARNING"
1-20
"RED AT NIGHT, BEAGLES DELIGHT"
?
SOMETHING ABOUT BIRDS AND WORMS, BUT I NEVER BELIEVED IT..
SCHULZ
www.unitedmedia.com
© 1998 United Feature Syndicate, Inc.

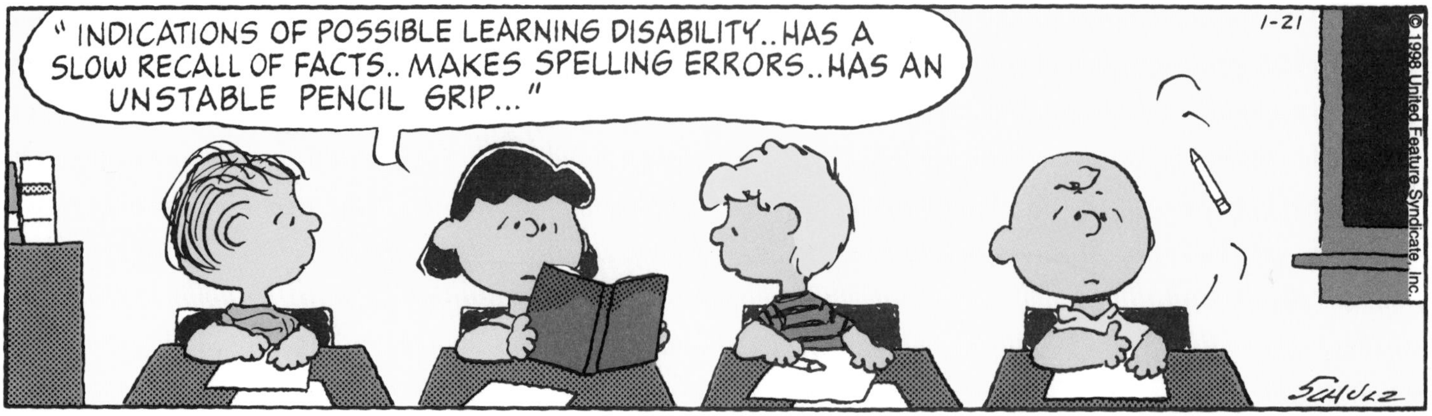
"INDICATIONS OF POSSIBLE LEARNING DISABILITY..HAS A SLOW RECALL OF FACTS..MAKES SPELLING ERRORS..HAS AN UNSTABLE PENCIL GRIP..."
1-21
SCHULZ
© 1998 United Feature Syndicate, Inc.

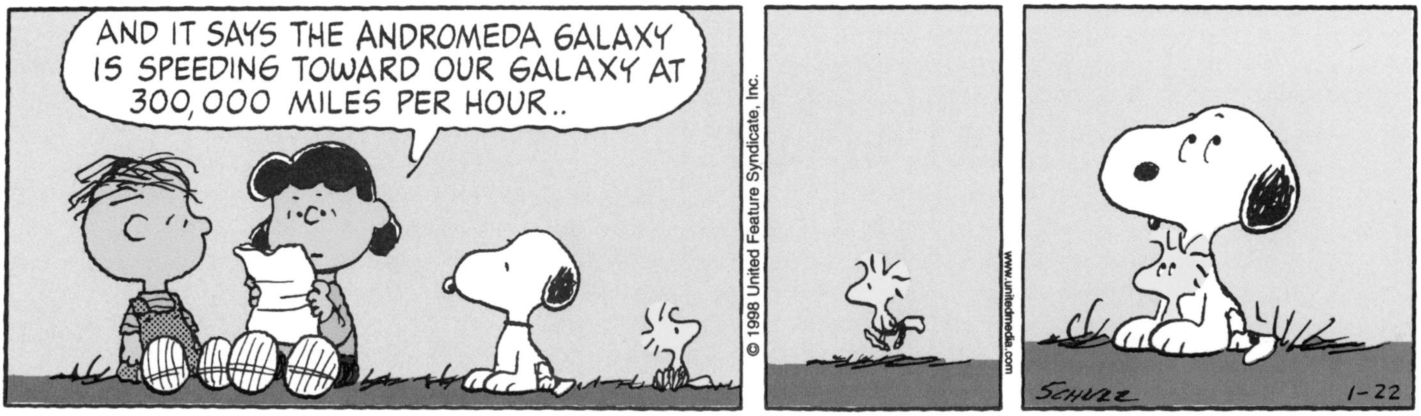
AND IT SAYS THE ANDROMEDA GALAXY IS SPEEDING TOWARD OUR GALAXY AT 300,000 MILES PER HOUR..
© 1998 United Feature Syndicate, Inc.
www.unitedmedia.com
SCHULZ
1-22

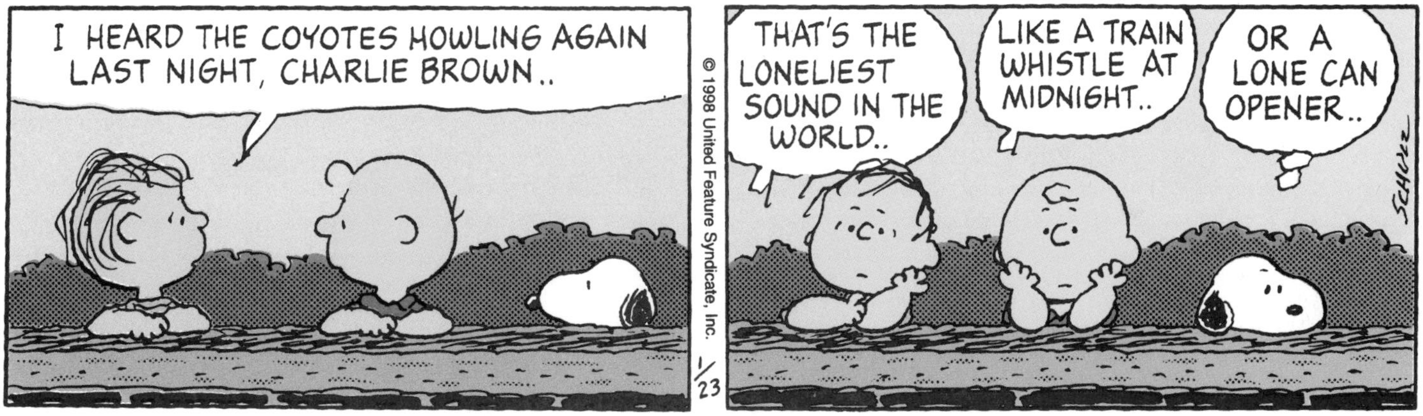
I HEARD THE COYOTES HOWLING AGAIN LAST NIGHT, CHARLIE BROWN..
© 1998 United Feature Syndicate, Inc.
1/23
THAT'S THE LONELIEST SOUND IN THE WORLD..
LIKE A TRAIN WHISTLE AT MIDNIGHT..
OR A LONE CAN OPENER..
SCHULZ

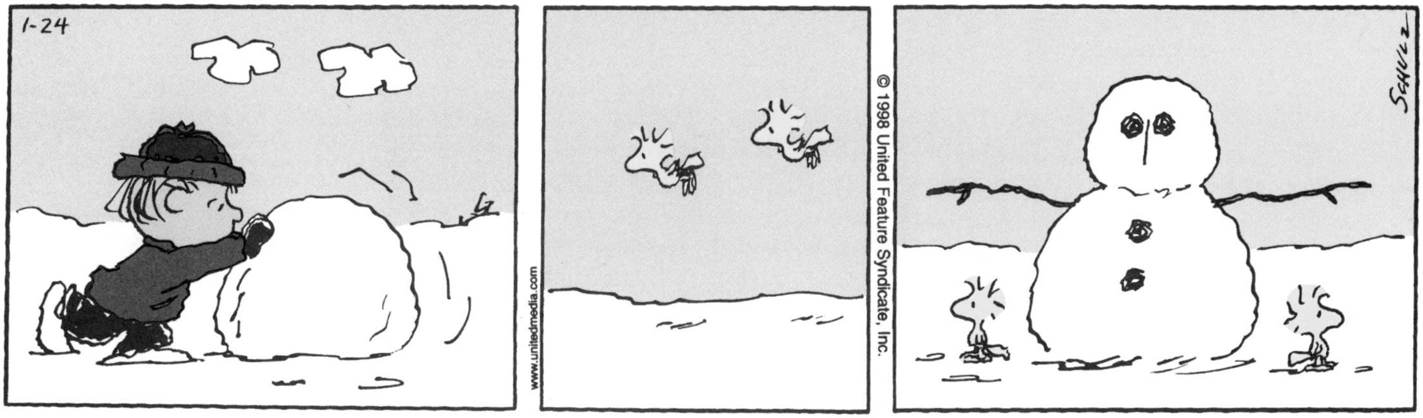
1-24
www.unitedmedia.com
© 1998 United Feature Syndicate, Inc.
SCHULZ

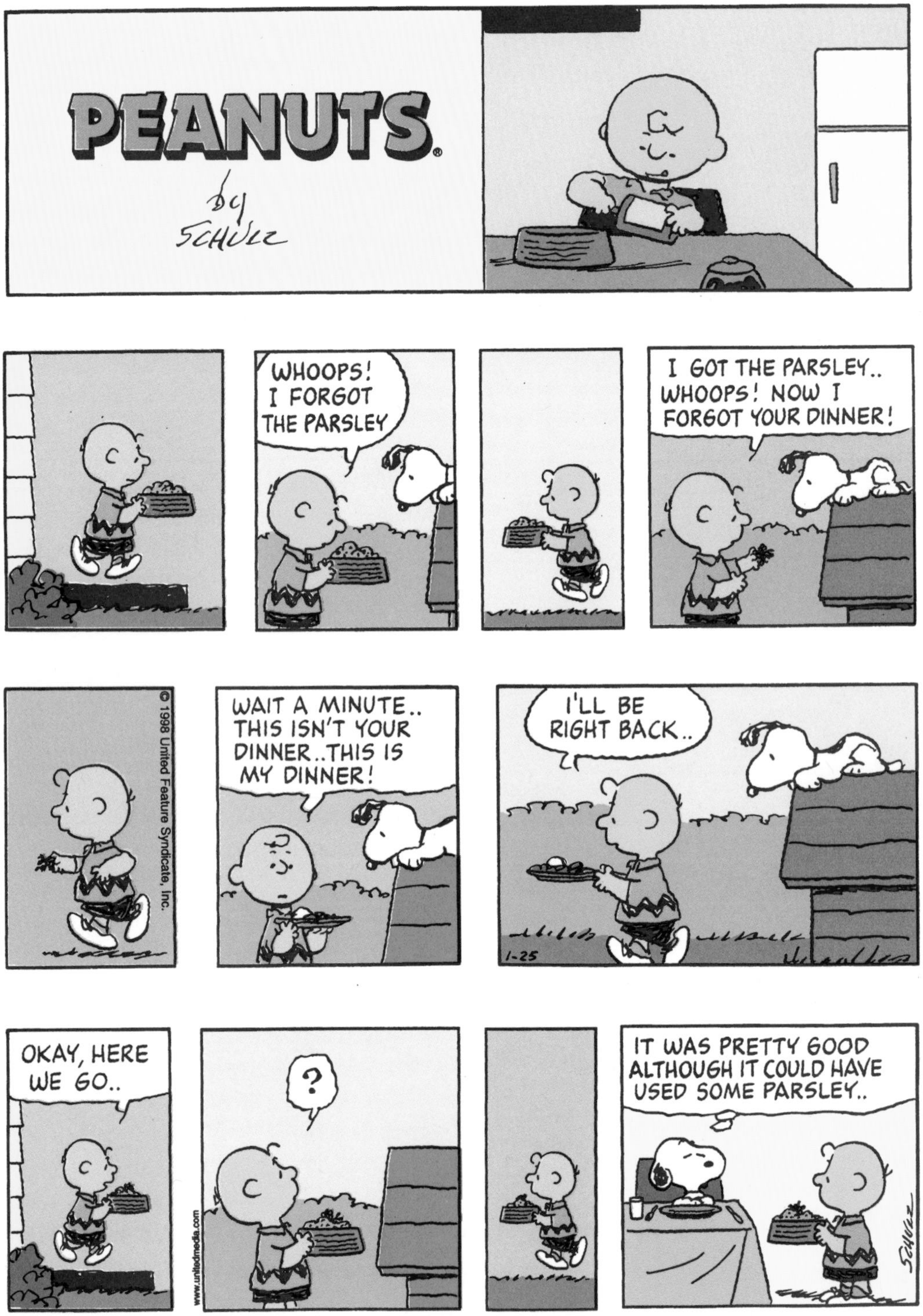
PEANUTS
by SCHULZ
WHOOPS! I FORGOT THE PARSLEY
I GOT THE PARSLEY.. WHOOPS! NOW I FORGOT YOUR DINNER!
© 1998 United Feature Syndicate, Inc.
WAIT A MINUTE.. THIS ISN'T YOUR DINNER..THIS IS MY DINNER!
I'LL BE RIGHT BACK..
1-25
OKAY, HERE WE GO..
?
www.unitedmedia.com
IT WAS PRETTY GOOD ALTHOUGH IT COULD HAVE USED SOME PARSLEY..
SCHULZ

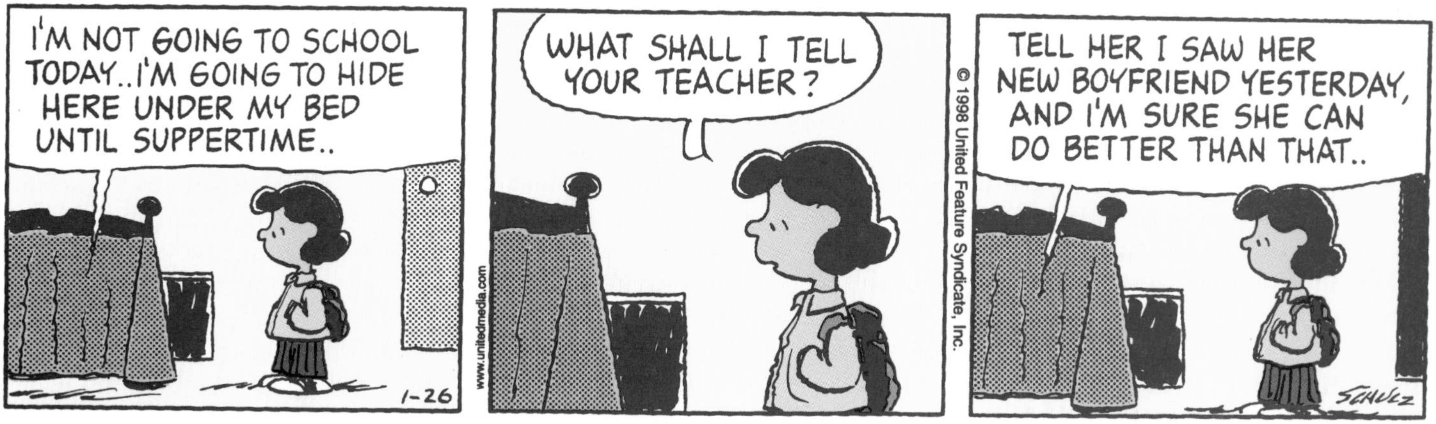
I'M NOT GOING TO SCHOOL TODAY..I'M GOING TO HIDE HERE UNDER MY BED UNTIL SUPPERTIME..
1-26
www.unitedmedia.com
WHAT SHALL I TELL YOUR TEACHER?
© 1998 United Feature Syndicate, Inc.
TELL HER I SAW HER NEW BOYFRIEND YESTERDAY, AND I'M SURE SHE CAN DO BETTER THAN THAT..
SCHULZ

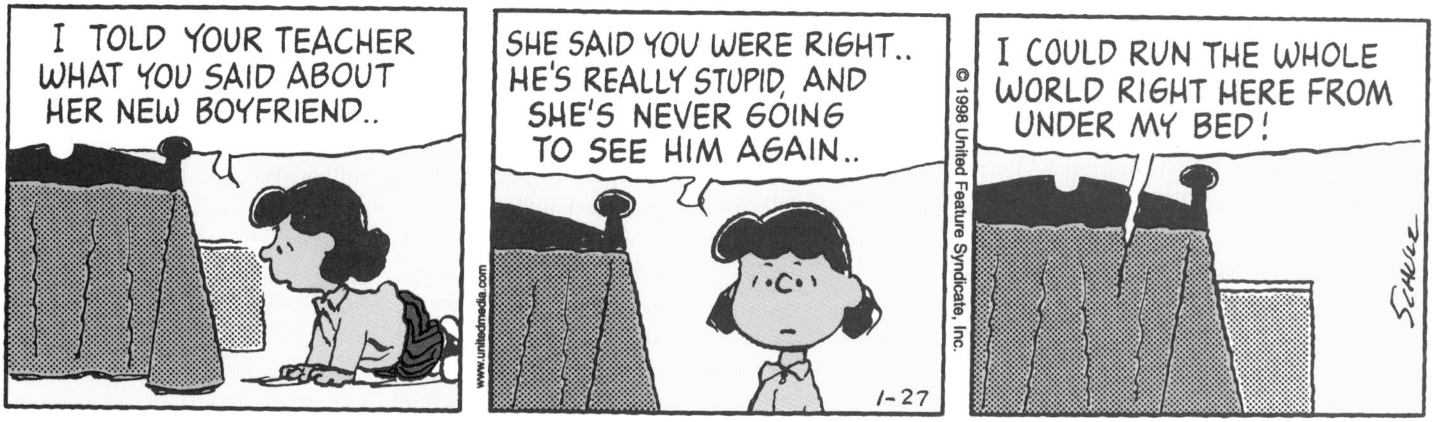
I TOLD YOUR TEACHER WHAT YOU SAID ABOUT HER NEW BOYFRIEND..
www.unitedmedia.com
SHE SAID YOU WERE RIGHT.. HE'S REALLY STUPID, AND SHE'S NEVER GOING TO SEE HIM AGAIN..
1-27
© 1998 United Feature Syndicate, Inc.
I COULD RUN THE WHOLE WORLD RIGHT HERE FROM UNDER MY BED!
SCHULZ

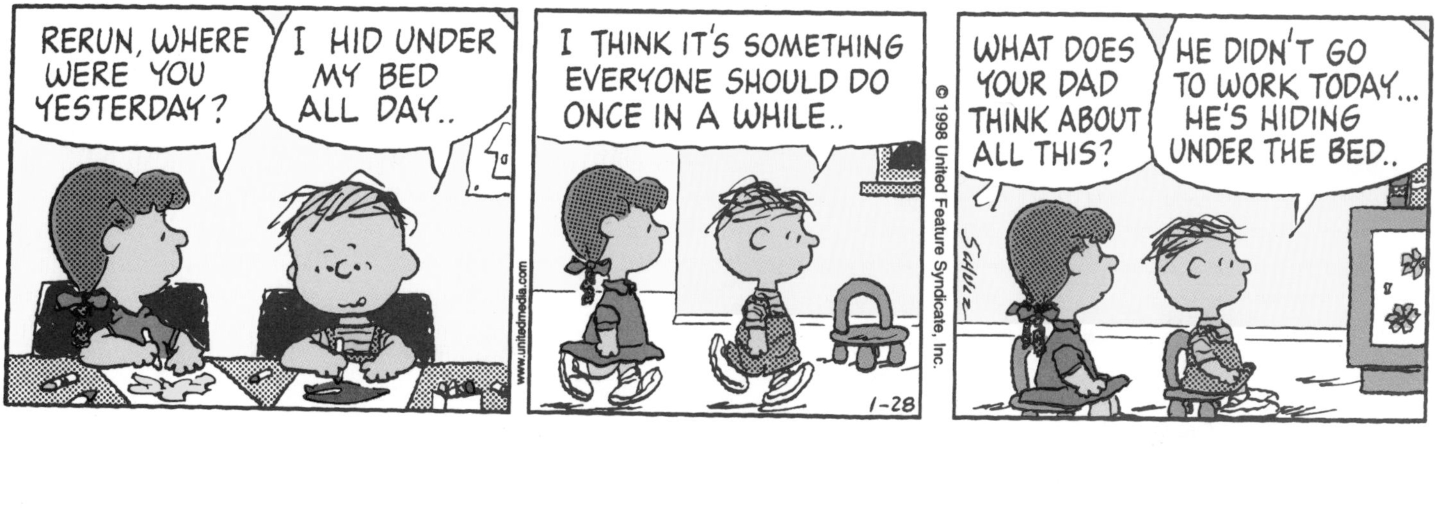
RERUN, WHERE WERE YOU YESTERDAY?
I HID UNDER MY BED ALL DAY..
www.unitedmedia.com
I THINK IT'S SOMETHING EVERYONE SHOULD DO ONCE IN A WHILE..
1-28
© 1998 United Feature Syndicate, Inc.
WHAT DOES YOUR DAD THINK ABOUT ALL THIS?
HE DIDN'T GO TO WORK TODAY... HE'S HIDING UNDER THE BED..
SCHULZ

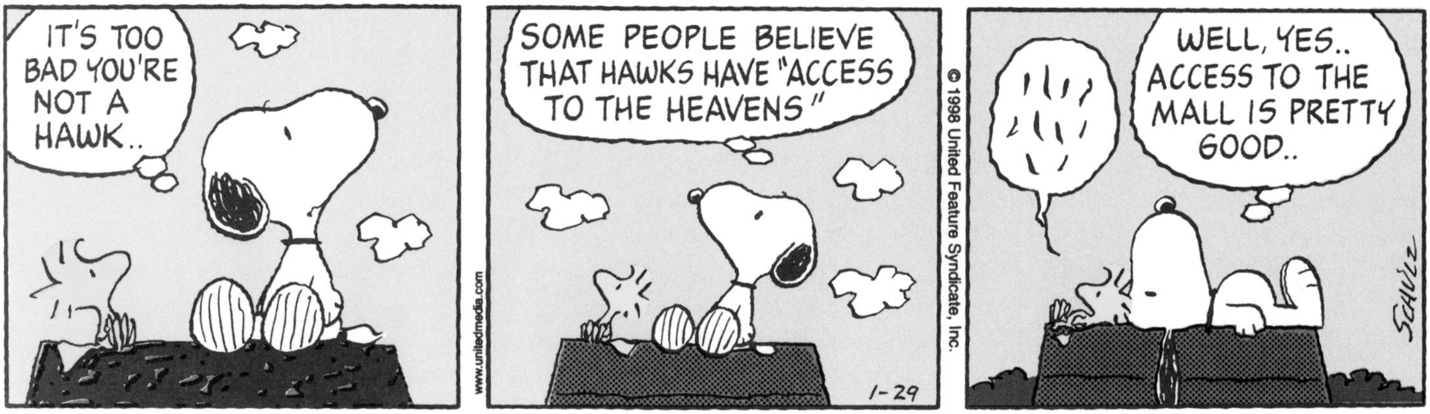
IT'S TOO BAD YOU'RE NOT A HAWK..
www.unitedmedia.com
SOME PEOPLE BELIEVE THAT HAWKS HAVE "ACCESS TO THE HEAVENS"
1-29
© 1998 United Feature Syndicate, Inc.
WELL, YES.. ACCESS TO THE MALL IS PRETTY GOOD..
SCHULZ

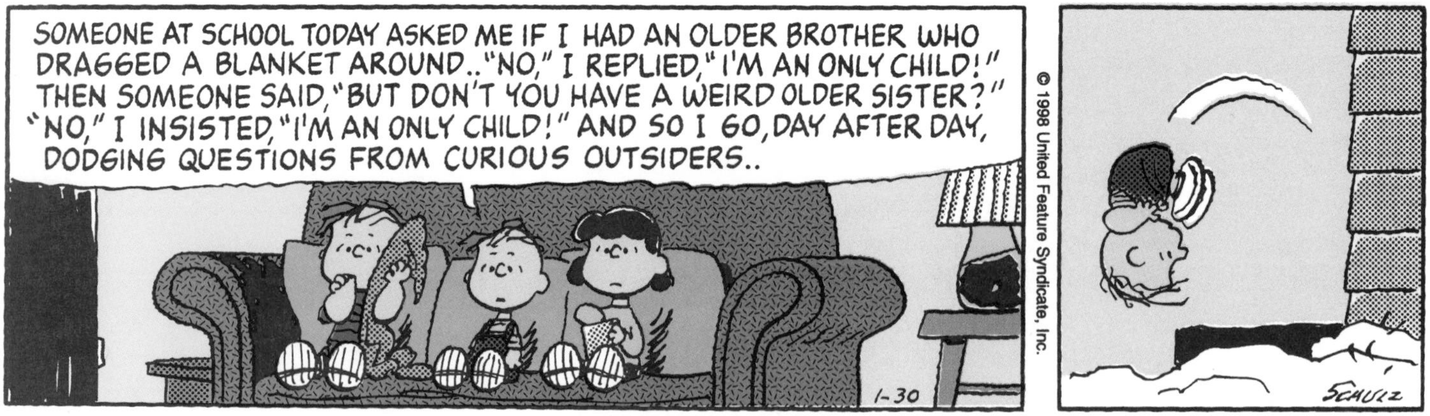
SOMEONE AT SCHOOL TODAY ASKED ME IF I HAD AN OLDER BROTHER WHO DRAGGED A BLANKET AROUND.."NO," I REPLIED, "I'M AN ONLY CHILD!" THEN SOMEONE SAID, "BUT DON'T YOU HAVE A WEIRD OLDER SISTER?" "NO," I INSISTED, "I'M AN ONLY CHILD!" AND SO I GO, DAY AFTER DAY, DODGING QUESTIONS FROM CURIOUS OUTSIDERS..
1-30
© 1998 United Feature Syndicate, Inc.
SCHULZ

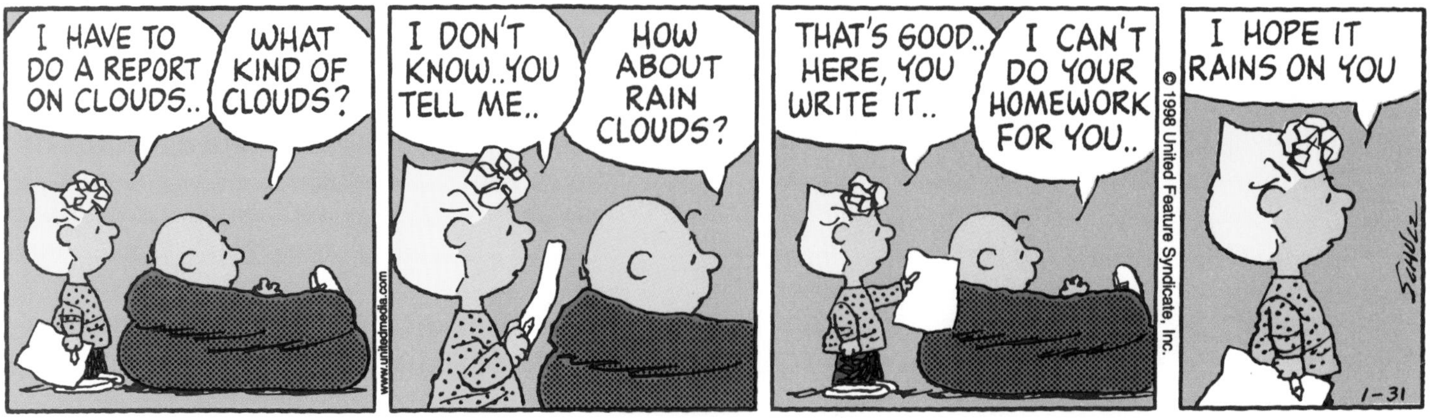
I HAVE TO DO A REPORT ON CLOUDS..
WHAT KIND OF CLOUDS?
www.unitedmedia.com
I DON'T KNOW..YOU TELL ME..
HOW ABOUT RAIN CLOUDS?
THAT'S GOOD.. HERE, YOU WRITE IT..
I CAN'T DO YOUR HOMEWORK FOR YOU..
© 1998 United Feature Syndicate, Inc.
I HOPE IT RAINS ON YOU
SCHULZ
1-31

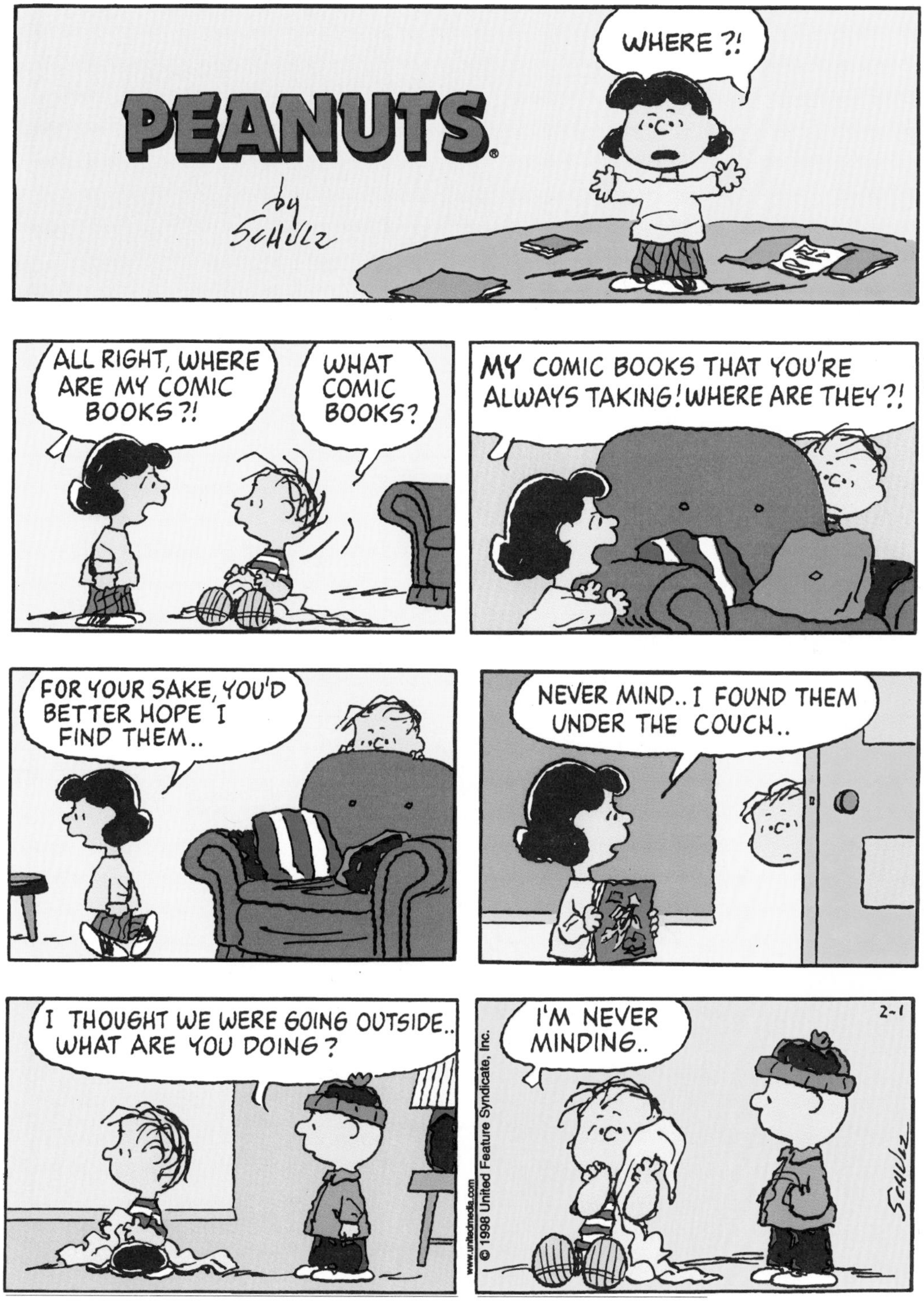
PEANUTS
by SCHULZ
WHERE ?!
ALL RIGHT, WHERE ARE MY COMIC BOOKS ?!
WHAT COMIC BOOKS?
MY COMIC BOOKS THAT YOU'RE ALWAYS TAKING! WHERE ARE THEY ?!
FOR YOUR SAKE, YOU'D BETTER HOPE I FIND THEM..
NEVER MIND.. I FOUND THEM UNDER THE COUCH..
I THOUGHT WE WERE GOING OUTSIDE.. WHAT ARE YOU DOING ?
I'M NEVER MINDING..
2-1
SCHULZ
© 1998 United Feature Syndicate, Inc.
www.unitedmedia.com

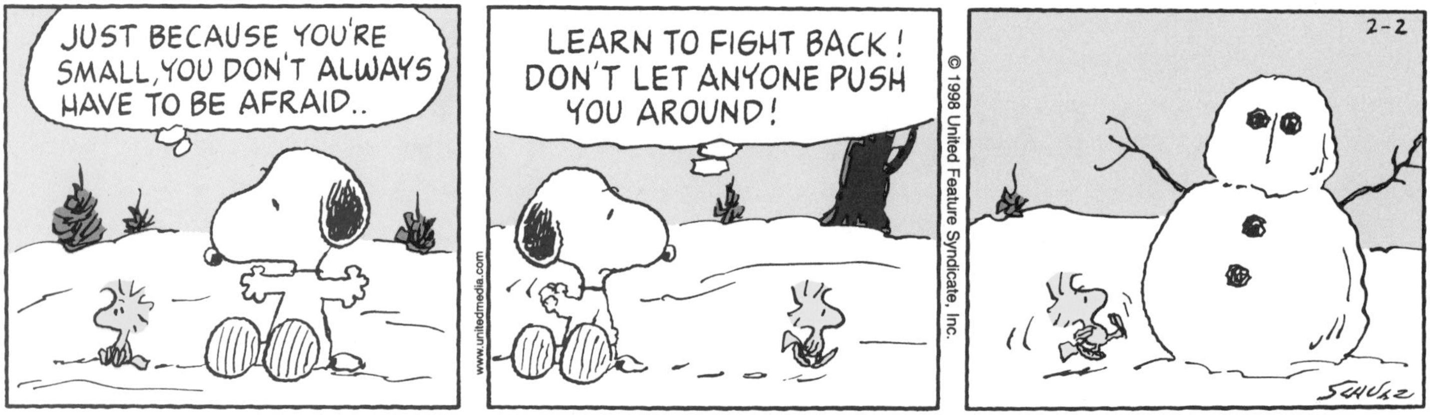
JUST BECAUSE YOU'RE SMALL, YOU DON'T ALWAYS HAVE TO BE AFRAID..
LEARN TO FIGHT BACK! DON'T LET ANYONE PUSH YOU AROUND!
2-2
© 1998 United Feature Syndicate, Inc.
www.unitedmedia.com
SCHULZ

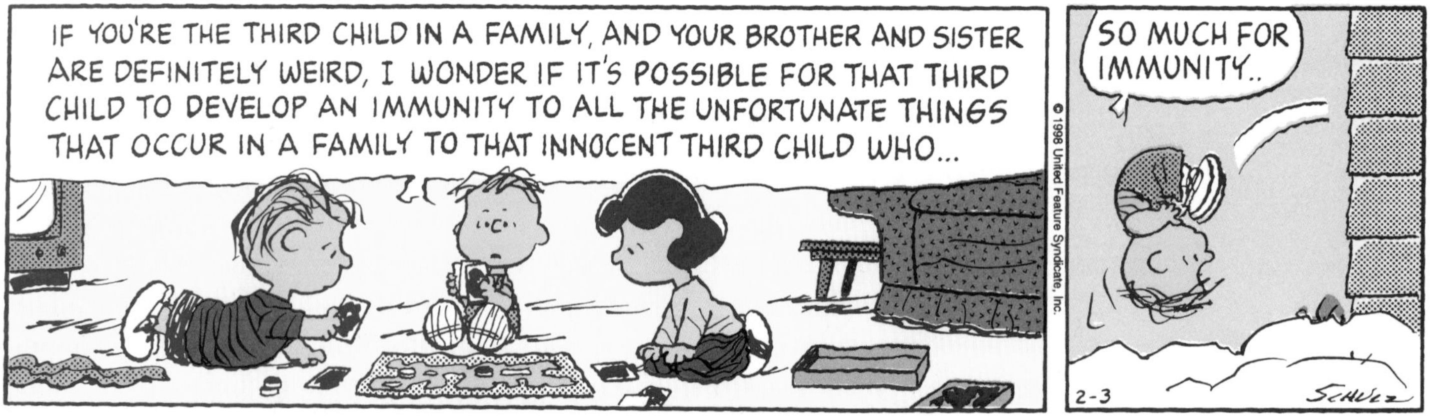
IF YOU'RE THE THIRD CHILD IN A FAMILY, AND YOUR BROTHER AND SISTER ARE DEFINITELY WEIRD, I WONDER IF IT'S POSSIBLE FOR THAT THIRD CHILD TO DEVELOP AN IMMUNITY TO ALL THE UNFORTUNATE THINGS THAT OCCUR IN A FAMILY TO THAT INNOCENT THIRD CHILD WHO...
SO MUCH FOR IMMUNITY..
© 1998 United Feature Syndicate, Inc.
2-3
SCHULZ

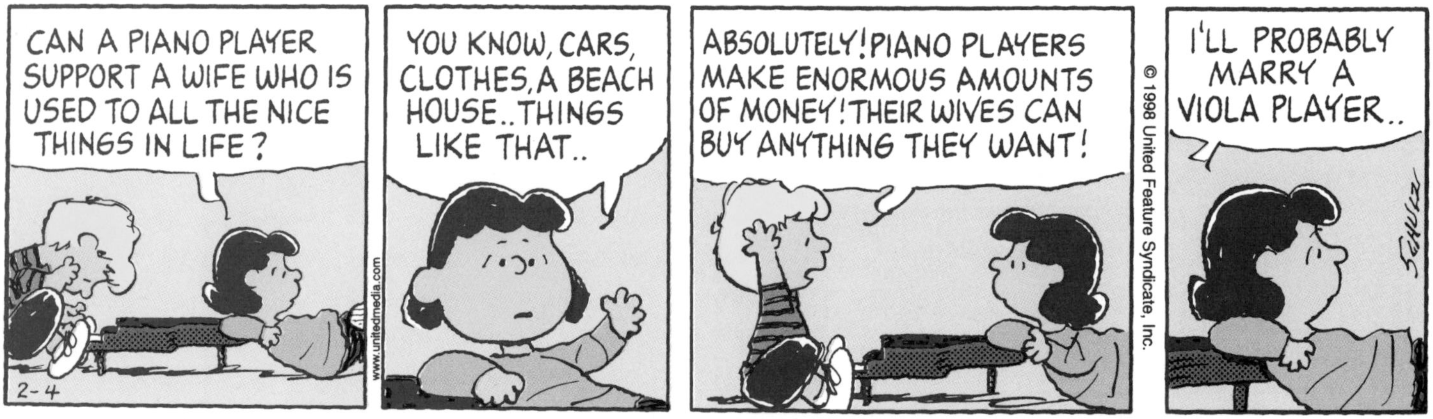
CAN A PIANO PLAYER SUPPORT A WIFE WHO IS USED TO ALL THE NICE THINGS IN LIFE?
YOU KNOW, CARS, CLOTHES, A BEACH HOUSE..THINGS LIKE THAT..
ABSOLUTELY! PIANO PLAYERS MAKE ENORMOUS AMOUNTS OF MONEY! THEIR WIVES CAN BUY ANYTHING THEY WANT!
I'LL PROBABLY MARRY A VIOLA PLAYER..
2-4
www.unitedmedia.com
© 1998 United Feature Syndicate, Inc.
SCHULZ

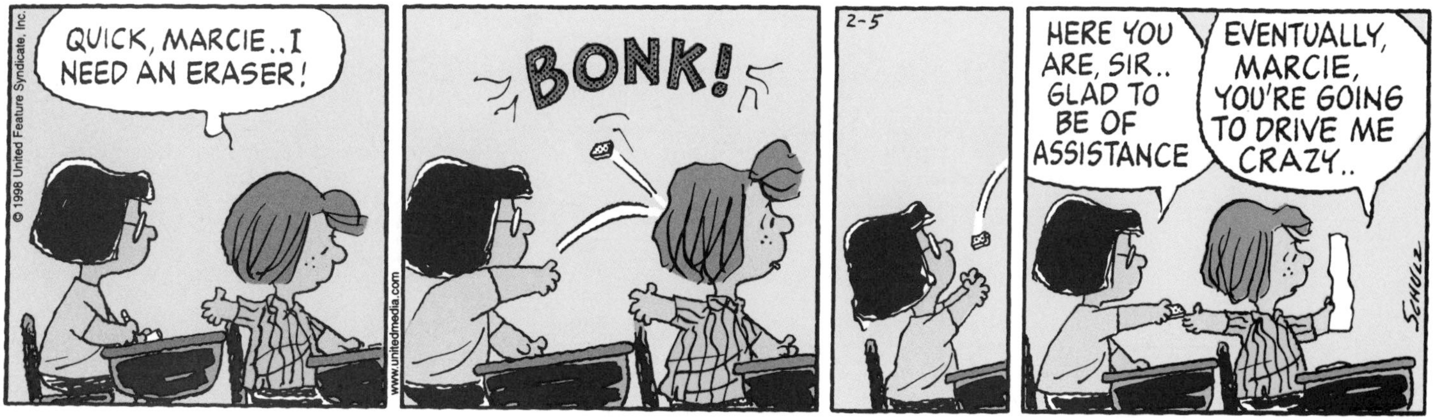
© 1998 United Feature Syndicate, Inc.
QUICK, MARCIE..I NEED AN ERASER!
BONK!
www.unitedmedia.com
2-5
HERE YOU ARE, SIR.. GLAD TO BE OF ASSISTANCE
EVENTUALLY, MARCIE, YOU'RE GOING TO DRIVE ME CRAZY..
SCHULZ

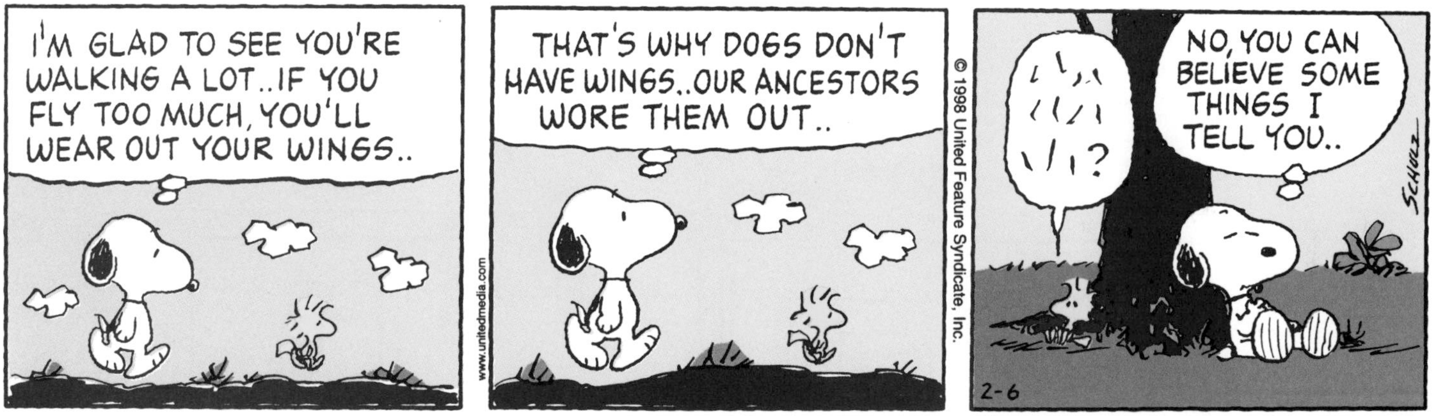
I'M GLAD TO SEE YOU'RE WALKING A LOT..IF YOU FLY TOO MUCH, YOU'LL WEAR OUT YOUR WINGS..
www.unitedmedia.com
THAT'S WHY DOGS DON'T HAVE WINGS..OUR ANCESTORS WORE THEM OUT..
© 1998 United Feature Syndicate, Inc.
?
NO, YOU CAN BELIEVE SOME THINGS I TELL YOU..
SCHULZ
2-6

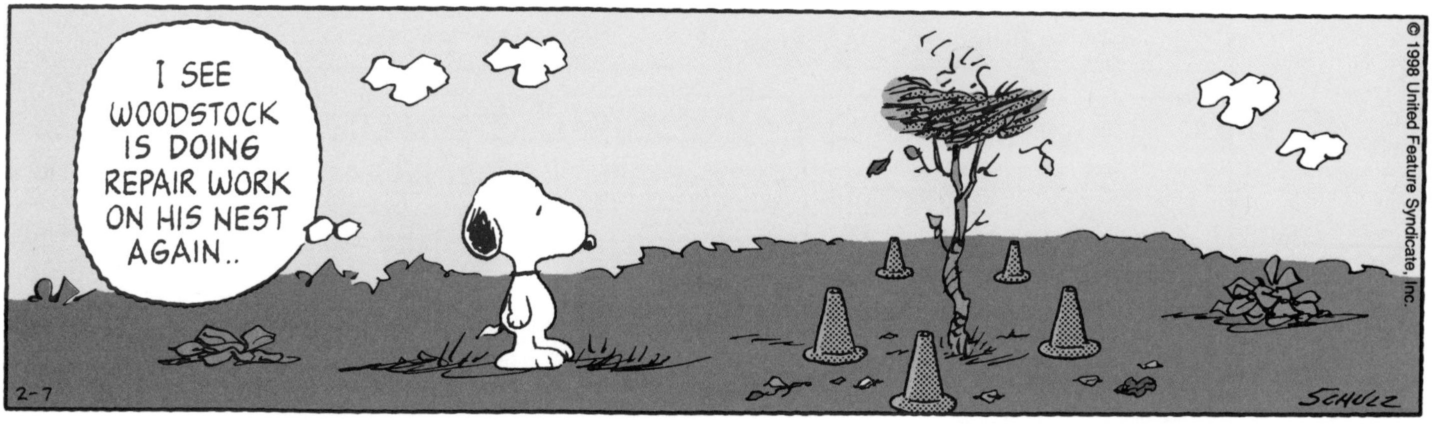
I SEE WOODSTOCK IS DOING REPAIR WORK ON HIS NEST AGAIN..
© 1998 United Feature Syndicate, Inc.
2-7
SCHULZ

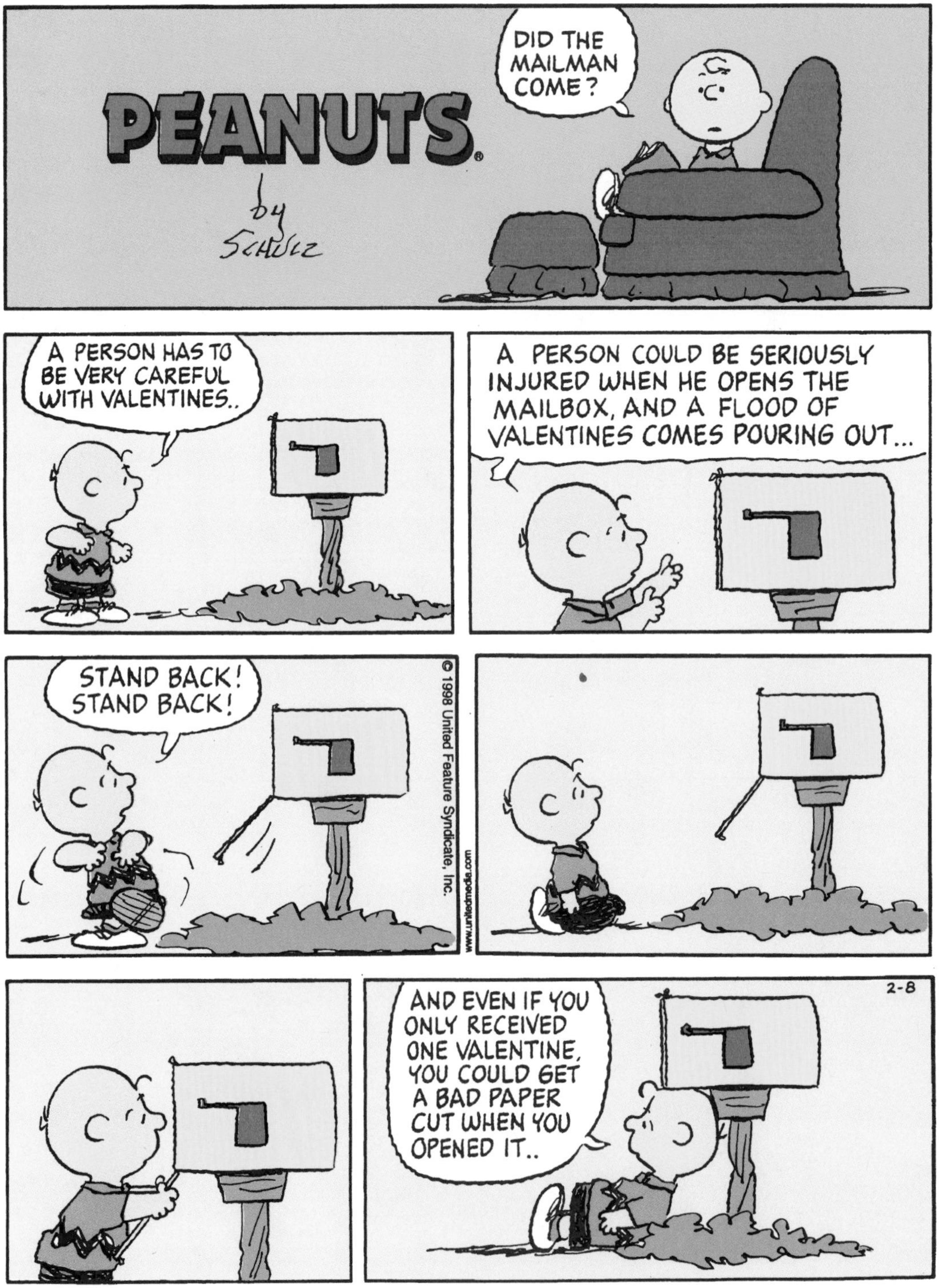
PEANUTS®
by SCHULZ
DID THE MAILMAN COME?
A PERSON HAS TO BE VERY CAREFUL WITH VALENTINES..
A PERSON COULD BE SERIOUSLY INJURED WHEN HE OPENS THE MAILBOX, AND A FLOOD OF VALENTINES COMES POURING OUT...
STAND BACK! STAND BACK!
© 1998 United Feature Syndicate, Inc.
www.unitedmedia.com
2-8
AND EVEN IF YOU ONLY RECEIVED ONE VALENTINE, YOU COULD GET A BAD PAPER CUT WHEN YOU OPENED IT..

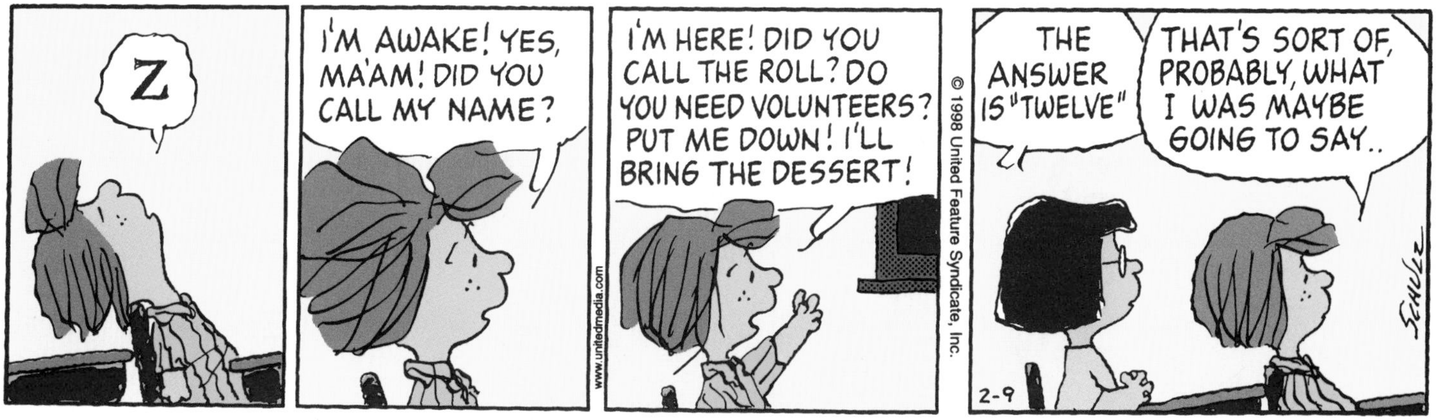
Z
I'M AWAKE! YES, MA'AM! DID YOU CALL MY NAME?
www.unitedmedia.com
I'M HERE! DID YOU CALL THE ROLL? DO YOU NEED VOLUNTEERS? PUT ME DOWN! I'LL BRING THE DESSERT!
© 1998 United Feature Syndicate, Inc.
THE ANSWER IS "TWELVE"
THAT'S SORT OF, PROBABLY, WHAT I WAS MAYBE GOING TO SAY..
SCHULZ
2-9

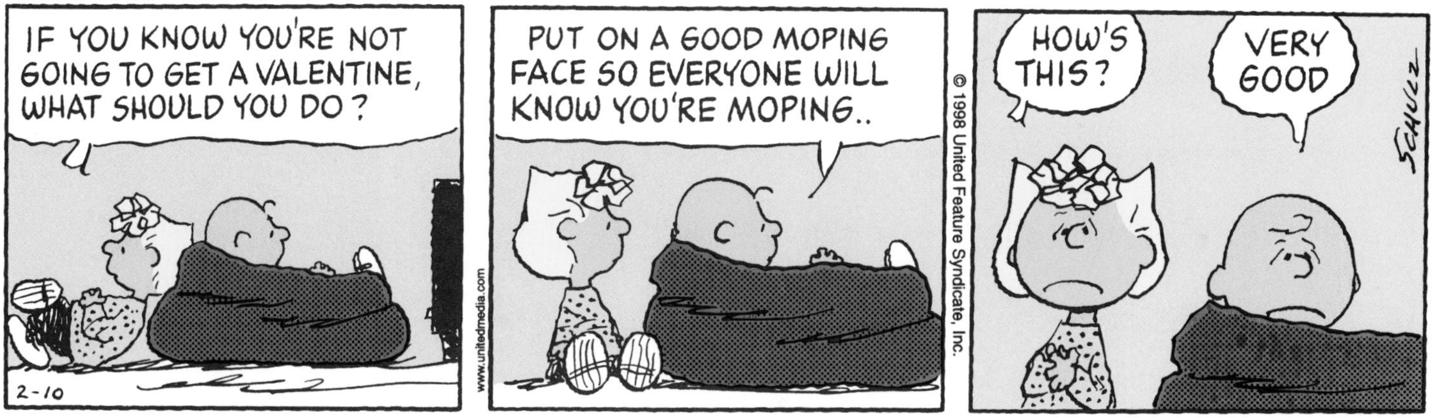
IF YOU KNOW YOU'RE NOT GOING TO GET A VALENTINE, WHAT SHOULD YOU DO?
2-10
www.unitedmedia.com
PUT ON A GOOD MOPING FACE SO EVERYONE WILL KNOW YOU'RE MOPING..
© 1998 United Feature Syndicate, Inc.
HOW'S THIS?
VERY GOOD
SCHULZ

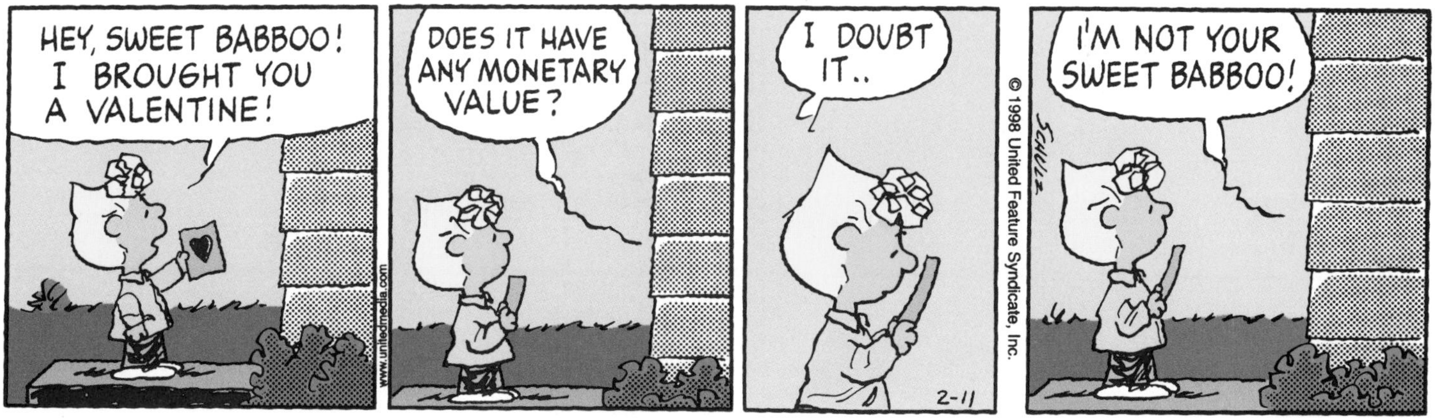
HEY, SWEET BABBOO! I BROUGHT YOU A VALENTINE!
www.unitedmedia.com
DOES IT HAVE ANY MONETARY VALUE?
I DOUBT IT..
2-11
SCHULZ
© 1998 United Feature Syndicate, Inc.
I'M NOT YOUR SWEET BABBOO!

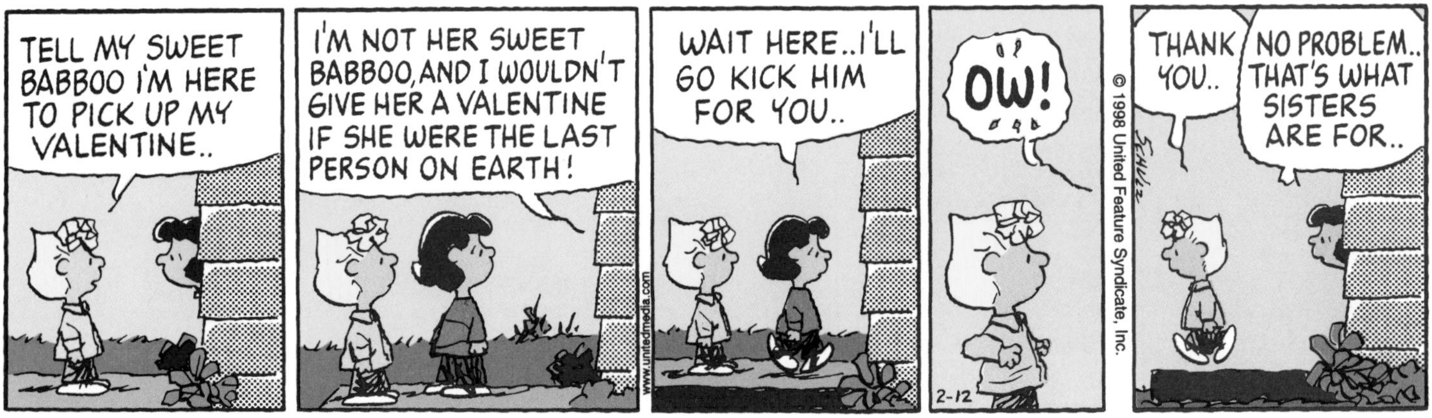
TELL MY SWEET BABBOO I'M HERE TO PICK UP MY VALENTINE..
I'M NOT HER SWEET BABBOO, AND I WOULDN'T GIVE HER A VALENTINE IF SHE WERE THE LAST PERSON ON EARTH!
WAIT HERE..I'LL GO KICK HIM FOR YOU..
OW!
THANK YOU..
NO PROBLEM.. THAT'S WHAT SISTERS ARE FOR..
2-12
© 1998 United Feature Syndicate, Inc.
www.unitedmedia.com

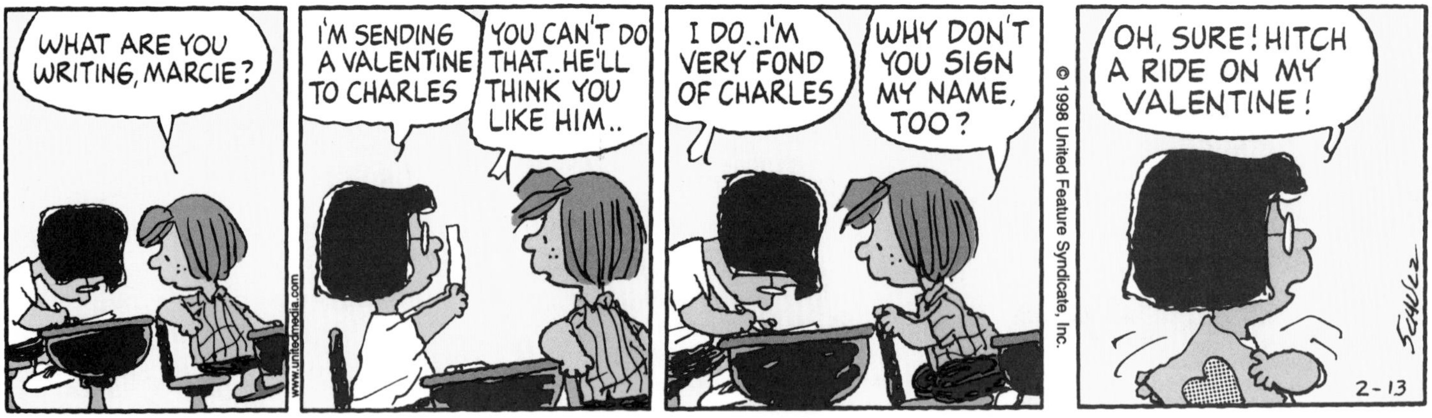
WHAT ARE YOU WRITING, MARCIE?
I'M SENDING A VALENTINE TO CHARLES
YOU CAN'T DO THAT..HE'LL THINK YOU LIKE HIM..
I DO..I'M VERY FOND OF CHARLES
WHY DON'T YOU SIGN MY NAME, TOO?
OH, SURE! HITCH A RIDE ON MY VALENTINE!
2-13
© 1998 United Feature Syndicate, Inc.
www.unitedmedia.com

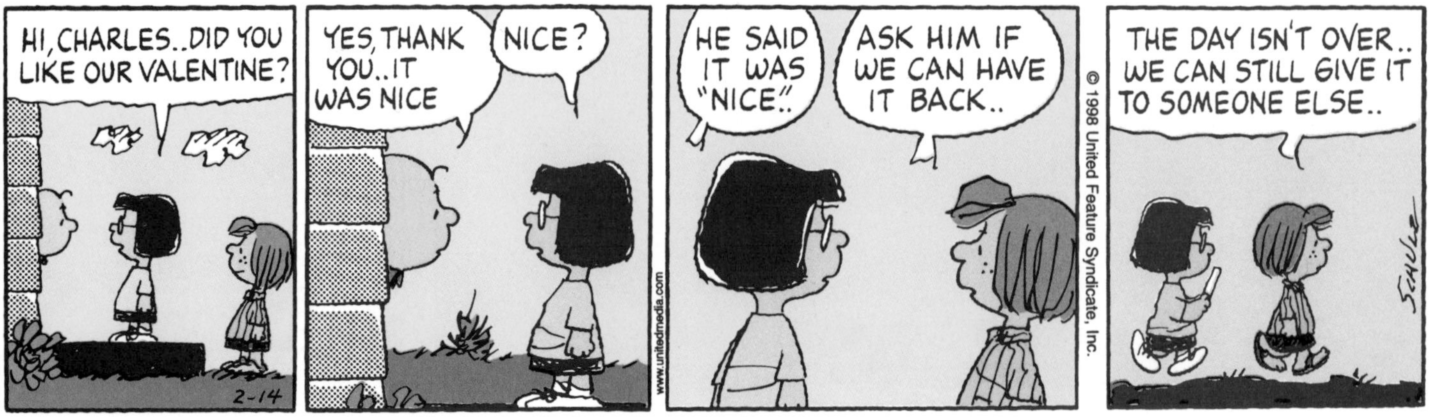
HI, CHARLES..DID YOU LIKE OUR VALENTINE?
YES, THANK YOU..IT WAS NICE
NICE?
HE SAID IT WAS "NICE"
ASK HIM IF WE CAN HAVE IT BACK..
THE DAY ISN'T OVER.. WE CAN STILL GIVE IT TO SOMEONE ELSE..
2-14
© 1998 United Feature Syndicate, Inc.
www.unitedmedia.com

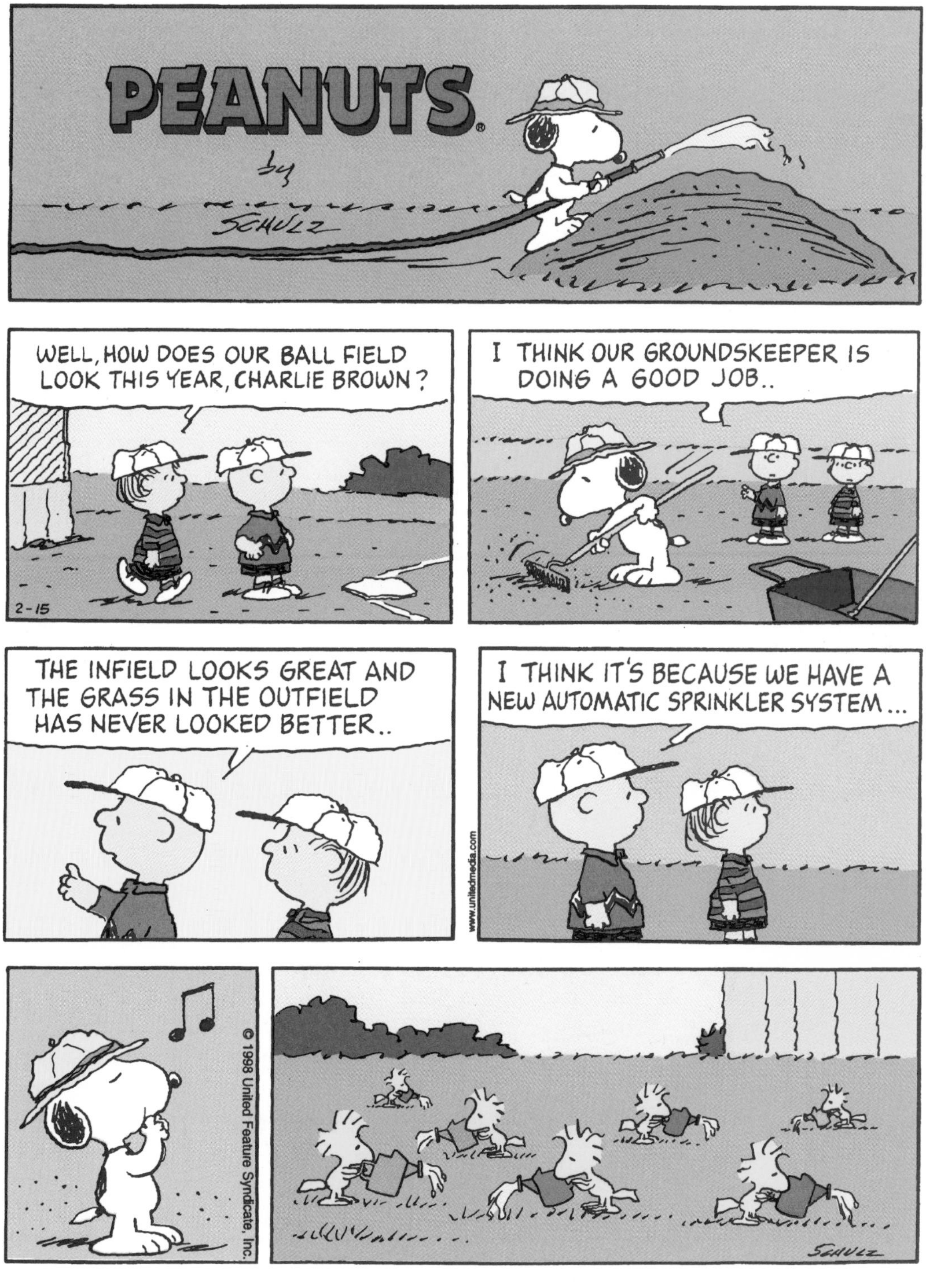

PEANUTS
by SCHULZ
WELL, HOW DOES OUR BALL FIELD LOOK THIS YEAR, CHARLIE BROWN?
2-15
I THINK OUR GROUNDSKEEPER IS DOING A GOOD JOB..
THE INFIELD LOOKS GREAT AND THE GRASS IN THE OUTFIELD HAS NEVER LOOKED BETTER..
www.unitedmedia.com
I THINK IT'S BECAUSE WE HAVE A NEW AUTOMATIC SPRINKLER SYSTEM...
© 1998 United Feature Syndicate, Inc.
SCHULZ

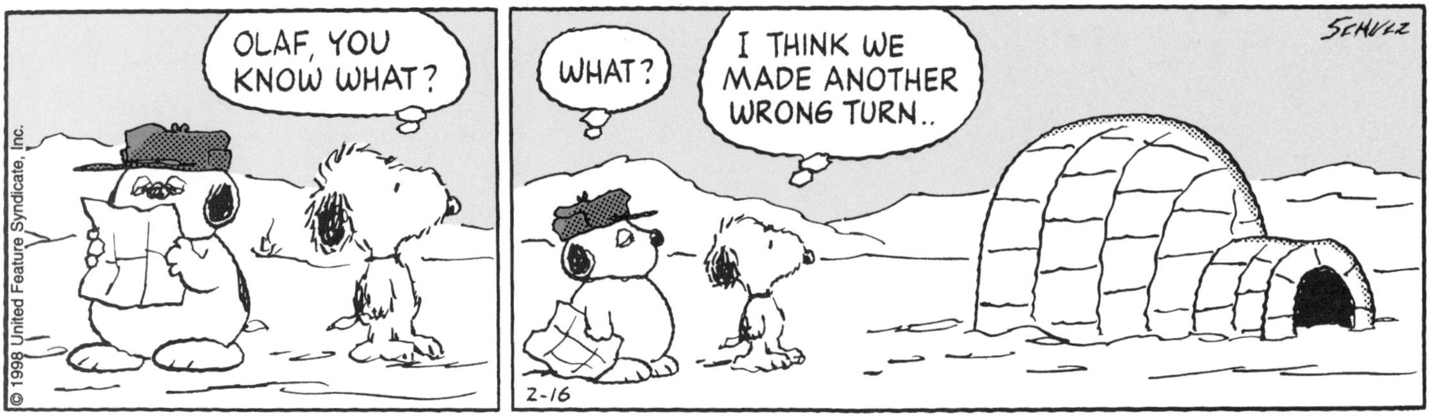
OLAF, YOU KNOW WHAT?
WHAT?
I THINK WE MADE ANOTHER WRONG TURN..
SCHULZ
2-16
© 1998 United Feature Syndicate, Inc.

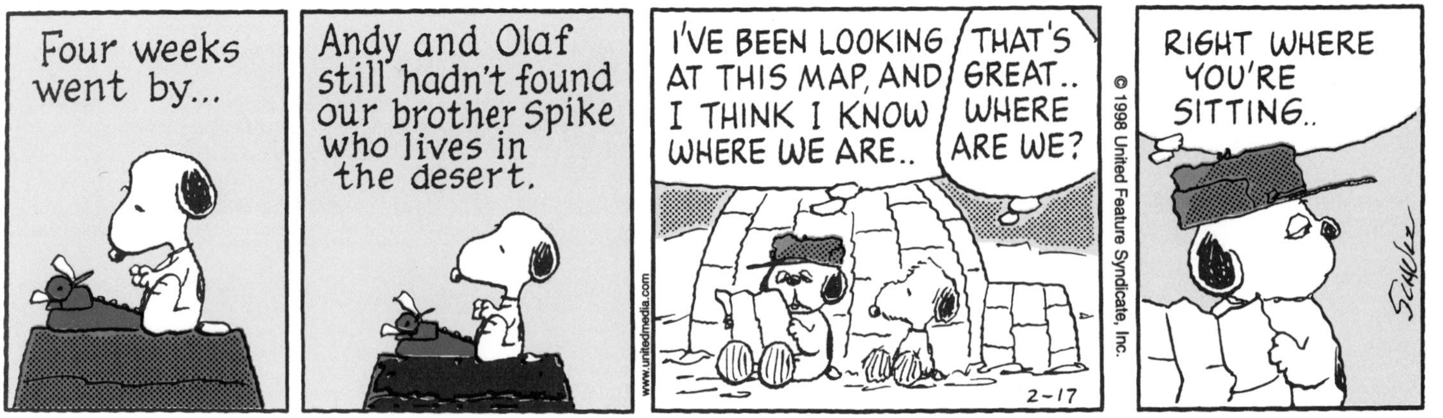
Four weeks went by...
Andy and Olaf still hadn't found our brother Spike who lives in the desert.
www.unitedmedia.com
I'VE BEEN LOOKING AT THIS MAP, AND I THINK I KNOW WHERE WE ARE..
THAT'S GREAT.. WHERE ARE WE?
2-17
© 1998 United Feature Syndicate, Inc.
RIGHT WHERE YOU'RE SITTING..
SCHULZ

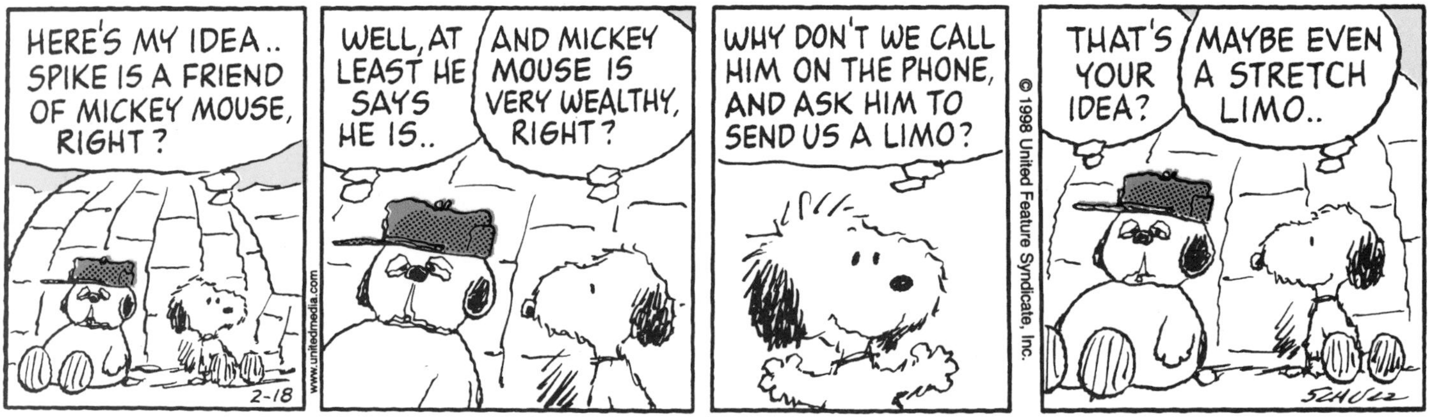
HERE'S MY IDEA.. SPIKE IS A FRIEND OF MICKEY MOUSE, RIGHT?
2-18
www.unitedmedia.com
WELL, AT LEAST HE SAYS HE IS..
AND MICKEY MOUSE IS VERY WEALTHY, RIGHT?
WHY DON'T WE CALL HIM ON THE PHONE, AND ASK HIM TO SEND US A LIMO?
© 1998 United Feature Syndicate, Inc.
THAT'S YOUR IDEA?
MAYBE EVEN A STRETCH LIMO..
SCHULZ

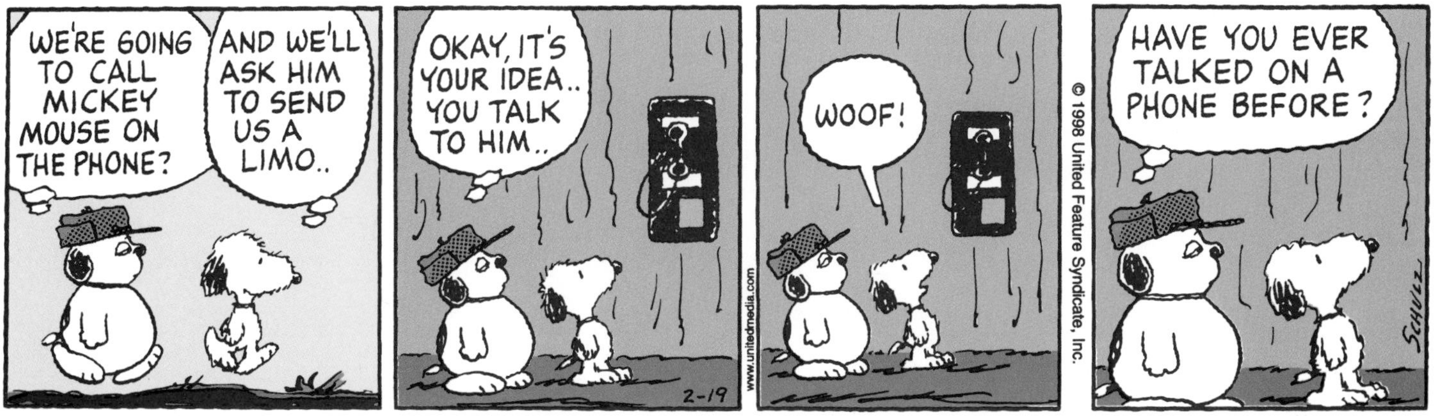
WE'RE GOING TO CALL MICKEY MOUSE ON THE PHONE?
AND WE'LL ASK HIM TO SEND US A LIMO..
OKAY, IT'S YOUR IDEA.. YOU TALK TO HIM..
2-19
www.unitedmedia.com
WOOF!
© 1998 United Feature Syndicate, Inc.
HAVE YOU EVER TALKED ON A PHONE BEFORE?
SCHULZ

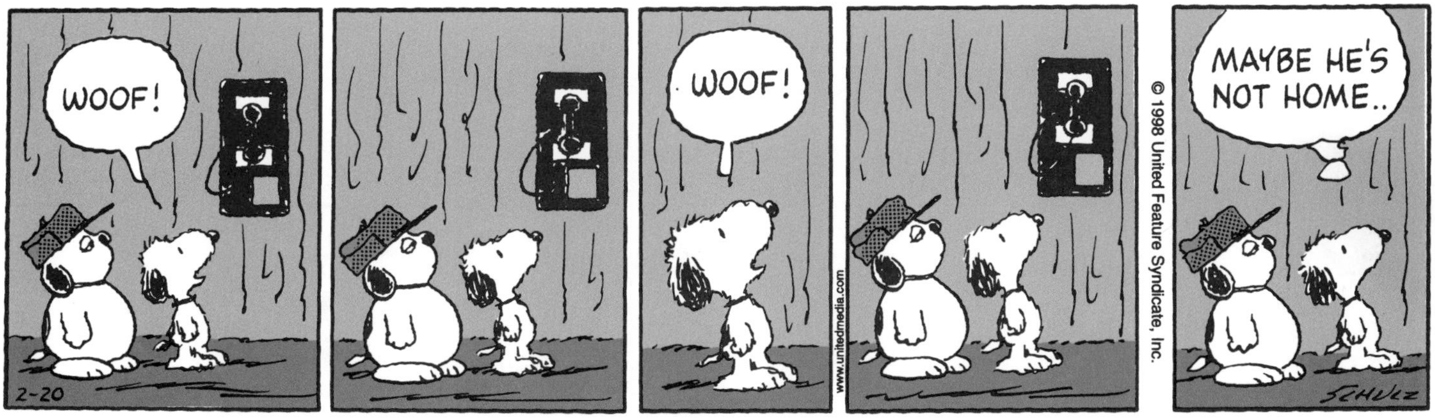
WOOF!
2-20
WOOF!
www.unitedmedia.com
© 1998 United Feature Syndicate, Inc.
MAYBE HE'S NOT HOME..
SCHULZ

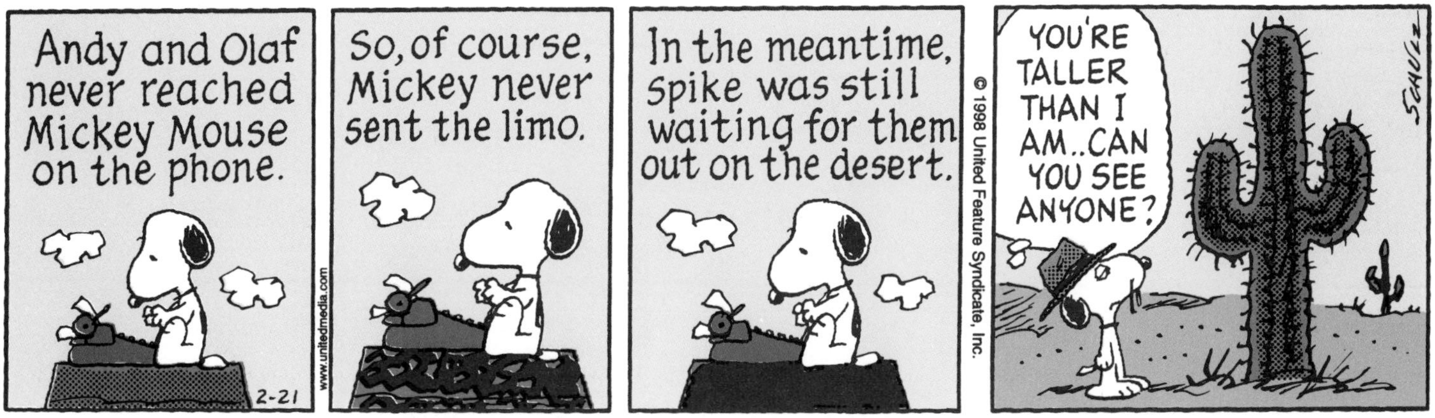
Andy and Olaf never reached Mickey Mouse on the phone.
2-21
www.unitedmedia.com
So, of course, Mickey never sent the limo.
In the meantime, Spike was still waiting for them out on the desert.
© 1998 United Feature Syndicate, Inc.
YOU'RE TALLER THAN I AM..CAN YOU SEE ANYONE?
SCHULZ

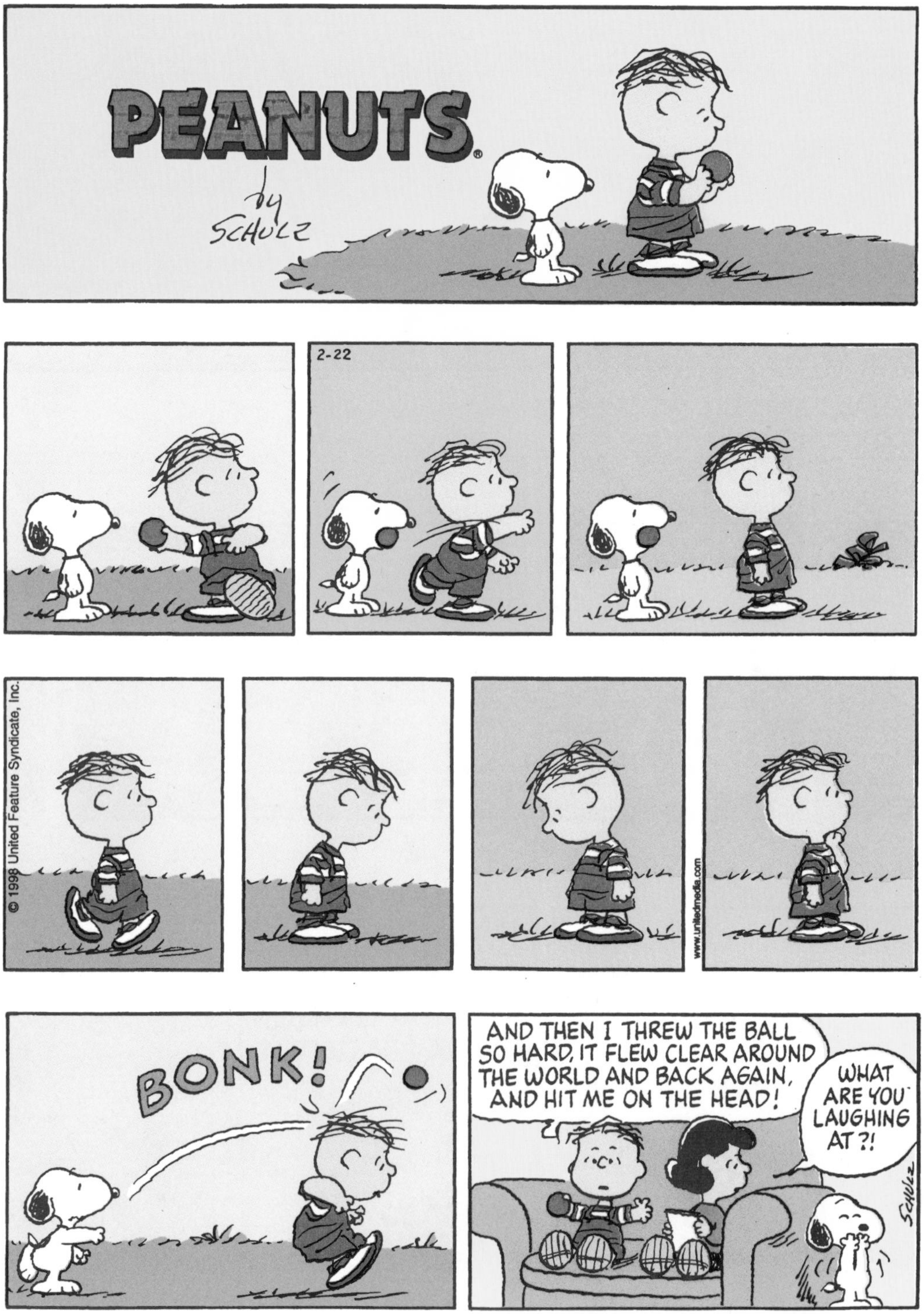
PEANUTS
by SCHULZ
2-22
© 1998 United Feature Syndicate, Inc.
www.unitedmedia.com
BONK!
AND THEN I THREW THE BALL SO HARD, IT FLEW CLEAR AROUND THE WORLD AND BACK AGAIN, AND HIT ME ON THE HEAD!
WHAT ARE YOU LAUGHING AT ?!
SCHULZ

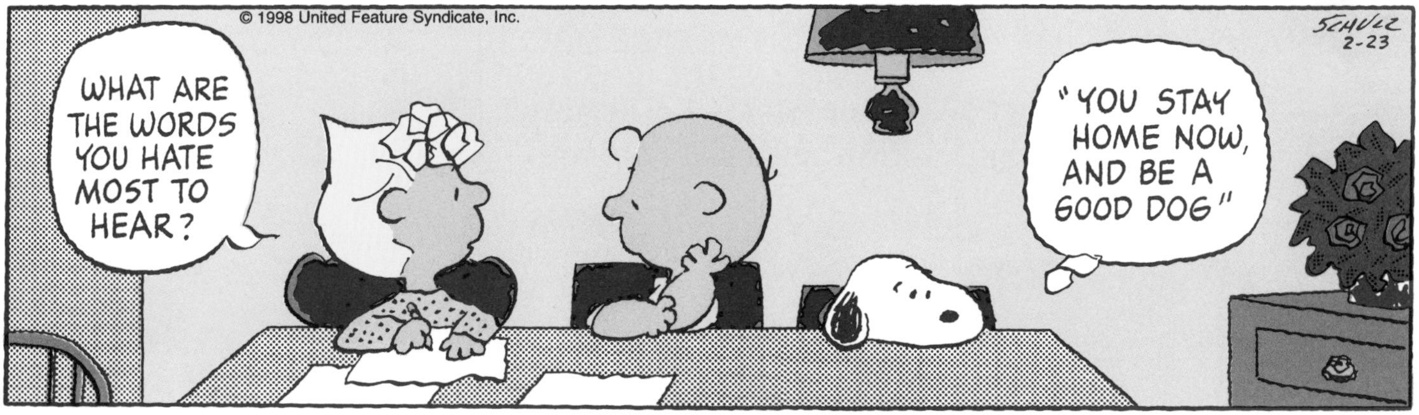
© 1998 United Feature Syndicate, Inc.
SCHULZ 2-23
WHAT ARE THE WORDS YOU HATE MOST TO HEAR?
"YOU STAY HOME NOW, AND BE A GOOD DOG"

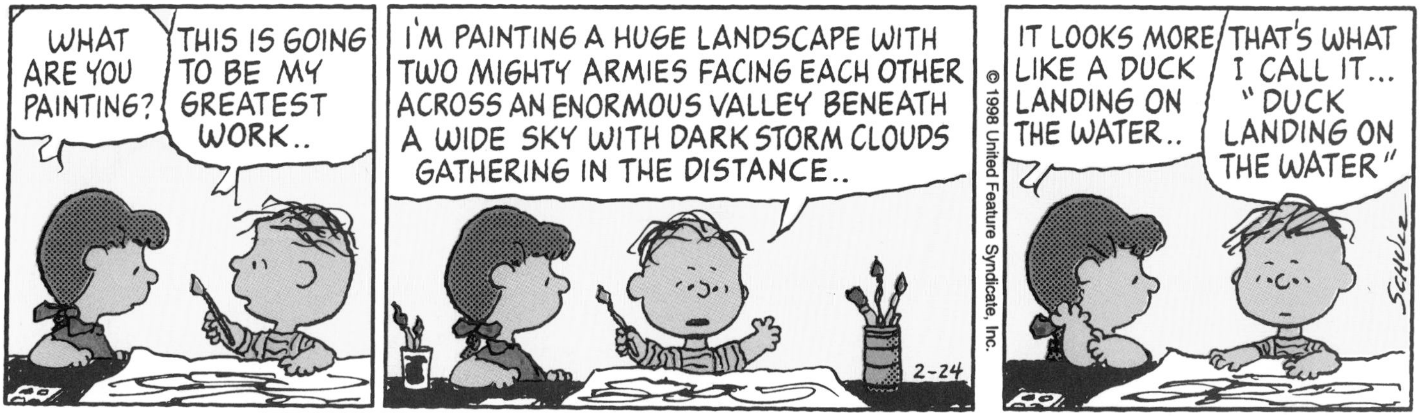
WHAT ARE YOU PAINTING?
THIS IS GOING TO BE MY GREATEST WORK..
I'M PAINTING A HUGE LANDSCAPE WITH TWO MIGHTY ARMIES FACING EACH OTHER ACROSS AN ENORMOUS VALLEY BENEATH A WIDE SKY WITH DARK STORM CLOUDS GATHERING IN THE DISTANCE..
2-24
© 1998 United Feature Syndicate, Inc.
IT LOOKS MORE LIKE A DUCK LANDING ON THE WATER..
THAT'S WHAT I CALL IT... "DUCK LANDING ON THE WATER"
SCHULZ

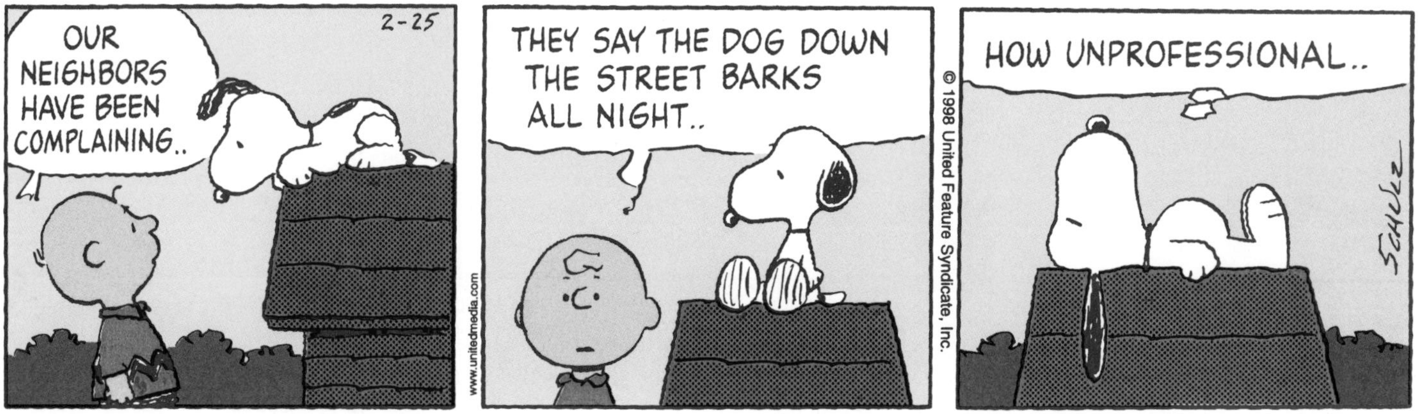
2-25
OUR NEIGHBORS HAVE BEEN COMPLAINING..
www.unitedmedia.com
THEY SAY THE DOG DOWN THE STREET BARKS ALL NIGHT..
© 1998 United Feature Syndicate, Inc.
HOW UNPROFESSIONAL..
SCHULZ

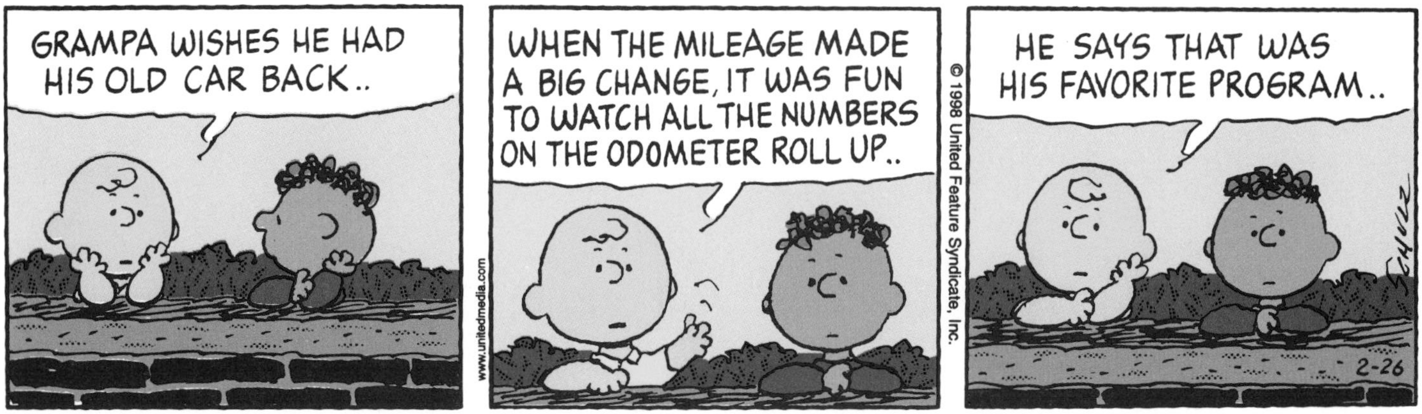
GRAMPA WISHES HE HAD HIS OLD CAR BACK..
WHEN THE MILEAGE MADE A BIG CHANGE, IT WAS FUN TO WATCH ALL THE NUMBERS ON THE ODOMETER ROLL UP..
HE SAYS THAT WAS HIS FAVORITE PROGRAM..
www.unitedmedia.com
© 1998 United Feature Syndicate, Inc.
SCHULZ
2-26

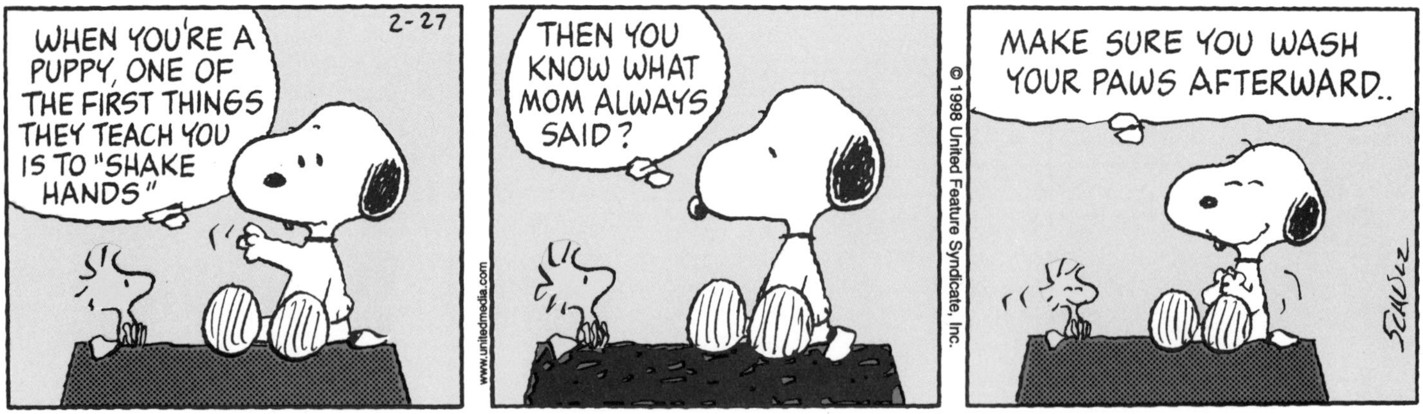
2-27
WHEN YOU'RE A PUPPY, ONE OF THE FIRST THINGS THEY TEACH YOU IS TO "SHAKE HANDS"
THEN YOU KNOW WHAT MOM ALWAYS SAID?
MAKE SURE YOU WASH YOUR PAWS AFTERWARD..
www.unitedmedia.com
© 1998 United Feature Syndicate, Inc.
SCHULZ

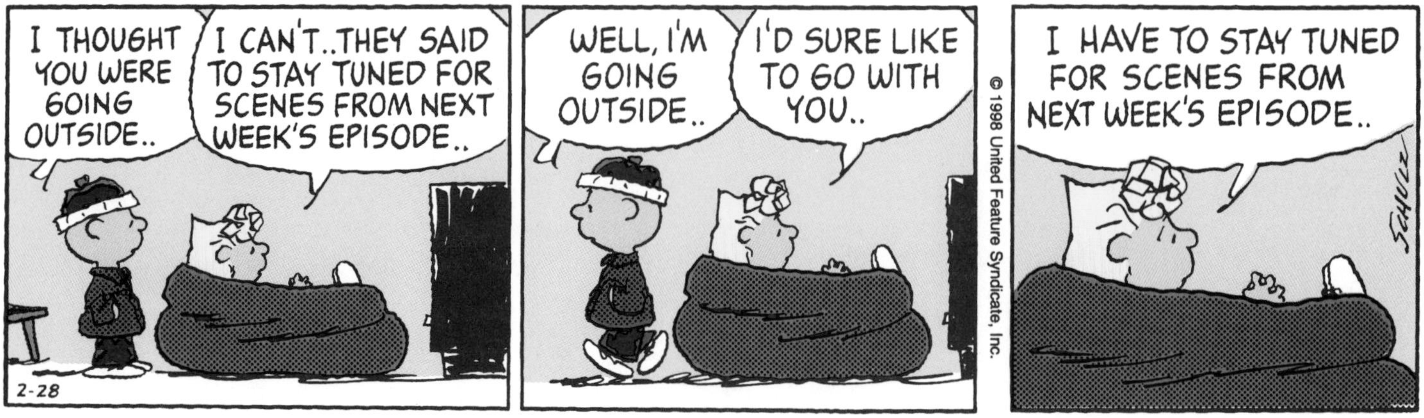
I THOUGHT YOU WERE GOING OUTSIDE..
I CAN'T..THEY SAID TO STAY TUNED FOR SCENES FROM NEXT WEEK'S EPISODE..
WELL, I'M GOING OUTSIDE..
I'D SURE LIKE TO GO WITH YOU..
I HAVE TO STAY TUNED FOR SCENES FROM NEXT WEEK'S EPISODE..
2-28
© 1998 United Feature Syndicate, Inc.
SCHULZ

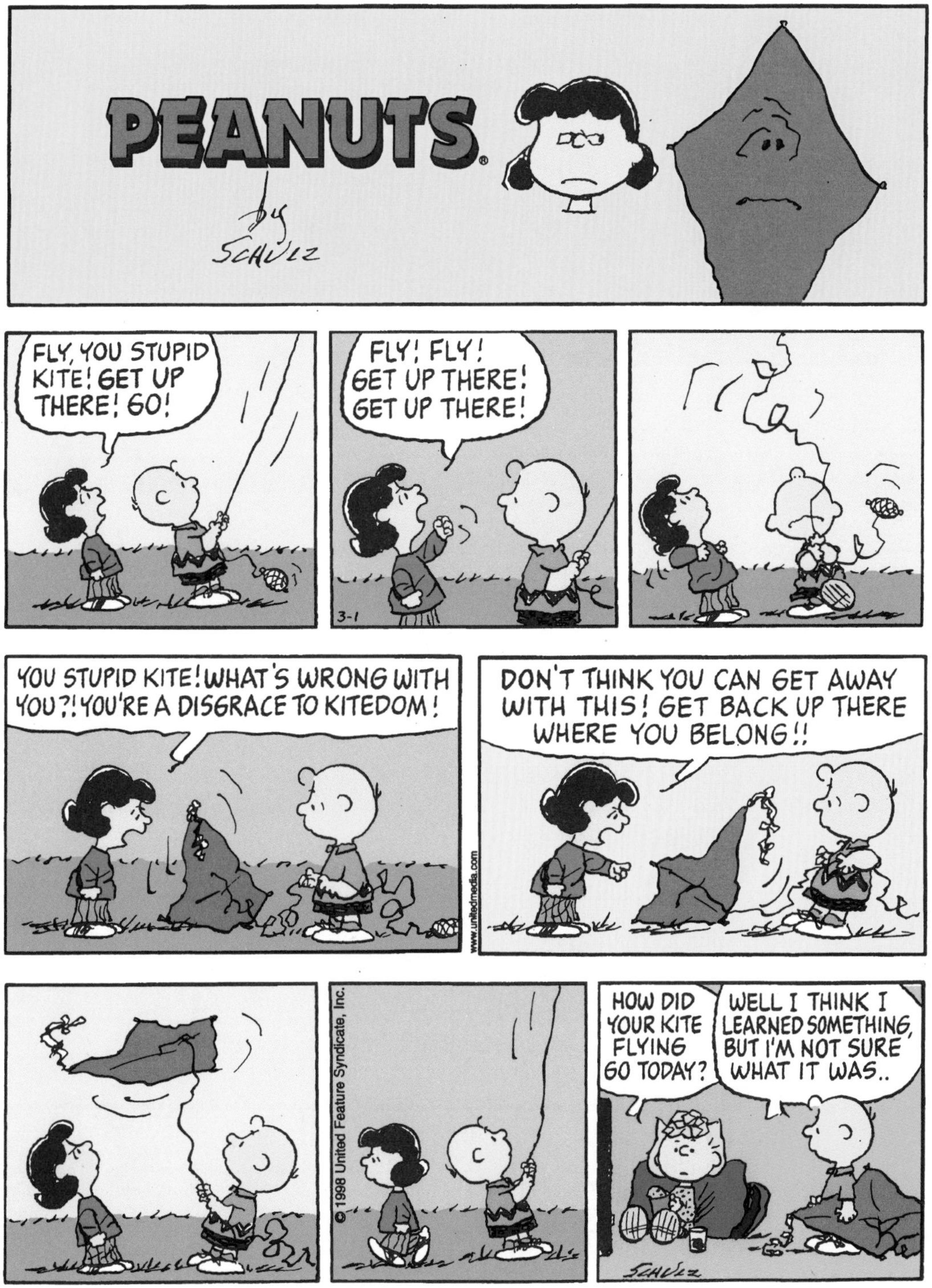
PEANUTS
by Schulz
FLY, YOU STUPID KITE! GET UP THERE! GO!
FLY! FLY! GET UP THERE! GET UP THERE!
3-1
YOU STUPID KITE! WHAT'S WRONG WITH YOU?! YOU'RE A DISGRACE TO KITEDOM!
www.unitedmedia.com
DON'T THINK YOU CAN GET AWAY WITH THIS! GET BACK UP THERE WHERE YOU BELONG!!
© 1998 United Feature Syndicate, Inc.
HOW DID YOUR KITE FLYING GO TODAY?
WELL I THINK I LEARNED SOMETHING, BUT I'M NOT SURE WHAT IT WAS..
SCHULZ

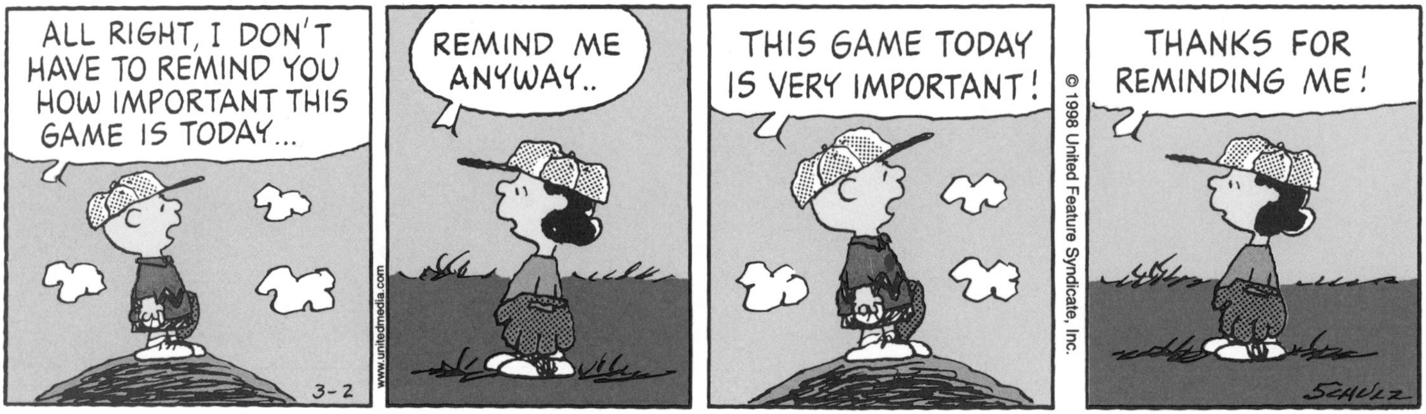
ALL RIGHT, I DON'T HAVE TO REMIND YOU HOW IMPORTANT THIS GAME IS TODAY...
3-2
www.unitedmedia.com
REMIND ME ANYWAY..
THIS GAME TODAY IS VERY IMPORTANT!
© 1998 United Feature Syndicate, Inc.
THANKS FOR REMINDING ME!
SCHULZ

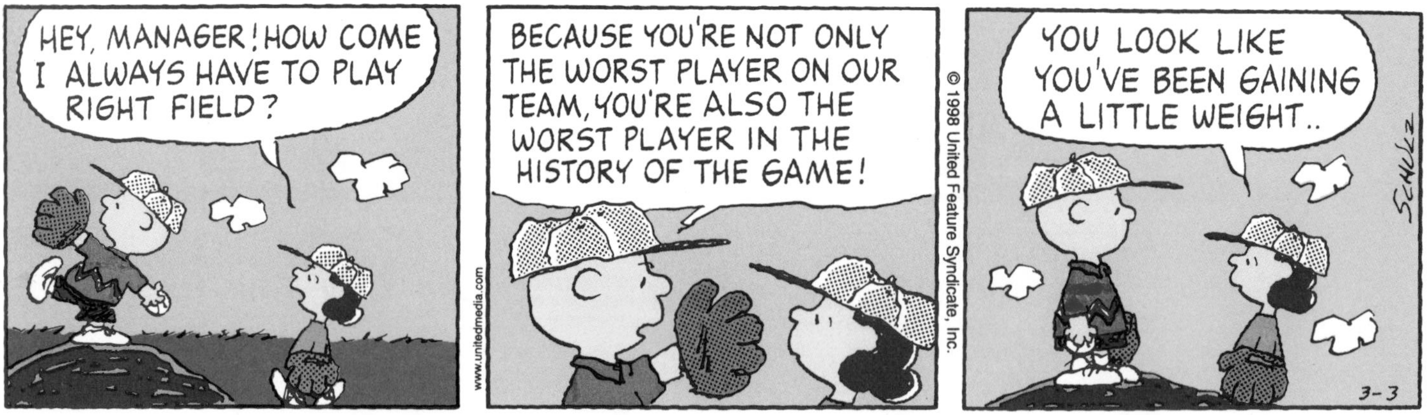
HEY, MANAGER! HOW COME I ALWAYS HAVE TO PLAY RIGHT FIELD?
www.unitedmedia.com
BECAUSE YOU'RE NOT ONLY THE WORST PLAYER ON OUR TEAM, YOU'RE ALSO THE WORST PLAYER IN THE HISTORY OF THE GAME!
© 1998 United Feature Syndicate, Inc.
YOU LOOK LIKE YOU'VE BEEN GAINING A LITTLE WEIGHT..
SCHULZ
3-3

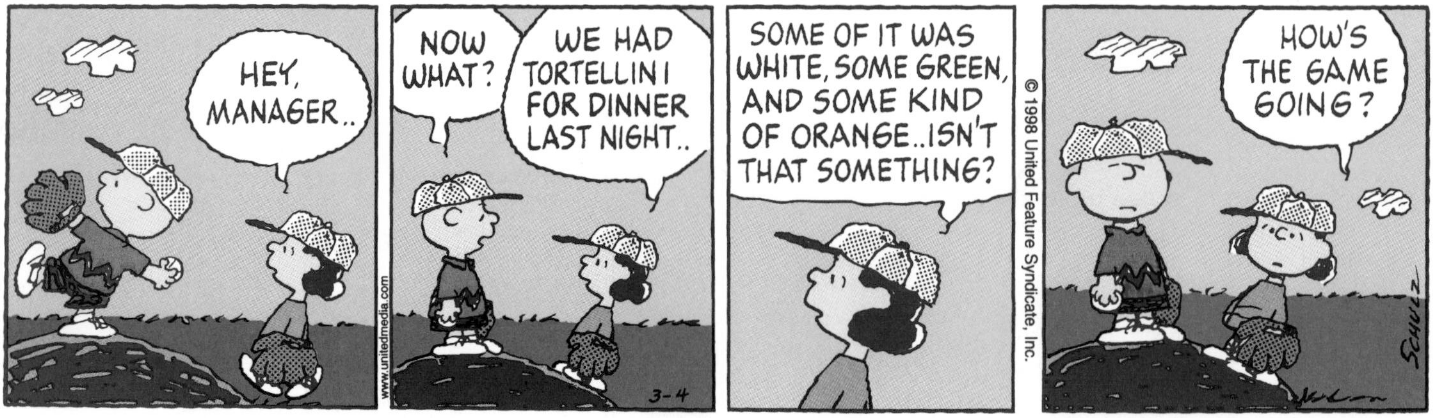
HEY, MANAGER..
www.unitedmedia.com
NOW WHAT?
WE HAD TORTELLINI FOR DINNER LAST NIGHT..
3-4
SOME OF IT WAS WHITE, SOME GREEN, AND SOME KIND OF ORANGE..ISN'T THAT SOMETHING?
© 1998 United Feature Syndicate, Inc.
HOW'S THE GAME GOING?
SCHULZ

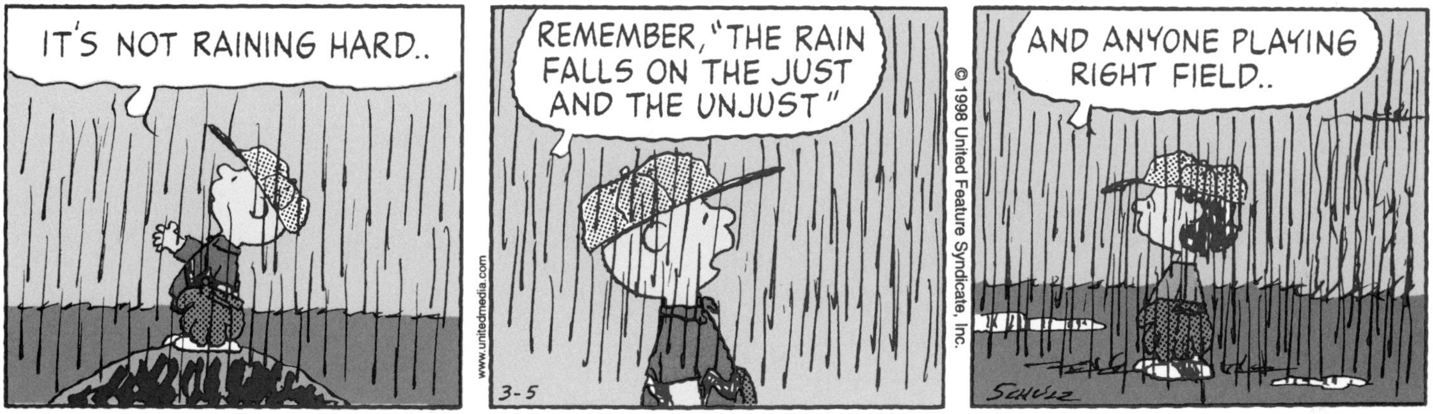
IT'S NOT RAINING HARD..
REMEMBER, "THE RAIN FALLS ON THE JUST AND THE UNJUST"
AND ANYONE PLAYING RIGHT FIELD..
3-5
www.unitedmedia.com
© 1998 United Feature Syndicate, Inc.
SCHULZ

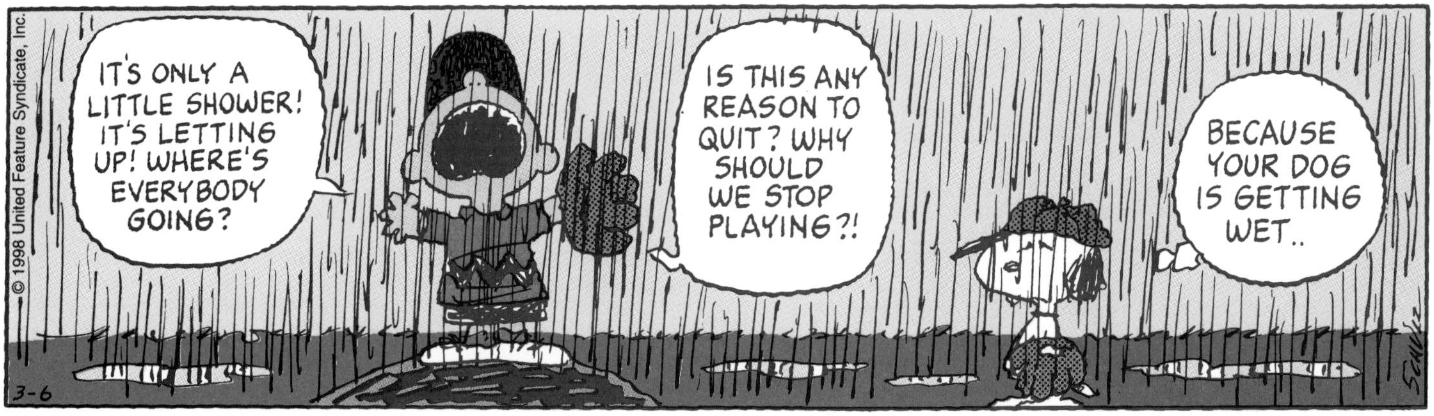
IT'S ONLY A LITTLE SHOWER! IT'S LETTING UP! WHERE'S EVERYBODY GOING?
IS THIS ANY REASON TO QUIT? WHY SHOULD WE STOP PLAYING?!
BECAUSE YOUR DOG IS GETTING WET..
3-6
© 1998 United Feature Syndicate, Inc.
SCHULZ

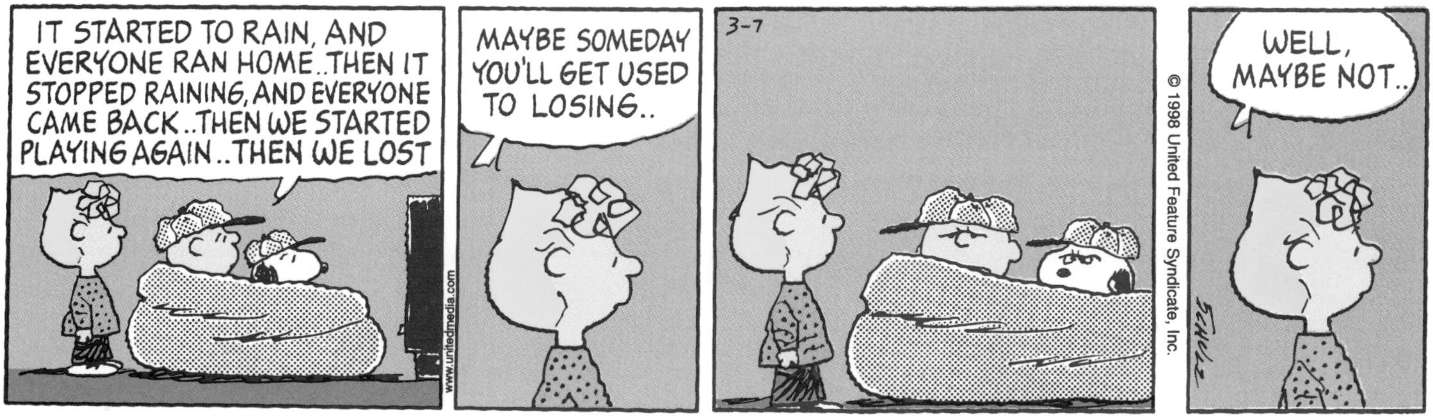
IT STARTED TO RAIN, AND EVERYONE RAN HOME..THEN IT STOPPED RAINING, AND EVERYONE CAME BACK..THEN WE STARTED PLAYING AGAIN..THEN WE LOST
MAYBE SOMEDAY YOU'LL GET USED TO LOSING..
WELL, MAYBE NOT..
3-7
www.unitedmedia.com
© 1998 United Feature Syndicate, Inc.
SCHULZ

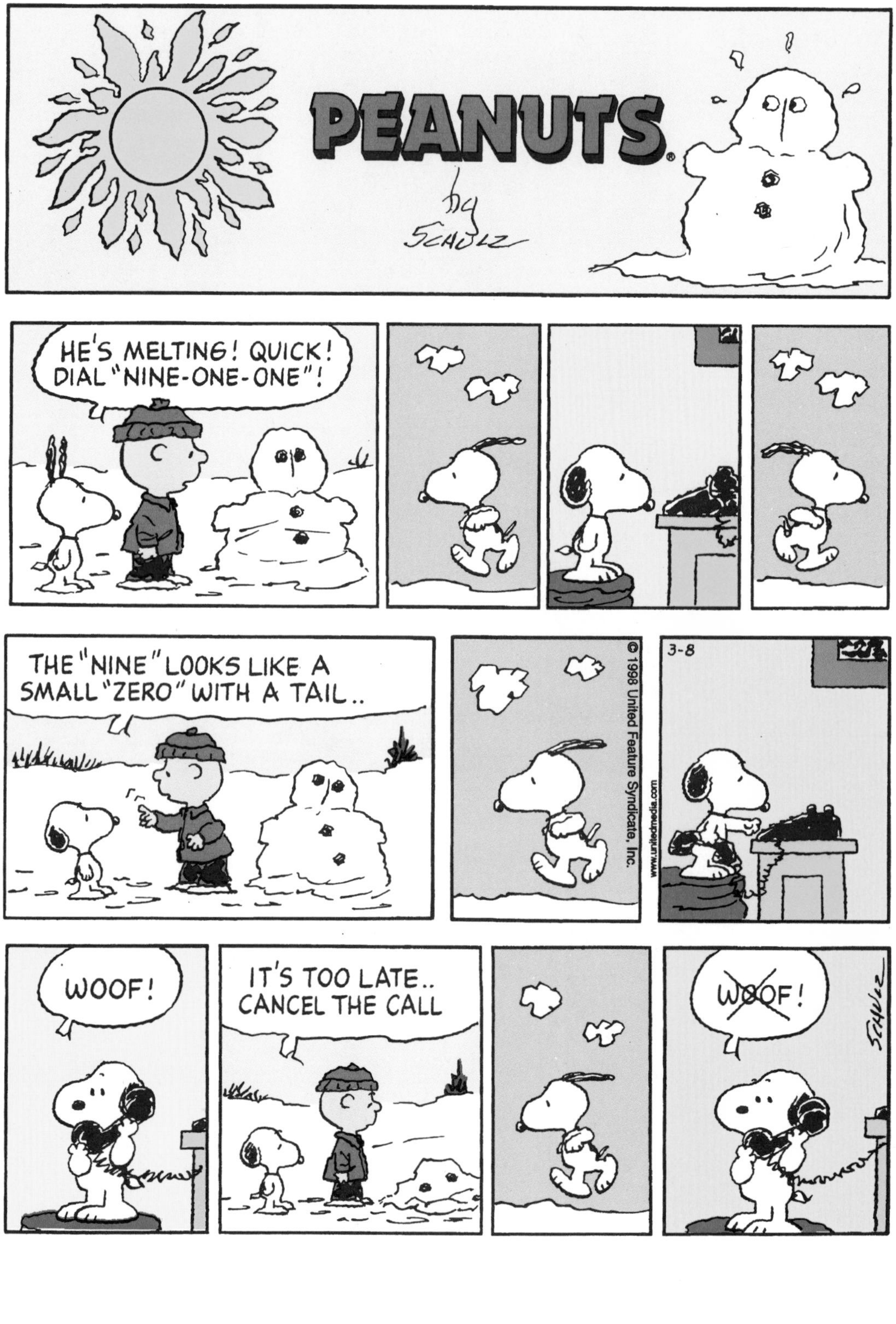
PEANUTS
by SCHULZ
HE'S MELTING! QUICK! DIAL "NINE-ONE-ONE"!
THE "NINE" LOOKS LIKE A SMALL "ZERO" WITH A TAIL..
© 1998 United Feature Syndicate, Inc.
www.unitedmedia.com
3-8
WOOF!
IT'S TOO LATE.. CANCEL THE CALL
WOOF!
SCHULZ

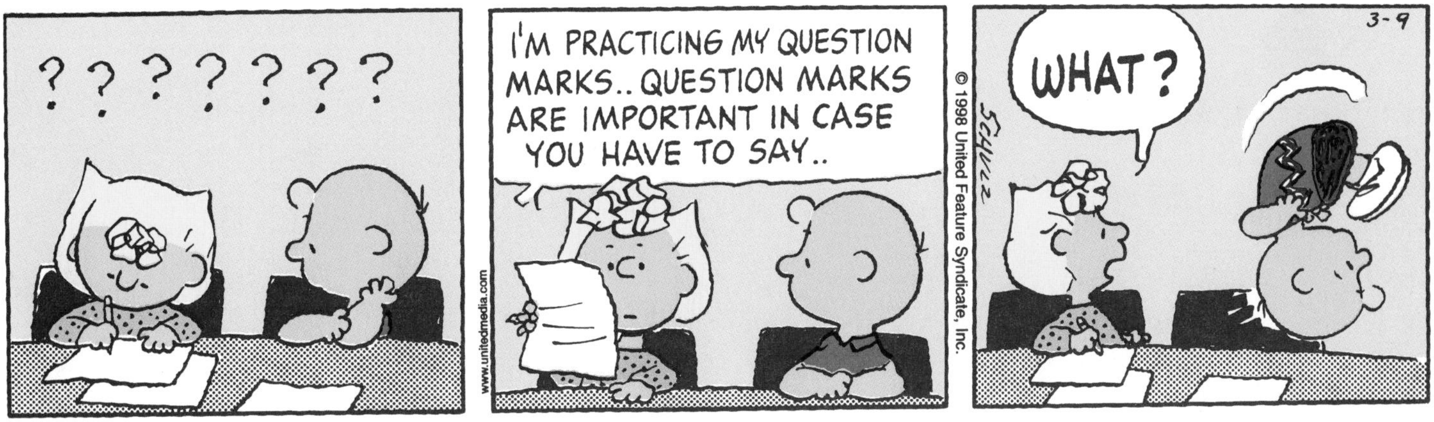
? ? ? ? ? ? ?
I'M PRACTICING MY QUESTION MARKS.. QUESTION MARKS ARE IMPORTANT IN CASE YOU HAVE TO SAY..
3-9
WHAT?
© 1998 United Feature Syndicate, Inc.
www.unitedmedia.com

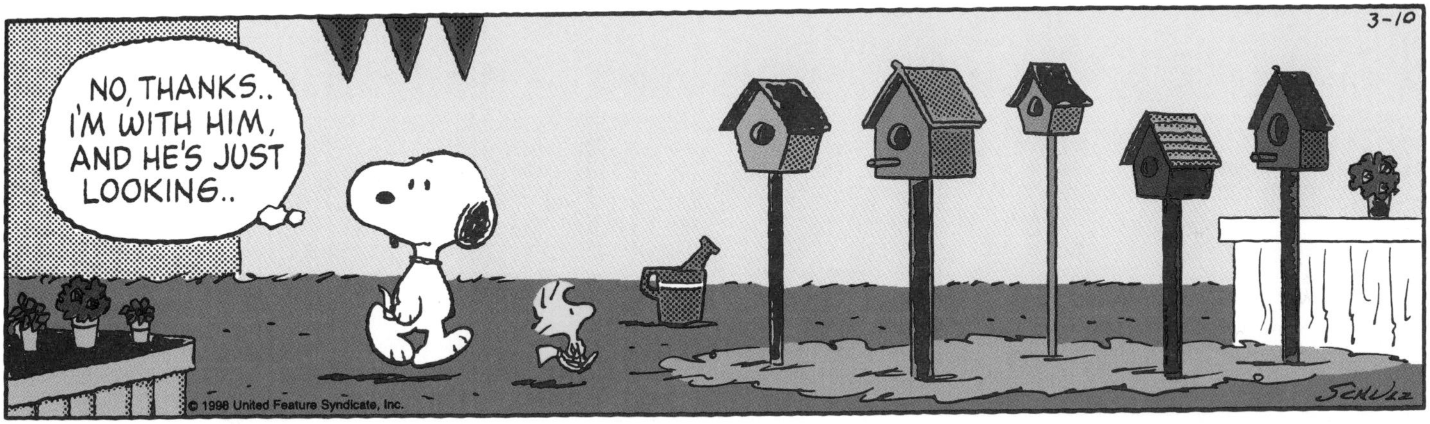
3-10
NO, THANKS.. I'M WITH HIM, AND HE'S JUST LOOKING..
© 1998 United Feature Syndicate, Inc.

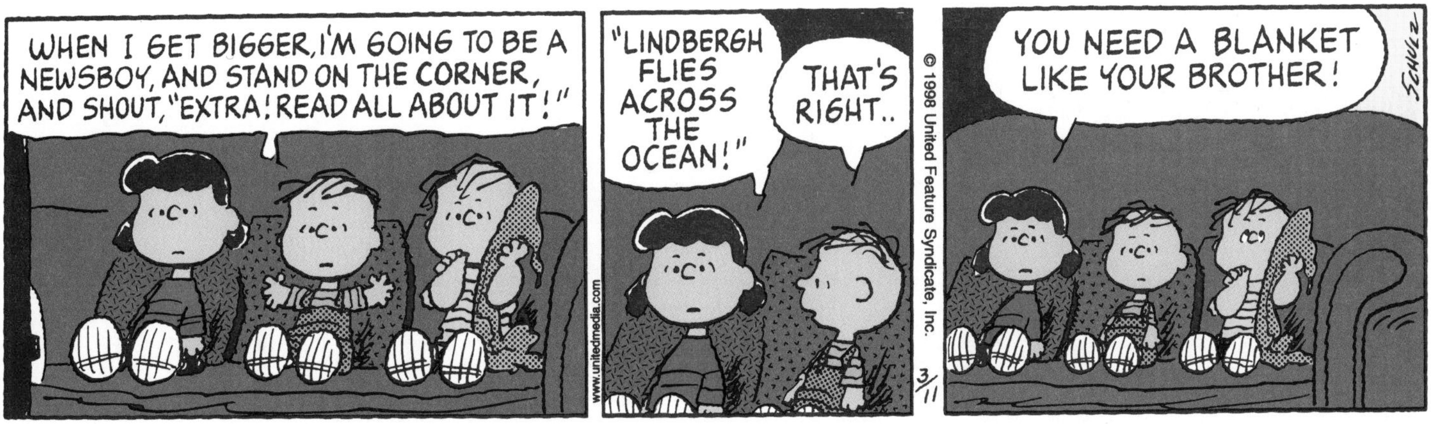
WHEN I GET BIGGER, I'M GOING TO BE A NEWSBOY, AND STAND ON THE CORNER, AND SHOUT, "EXTRA! READ ALL ABOUT IT!"
"LINDBERGH FLIES ACROSS THE OCEAN!"
THAT'S RIGHT..
3/11
YOU NEED A BLANKET LIKE YOUR BROTHER!
© 1998 United Feature Syndicate, Inc.
www.unitedmedia.com

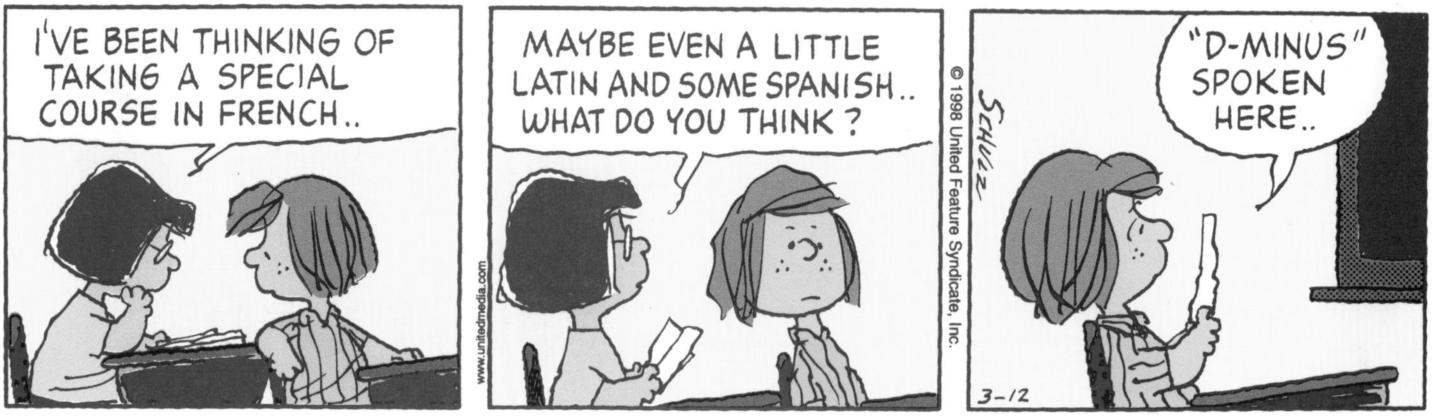
I'VE BEEN THINKING OF TAKING A SPECIAL COURSE IN FRENCH..
MAYBE EVEN A LITTLE LATIN AND SOME SPANISH.. WHAT DO YOU THINK?
"D-MINUS" SPOKEN HERE..
SCHULZ
3-12
www.unitedmedia.com
© 1998 United Feature Syndicate, Inc.

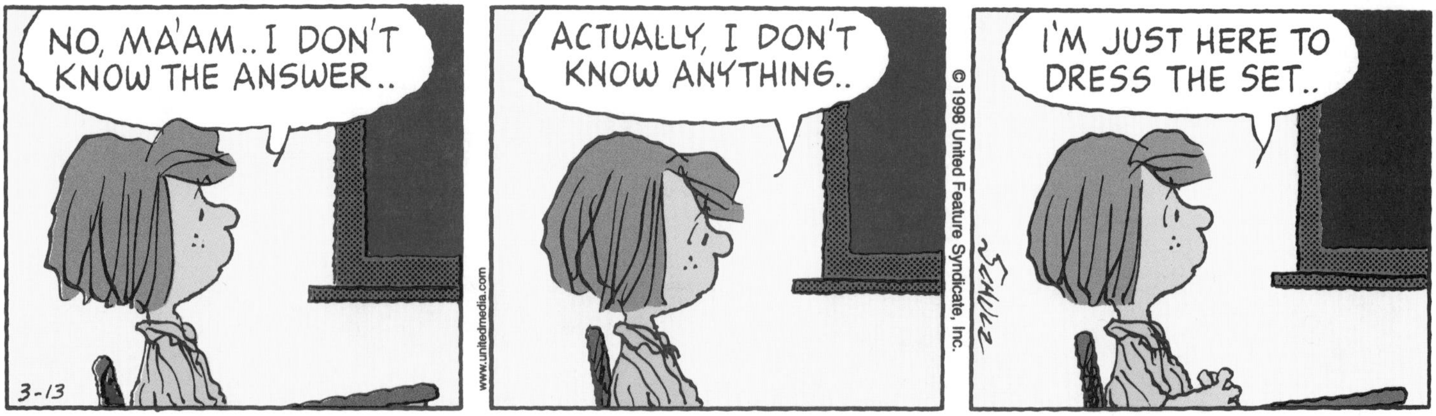
NO, MA'AM.. I DON'T KNOW THE ANSWER..
ACTUALLY, I DON'T KNOW ANYTHING..
I'M JUST HERE TO DRESS THE SET..
SCHULZ
3-13
www.unitedmedia.com
© 1998 United Feature Syndicate, Inc.

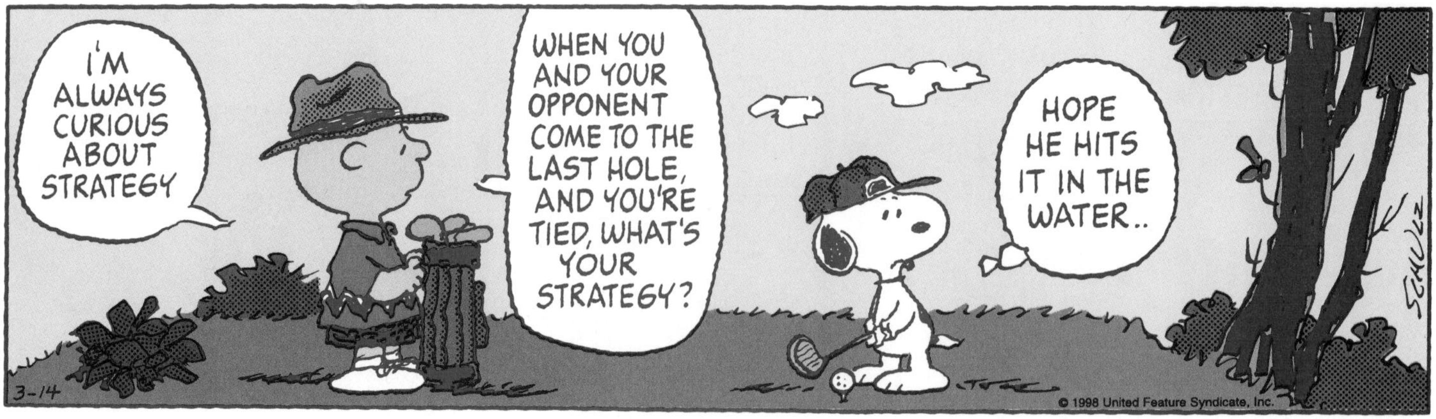
I'M ALWAYS CURIOUS ABOUT STRATEGY
WHEN YOU AND YOUR OPPONENT COME TO THE LAST HOLE, AND YOU'RE TIED, WHAT'S YOUR STRATEGY?
HOPE HE HITS IT IN THE WATER..
SCHULZ
3-14
© 1998 United Feature Syndicate, Inc.

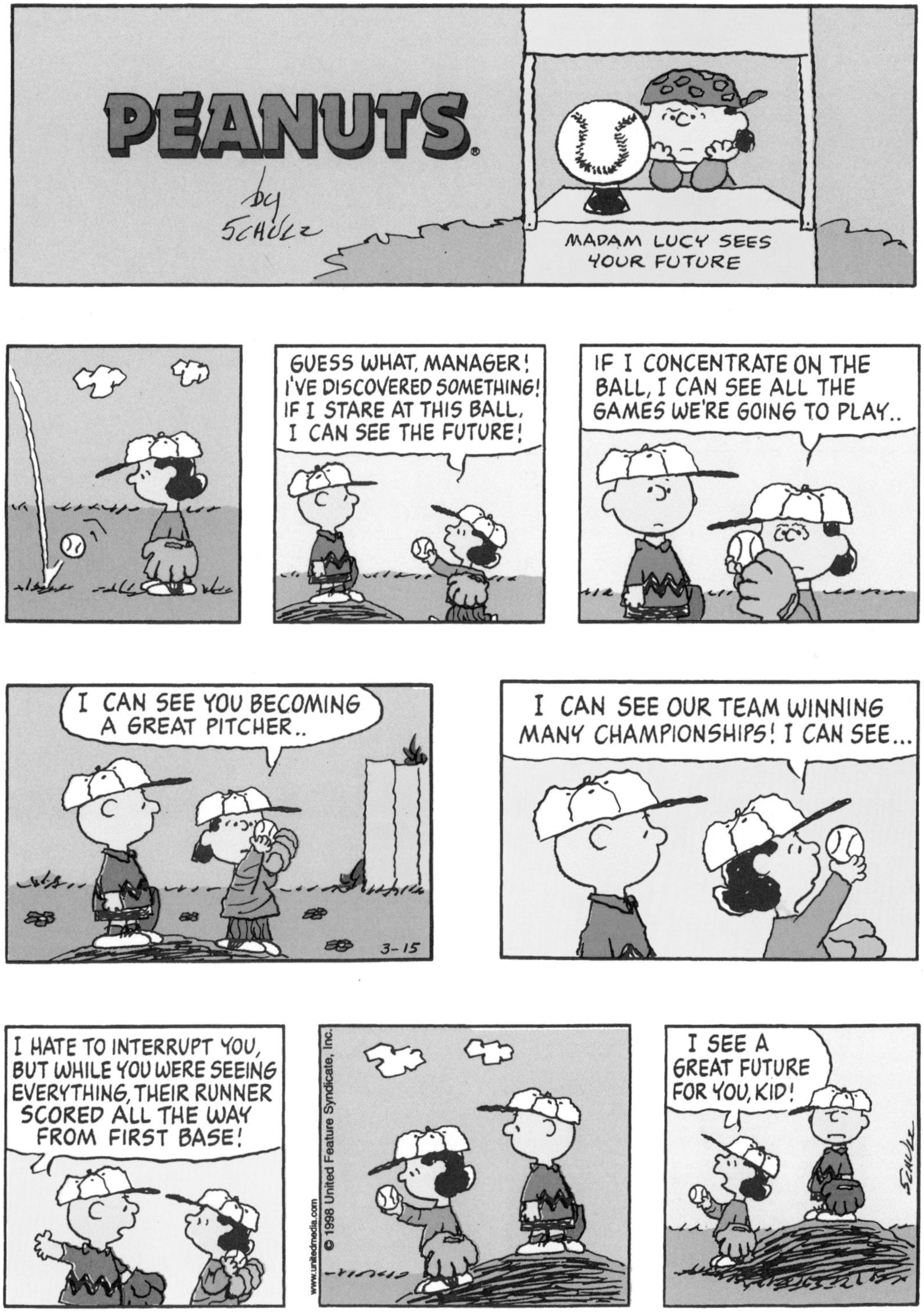

PEANUTS
by SCHULZ
MADAM LUCY SEES YOUR FUTURE
GUESS WHAT, MANAGER! I'VE DISCOVERED SOMETHING! IF I STARE AT THIS BALL, I CAN SEE THE FUTURE!
IF I CONCENTRATE ON THE BALL, I CAN SEE ALL THE GAMES WE'RE GOING TO PLAY..
I CAN SEE YOU BECOMING A GREAT PITCHER..
3-15
I CAN SEE OUR TEAM WINNING MANY CHAMPIONSHIPS! I CAN SEE...
I HATE TO INTERRUPT YOU, BUT WHILE YOU WERE SEEING EVERYTHING, THEIR RUNNER SCORED ALL THE WAY FROM FIRST BASE!
www.unitedmedia.com © 1998 United Feature Syndicate, Inc.
I SEE A GREAT FUTURE FOR YOU, KID!
SCHULZ

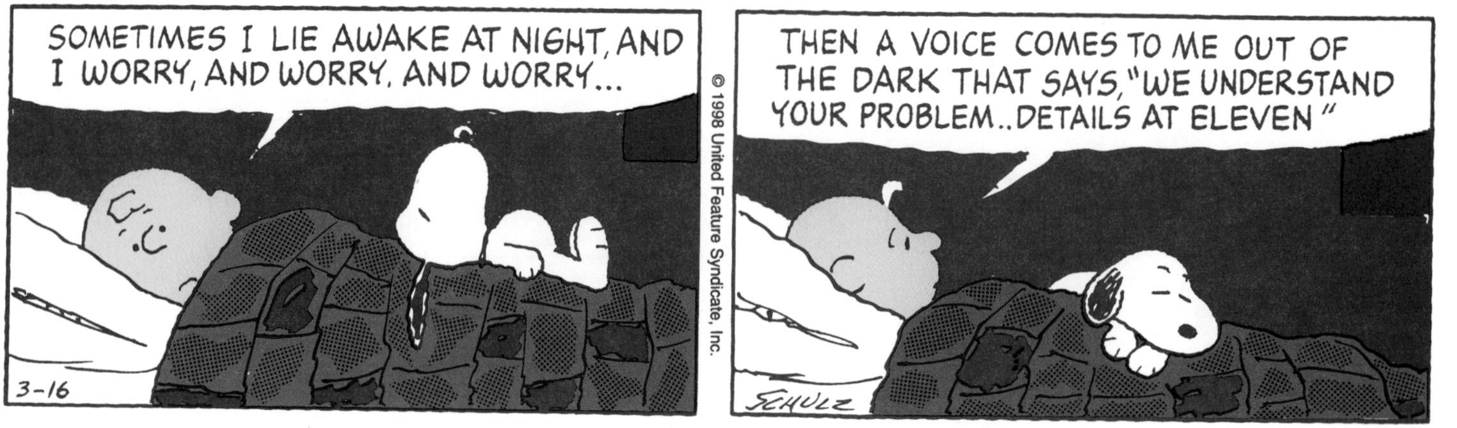
SOMETIMES I LIE AWAKE AT NIGHT, AND I WORRY, AND WORRY, AND WORRY...
THEN A VOICE COMES TO ME OUT OF THE DARK THAT SAYS, "WE UNDERSTAND YOUR PROBLEM..DETAILS AT ELEVEN"
3-16
SCHULZ
© 1998 United Feature Syndicate, Inc.

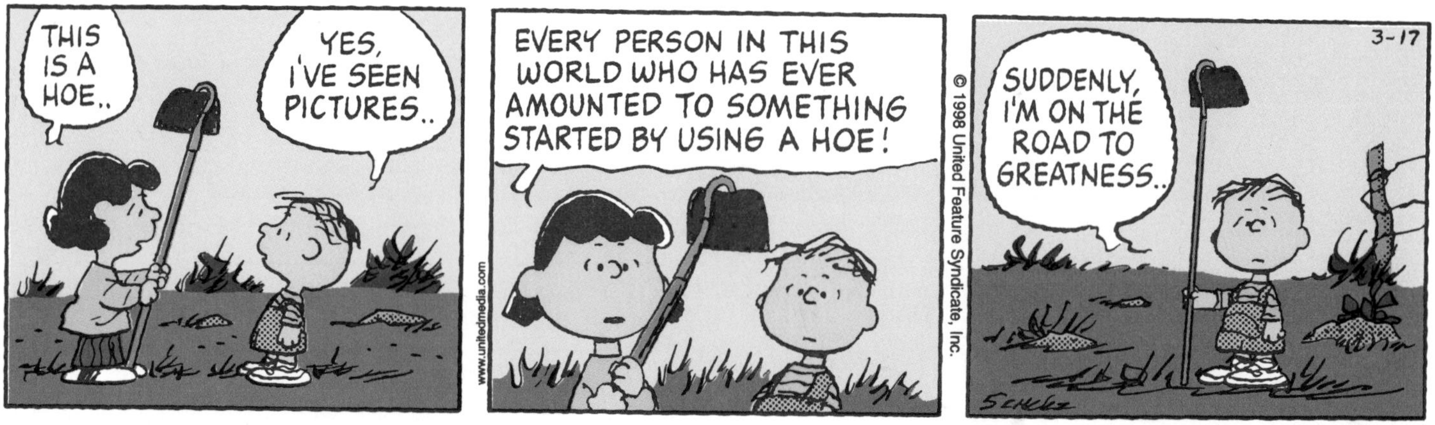
THIS IS A HOE..
YES, I'VE SEEN PICTURES..
EVERY PERSON IN THIS WORLD WHO HAS EVER AMOUNTED TO SOMETHING STARTED BY USING A HOE!
SUDDENLY, I'M ON THE ROAD TO GREATNESS..
3-17
SCHULZ
www.unitedmedia.com
© 1998 United Feature Syndicate, Inc.

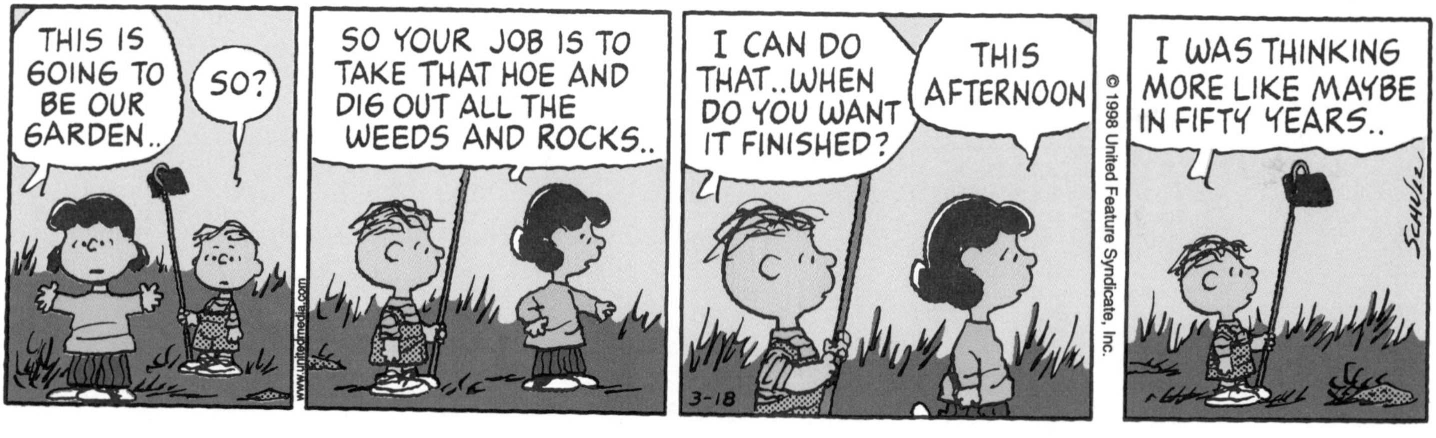
THIS IS GOING TO BE OUR GARDEN..
SO?
SO YOUR JOB IS TO TAKE THAT HOE AND DIG OUT ALL THE WEEDS AND ROCKS..
I CAN DO THAT..WHEN DO YOU WANT IT FINISHED?
THIS AFTERNOON
I WAS THINKING MORE LIKE MAYBE IN FIFTY YEARS..
3-18
SCHULZ
www.unitedmedia.com
© 1998 United Feature Syndicate, Inc.

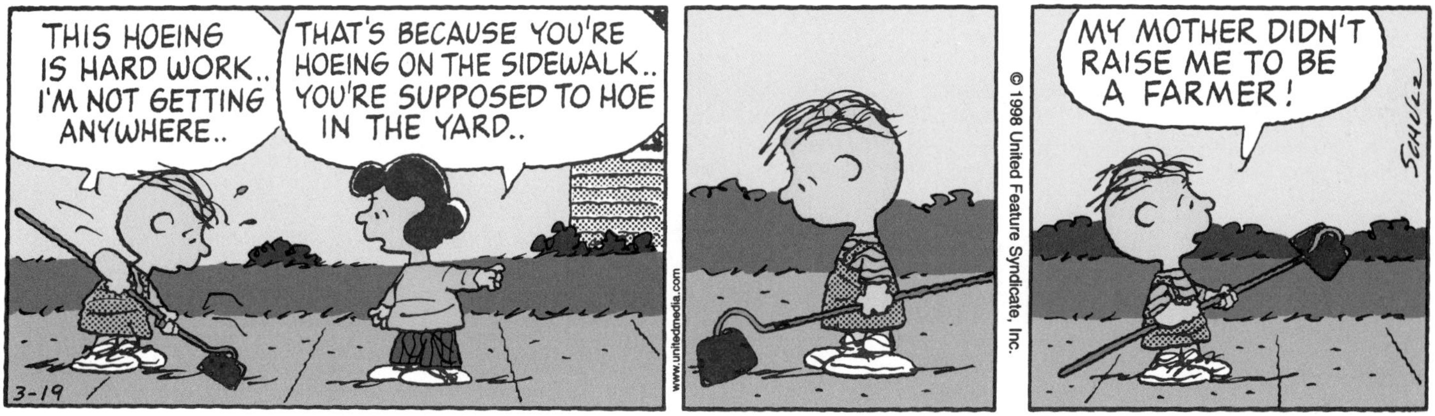
THIS HOEING IS HARD WORK.. I'M NOT GETTING ANYWHERE..
THAT'S BECAUSE YOU'RE HOEING ON THE SIDEWALK.. YOU'RE SUPPOSED TO HOE IN THE YARD..
MY MOTHER DIDN'T RAISE ME TO BE A FARMER!
3-19
www.unitedmedia.com
© 1998 United Feature Syndicate, Inc.
SCHULZ

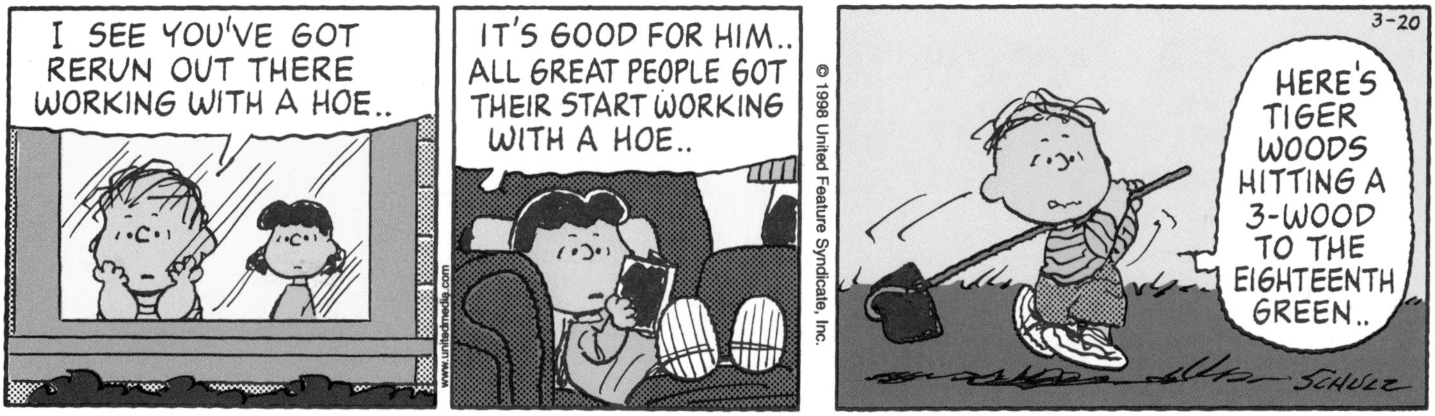
I SEE YOU'VE GOT RERUN OUT THERE WORKING WITH A HOE..
IT'S GOOD FOR HIM.. ALL GREAT PEOPLE GOT THEIR START WORKING WITH A HOE..
HERE'S TIGER WOODS HITTING A 3-WOOD TO THE EIGHTEENTH GREEN..
3-20
www.unitedmedia.com
© 1998 United Feature Syndicate, Inc.
SCHULZ

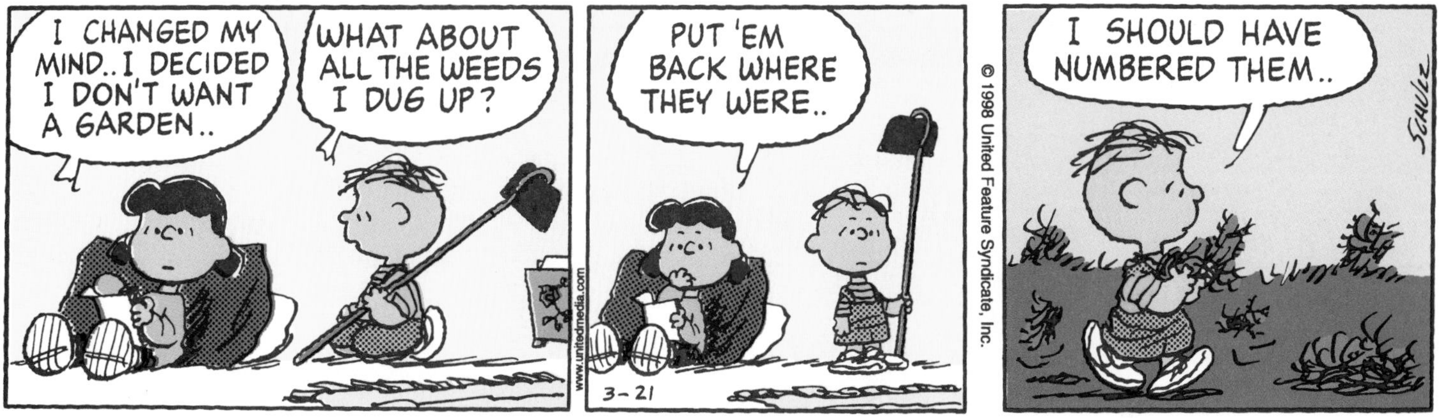
I CHANGED MY MIND.. I DECIDED I DON'T WANT A GARDEN..
WHAT ABOUT ALL THE WEEDS I DUG UP?
PUT 'EM BACK WHERE THEY WERE..
I SHOULD HAVE NUMBERED THEM..
3-21
www.unitedmedia.com
© 1998 United Feature Syndicate, Inc.
SCHULZ

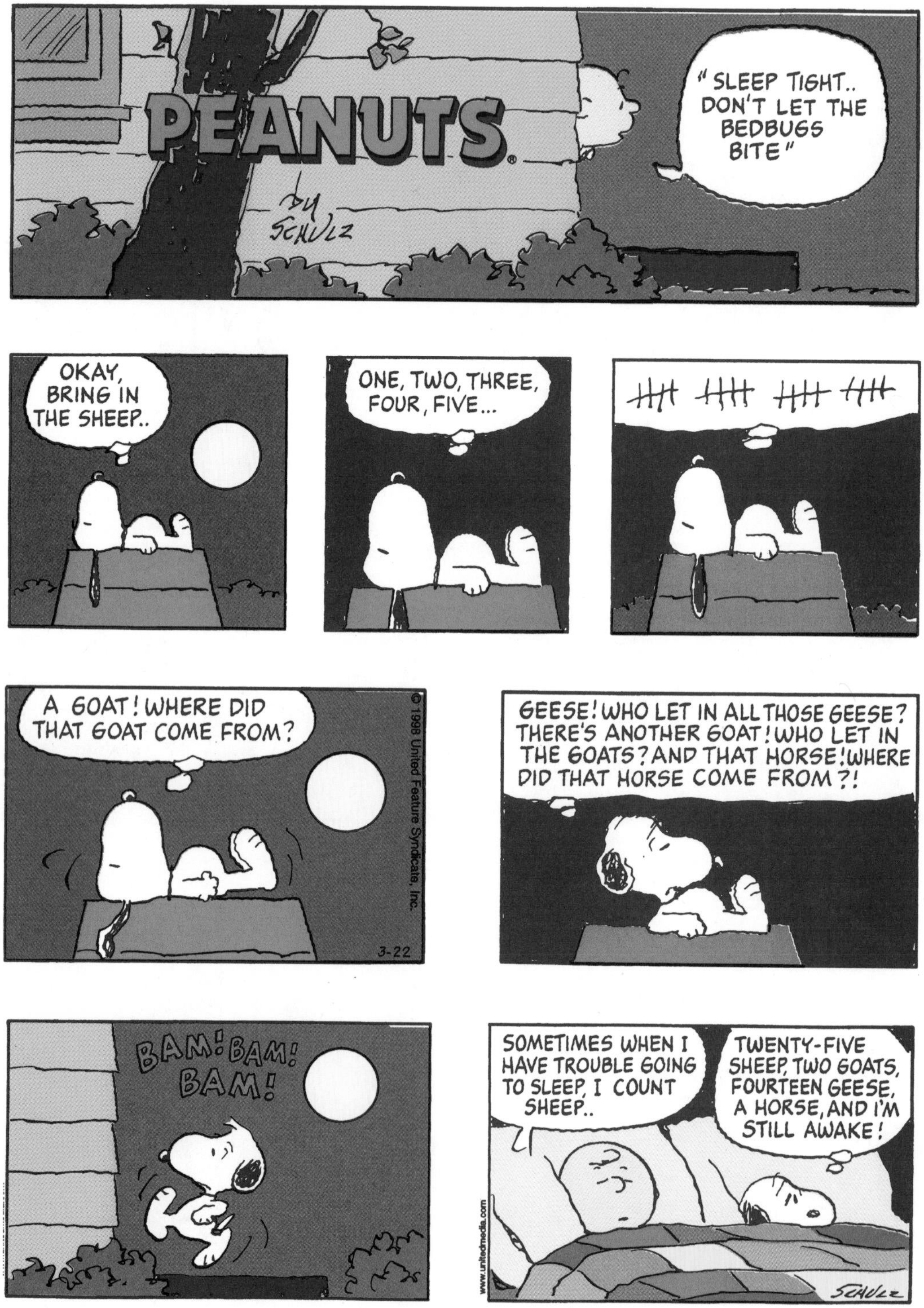
PEANUTS
by SCHULZ
"SLEEP TIGHT.. DON'T LET THE BEDBUGS BITE"
OKAY, BRING IN THE SHEEP..
ONE, TWO, THREE, FOUR, FIVE...
A GOAT! WHERE DID THAT GOAT COME FROM?
© 1998 United Feature Syndicate, Inc.
3-22
GEESE! WHO LET IN ALL THOSE GEESE? THERE'S ANOTHER GOAT! WHO LET IN THE GOATS? AND THAT HORSE! WHERE DID THAT HORSE COME FROM?!
BAM! BAM! BAM!
SOMETIMES WHEN I HAVE TROUBLE GOING TO SLEEP, I COUNT SHEEP..
TWENTY-FIVE SHEEP, TWO GOATS, FOURTEEN GEESE, A HORSE, AND I'M STILL AWAKE!
www.unitedmedia.com
SCHULZ

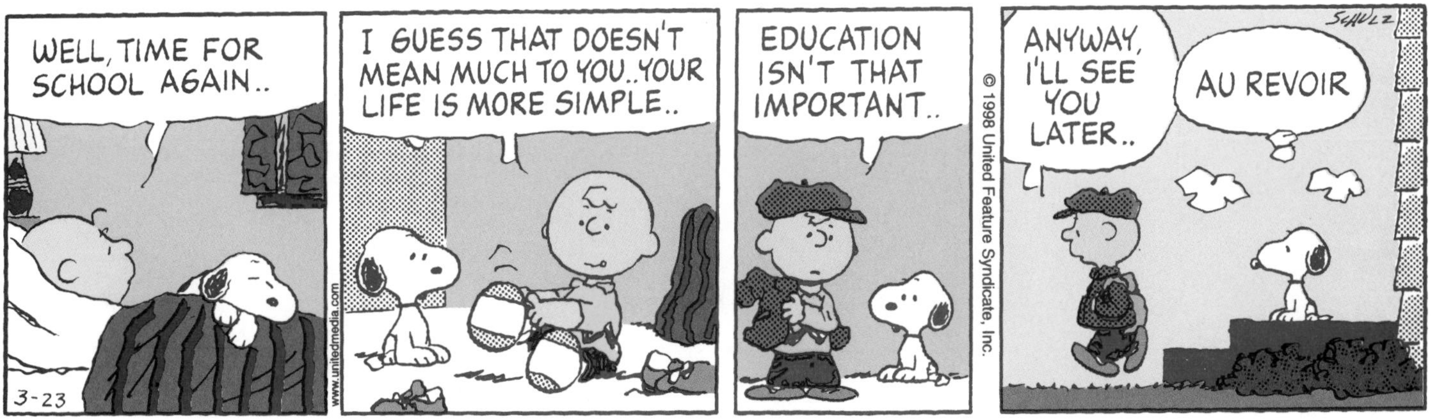
WELL, TIME FOR SCHOOL AGAIN..
3-23
I GUESS THAT DOESN'T MEAN MUCH TO YOU..YOUR LIFE IS MORE SIMPLE..
EDUCATION ISN'T THAT IMPORTANT..
ANYWAY, I'LL SEE YOU LATER..
AU REVOIR
SCHULZ
© 1998 United Feature Syndicate, Inc.
www.unitedmedia.com

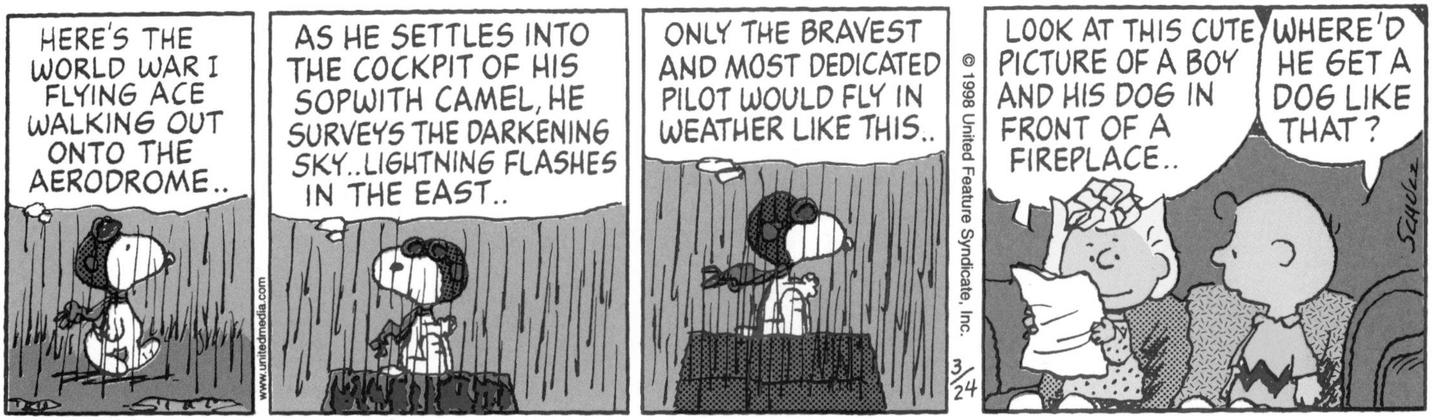
HERE'S THE WORLD WAR I FLYING ACE WALKING OUT ONTO THE AERODROME..
AS HE SETTLES INTO THE COCKPIT OF HIS SOPWITH CAMEL, HE SURVEYS THE DARKENING SKY..LIGHTNING FLASHES IN THE EAST..
ONLY THE BRAVEST AND MOST DEDICATED PILOT WOULD FLY IN WEATHER LIKE THIS..
3/24
LOOK AT THIS CUTE PICTURE OF A BOY AND HIS DOG IN FRONT OF A FIREPLACE..
WHERE'D HE GET A DOG LIKE THAT?
SCHULZ
© 1998 United Feature Syndicate, Inc.
www.unitedmedia.com

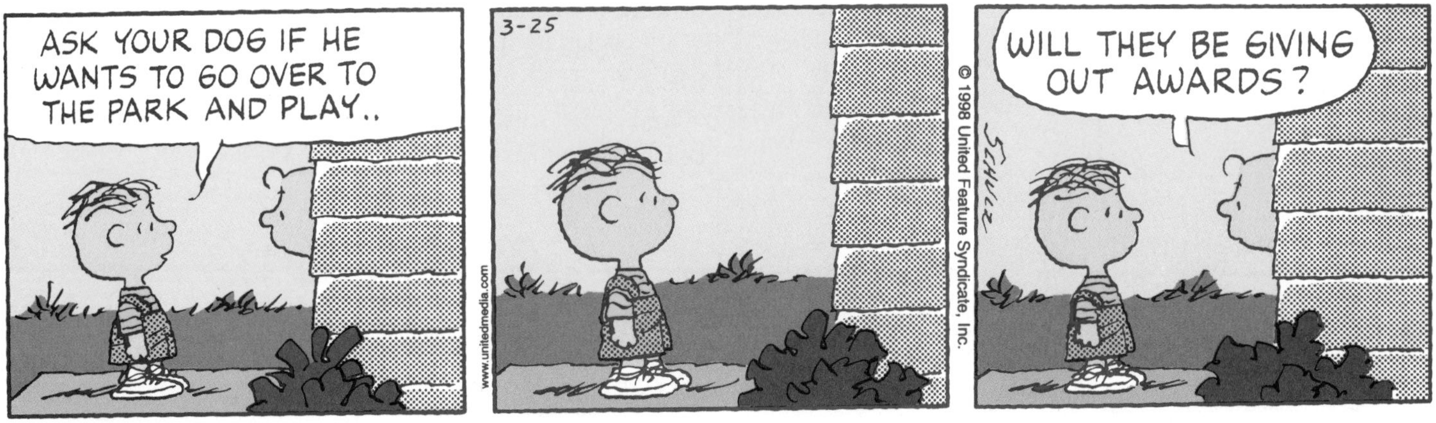
ASK YOUR DOG IF HE WANTS TO GO OVER TO THE PARK AND PLAY..
3-25
WILL THEY BE GIVING OUT AWARDS?
SCHULZ
© 1998 United Feature Syndicate, Inc.
www.unitedmedia.com

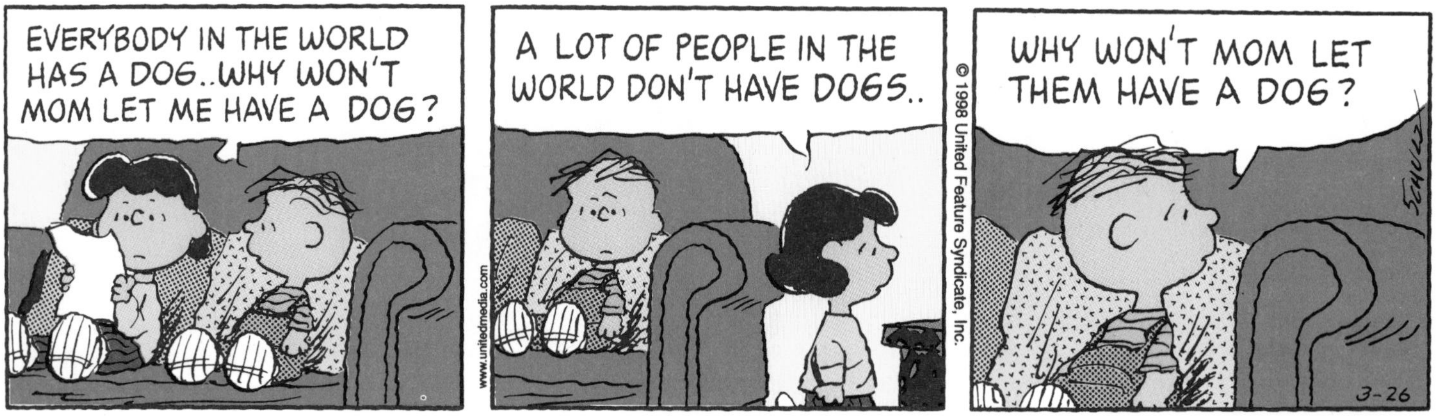
EVERYBODY IN THE WORLD HAS A DOG..WHY WON'T MOM LET ME HAVE A DOG?
A LOT OF PEOPLE IN THE WORLD DON'T HAVE DOGS..
WHY WON'T MOM LET THEM HAVE A DOG?
© 1998 United Feature Syndicate, Inc.
www.unitedmedia.com
SCHULZ
3-26

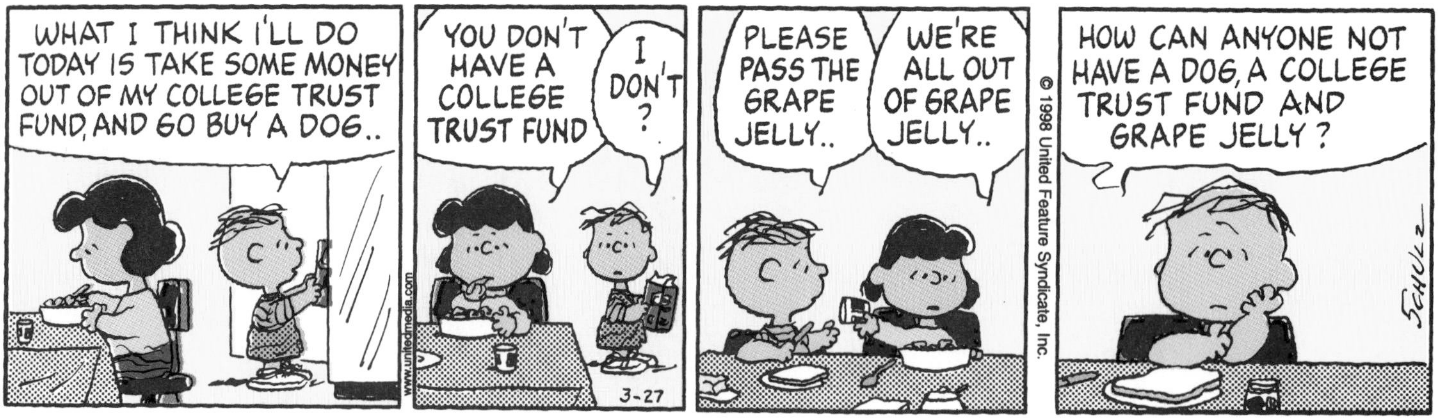
WHAT I THINK I'LL DO TODAY IS TAKE SOME MONEY OUT OF MY COLLEGE TRUST FUND, AND GO BUY A DOG..
YOU DON'T HAVE A COLLEGE TRUST FUND
I DON'T ?
PLEASE PASS THE GRAPE JELLY..
WE'RE ALL OUT OF GRAPE JELLY..
HOW CAN ANYONE NOT HAVE A DOG, A COLLEGE TRUST FUND AND GRAPE JELLY?
© 1998 United Feature Syndicate, Inc.
www.unitedmedia.com
SCHULZ
3-27

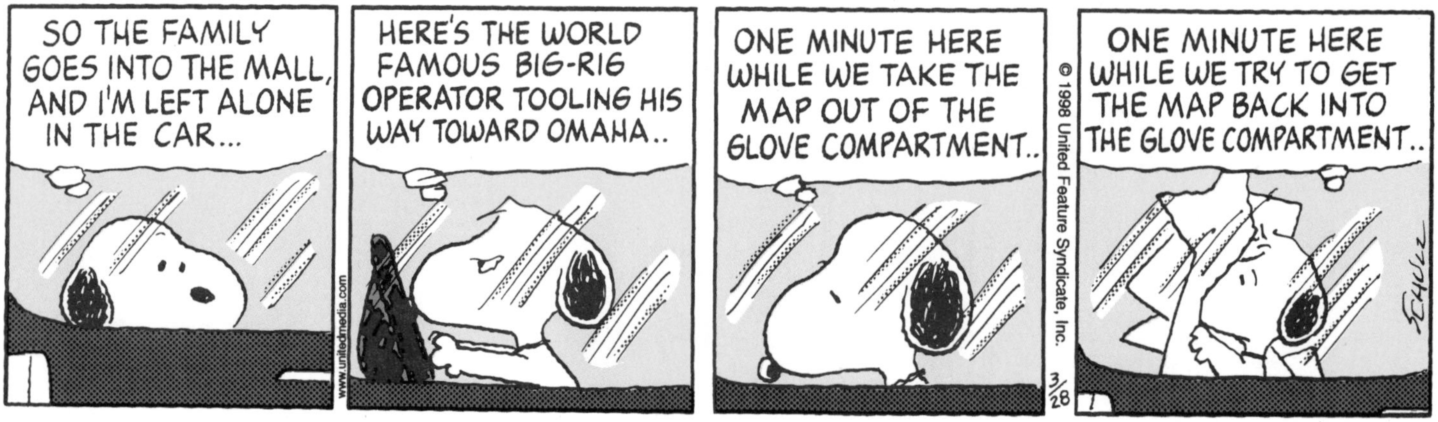
SO THE FAMILY GOES INTO THE MALL, AND I'M LEFT ALONE IN THE CAR...
HERE'S THE WORLD FAMOUS BIG-RIG OPERATOR TOOLING HIS WAY TOWARD OMAHA..
ONE MINUTE HERE WHILE WE TAKE THE MAP OUT OF THE GLOVE COMPARTMENT..
ONE MINUTE HERE WHILE WE TRY TO GET THE MAP BACK INTO THE GLOVE COMPARTMENT..
© 1998 United Feature Syndicate, Inc.
www.unitedmedia.com
SCHULZ
3/28

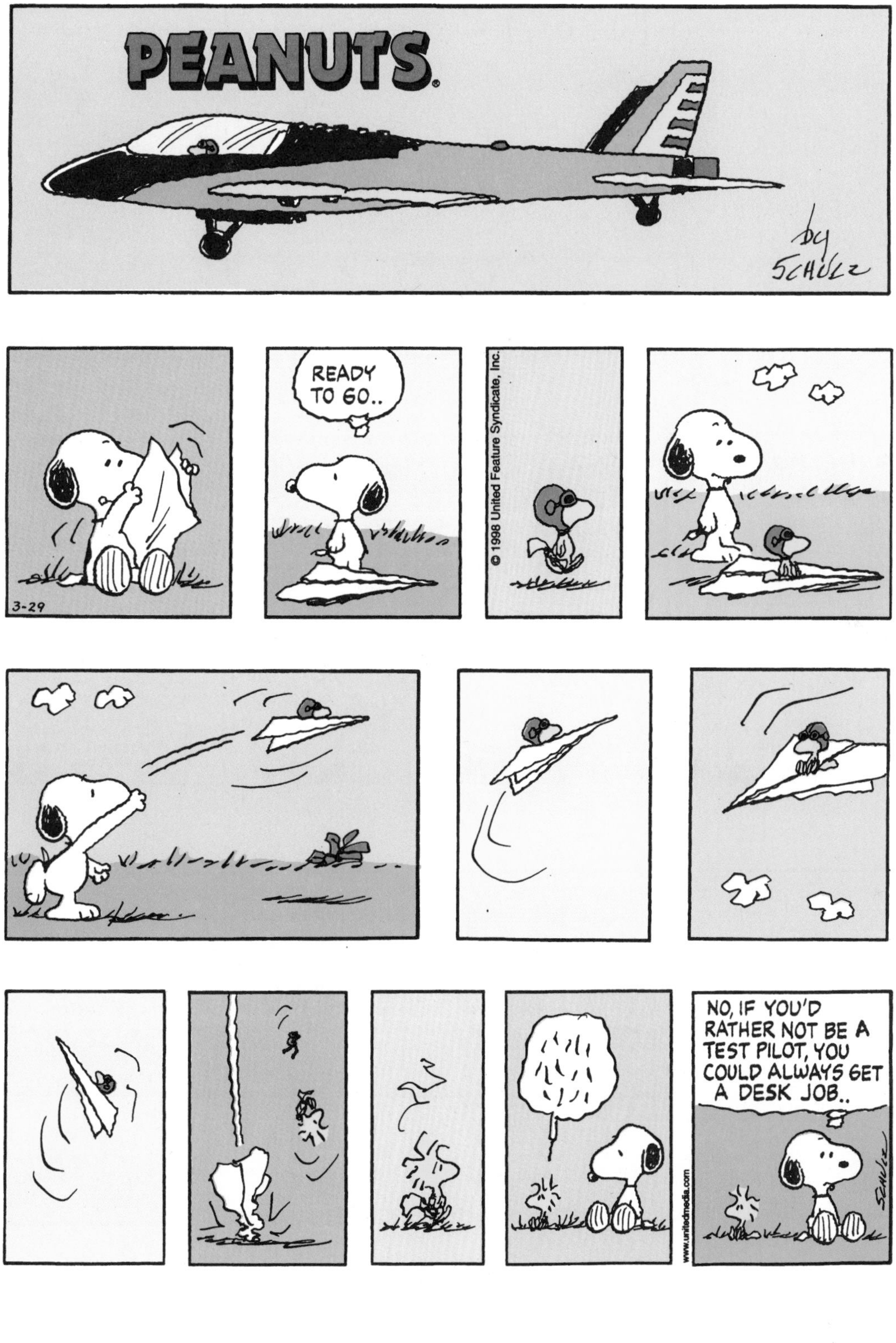
PEANUTS
by SCHULZ
3-29
READY TO GO..
© 1998 United Feature Syndicate, Inc.
www.unitedmedia.com
NO, IF YOU'D RATHER NOT BE A TEST PILOT, YOU COULD ALWAYS GET A DESK JOB..
SCHULZ

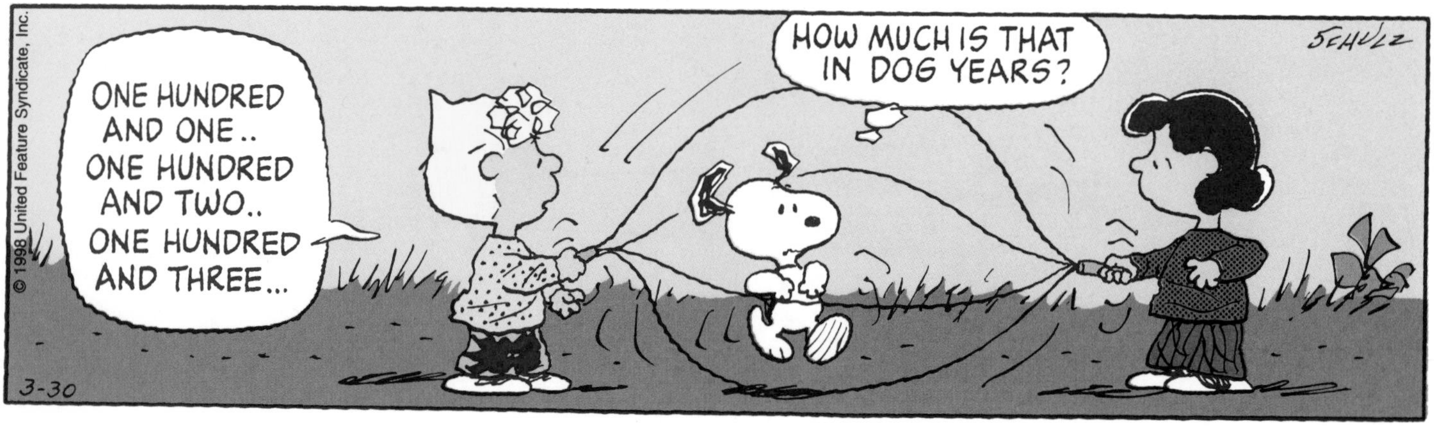
© 1998 United Feature Syndicate, Inc.
ONE HUNDRED AND ONE.. ONE HUNDRED AND TWO.. ONE HUNDRED AND THREE...
HOW MUCH IS THAT IN DOG YEARS?
SCHULZ
3-30

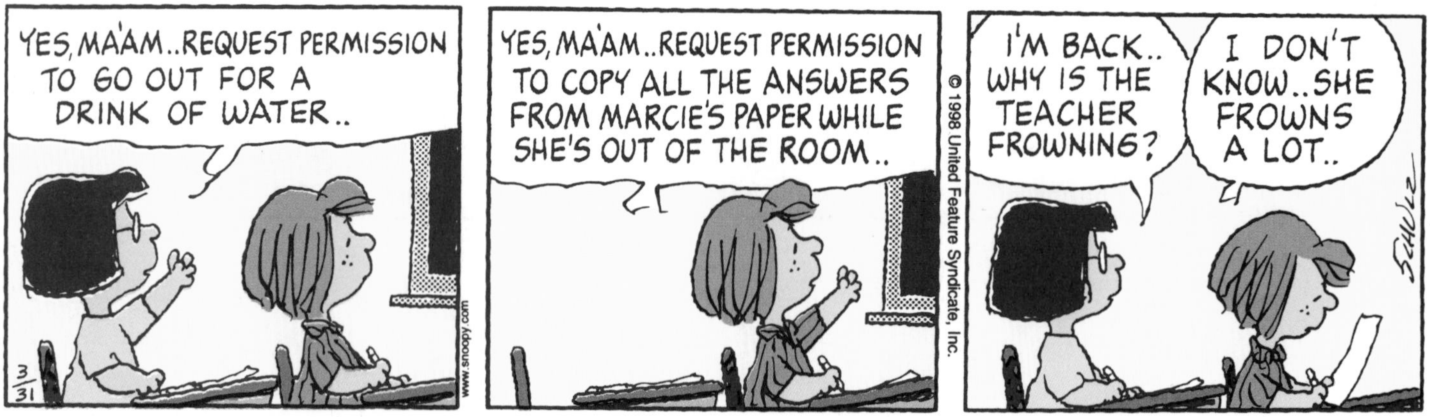
YES, MA'AM..REQUEST PERMISSION TO GO OUT FOR A DRINK OF WATER..
3/31
www.snoopy.com
YES, MA'AM..REQUEST PERMISSION TO COPY ALL THE ANSWERS FROM MARCIE'S PAPER WHILE SHE'S OUT OF THE ROOM..
© 1998 United Feature Syndicate, Inc.
I'M BACK.. WHY IS THE TEACHER FROWNING?
I DON'T KNOW..SHE FROWNS A LOT..
SCHULZ

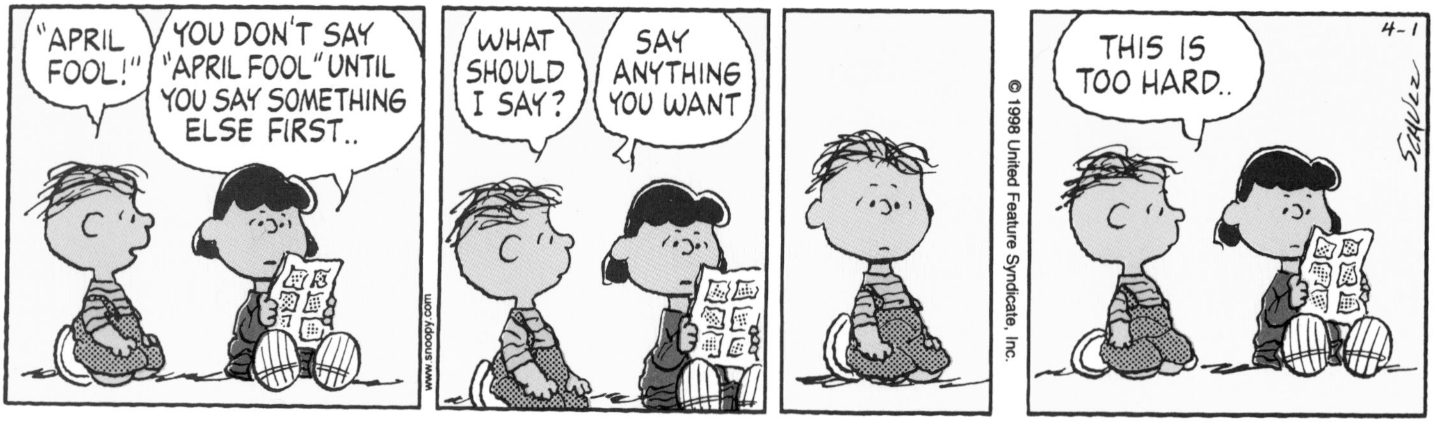
"APRIL FOOL!"
YOU DON'T SAY "APRIL FOOL" UNTIL YOU SAY SOMETHING ELSE FIRST..
www.snoopy.com
WHAT SHOULD I SAY?
SAY ANYTHING YOU WANT
© 1998 United Feature Syndicate, Inc.
4-1
THIS IS TOO HARD..
SCHULZ

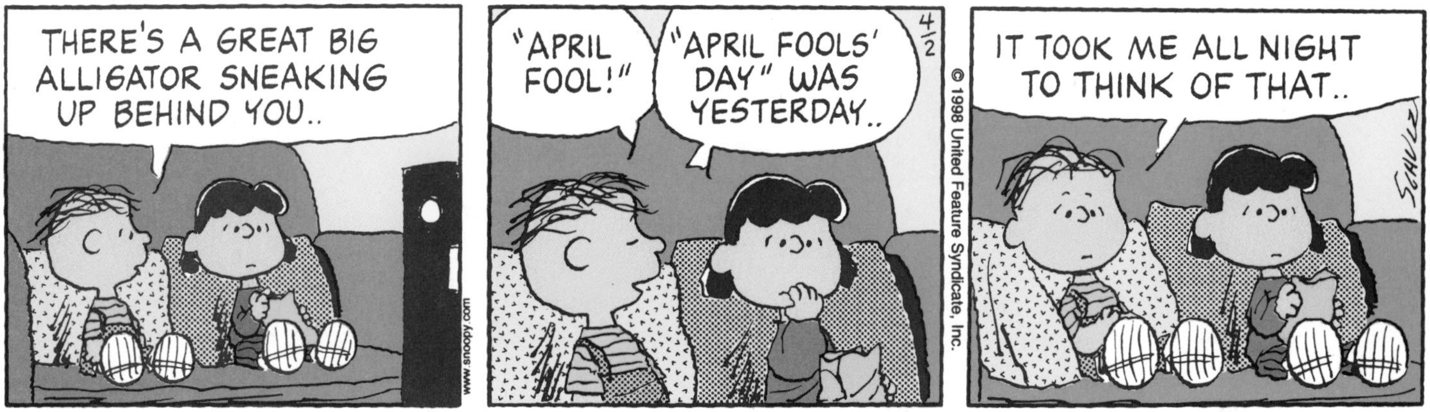
THERE'S A GREAT BIG ALLIGATOR SNEAKING UP BEHIND YOU..
"APRIL FOOL!"
"APRIL FOOLS' DAY" WAS YESTERDAY..
IT TOOK ME ALL NIGHT TO THINK OF THAT..
4/2
© 1998 United Feature Syndicate, Inc.
www.snoopy.com
SCHULZ

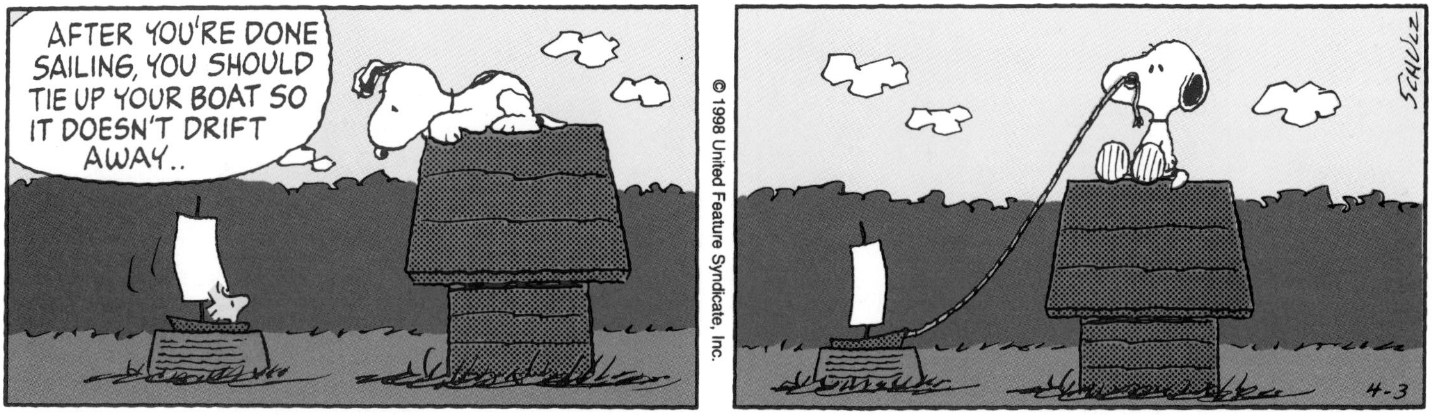
AFTER YOU'RE DONE SAILING, YOU SHOULD TIE UP YOUR BOAT SO IT DOESN'T DRIFT AWAY..
© 1998 United Feature Syndicate, Inc.
SCHULZ
4-3

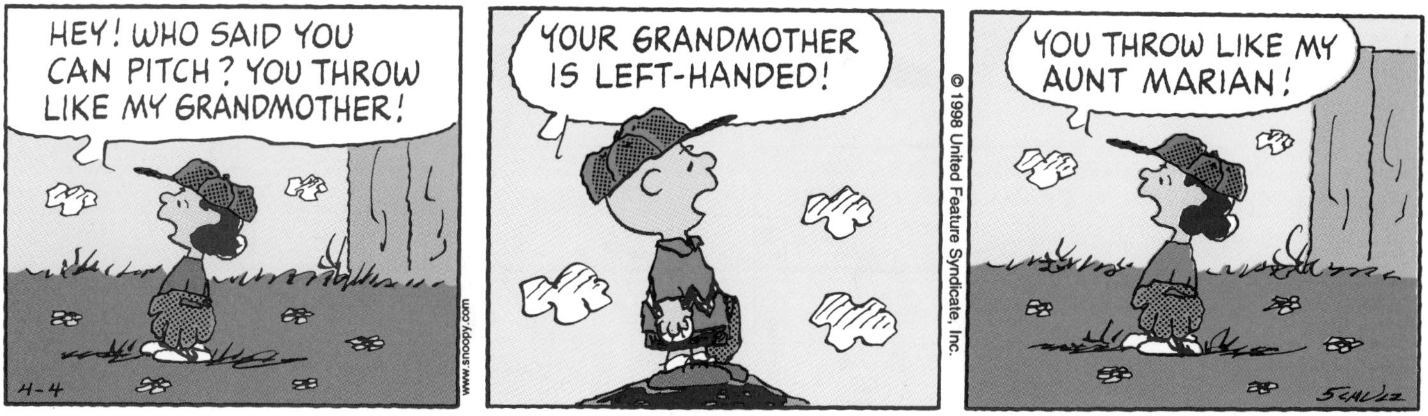
HEY! WHO SAID YOU CAN PITCH? YOU THROW LIKE MY GRANDMOTHER!
YOUR GRANDMOTHER IS LEFT-HANDED!
YOU THROW LIKE MY AUNT MARIAN!
4-4
www.snoopy.com
© 1998 United Feature Syndicate, Inc.
SCHULZ

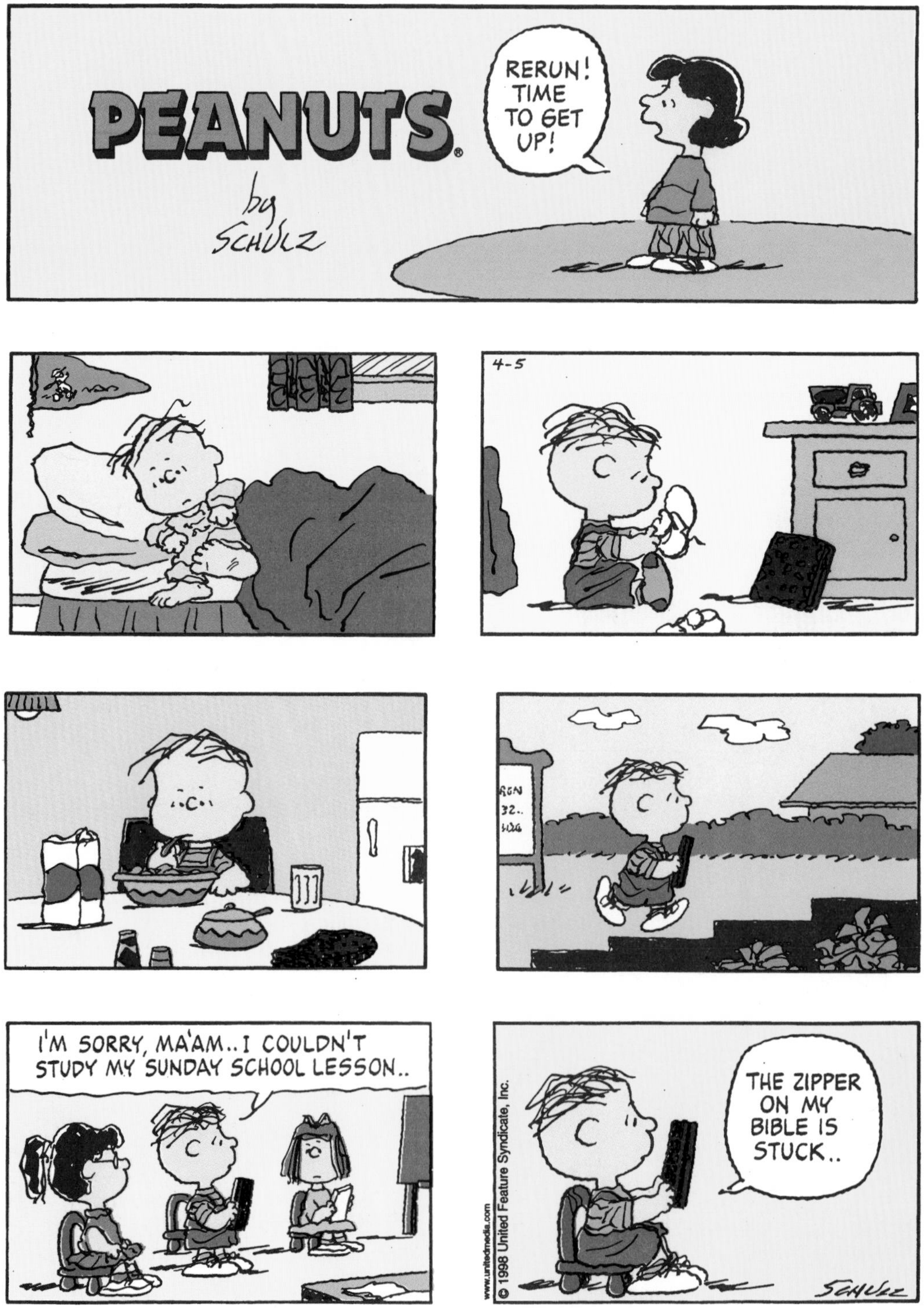
PEANUTS
by SCHULZ
RERUN! TIME TO GET UP!
4-5
I'M SORRY, MA'AM..I COULDN'T STUDY MY SUNDAY SCHOOL LESSON..
THE ZIPPER ON MY BIBLE IS STUCK..
© 1998 United Feature Syndicate, Inc.
www.unitedmedia.com
SCHULZ

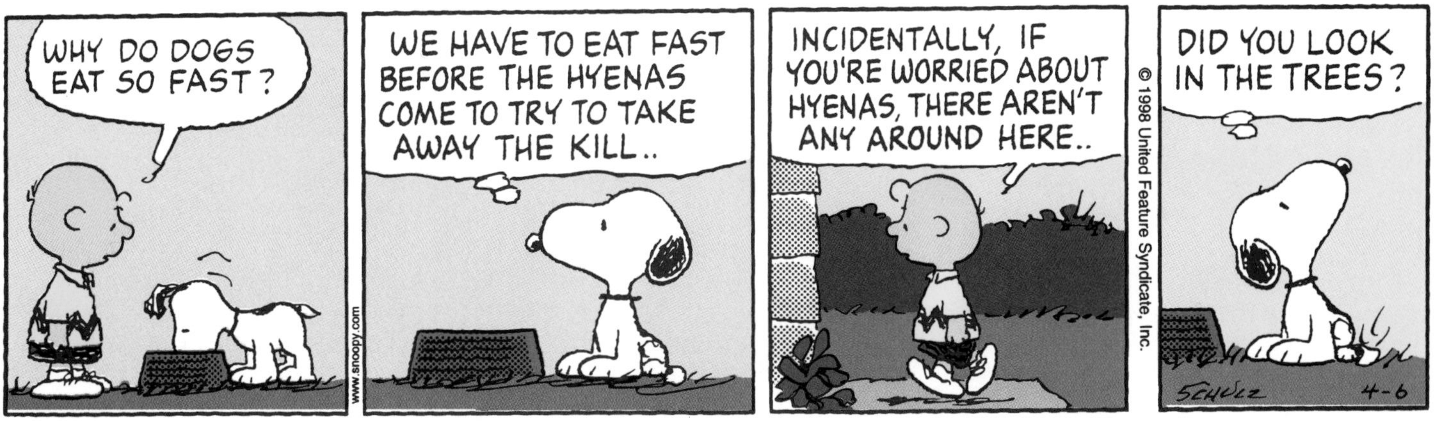
WHY DO DOGS EAT SO FAST?
WE HAVE TO EAT FAST BEFORE THE HYENAS COME TO TRY TO TAKE AWAY THE KILL..
INCIDENTALLY, IF YOU'RE WORRIED ABOUT HYENAS, THERE AREN'T ANY AROUND HERE..
DID YOU LOOK IN THE TREES?
www.snoopy.com
© 1998 United Feature Syndicate, Inc.
SCHULZ 4-6

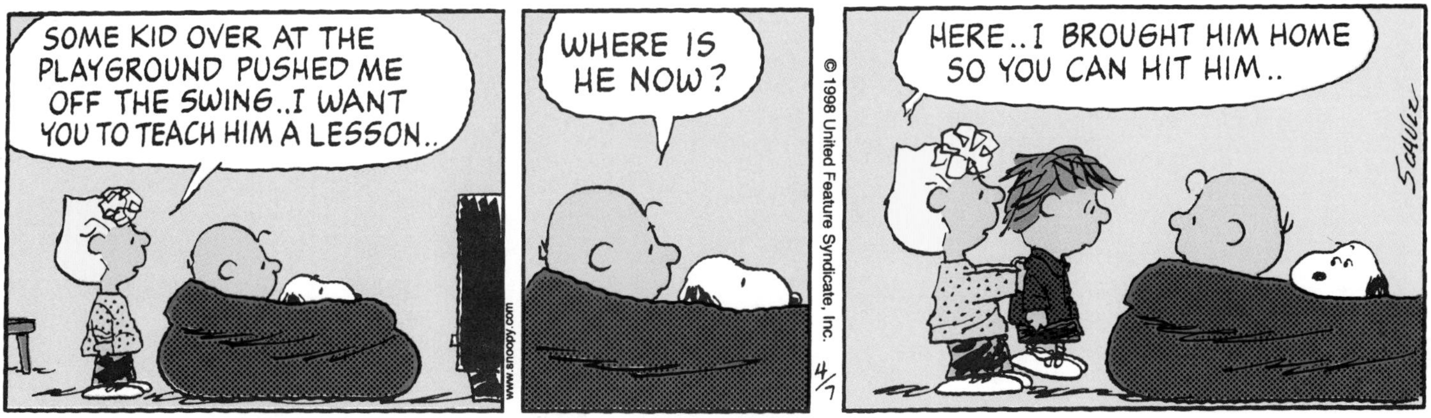
SOME KID OVER AT THE PLAYGROUND PUSHED ME OFF THE SWING..I WANT YOU TO TEACH HIM A LESSON..
WHERE IS HE NOW?
HERE..I BROUGHT HIM HOME SO YOU CAN HIT HIM..
www.snoopy.com
© 1998 United Feature Syndicate, Inc.
4/7
SCHULZ

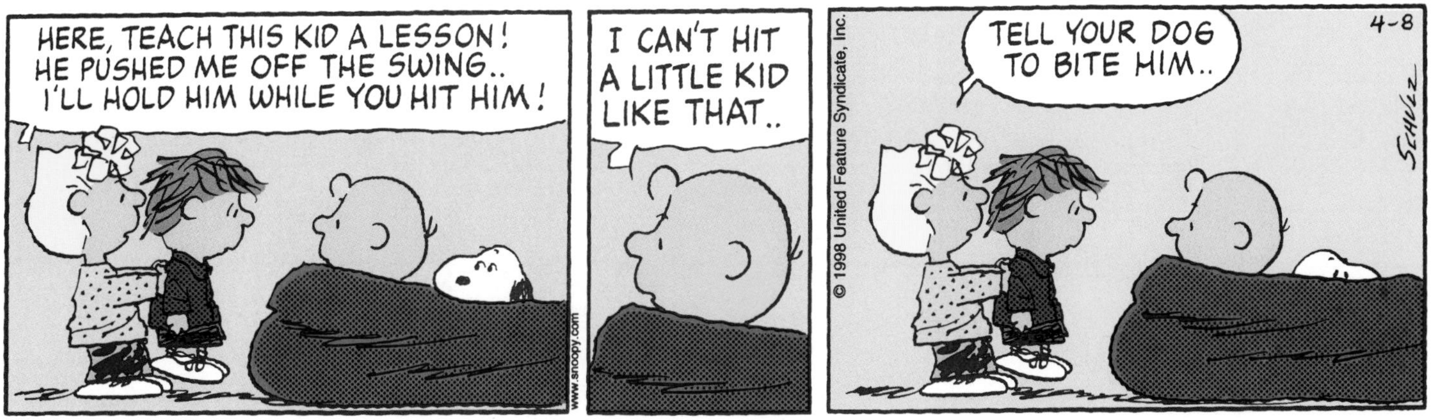
HERE, TEACH THIS KID A LESSON! HE PUSHED ME OFF THE SWING.. I'LL HOLD HIM WHILE YOU HIT HIM!
I CAN'T HIT A LITTLE KID LIKE THAT..
TELL YOUR DOG TO BITE HIM..
www.snoopy.com
© 1998 United Feature Syndicate, Inc.
4-8
SCHULZ

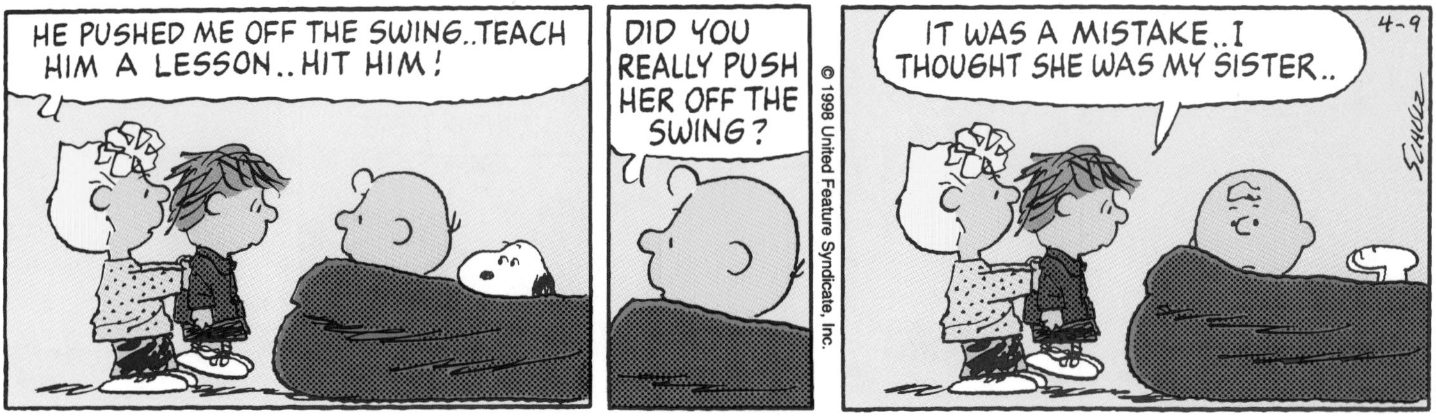
HE PUSHED ME OFF THE SWING..TEACH HIM A LESSON..HIT HIM!
DID YOU REALLY PUSH HER OFF THE SWING?
© 1998 United Feature Syndicate, Inc.
4-9
IT WAS A MISTAKE..I THOUGHT SHE WAS MY SISTER..
SCHULZ

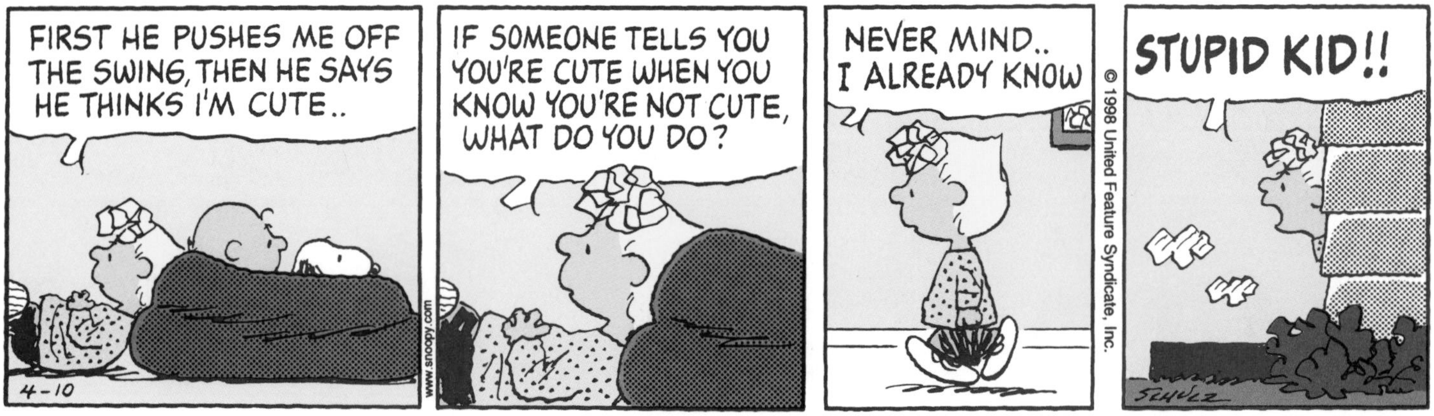
FIRST HE PUSHES ME OFF THE SWING, THEN HE SAYS HE THINKS I'M CUTE..
4-10
www.snoopy.com
IF SOMEONE TELLS YOU YOU'RE CUTE WHEN YOU KNOW YOU'RE NOT CUTE, WHAT DO YOU DO?
NEVER MIND.. I ALREADY KNOW
© 1998 United Feature Syndicate, Inc.
STUPID KID!!
SCHULZ

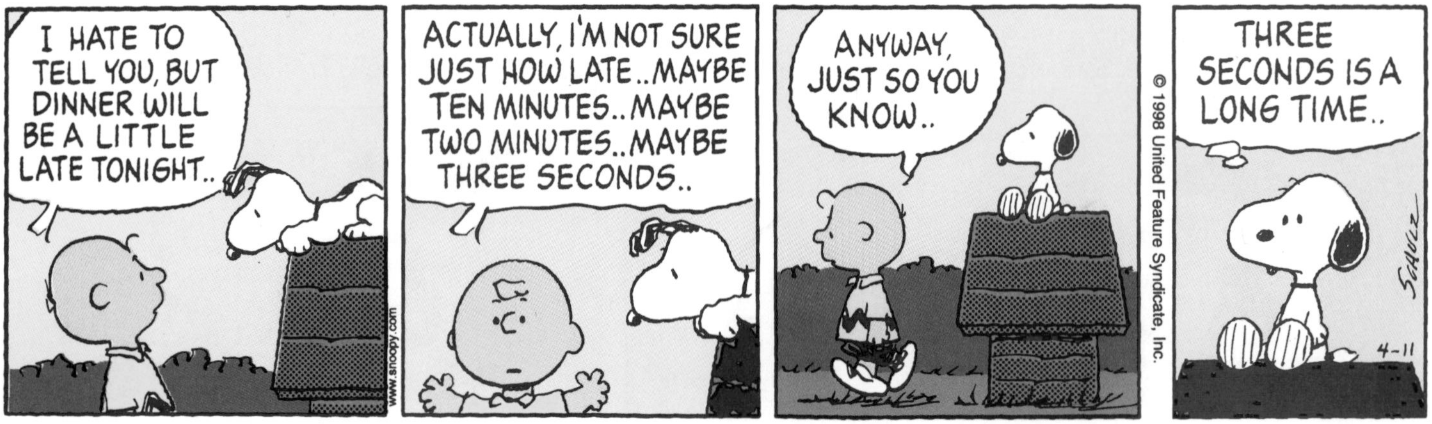
I HATE TO TELL YOU, BUT DINNER WILL BE A LITTLE LATE TONIGHT..
www.snoopy.com
ACTUALLY, I'M NOT SURE JUST HOW LATE..MAYBE TEN MINUTES..MAYBE TWO MINUTES..MAYBE THREE SECONDS..
ANYWAY, JUST SO YOU KNOW..
© 1998 United Feature Syndicate, Inc.
THREE SECONDS IS A LONG TIME..
SCHULZ
4-11

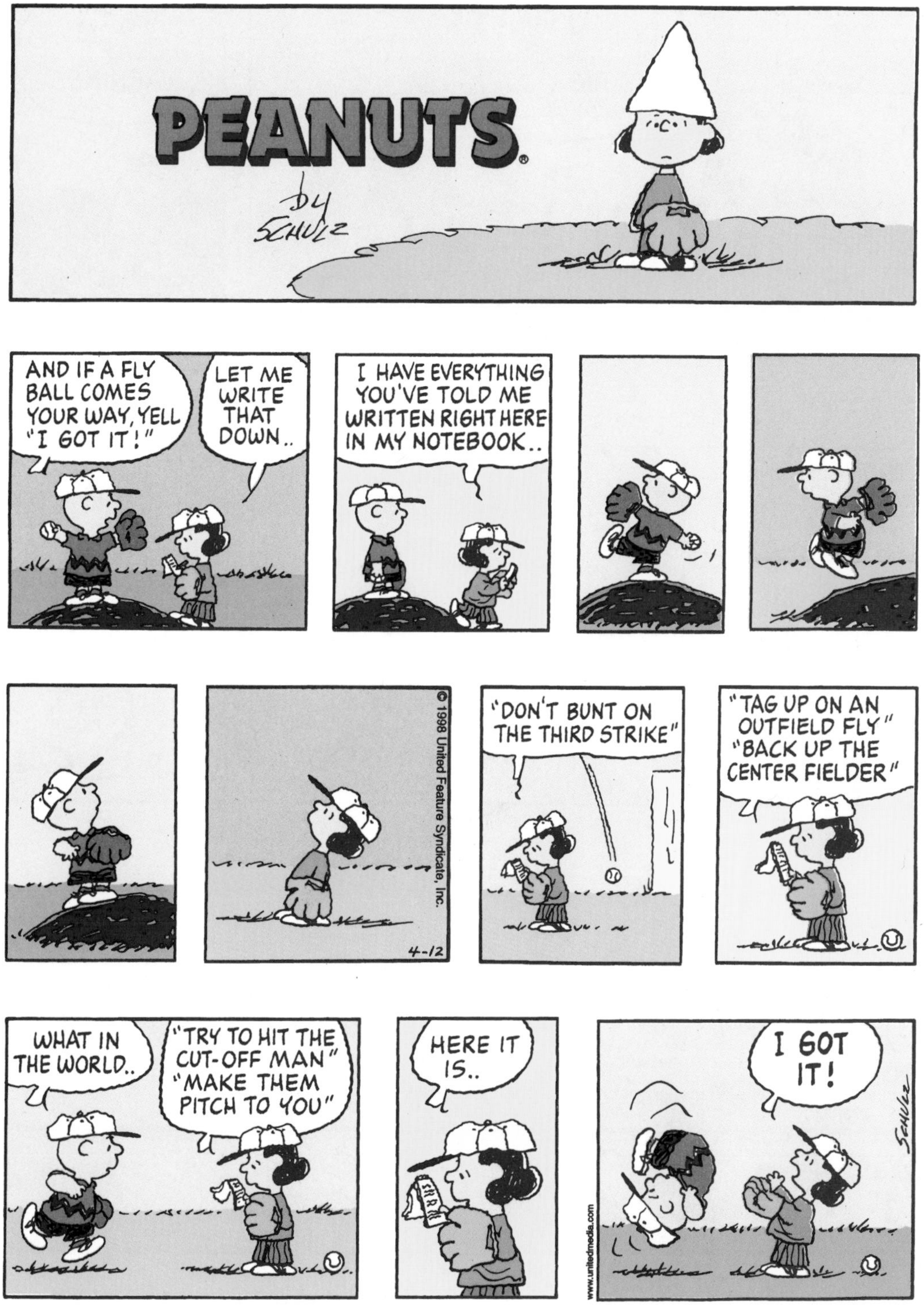
PEANUTS
by SCHULZ
AND IF A FLY BALL COMES YOUR WAY, YELL "I GOT IT!"
LET ME WRITE THAT DOWN..
I HAVE EVERYTHING YOU'VE TOLD ME WRITTEN RIGHT HERE IN MY NOTEBOOK..
© 1998 United Feature Syndicate, Inc.
4-12
"DON'T BUNT ON THE THIRD STRIKE"
"TAG UP ON AN OUTFIELD FLY" "BACK UP THE CENTER FIELDER"
WHAT IN THE WORLD..
"TRY TO HIT THE CUT-OFF MAN" "MAKE THEM PITCH TO YOU"
HERE IT IS..
www.unitedmedia.com
I GOT IT!
SCHULZ

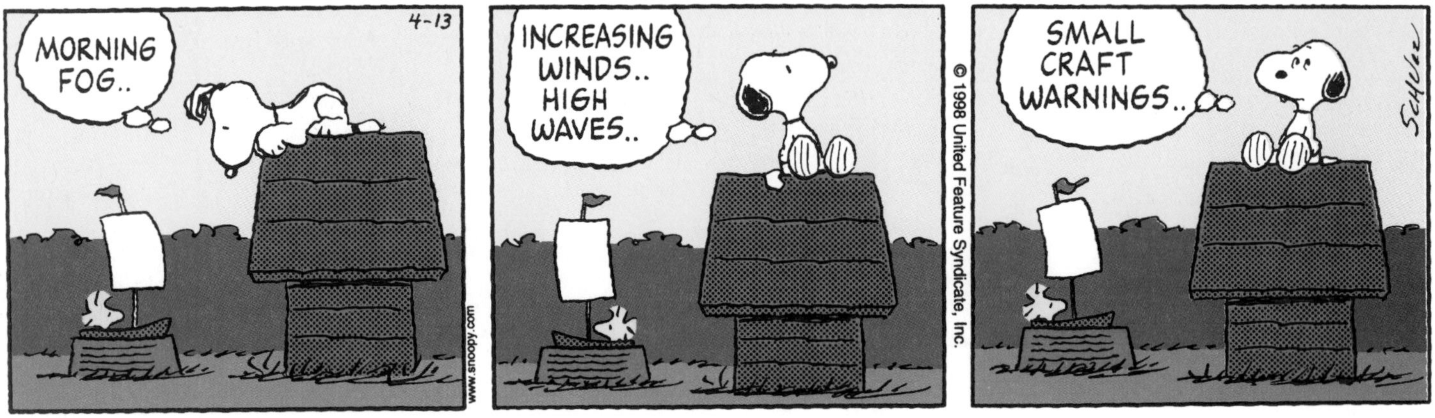
4-13
MORNING FOG..
INCREASING WINDS.. HIGH WAVES..
SMALL CRAFT WARNINGS..
SCHULZ
www.snoopy.com
© 1998 United Feature Syndicate, Inc.

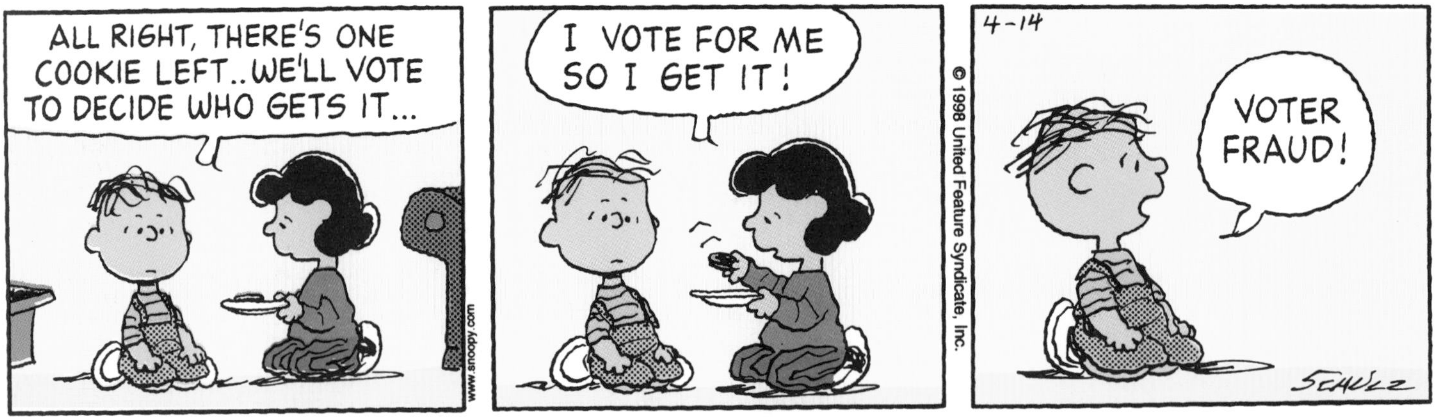
ALL RIGHT, THERE'S ONE COOKIE LEFT..WE'LL VOTE TO DECIDE WHO GETS IT...
I VOTE FOR ME SO I GET IT!
4-14
VOTER FRAUD!
SCHULZ
www.snoopy.com
© 1998 United Feature Syndicate, Inc.

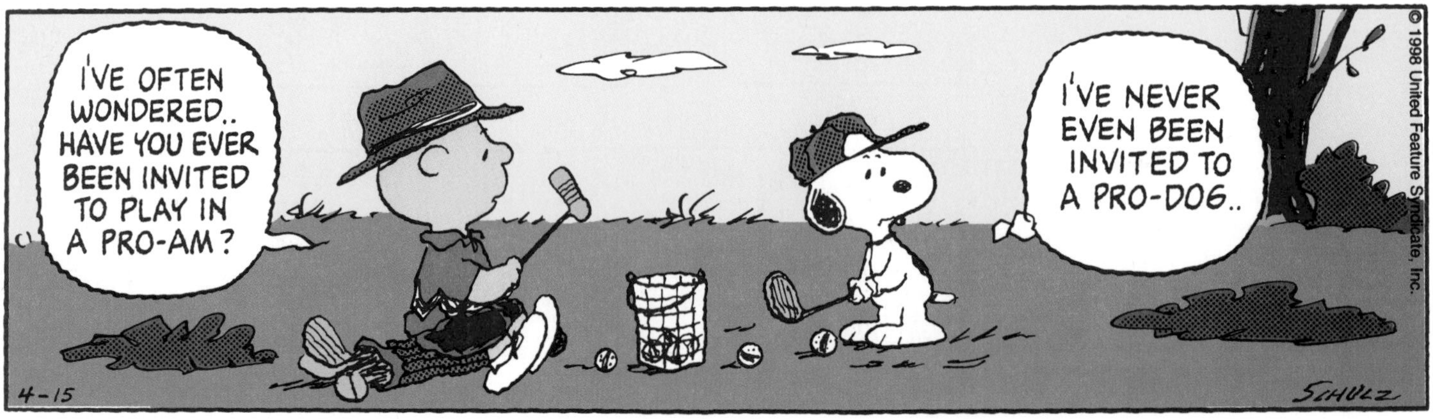
I'VE OFTEN WONDERED.. HAVE YOU EVER BEEN INVITED TO PLAY IN A PRO-AM?
I'VE NEVER EVEN BEEN INVITED TO A PRO-DOG..
4-15
SCHULZ
© 1998 United Feature Syndicate, Inc.

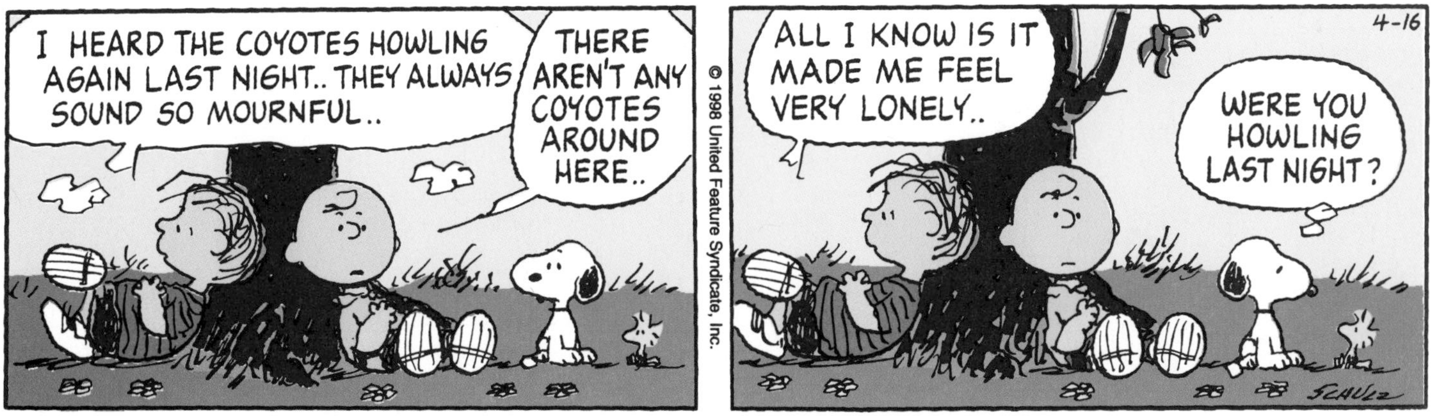
I HEARD THE COYOTES HOWLING AGAIN LAST NIGHT.. THEY ALWAYS SOUND SO MOURNFUL..
THERE AREN'T ANY COYOTES AROUND HERE..
© 1998 United Feature Syndicate, Inc.
4-16
ALL I KNOW IS IT MADE ME FEEL VERY LONELY..
WERE YOU HOWLING LAST NIGHT?
SCHULZ

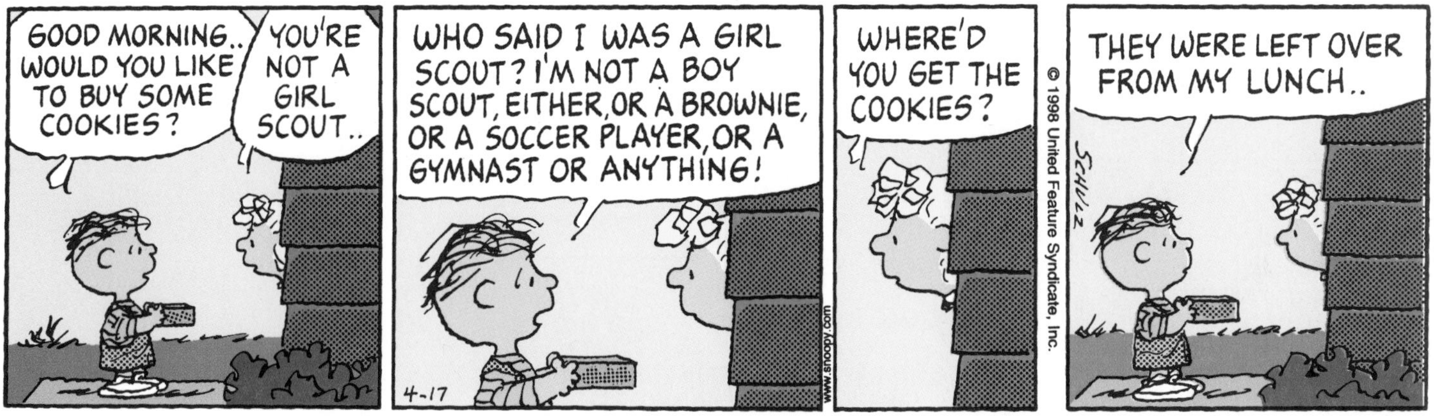
GOOD MORNING.. WOULD YOU LIKE TO BUY SOME COOKIES?
YOU'RE NOT A GIRL SCOUT..
WHO SAID I WAS A GIRL SCOUT? I'M NOT A BOY SCOUT, EITHER, OR A BROWNIE, OR A SOCCER PLAYER, OR A GYMNAST OR ANYTHING!
4-17
www.snoopy.com
WHERE'D YOU GET THE COOKIES?
© 1998 United Feature Syndicate, Inc.
SCHULZ
THEY WERE LEFT OVER FROM MY LUNCH..

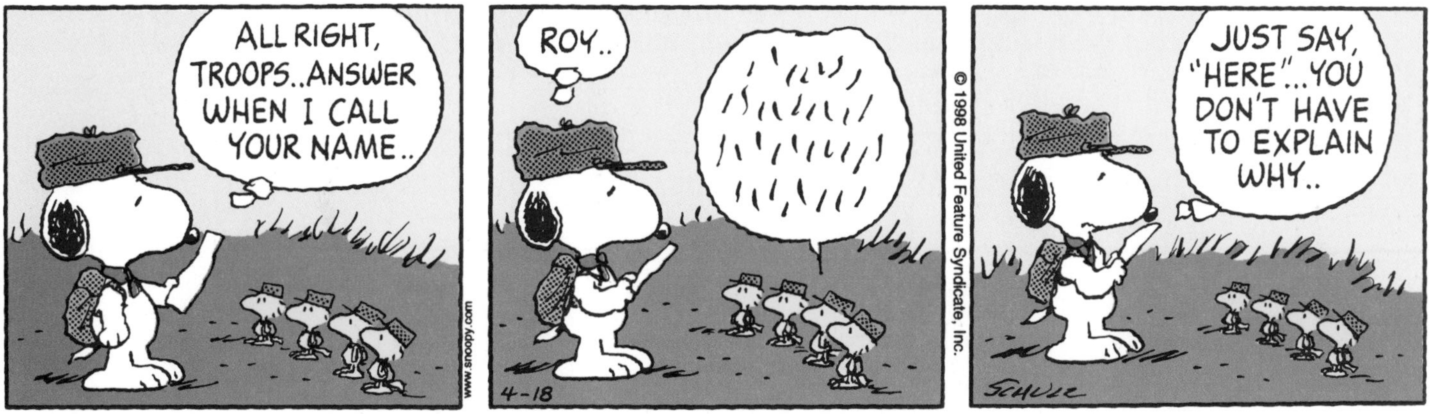
ALL RIGHT, TROOPS..ANSWER WHEN I CALL YOUR NAME..
www.snoopy.com
ROY..
4-18
© 1998 United Feature Syndicate, Inc.
JUST SAY, "HERE"...YOU DON'T HAVE TO EXPLAIN WHY..
SCHULZ

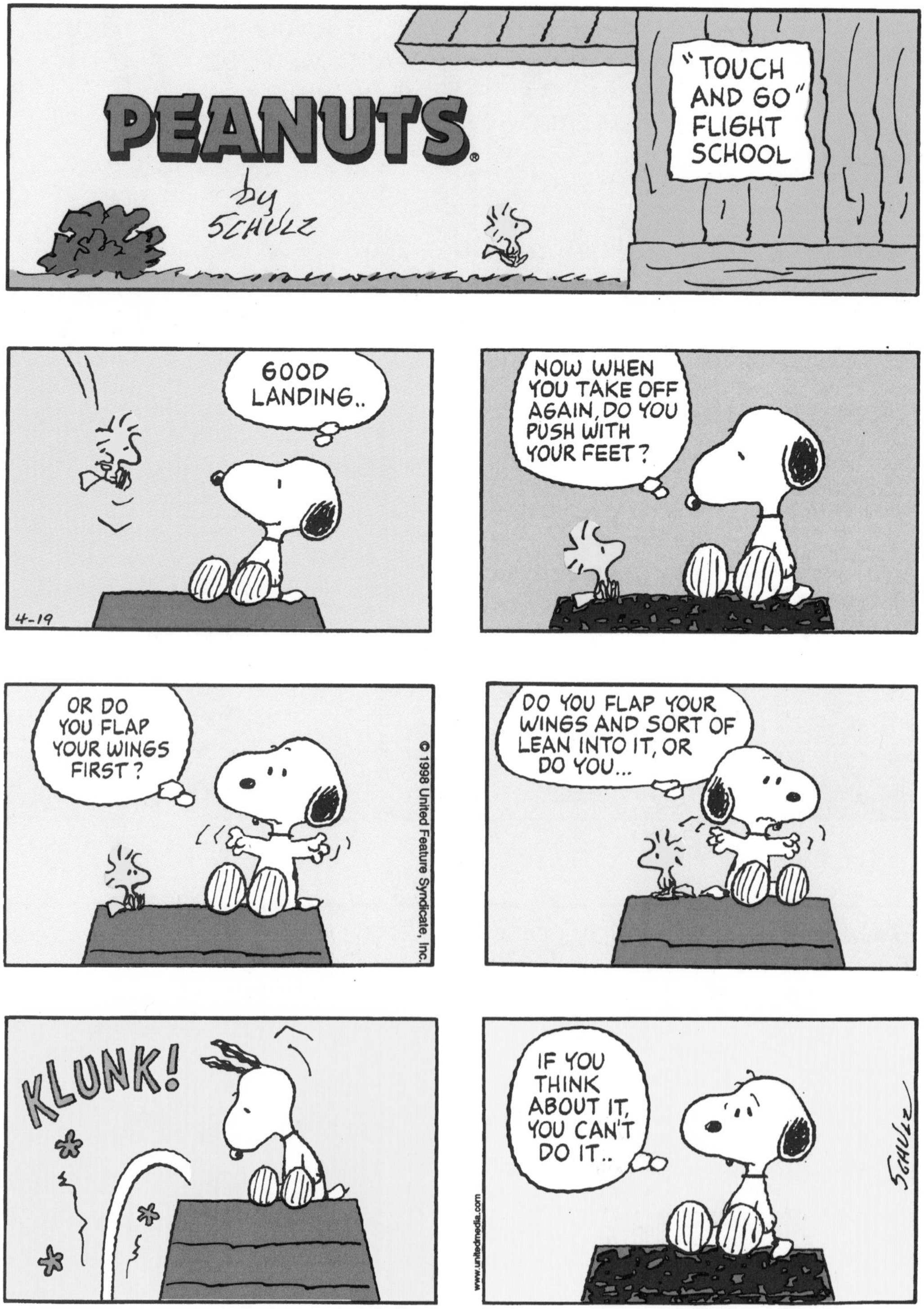
"TOUCH AND GO" FLIGHT SCHOOL
PEANUTS
by SCHULZ
4-19
GOOD LANDING..
NOW WHEN YOU TAKE OFF AGAIN, DO YOU PUSH WITH YOUR FEET?
OR DO YOU FLAP YOUR WINGS FIRST?
© 1998 United Feature Syndicate, Inc.
DO YOU FLAP YOUR WINGS AND SORT OF LEAN INTO IT, OR DO YOU...
KLUNK!
www.unitedmedia.com
IF YOU THINK ABOUT IT, YOU CAN'T DO IT..
SCHULZ

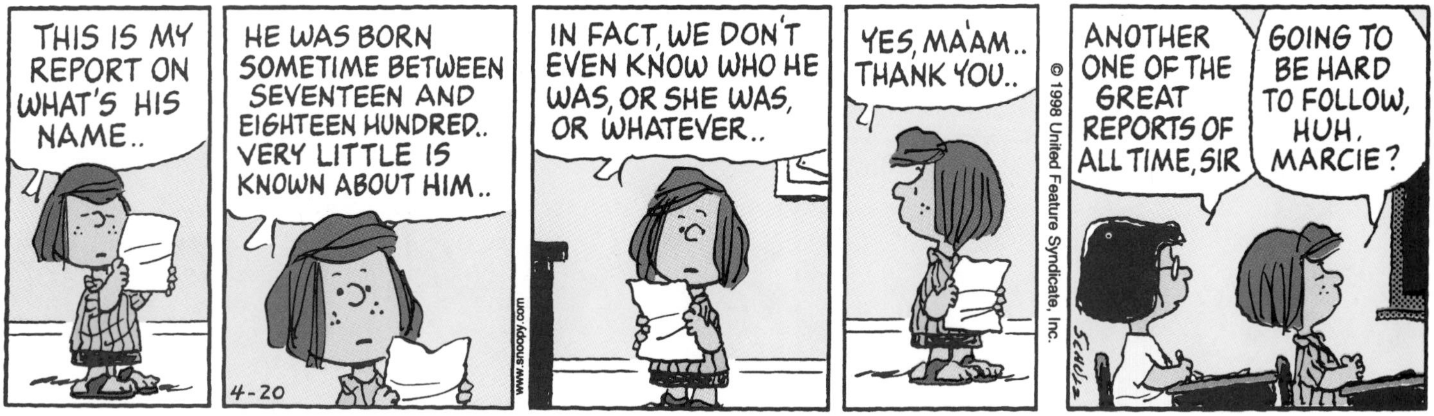
THIS IS MY REPORT ON WHAT'S HIS NAME..
HE WAS BORN SOMETIME BETWEEN SEVENTEEN AND EIGHTEEN HUNDRED.. VERY LITTLE IS KNOWN ABOUT HIM..
4-20
IN FACT, WE DON'T EVEN KNOW WHO HE WAS, OR SHE WAS, OR WHATEVER..
YES, MA'AM.. THANK YOU..
© 1998 United Feature Syndicate, Inc.
ANOTHER ONE OF THE GREAT REPORTS OF ALL TIME, SIR
GOING TO BE HARD TO FOLLOW, HUH, MARCIE?

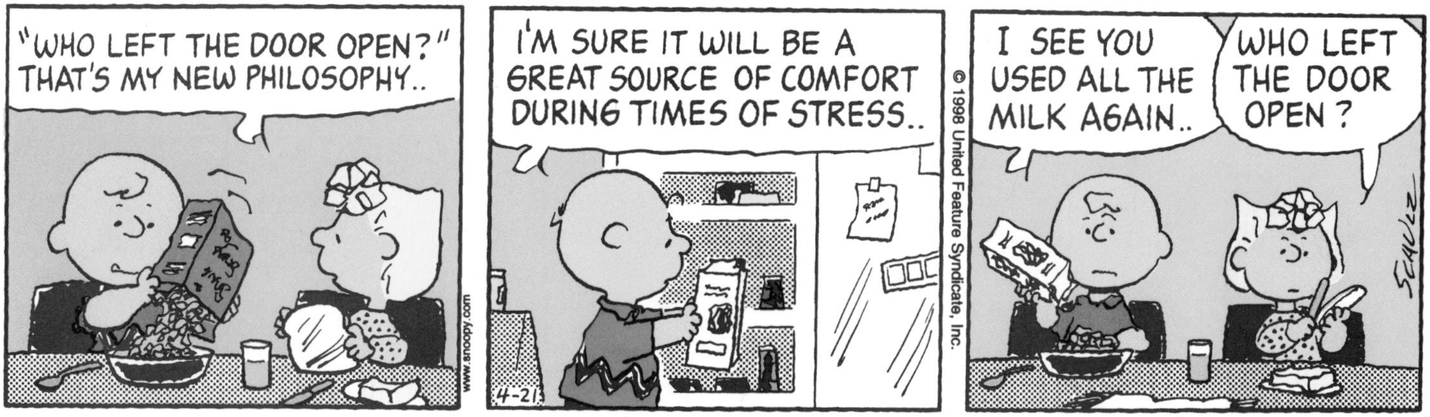
"WHO LEFT THE DOOR OPEN?" THAT'S MY NEW PHILOSOPHY..
I'M SURE IT WILL BE A GREAT SOURCE OF COMFORT DURING TIMES OF STRESS..
4-21
© 1998 United Feature Syndicate, Inc.
I SEE YOU USED ALL THE MILK AGAIN..
WHO LEFT THE DOOR OPEN?

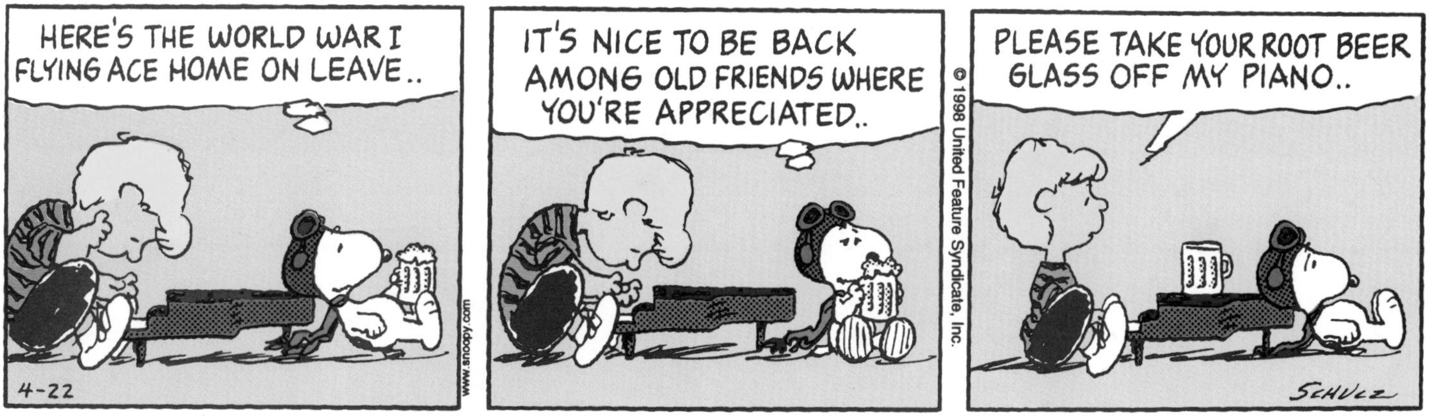
HERE'S THE WORLD WAR I FLYING ACE HOME ON LEAVE..
4-22
IT'S NICE TO BE BACK AMONG OLD FRIENDS WHERE YOU'RE APPRECIATED..
© 1998 United Feature Syndicate, Inc.
PLEASE TAKE YOUR ROOT BEER GLASS OFF MY PIANO..

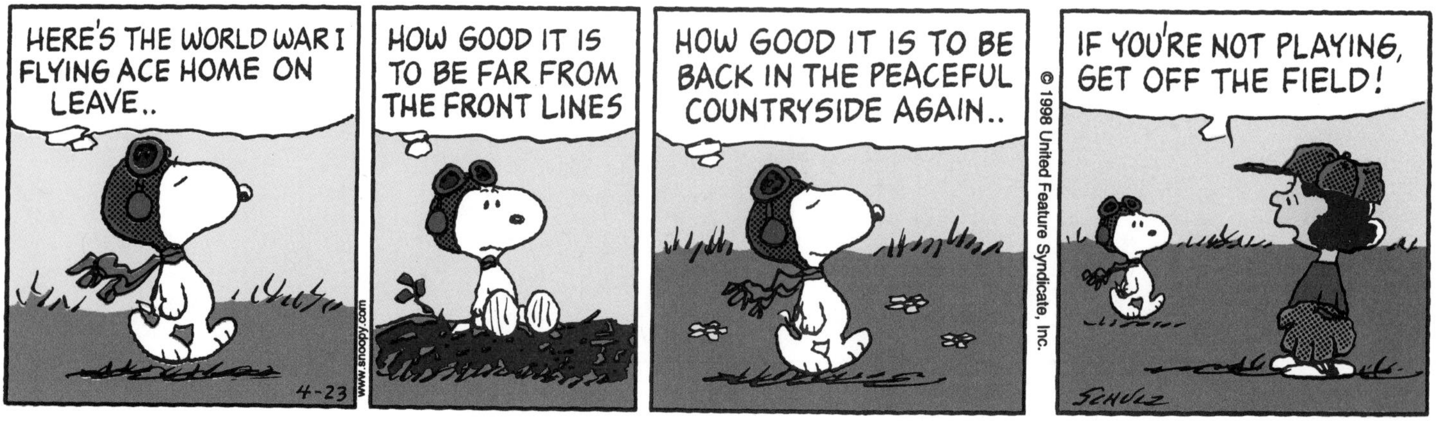
HERE'S THE WORLD WAR I FLYING ACE HOME ON LEAVE..
4-23
www.snoopy.com
HOW GOOD IT IS TO BE FAR FROM THE FRONT LINES
HOW GOOD IT IS TO BE BACK IN THE PEACEFUL COUNTRYSIDE AGAIN..
© 1998 United Feature Syndicate, Inc.
IF YOU'RE NOT PLAYING, GET OFF THE FIELD!
SCHULZ

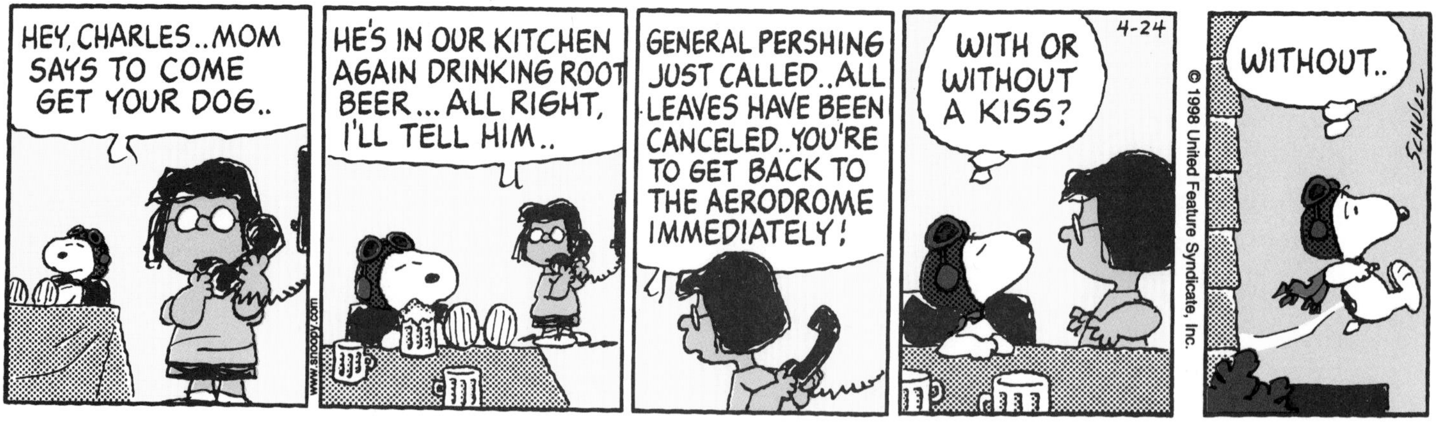
HEY, CHARLES..MOM SAYS TO COME GET YOUR DOG..
www.snoopy.com
HE'S IN OUR KITCHEN AGAIN DRINKING ROOT BEER....ALL RIGHT, I'LL TELL HIM..
GENERAL PERSHING JUST CALLED..ALL LEAVES HAVE BEEN CANCELED..YOU'RE TO GET BACK TO THE AERODROME IMMEDIATELY!
4-24
WITH OR WITHOUT A KISS?
© 1998 United Feature Syndicate, Inc.
WITHOUT..
SCHULZ

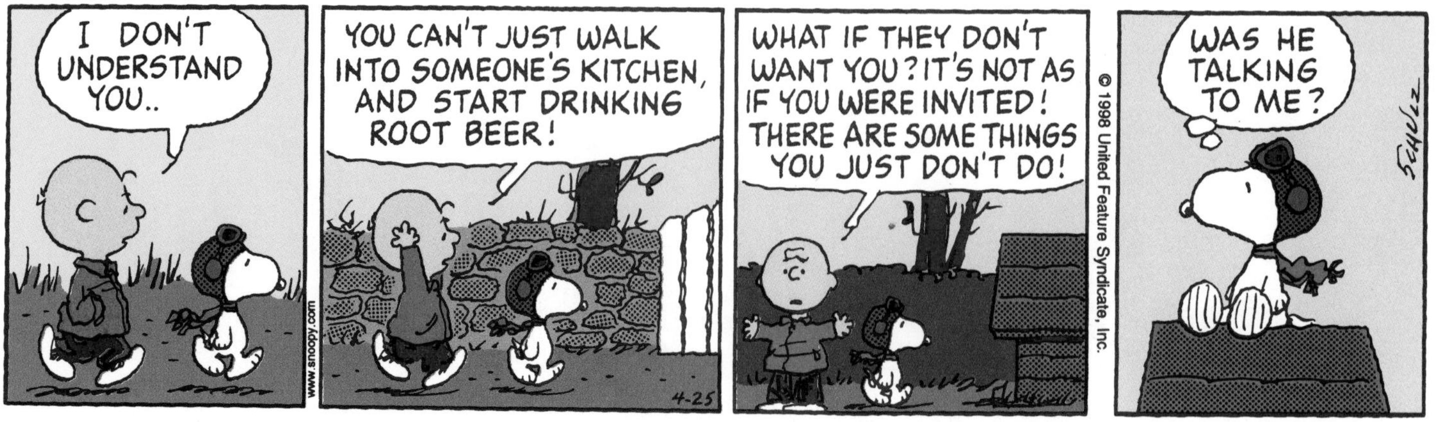
I DON'T UNDERSTAND YOU..
www.snoopy.com
YOU CAN'T JUST WALK INTO SOMEONE'S KITCHEN, AND START DRINKING ROOT BEER!
4-25
WHAT IF THEY DON'T WANT YOU? IT'S NOT AS IF YOU WERE INVITED! THERE ARE SOME THINGS YOU JUST DON'T DO!
© 1998 United Feature Syndicate, Inc.
WAS HE TALKING TO ME?
SCHULZ

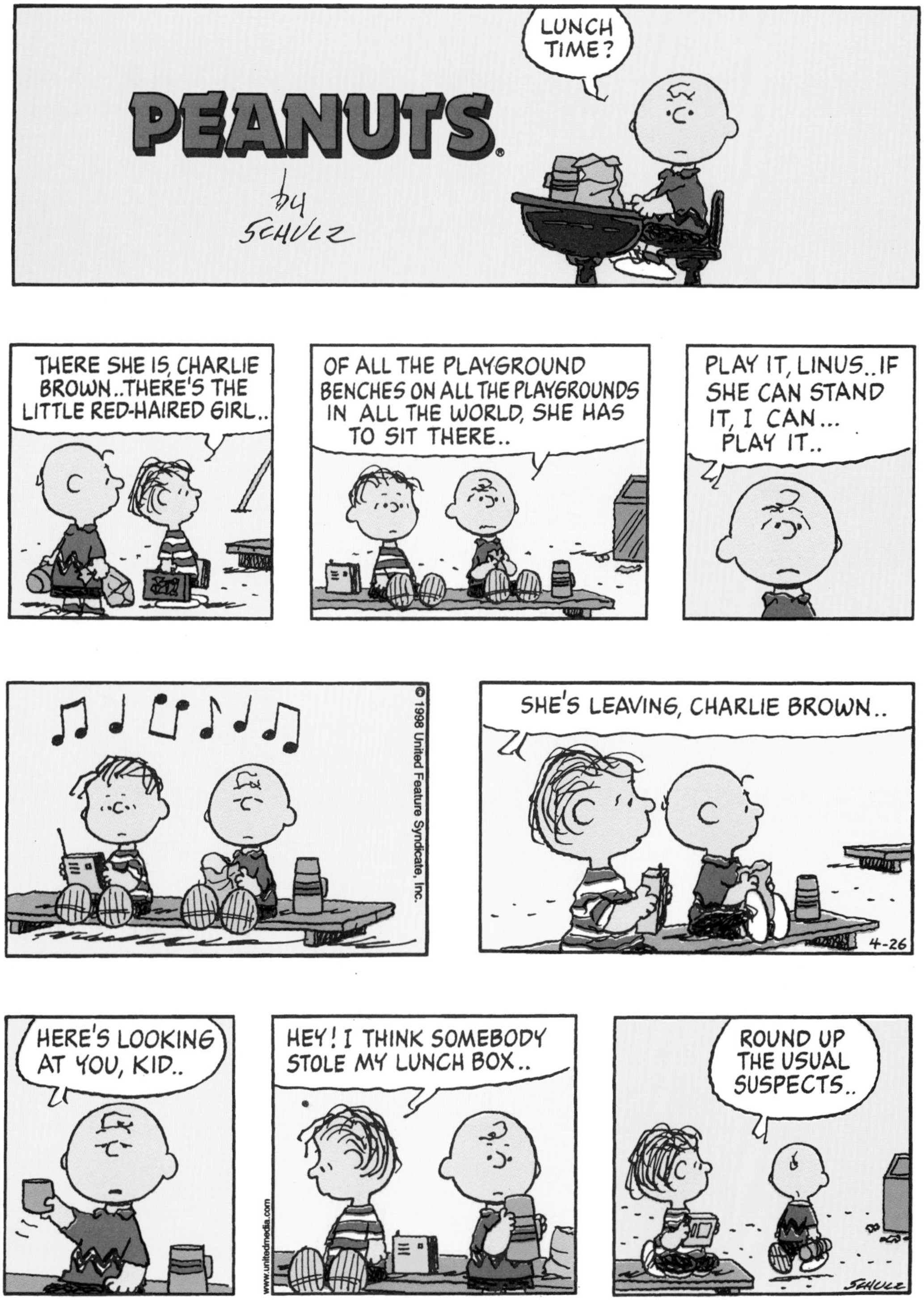
LUNCH TIME?
PEANUTS
by SCHULZ
THERE SHE IS, CHARLIE BROWN..THERE'S THE LITTLE RED-HAIRED GIRL..
OF ALL THE PLAYGROUND BENCHES ON ALL THE PLAYGROUNDS IN ALL THE WORLD, SHE HAS TO SIT THERE..
PLAY IT, LINUS..IF SHE CAN STAND IT, I CAN... PLAY IT..
© 1998 United Feature Syndicate, Inc.
SHE'S LEAVING, CHARLIE BROWN..
4-26
HERE'S LOOKING AT YOU, KID..
www.unitedmedia.com
HEY! I THINK SOMEBODY STOLE MY LUNCH BOX..
ROUND UP THE USUAL SUSPECTS..
SCHULZ

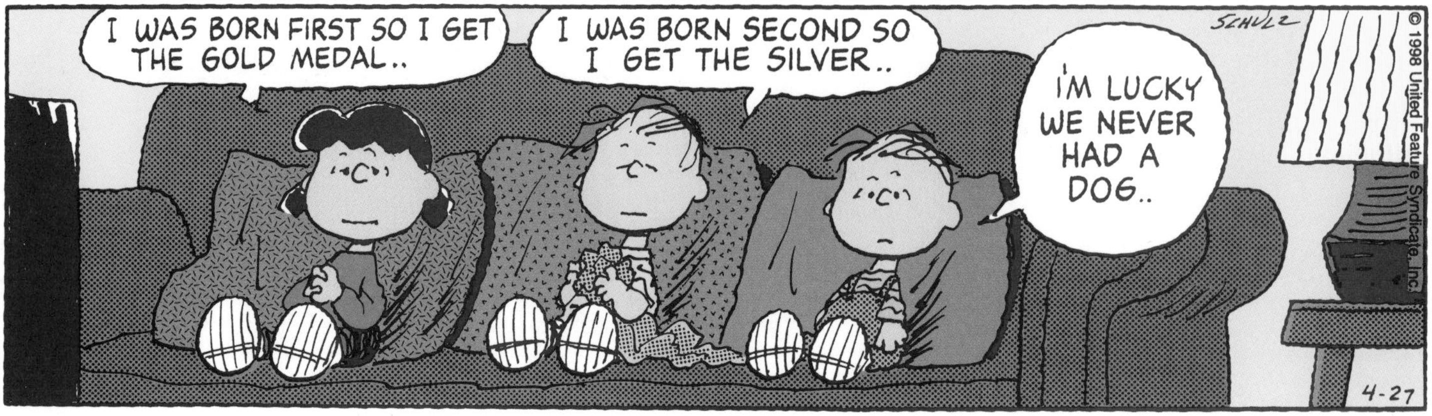
I WAS BORN FIRST SO I GET THE GOLD MEDAL..
I WAS BORN SECOND SO I GET THE SILVER..
I'M LUCKY WE NEVER HAD A DOG..
SCHULZ
© 1998 United Feature Syndicate, Inc.
4-27

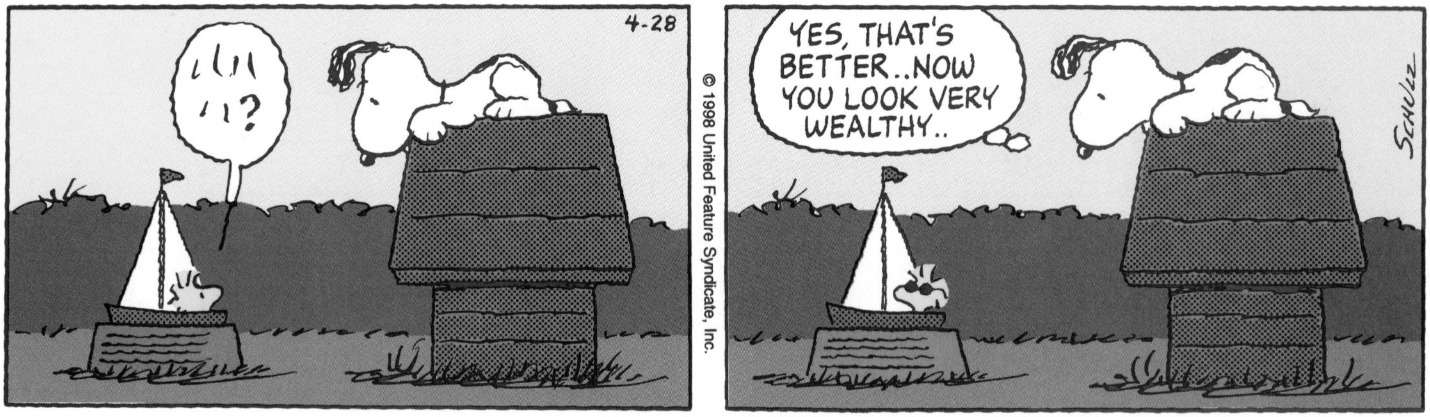
4-28
© 1998 United Feature Syndicate, Inc.
YES, THAT'S BETTER..NOW YOU LOOK VERY WEALTHY..
SCHULZ

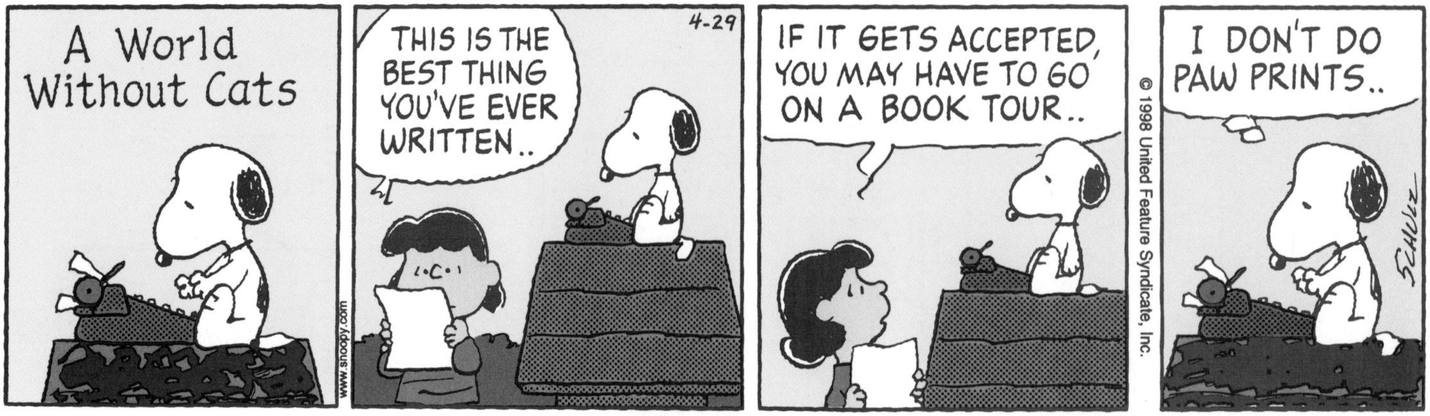
A World Without Cats
www.snoopy.com
THIS IS THE BEST THING YOU'VE EVER WRITTEN..
4-29
IF IT GETS ACCEPTED, YOU MAY HAVE TO GO ON A BOOK TOUR..
© 1998 United Feature Syndicate, Inc.
I DON'T DO PAW PRINTS..
SCHULZ

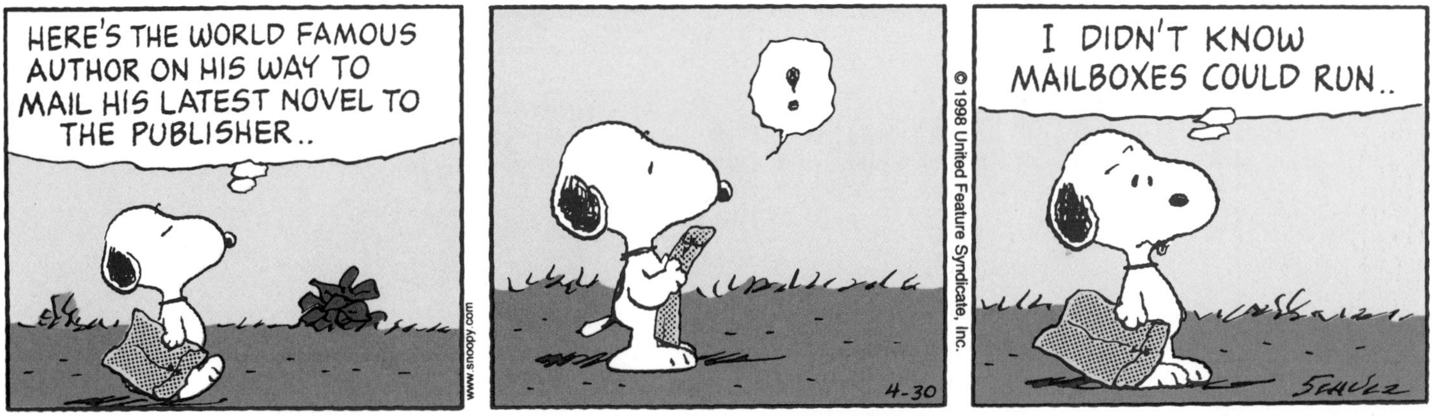
HERE'S THE WORLD FAMOUS AUTHOR ON HIS WAY TO MAIL HIS LATEST NOVEL TO THE PUBLISHER..
!
I DIDN'T KNOW MAILBOXES COULD RUN..
www.snoopy.com
© 1998 United Feature Syndicate, Inc.
4-30
SCHULZ

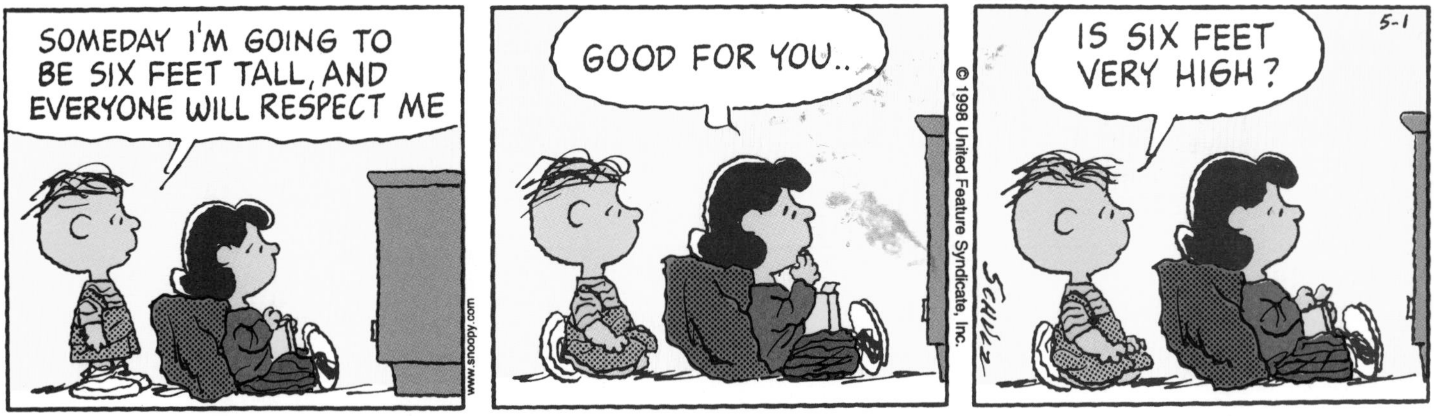
SOMEDAY I'M GOING TO BE SIX FEET TALL, AND EVERYONE WILL RESPECT ME
GOOD FOR YOU..
IS SIX FEET VERY HIGH?
www.snoopy.com
© 1998 United Feature Syndicate, Inc.
SCHULZ
5-1

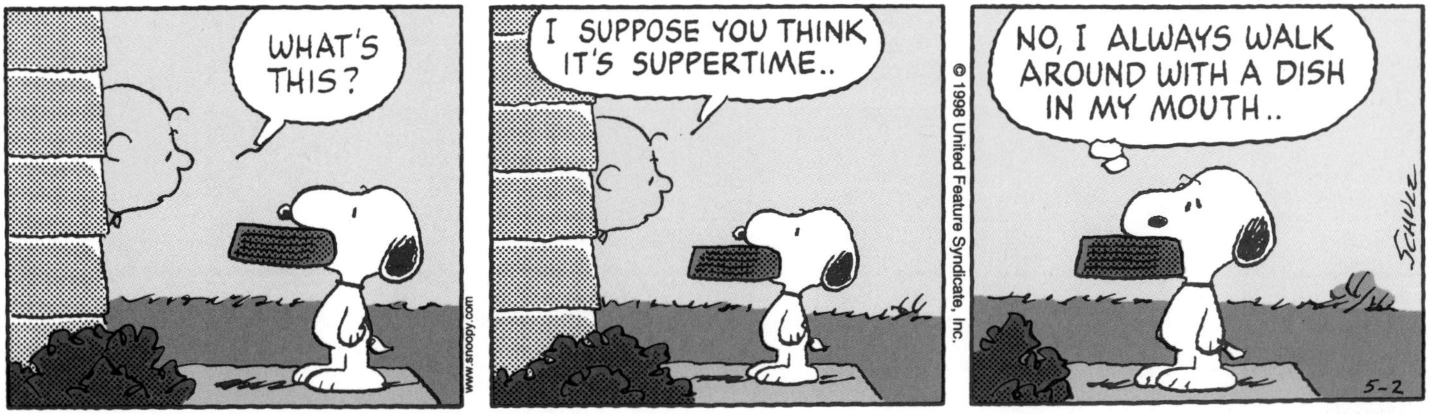
WHAT'S THIS?
I SUPPOSE YOU THINK IT'S SUPPERTIME..
NO, I ALWAYS WALK AROUND WITH A DISH IN MY MOUTH..
www.snoopy.com
© 1998 United Feature Syndicate, Inc.
SCHULZ
5-2

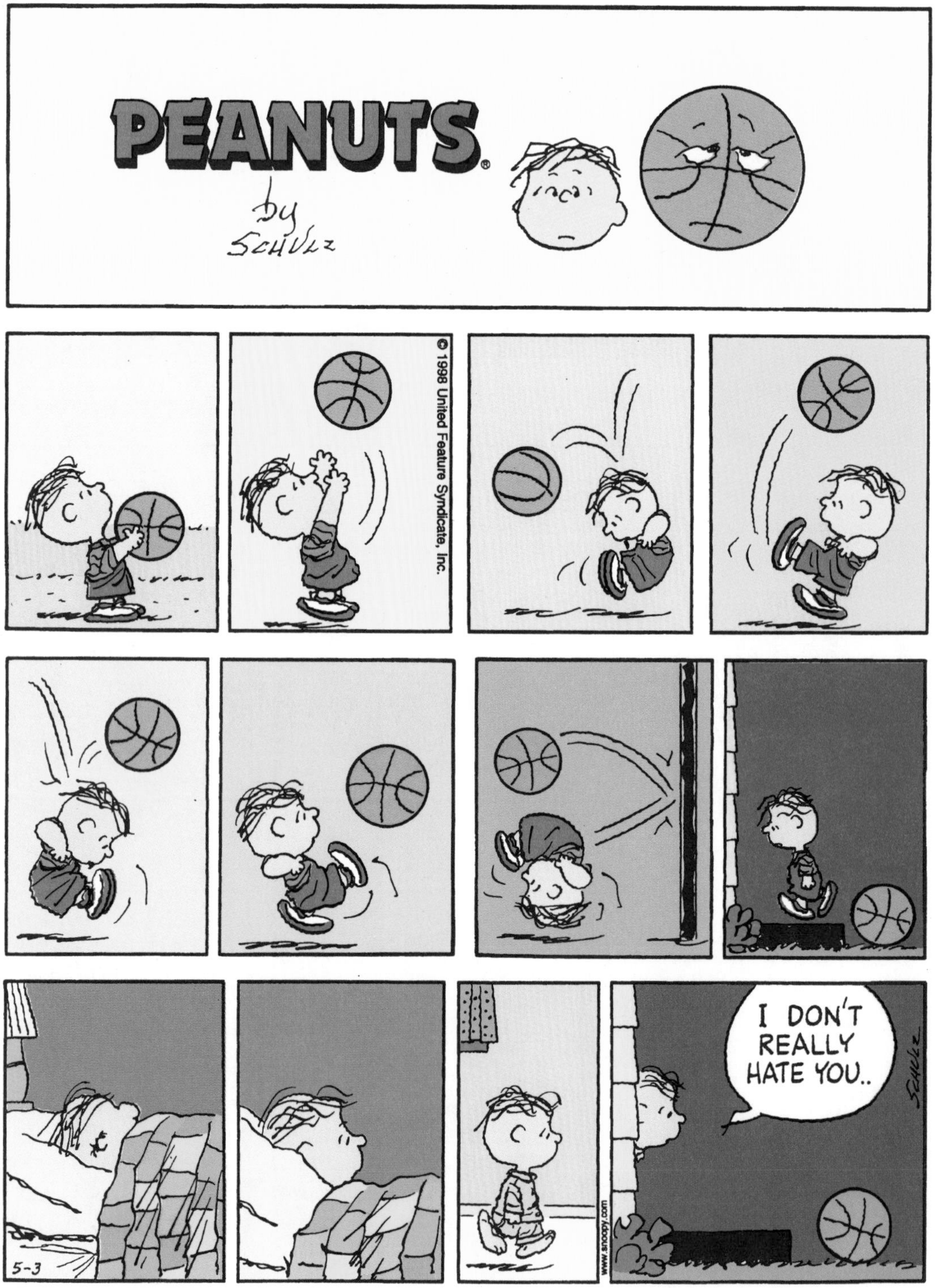
PEANUTS
by SCHULZ
© 1998 United Feature Syndicate, Inc.
5-3
www.snoopy.com
I DON'T REALLY HATE YOU..
SCHULZ

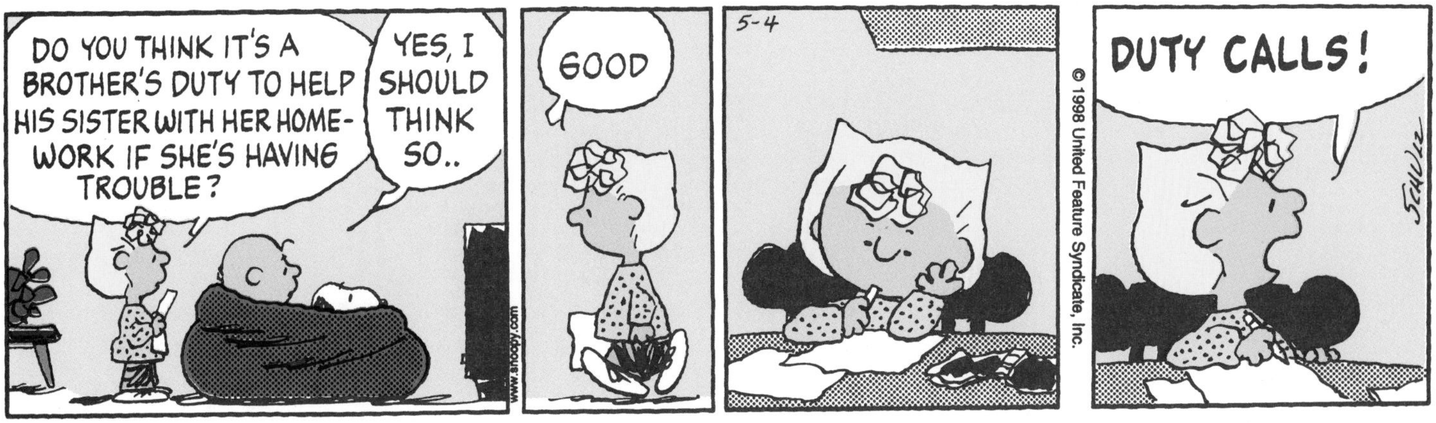
DO YOU THINK IT'S A BROTHER'S DUTY TO HELP HIS SISTER WITH HER HOME-WORK IF SHE'S HAVING TROUBLE?
YES, I SHOULD THINK SO..
GOOD
5-4
DUTY CALLS!
www.snoopy.com
© 1998 United Feature Syndicate, Inc.
SCHULZ

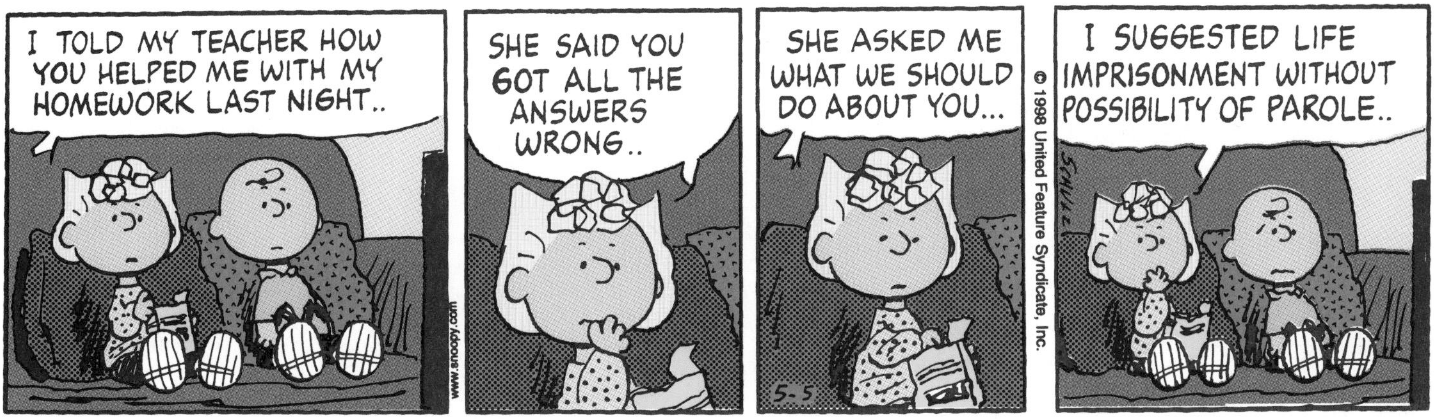
I TOLD MY TEACHER HOW YOU HELPED ME WITH MY HOMEWORK LAST NIGHT..
SHE SAID YOU GOT ALL THE ANSWERS WRONG..
SHE ASKED ME WHAT WE SHOULD DO ABOUT YOU...
I SUGGESTED LIFE IMPRISONMENT WITHOUT POSSIBILITY OF PAROLE..
5-5
www.snoopy.com
© 1998 United Feature Syndicate, Inc.
SCHULZ

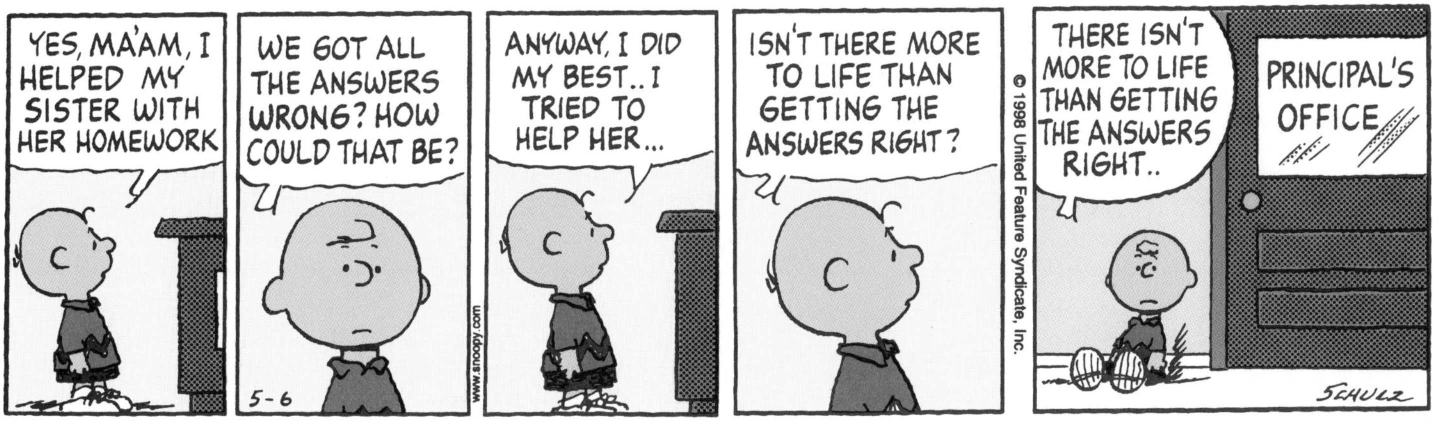
YES, MA'AM, I HELPED MY SISTER WITH HER HOMEWORK
WE GOT ALL THE ANSWERS WRONG? HOW COULD THAT BE?
ANYWAY, I DID MY BEST.. I TRIED TO HELP HER...
ISN'T THERE MORE TO LIFE THAN GETTING THE ANSWERS RIGHT?
THERE ISN'T MORE TO LIFE THAN GETTING THE ANSWERS RIGHT..
PRINCIPAL'S OFFICE
5-6
www.snoopy.com
© 1998 United Feature Syndicate, Inc.
SCHULZ

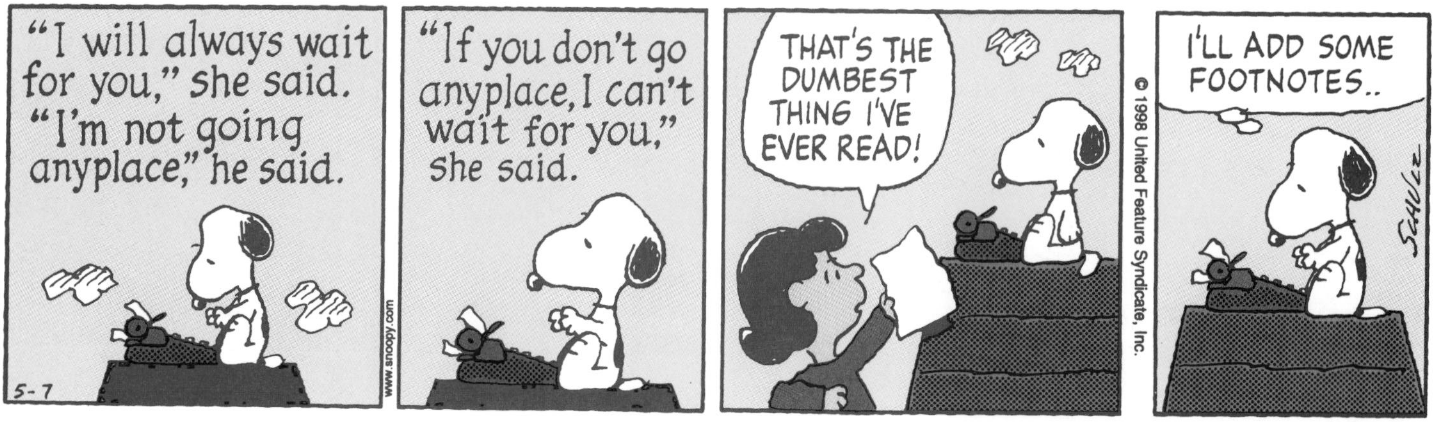
"I will always wait for you," she said. "I'm not going anyplace," he said.
5-7
"If you don't go anyplace, I can't wait for you," she said.
www.snoopy.com
THAT'S THE DUMBEST THING I'VE EVER READ!
© 1998 United Feature Syndicate, Inc.
I'LL ADD SOME FOOTNOTES..
SCHULZ

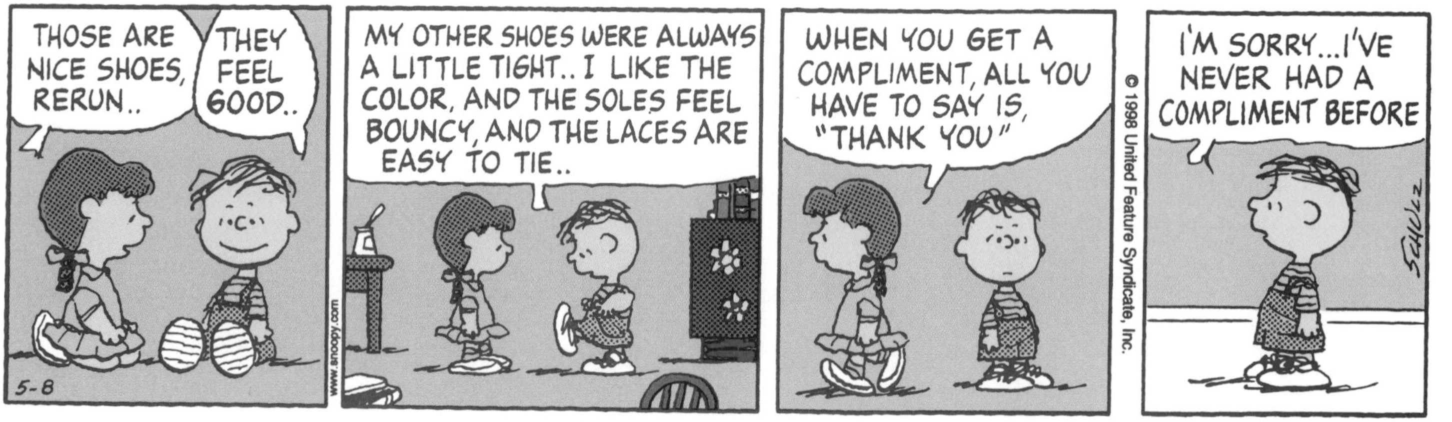
THOSE ARE NICE SHOES, RERUN..
THEY FEEL GOOD..
5-8
www.snoopy.com
MY OTHER SHOES WERE ALWAYS A LITTLE TIGHT.. I LIKE THE COLOR, AND THE SOLES FEEL BOUNCY, AND THE LACES ARE EASY TO TIE..
WHEN YOU GET A COMPLIMENT, ALL YOU HAVE TO SAY IS, "THANK YOU"
© 1998 United Feature Syndicate, Inc.
I'M SORRY...I'VE NEVER HAD A COMPLIMENT BEFORE
SCHULZ

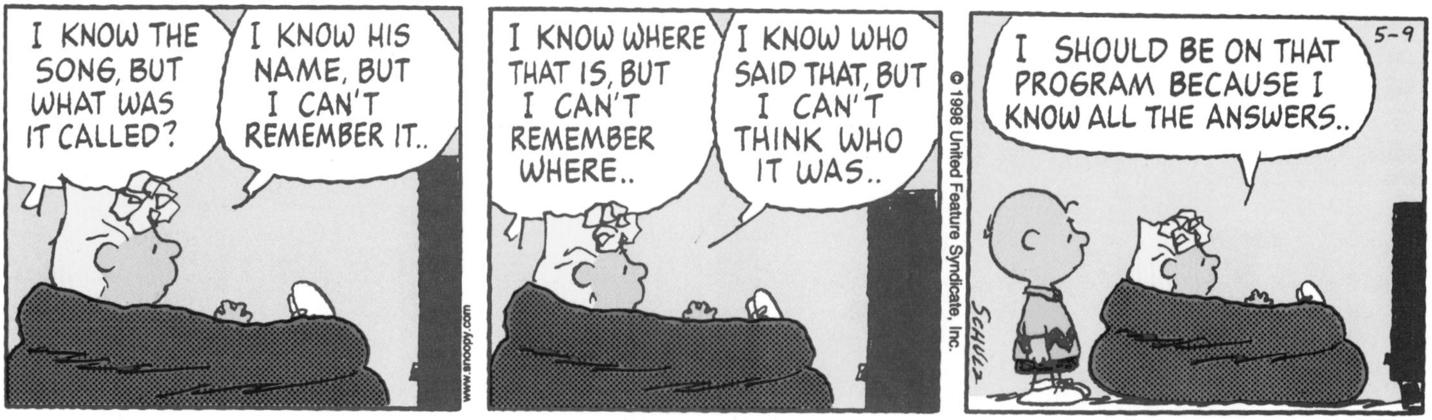
I KNOW THE SONG, BUT WHAT WAS IT CALLED?
I KNOW HIS NAME, BUT I CAN'T REMEMBER IT..
www.snoopy.com
I KNOW WHERE THAT IS, BUT I CAN'T REMEMBER WHERE..
I KNOW WHO SAID THAT, BUT I CAN'T THINK WHO IT WAS..
© 1998 United Feature Syndicate, Inc.
5-9
I SHOULD BE ON THAT PROGRAM BECAUSE I KNOW ALL THE ANSWERS..
SCHULZ

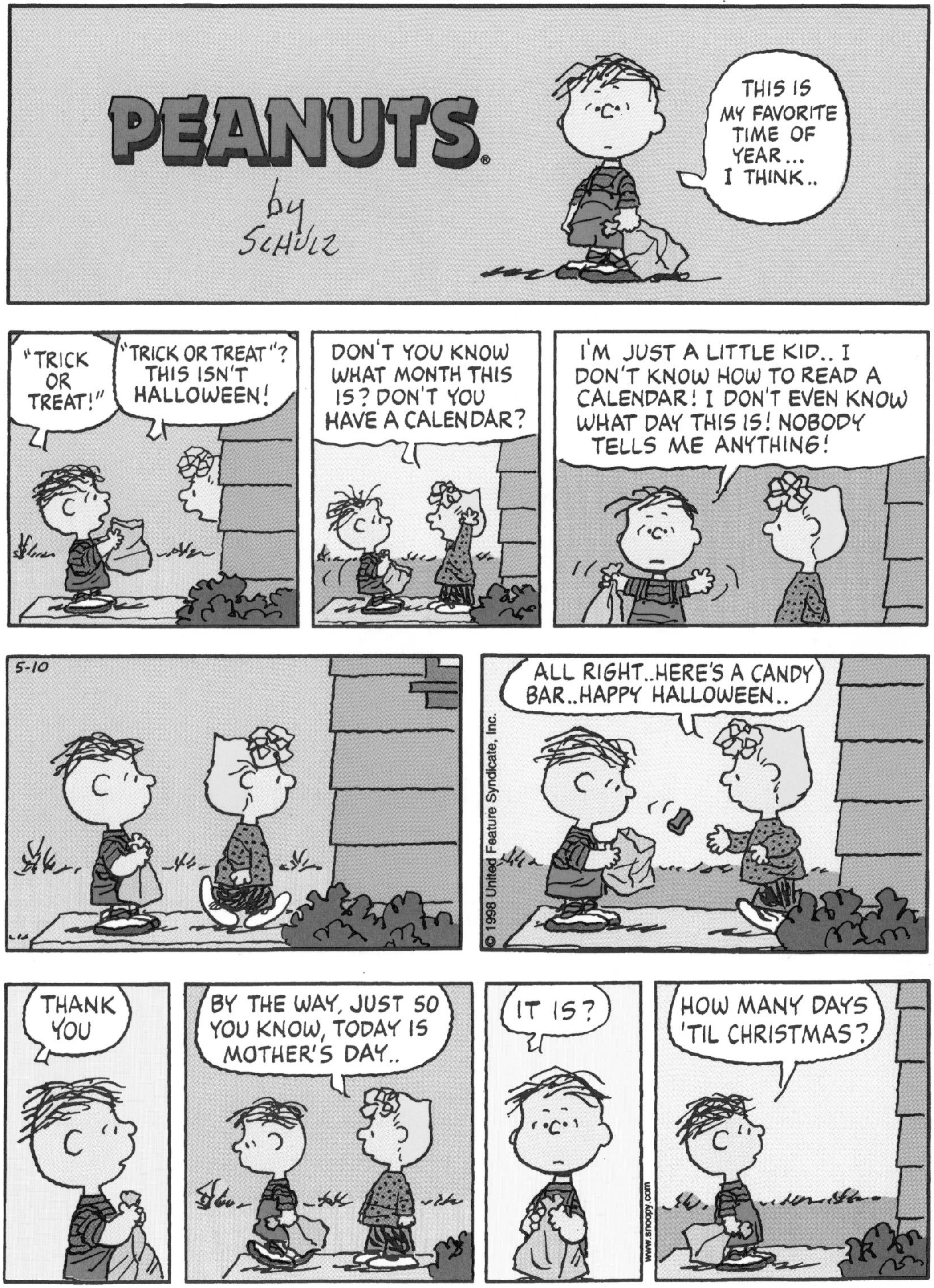
PEANUTS
by SCHULZ
THIS IS MY FAVORITE TIME OF YEAR... I THINK..
"TRICK OR TREAT!"
"TRICK OR TREAT"? THIS ISN'T HALLOWEEN!
DON'T YOU KNOW WHAT MONTH THIS IS? DON'T YOU HAVE A CALENDAR?
I'M JUST A LITTLE KID.. I DON'T KNOW HOW TO READ A CALENDAR! I DON'T EVEN KNOW WHAT DAY THIS IS! NOBODY TELLS ME ANYTHING!
5-10
ALL RIGHT..HERE'S A CANDY BAR..HAPPY HALLOWEEN..
© 1998 United Feature Syndicate, Inc.
THANK YOU
BY THE WAY, JUST SO YOU KNOW, TODAY IS MOTHER'S DAY..
IT IS?
www.snoopy.com
HOW MANY DAYS 'TIL CHRISTMAS?

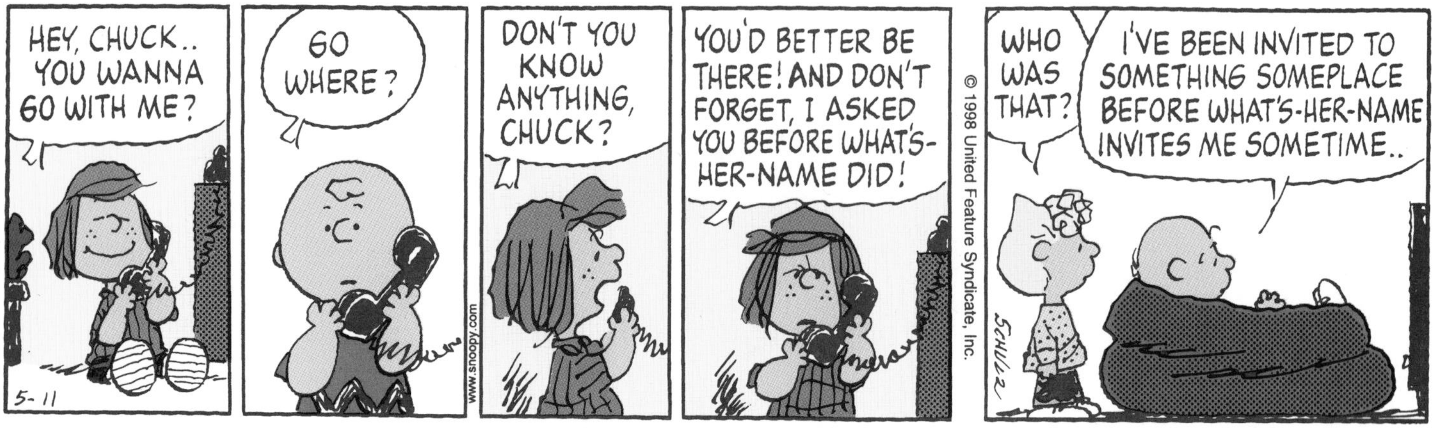
5-11
HEY, CHUCK.. YOU WANNA GO WITH ME?
GO WHERE?
DON'T YOU KNOW ANYTHING, CHUCK?
YOU'D BETTER BE THERE! AND DON'T FORGET, I ASKED YOU BEFORE WHAT'S-HER-NAME DID!
WHO WAS THAT?
I'VE BEEN INVITED TO SOMETHING SOMEPLACE BEFORE WHAT'S-HER-NAME INVITES ME SOMETIME..
www.snoopy.com
© 1998 United Feature Syndicate, Inc.
SCHULZ

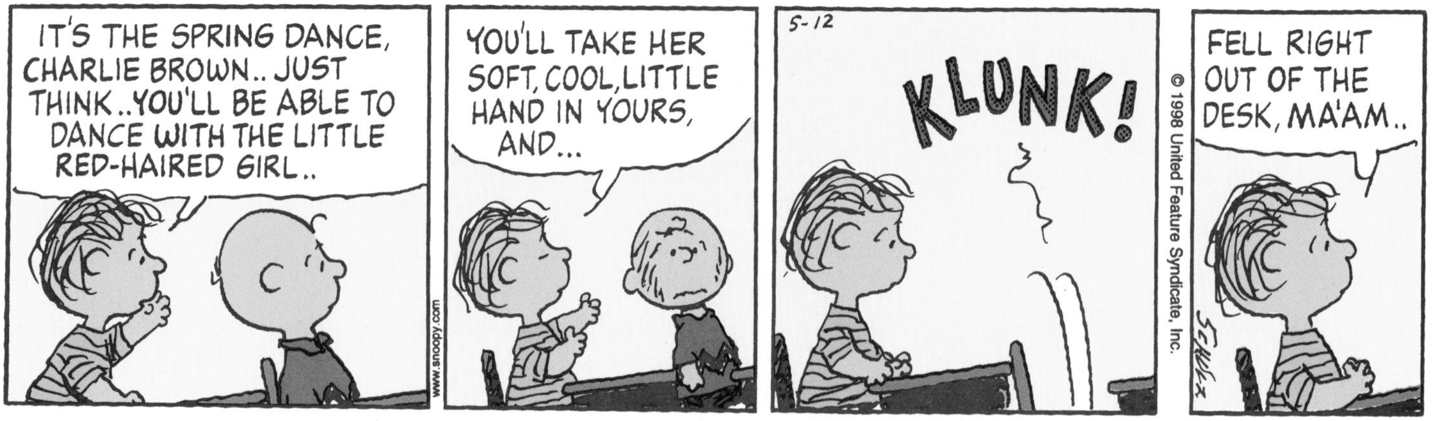
IT'S THE SPRING DANCE, CHARLIE BROWN.. JUST THINK..YOU'LL BE ABLE TO DANCE WITH THE LITTLE RED-HAIRED GIRL..
YOU'LL TAKE HER SOFT, COOL, LITTLE HAND IN YOURS, AND...
5-12
KLUNK!
FELL RIGHT OUT OF THE DESK, MA'AM..
www.snoopy.com
© 1998 United Feature Syndicate, Inc.
SCHULZ

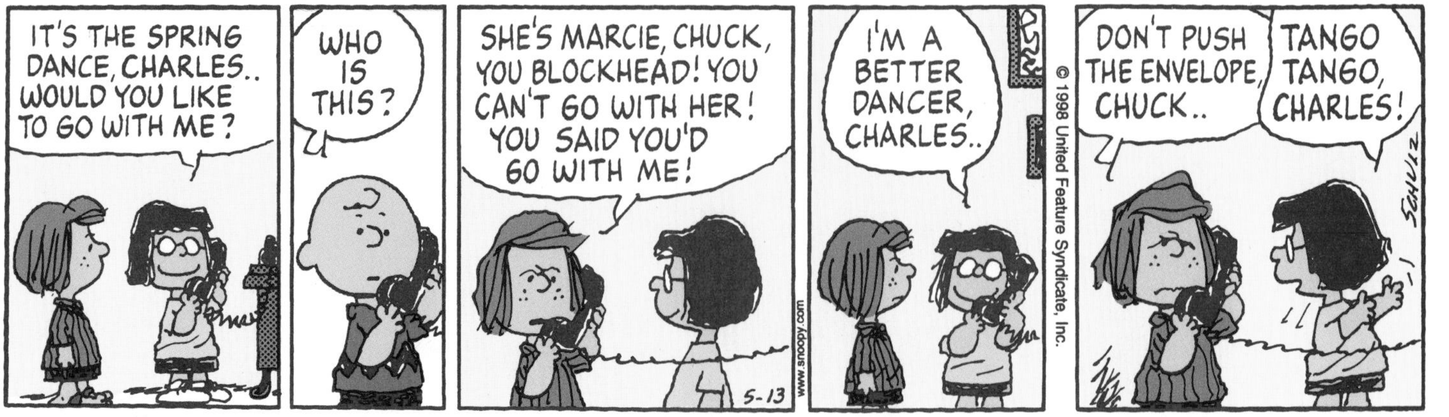
IT'S THE SPRING DANCE, CHARLES.. WOULD YOU LIKE TO GO WITH ME?
WHO IS THIS?
SHE'S MARCIE, CHUCK, YOU BLOCKHEAD! YOU CAN'T GO WITH HER! YOU SAID YOU'D GO WITH ME!
5-13
I'M A BETTER DANCER, CHARLES..
DON'T PUSH THE ENVELOPE, CHUCK..
TANGO TANGO, CHARLES!
www.snoopy.com
© 1998 United Feature Syndicate, Inc.
SCHULZ

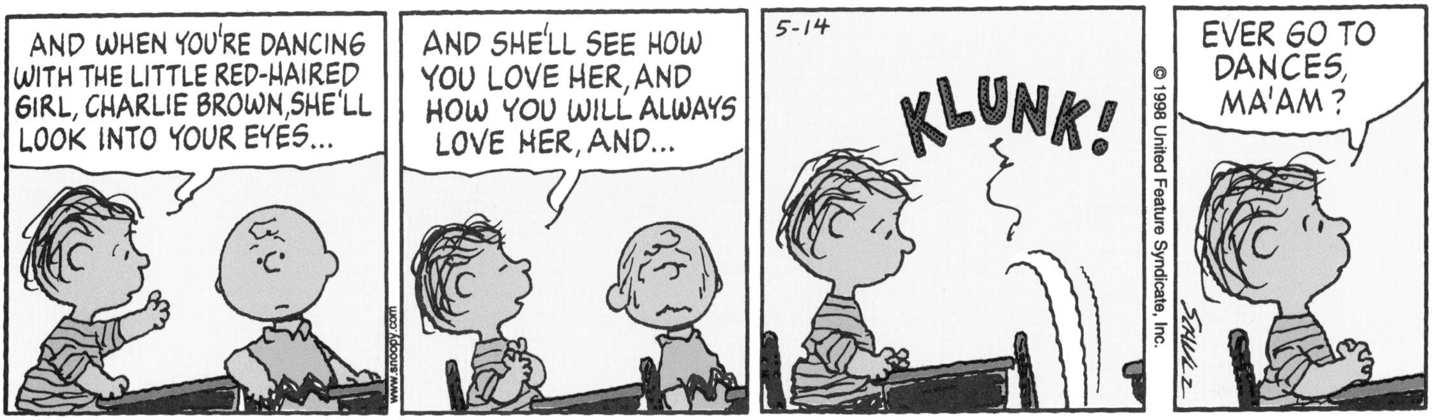
AND WHEN YOU'RE DANCING WITH THE LITTLE RED-HAIRED GIRL, CHARLIE BROWN, SHE'LL LOOK INTO YOUR EYES...
www.snoopy.com
AND SHE'LL SEE HOW YOU LOVE HER, AND HOW YOU WILL ALWAYS LOVE HER, AND...
5-14
KLUNK!
© 1998 United Feature Syndicate, Inc.
EVER GO TO DANCES, MA'AM?
SCHULZ

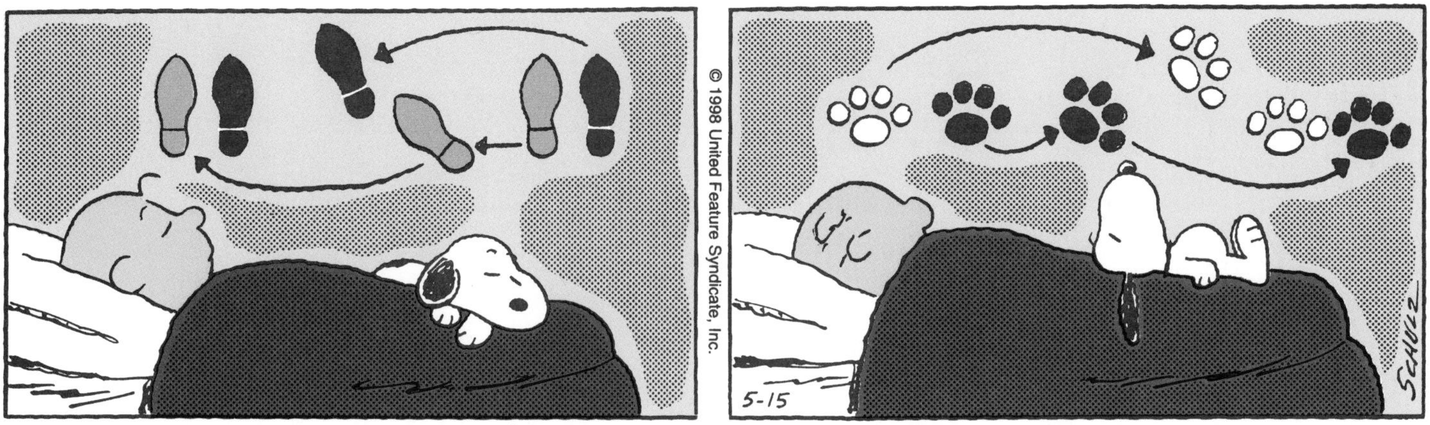
© 1998 United Feature Syndicate, Inc.
5-15
SCHULZ

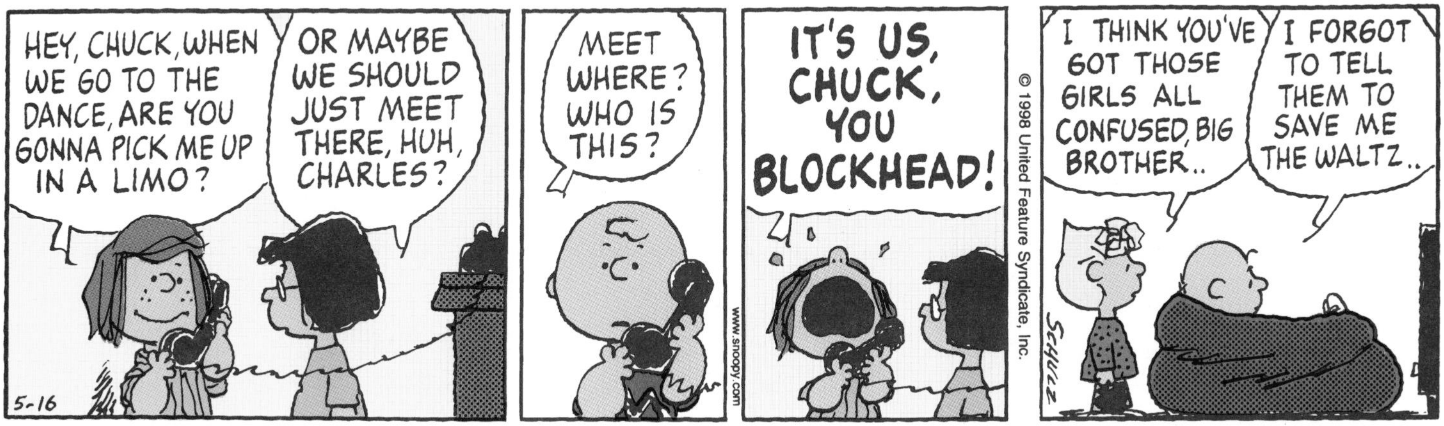
HEY, CHUCK, WHEN WE GO TO THE DANCE, ARE YOU GONNA PICK ME UP IN A LIMO?
OR MAYBE WE SHOULD JUST MEET THERE, HUH, CHARLES?
5-16
MEET WHERE? WHO IS THIS?
www.snoopy.com
IT'S US, CHUCK, YOU BLOCKHEAD!
© 1998 United Feature Syndicate, Inc.
I THINK YOU'VE GOT THOSE GIRLS ALL CONFUSED, BIG BROTHER..
I FORGOT TO TELL THEM TO SAVE ME THE WALTZ..
SCHULZ

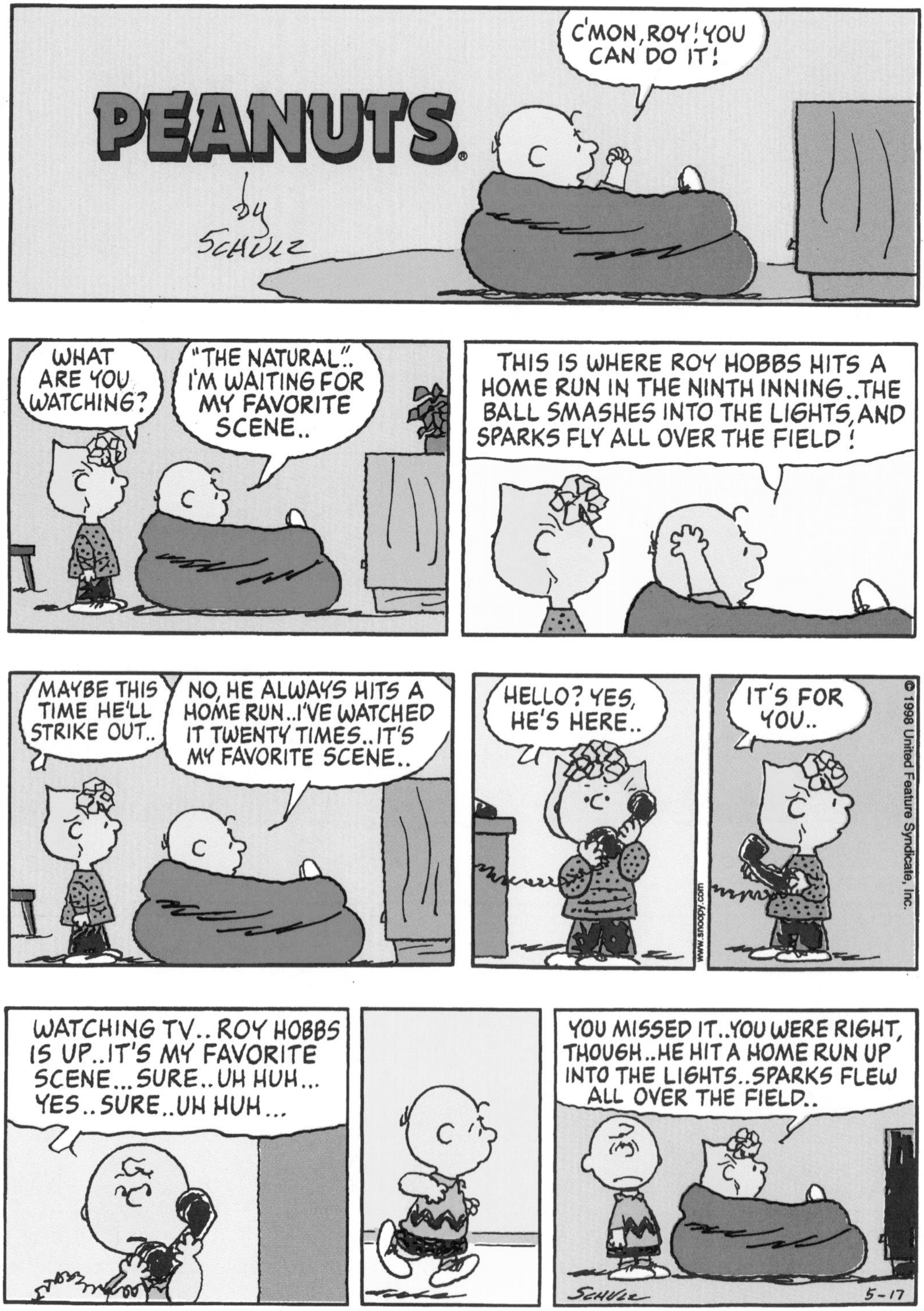
PEANUTS
by SCHULZ
C'MON, ROY! YOU CAN DO IT!
WHAT ARE YOU WATCHING?
"THE NATURAL".. I'M WAITING FOR MY FAVORITE SCENE..
THIS IS WHERE ROY HOBBS HITS A HOME RUN IN THE NINTH INNING..THE BALL SMASHES INTO THE LIGHTS, AND SPARKS FLY ALL OVER THE FIELD!
MAYBE THIS TIME HE'LL STRIKE OUT..
NO, HE ALWAYS HITS A HOME RUN..I'VE WATCHED IT TWENTY TIMES..IT'S MY FAVORITE SCENE..
HELLO? YES, HE'S HERE..
www.snoopy.com
IT'S FOR YOU..
© 1998 United Feature Syndicate, Inc.
WATCHING TV.. ROY HOBBS IS UP..IT'S MY FAVORITE SCENE...SURE..UH HUH... YES..SURE..UH HUH...
YOU MISSED IT..YOU WERE RIGHT, THOUGH..HE HIT A HOME RUN UP INTO THE LIGHTS..SPARKS FLEW ALL OVER THE FIELD..
SCHULZ
5-17

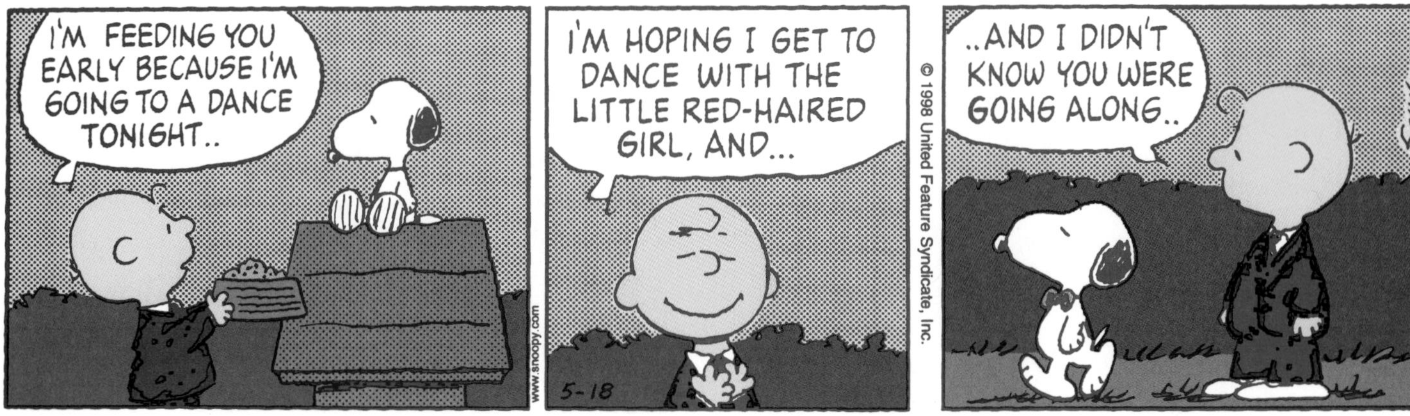
I'M FEEDING YOU EARLY BECAUSE I'M GOING TO A DANCE TONIGHT..
www.snoopy.com
I'M HOPING I GET TO DANCE WITH THE LITTLE RED-HAIRED GIRL, AND...
5-18
© 1998 United Feature Syndicate, Inc.
..AND I DIDN'T KNOW YOU WERE GOING ALONG..
SCHULZ

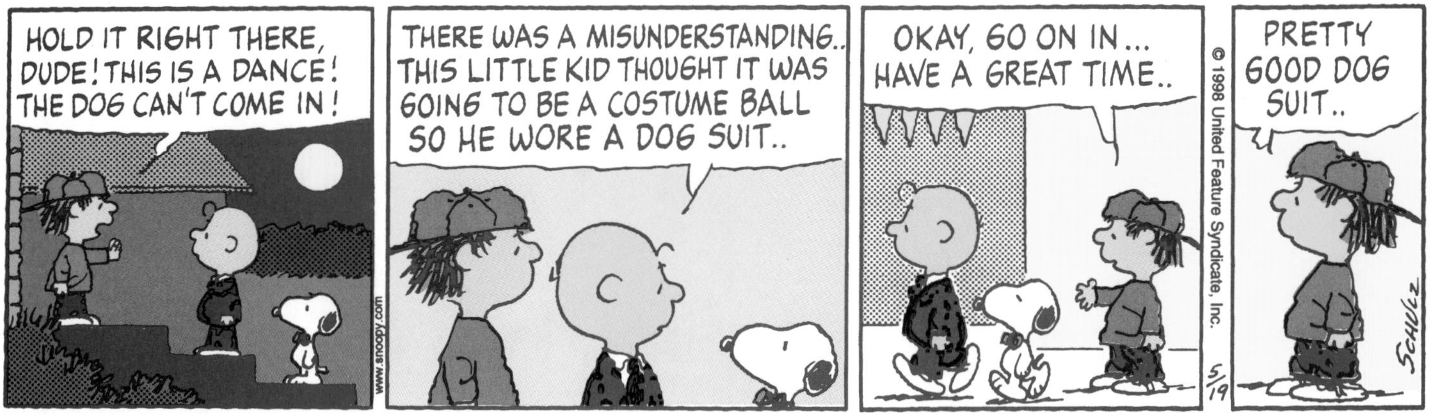
HOLD IT RIGHT THERE, DUDE! THIS IS A DANCE! THE DOG CAN'T COME IN!
www.snoopy.com
THERE WAS A MISUNDERSTANDING.. THIS LITTLE KID THOUGHT IT WAS GOING TO BE A COSTUME BALL SO HE WORE A DOG SUIT..
OKAY, GO ON IN... HAVE A GREAT TIME..
5/19
© 1998 United Feature Syndicate, Inc.
PRETTY GOOD DOG SUIT..
SCHULZ

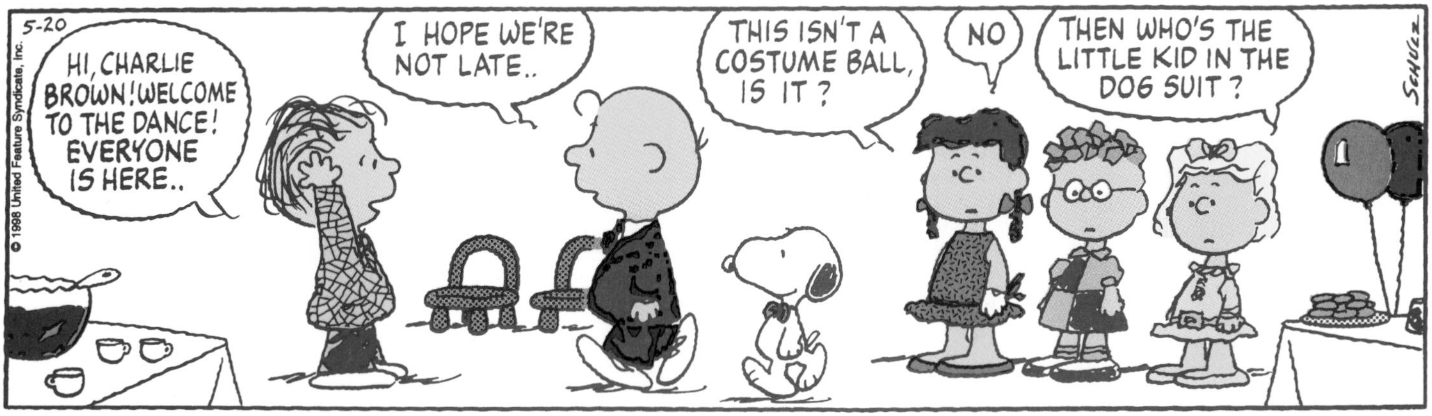
5-20
© 1998 United Feature Syndicate, Inc.
HI, CHARLIE BROWN! WELCOME TO THE DANCE! EVERYONE IS HERE..
I HOPE WE'RE NOT LATE..
THIS ISN'T A COSTUME BALL, IS IT?
NO
THEN WHO'S THE LITTLE KID IN THE DOG SUIT?
SCHULZ

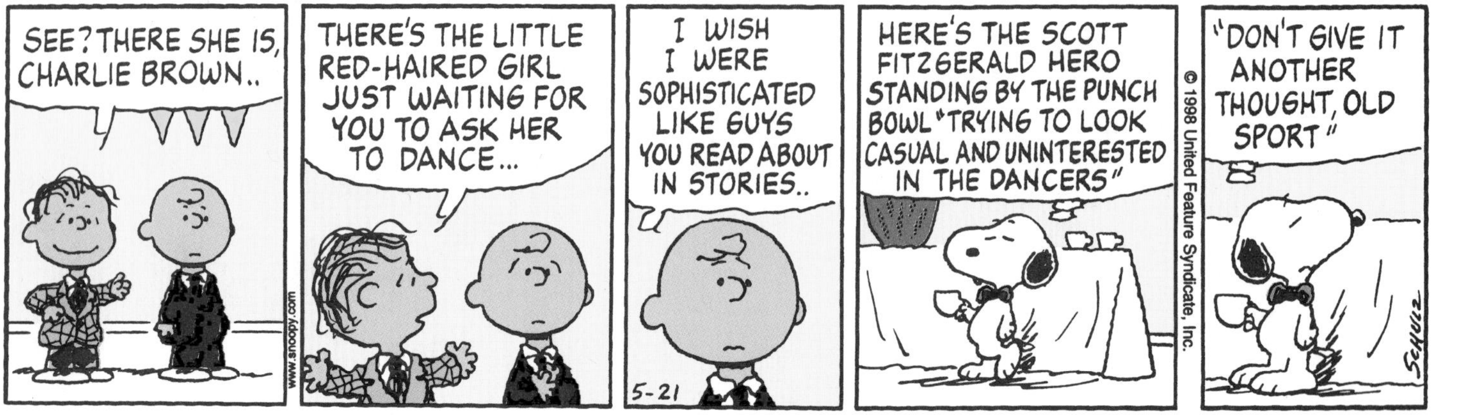
SEE? THERE SHE IS, CHARLIE BROWN..
THERE'S THE LITTLE RED-HAIRED GIRL JUST WAITING FOR YOU TO ASK HER TO DANCE...
I WISH I WERE SOPHISTICATED LIKE GUYS YOU READ ABOUT IN STORIES..
HERE'S THE SCOTT FITZGERALD HERO STANDING BY THE PUNCH BOWL "TRYING TO LOOK CASUAL AND UNINTERESTED IN THE DANCERS"
"DON'T GIVE IT ANOTHER THOUGHT, OLD SPORT"
5-21
www.snoopy.com
© 1998 United Feature Syndicate, Inc.
SCHULZ

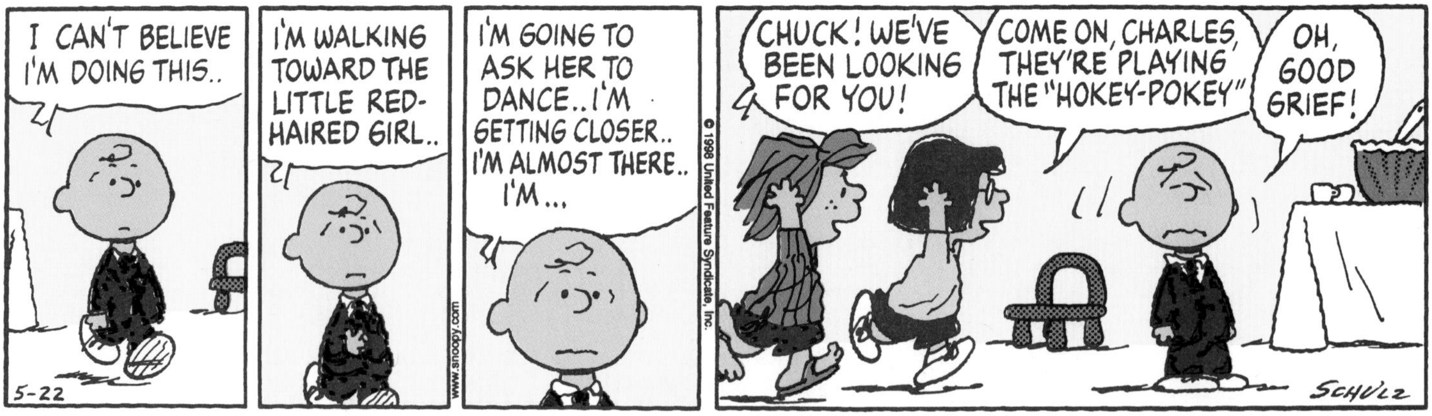
I CAN'T BELIEVE I'M DOING THIS..
I'M WALKING TOWARD THE LITTLE RED-HAIRED GIRL..
I'M GOING TO ASK HER TO DANCE..I'M GETTING CLOSER.. I'M ALMOST THERE.. I'M...
CHUCK! WE'VE BEEN LOOKING FOR YOU!
COME ON, CHARLES, THEY'RE PLAYING THE "HOKEY-POKEY"
OH, GOOD GRIEF!
5-22
www.snoopy.com
© 1998 United Feature Syndicate, Inc.
SCHULZ

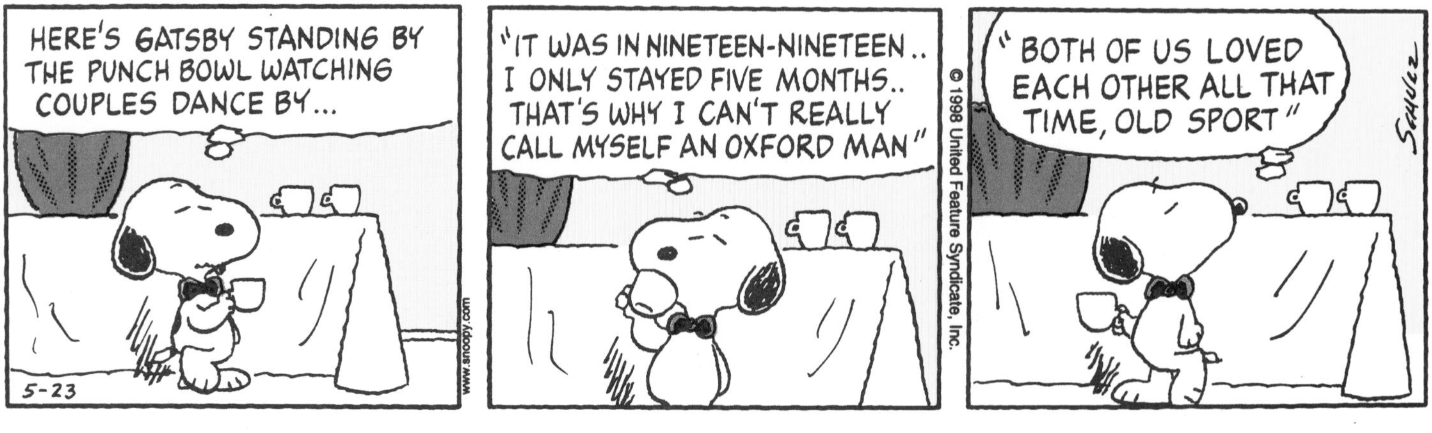
HERE'S GATSBY STANDING BY THE PUNCH BOWL WATCHING COUPLES DANCE BY...
"IT WAS IN NINETEEN-NINETEEN.. I ONLY STAYED FIVE MONTHS.. THAT'S WHY I CAN'T REALLY CALL MYSELF AN OXFORD MAN"
"BOTH OF US LOVED EACH OTHER ALL THAT TIME, OLD SPORT"
5-23
www.snoopy.com
© 1998 United Feature Syndicate, Inc.
SCHULZ

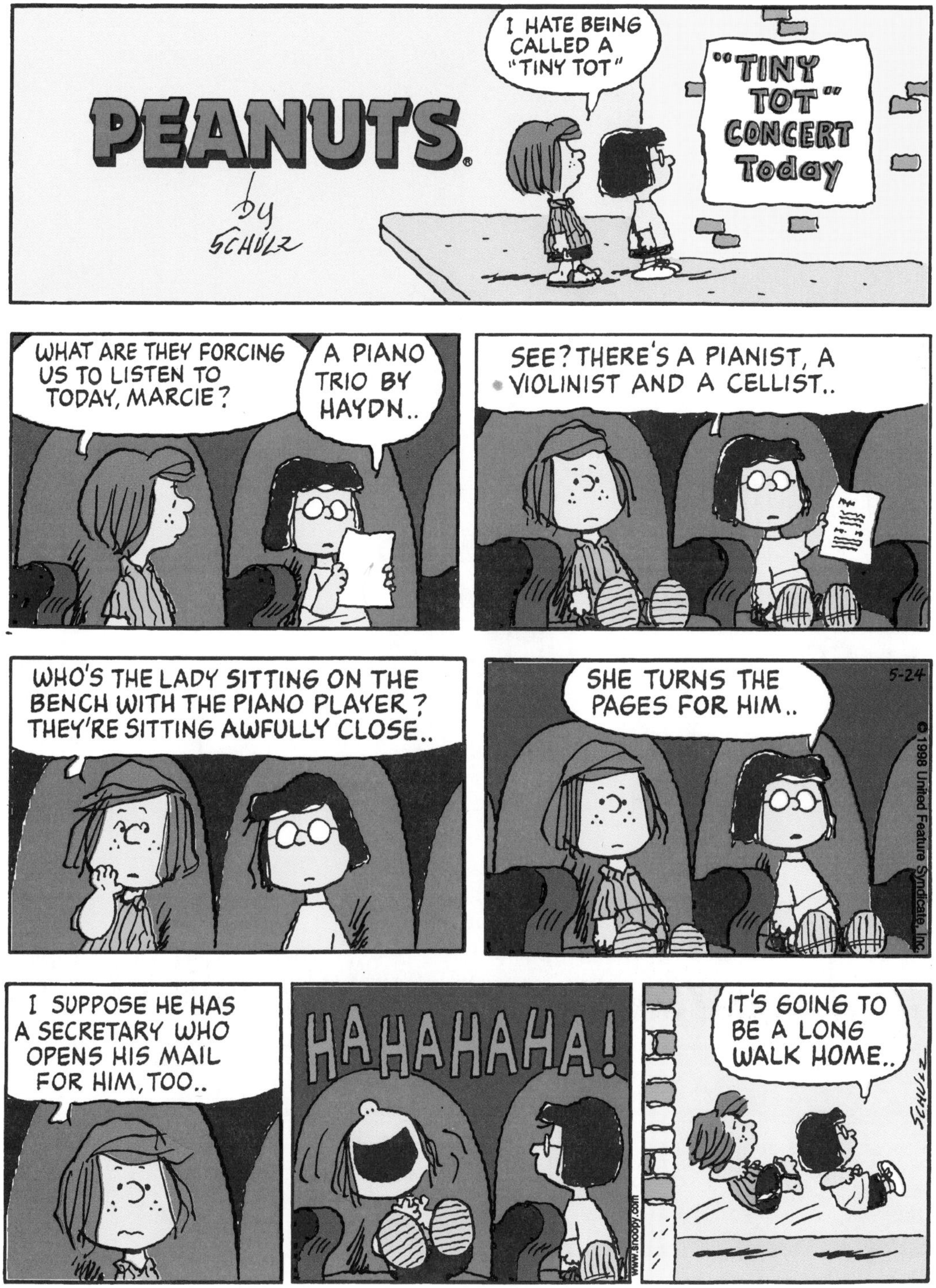

PEANUTS
by SCHULZ
I HATE BEING CALLED A "TINY TOT"
"TINY TOT" CONCERT Today
WHAT ARE THEY FORCING US TO LISTEN TO TODAY, MARCIE?
A PIANO TRIO BY HAYDN..
SEE? THERE'S A PIANIST, A VIOLINIST AND A CELLIST..
WHO'S THE LADY SITTING ON THE BENCH WITH THE PIANO PLAYER? THEY'RE SITTING AWFULLY CLOSE..
SHE TURNS THE PAGES FOR HIM..
5-24
© 1998 United Feature Syndicate, Inc.
I SUPPOSE HE HAS A SECRETARY WHO OPENS HIS MAIL FOR HIM, TOO..
HAHAHAHA!
www.snoopy.com
IT'S GOING TO BE A LONG WALK HOME..
SCHULZ

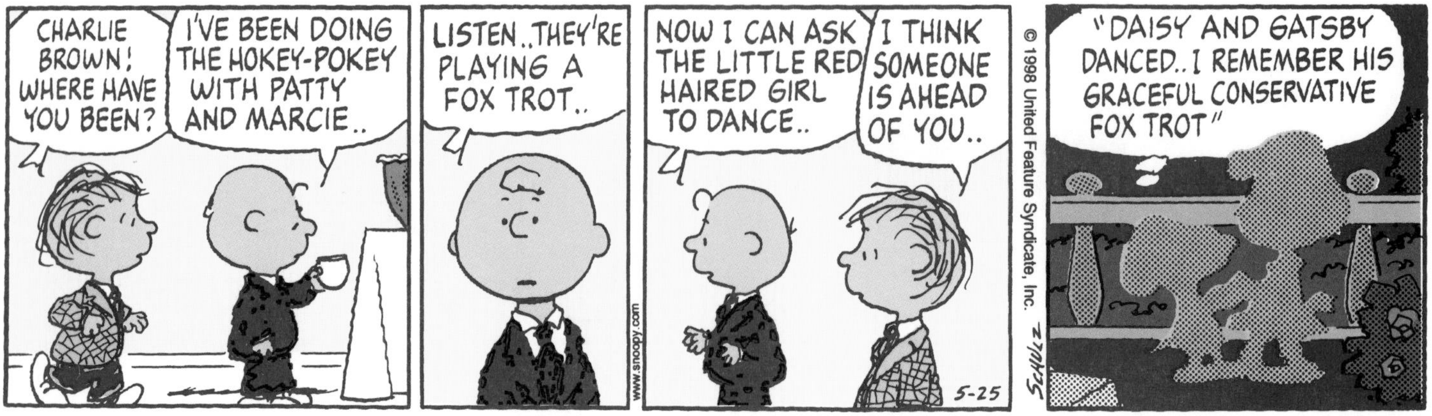
CHARLIE BROWN! WHERE HAVE YOU BEEN?
I'VE BEEN DOING THE HOKEY-POKEY WITH PATTY AND MARCIE..
LISTEN..THEY'RE PLAYING A FOX TROT..
NOW I CAN ASK THE LITTLE RED HAIRED GIRL TO DANCE..
I THINK SOMEONE IS AHEAD OF YOU..
"DAISY AND GATSBY DANCED.. I REMEMBER HIS GRACEFUL CONSERVATIVE FOX TROT"
© 1998 United Feature Syndicate, Inc.
www.snoopy.com
5-25
SCHULZ

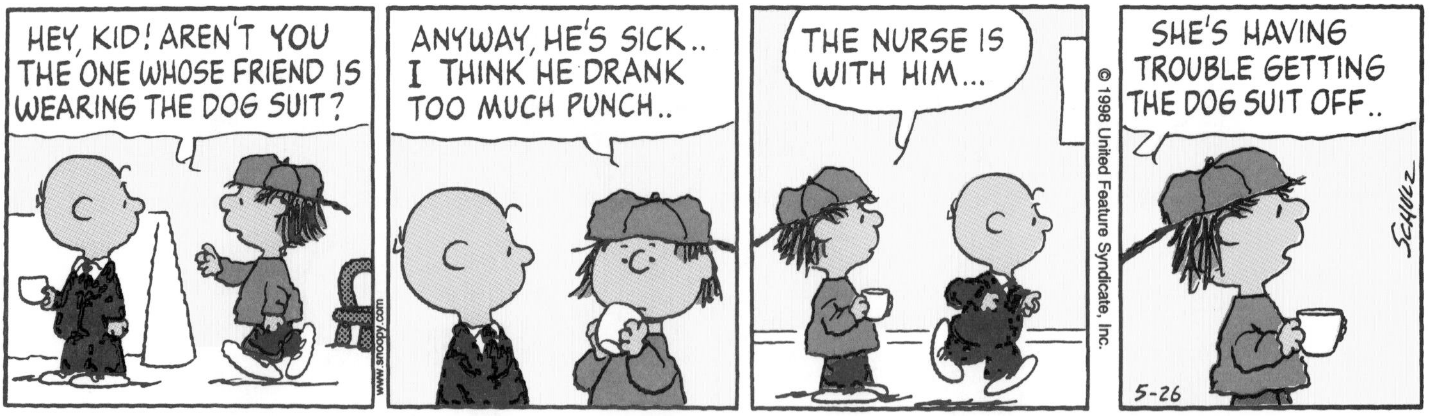
HEY, KID! AREN'T YOU THE ONE WHOSE FRIEND IS WEARING THE DOG SUIT?
ANYWAY, HE'S SICK.. I THINK HE DRANK TOO MUCH PUNCH..
THE NURSE IS WITH HIM...
SHE'S HAVING TROUBLE GETTING THE DOG SUIT OFF..
www.snoopy.com
© 1998 United Feature Syndicate, Inc.
5-26
SCHULZ

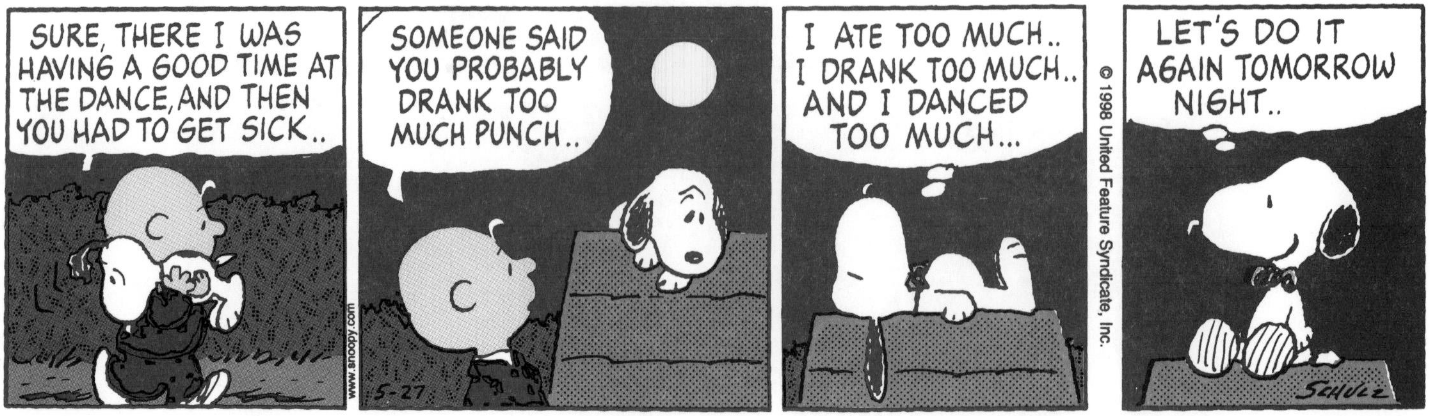
SURE, THERE I WAS HAVING A GOOD TIME AT THE DANCE, AND THEN YOU HAD TO GET SICK..
SOMEONE SAID YOU PROBABLY DRANK TOO MUCH PUNCH..
I ATE TOO MUCH.. I DRANK TOO MUCH.. AND I DANCED TOO MUCH...
LET'S DO IT AGAIN TOMORROW NIGHT..
www.snoopy.com
5-27
© 1998 United Feature Syndicate, Inc.
SCHULZ

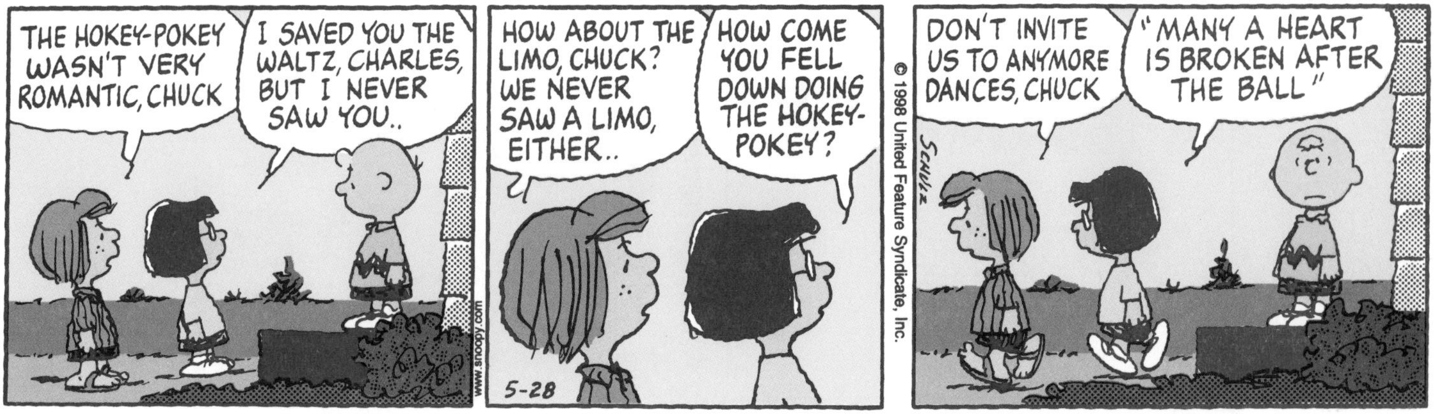
THE HOKEY-POKEY WASN'T VERY ROMANTIC, CHUCK
I SAVED YOU THE WALTZ, CHARLES, BUT I NEVER SAW YOU..
HOW ABOUT THE LIMO, CHUCK? WE NEVER SAW A LIMO, EITHER..
HOW COME YOU FELL DOWN DOING THE HOKEY-POKEY?
DON'T INVITE US TO ANYMORE DANCES, CHUCK
"MANY A HEART IS BROKEN AFTER THE BALL"
5-28
© 1998 United Feature Syndicate, Inc.
www.snoopy.com
SCHULZ

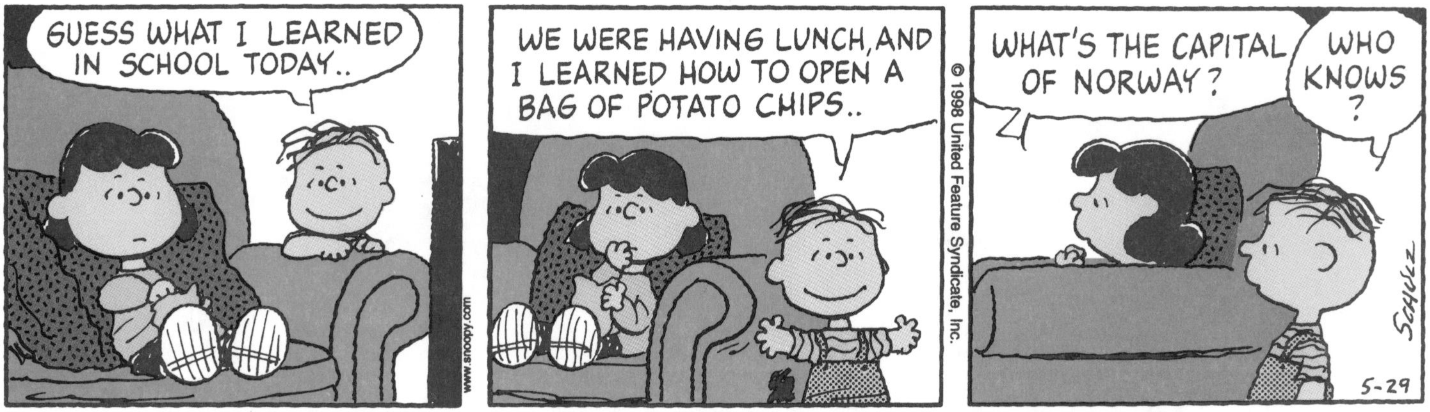
GUESS WHAT I LEARNED IN SCHOOL TODAY..
WE WERE HAVING LUNCH, AND I LEARNED HOW TO OPEN A BAG OF POTATO CHIPS..
WHAT'S THE CAPITAL OF NORWAY?
WHO KNOWS?
5-29
© 1998 United Feature Syndicate, Inc.
www.snoopy.com
SCHULZ

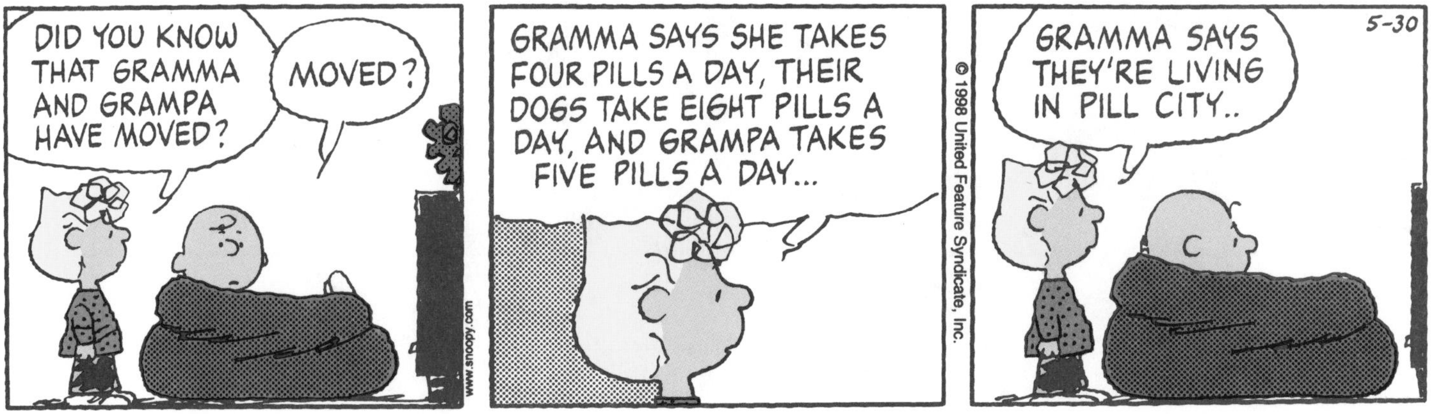
DID YOU KNOW THAT GRAMMA AND GRAMPA HAVE MOVED?
MOVED?
GRAMMA SAYS SHE TAKES FOUR PILLS A DAY, THEIR DOGS TAKE EIGHT PILLS A DAY, AND GRAMPA TAKES FIVE PILLS A DAY...
GRAMMA SAYS THEY'RE LIVING IN PILL CITY..
5-30
© 1998 United Feature Syndicate, Inc.
www.snoopy.com

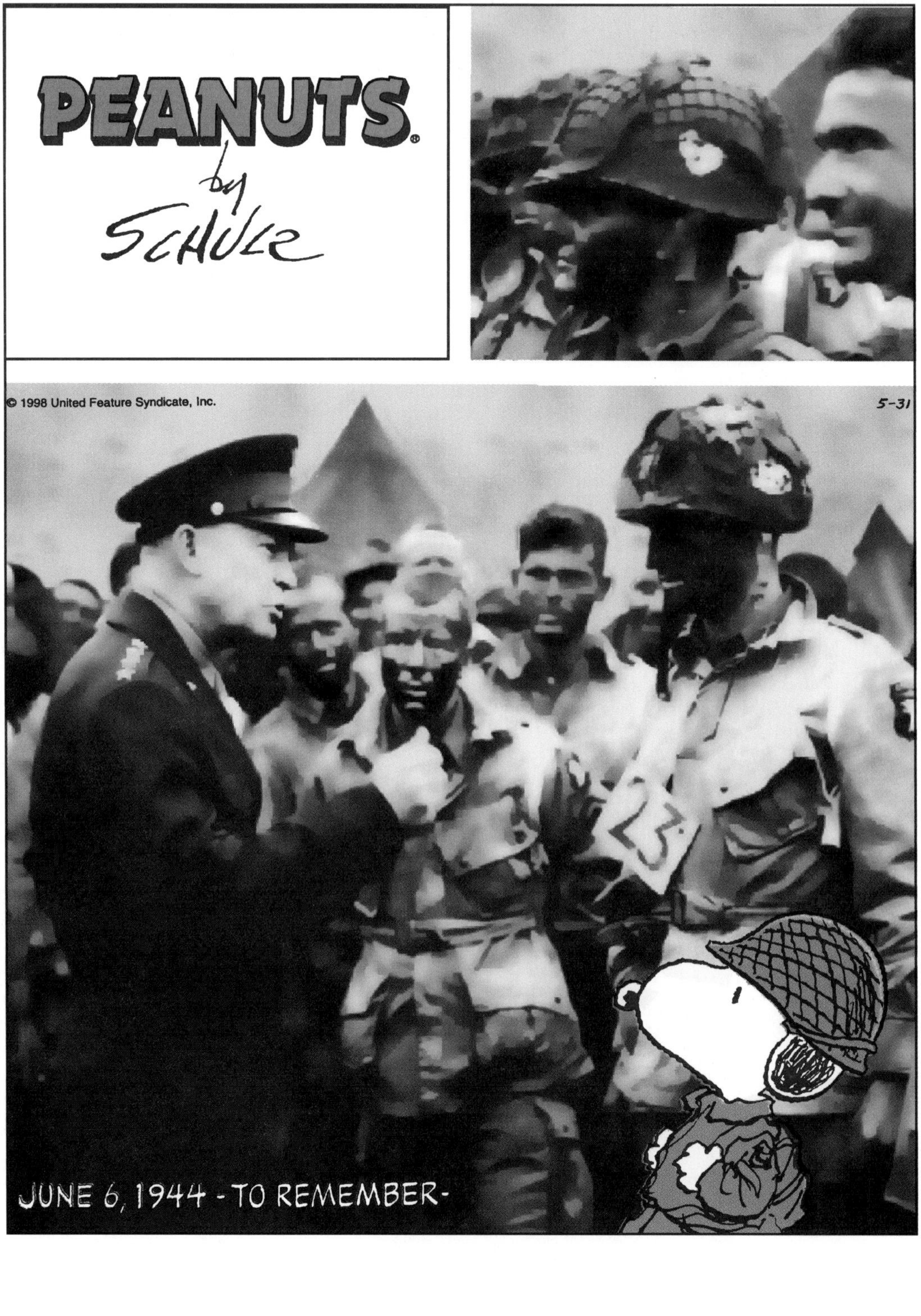
PEANUTS
by SCHULZ
© 1998 United Feature Syndicate, Inc.
5-31
23
JUNE 6, 1944 - TO REMEMBER -

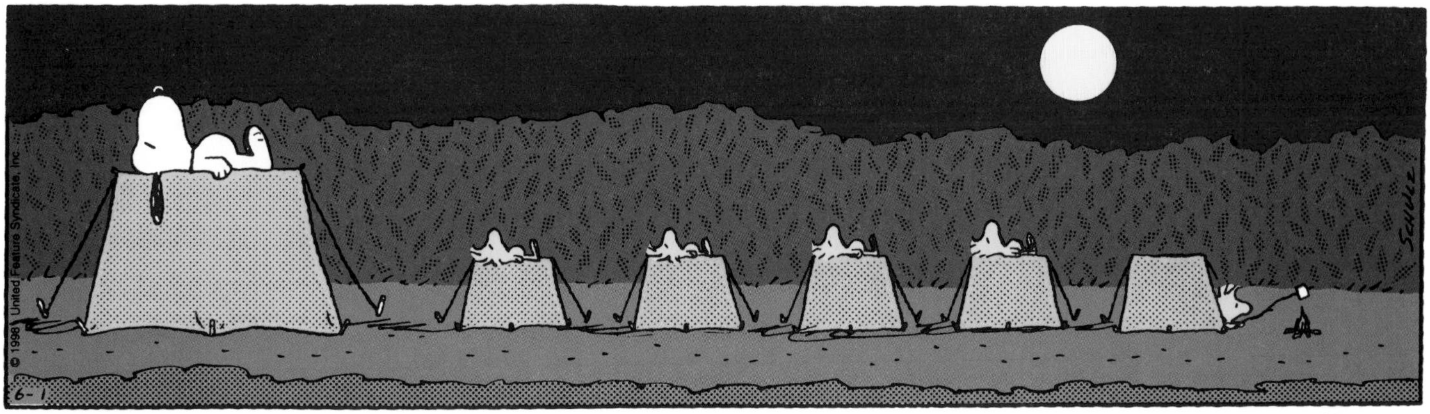
© 1998 United Feature Syndicate, Inc.
6-1
SCHULZ

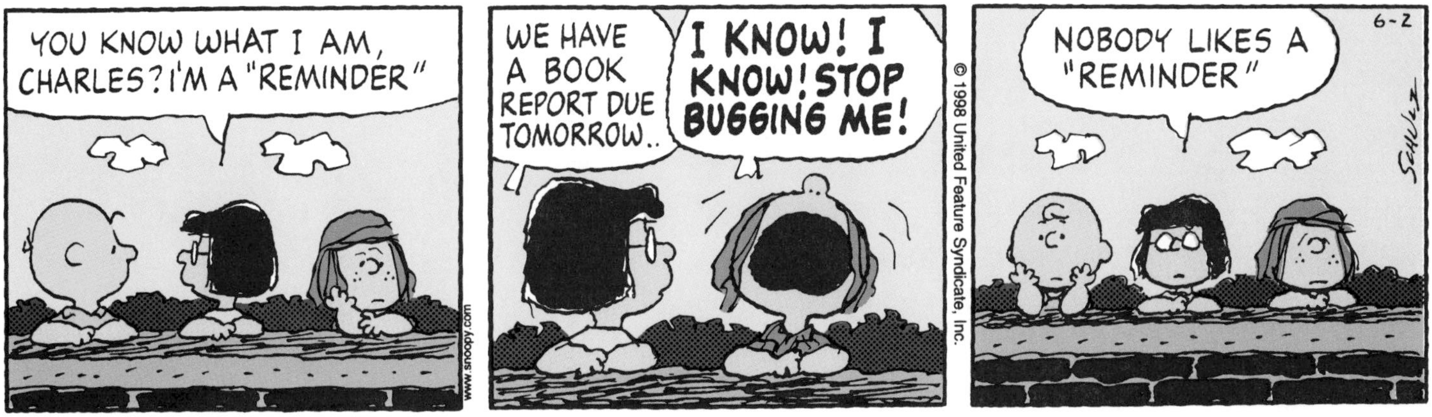
YOU KNOW WHAT I AM, CHARLES? I'M A "REMINDER"
WE HAVE A BOOK REPORT DUE TOMORROW..
I KNOW! I KNOW! STOP BUGGING ME!
NOBODY LIKES A "REMINDER"
6-2
SCHULZ
www.snoopy.com
© 1998 United Feature Syndicate, Inc.

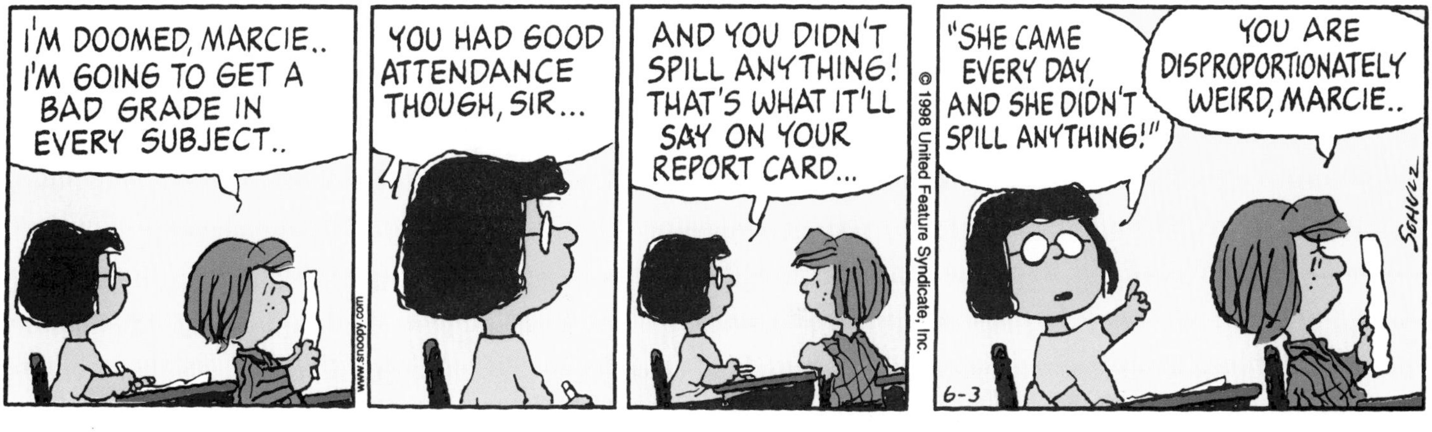
I'M DOOMED, MARCIE.. I'M GOING TO GET A BAD GRADE IN EVERY SUBJECT..
YOU HAD GOOD ATTENDANCE THOUGH, SIR...
AND YOU DIDN'T SPILL ANYTHING! THAT'S WHAT IT'LL SAY ON YOUR REPORT CARD...
"SHE CAME EVERY DAY, AND SHE DIDN'T SPILL ANYTHING!"
YOU ARE DISPROPORTIONATELY WEIRD, MARCIE..
6-3
SCHULZ
www.snoopy.com
© 1998 United Feature Syndicate, Inc.

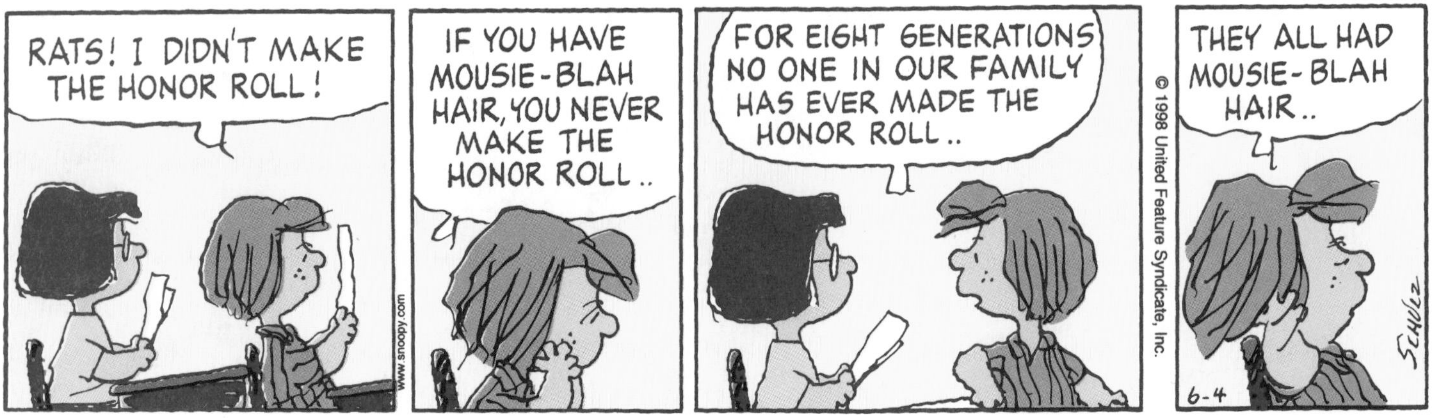
RATS! I DIDN'T MAKE THE HONOR ROLL!
IF YOU HAVE MOUSIE-BLAH HAIR, YOU NEVER MAKE THE HONOR ROLL..
FOR EIGHT GENERATIONS NO ONE IN OUR FAMILY HAS EVER MADE THE HONOR ROLL..
THEY ALL HAD MOUSIE-BLAH HAIR..
www.snoopy.com
© 1998 United Feature Syndicate, Inc.
SCHULZ
6-4

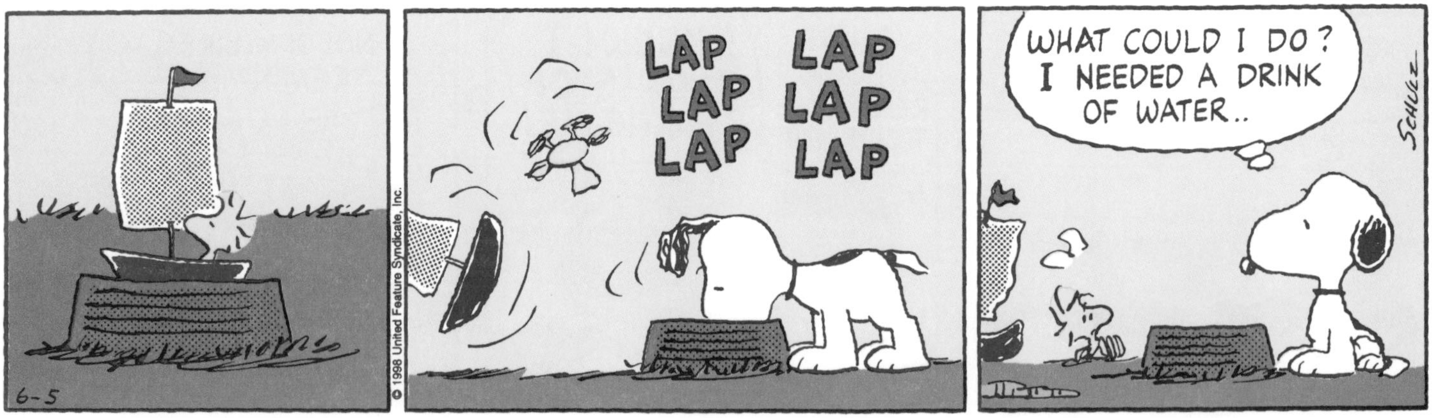
6-5
© 1998 United Feature Syndicate, Inc.
LAP LAP LAP
LAP LAP LAP
WHAT COULD I DO? I NEEDED A DRINK OF WATER..
SCHULZ

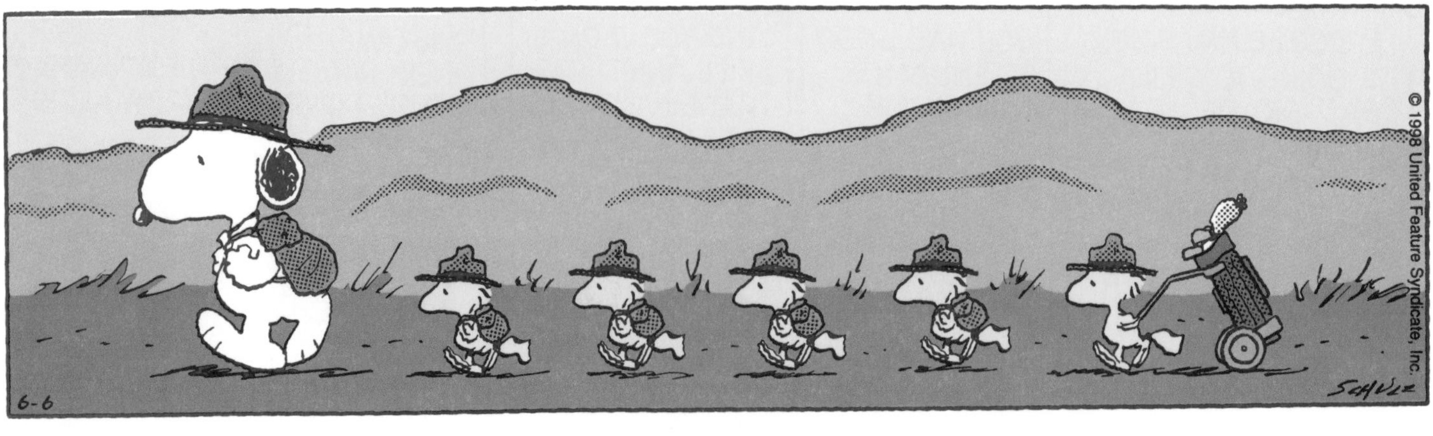
© 1998 United Feature Syndicate, Inc.
SCHULZ
6-6

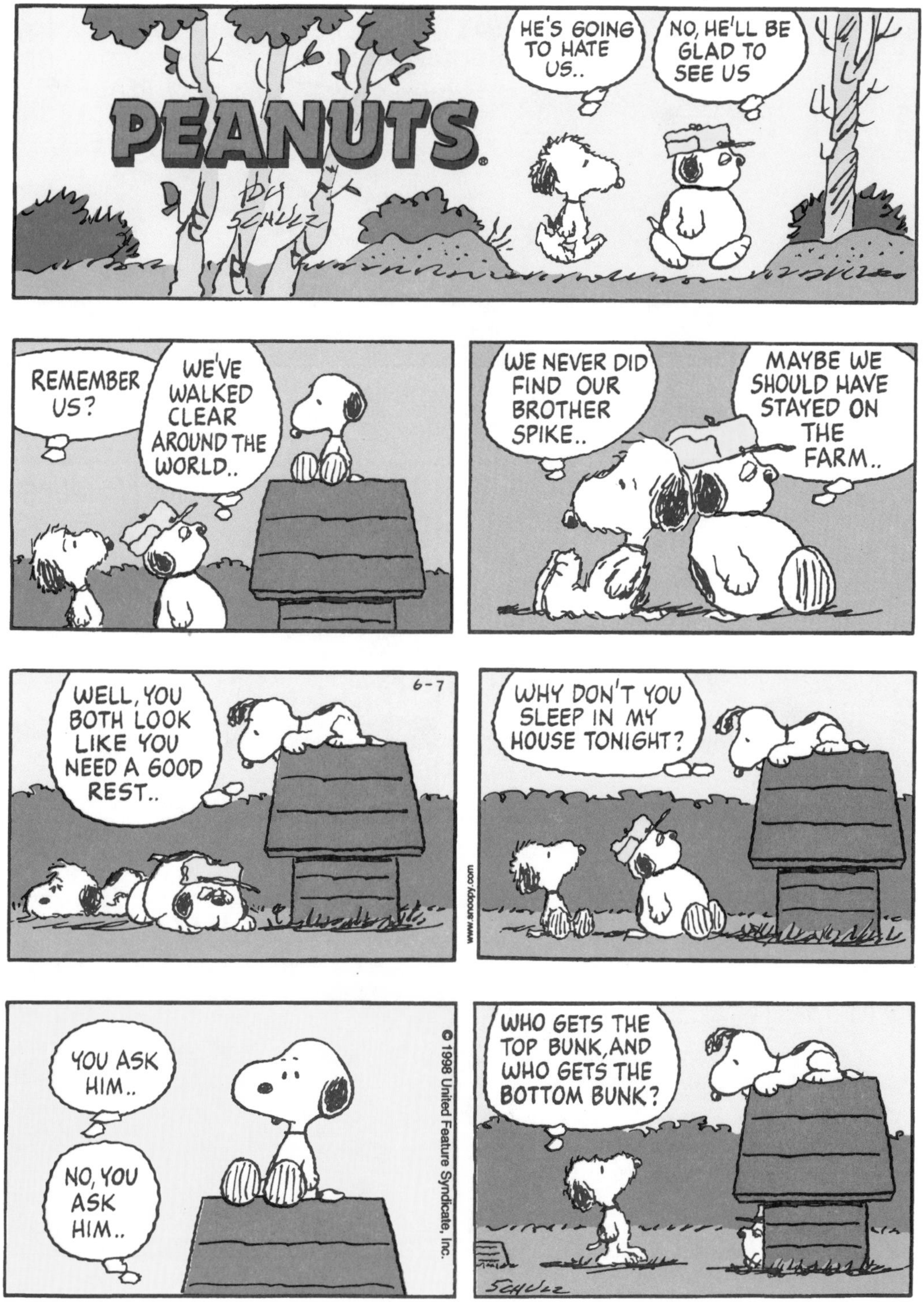
PEANUTS
by SCHULZ
HE'S GOING TO HATE US..
NO, HE'LL BE GLAD TO SEE US
REMEMBER US?
WE'VE WALKED CLEAR AROUND THE WORLD..
WE NEVER DID FIND OUR BROTHER SPIKE..
MAYBE WE SHOULD HAVE STAYED ON THE FARM..
6-7
WELL, YOU BOTH LOOK LIKE YOU NEED A GOOD REST..
www.snoopy.com
WHY DON'T YOU SLEEP IN MY HOUSE TONIGHT?
© 1998 United Feature Syndicate, Inc.
YOU ASK HIM..
NO, YOU ASK HIM..
WHO GETS THE TOP BUNK, AND WHO GETS THE BOTTOM BUNK?
SCHULZ

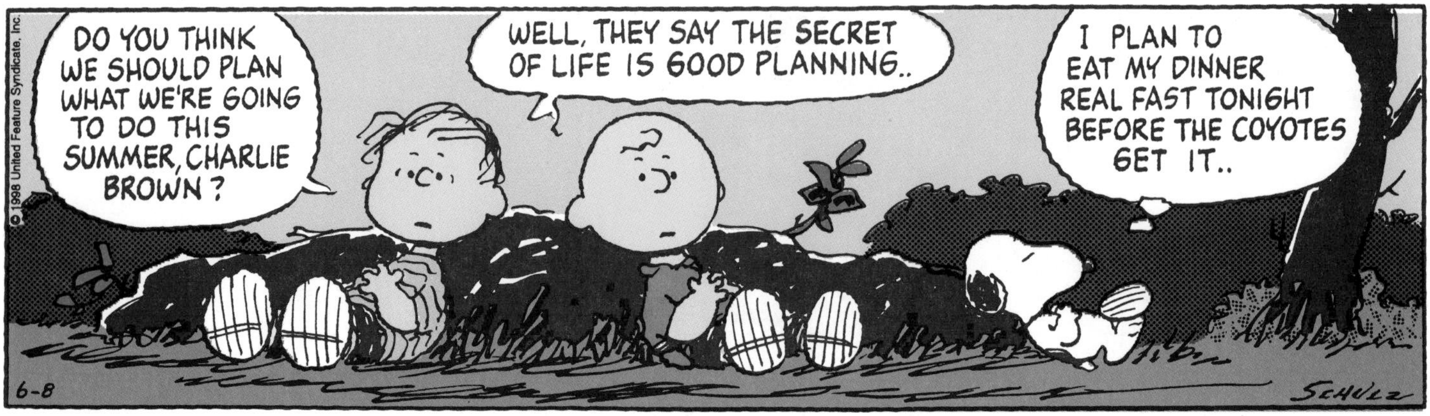
© 1998 United Feature Syndicate, Inc.
DO YOU THINK WE SHOULD PLAN WHAT WE'RE GOING TO DO THIS SUMMER, CHARLIE BROWN?
WELL, THEY SAY THE SECRET OF LIFE IS GOOD PLANNING..
I PLAN TO EAT MY DINNER REAL FAST TONIGHT BEFORE THE COYOTES GET IT..
6-8
SCHULZ

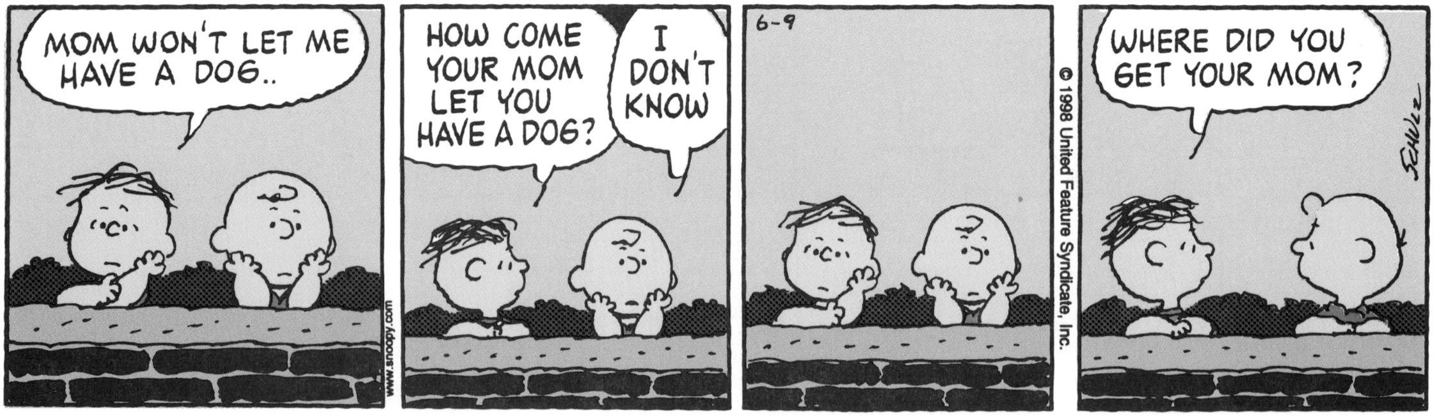
MOM WON'T LET ME HAVE A DOG..
www.snoopy.com
HOW COME YOUR MOM LET YOU HAVE A DOG?
I DON'T KNOW
6-9
© 1998 United Feature Syndicate, Inc.
WHERE DID YOU GET YOUR MOM?
SCHULZ

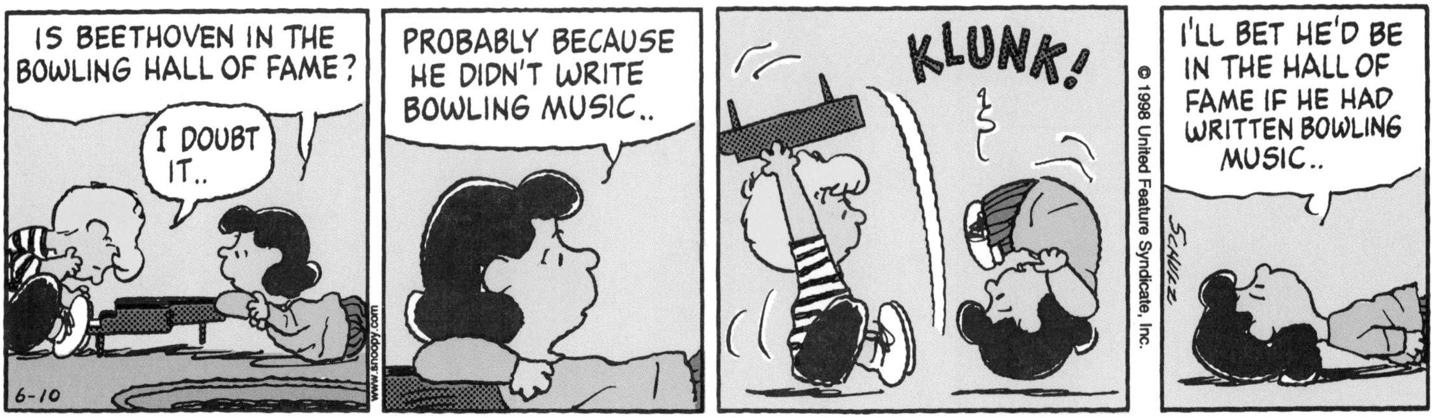
IS BEETHOVEN IN THE BOWLING HALL OF FAME?
I DOUBT IT..
6-10
www.snoopy.com
PROBABLY BECAUSE HE DIDN'T WRITE BOWLING MUSIC..
KLUNK!
© 1998 United Feature Syndicate, Inc.
I'LL BET HE'D BE IN THE HALL OF FAME IF HE HAD WRITTEN BOWLING MUSIC..
SCHULZ

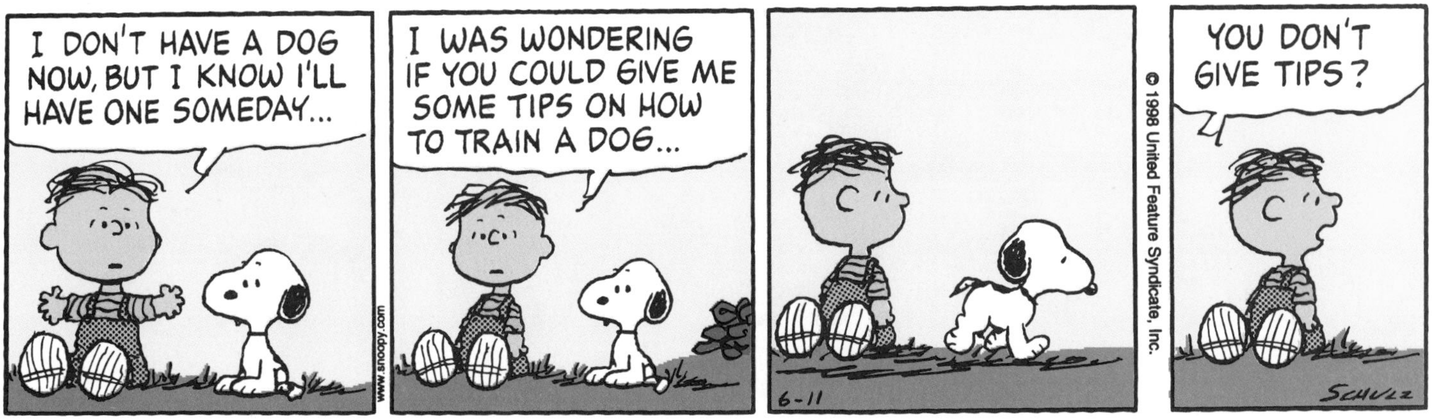
I DON'T HAVE A DOG NOW, BUT I KNOW I'LL HAVE ONE SOMEDAY...
I WAS WONDERING IF YOU COULD GIVE ME SOME TIPS ON HOW TO TRAIN A DOG...
YOU DON'T GIVE TIPS?
www.snoopy.com
© 1998 United Feature Syndicate, Inc.
6-11
SCHULZ

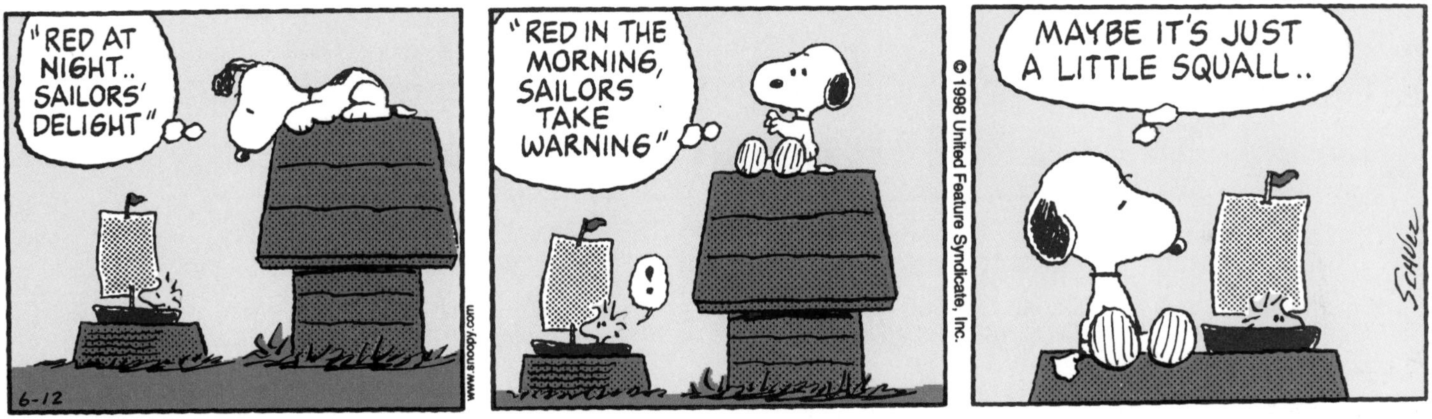
"RED AT NIGHT.. SAILORS' DELIGHT"
"RED IN THE MORNING, SAILORS TAKE WARNING"
!
MAYBE IT'S JUST A LITTLE SQUALL..
6-12
www.snoopy.com
© 1998 United Feature Syndicate, Inc.
SCHULZ

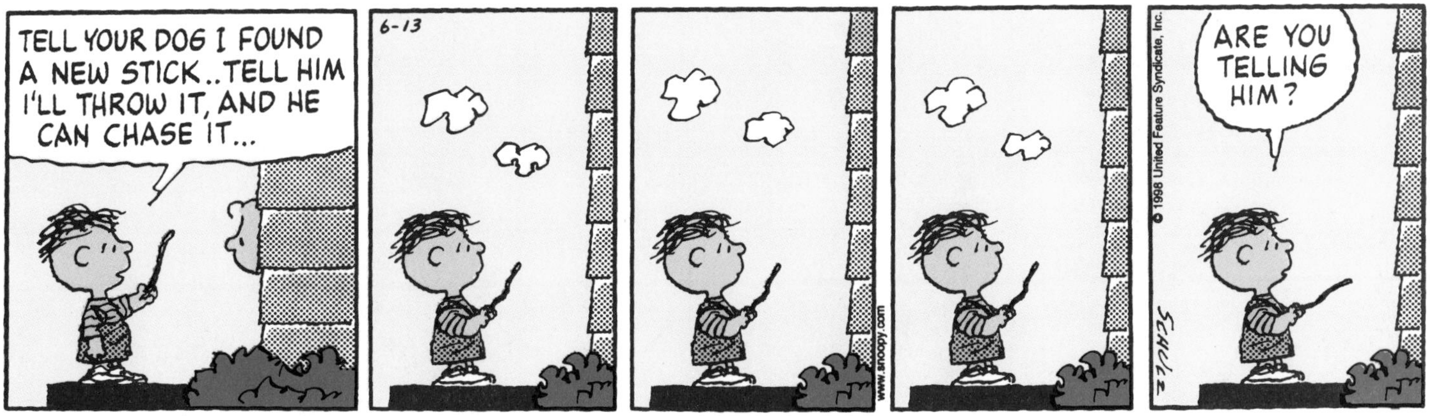
TELL YOUR DOG I FOUND A NEW STICK..TELL HIM I'LL THROW IT, AND HE CAN CHASE IT...
ARE YOU TELLING HIM?
6-13
www.snoopy.com
© 1998 United Feature Syndicate, Inc.
SCHULZ

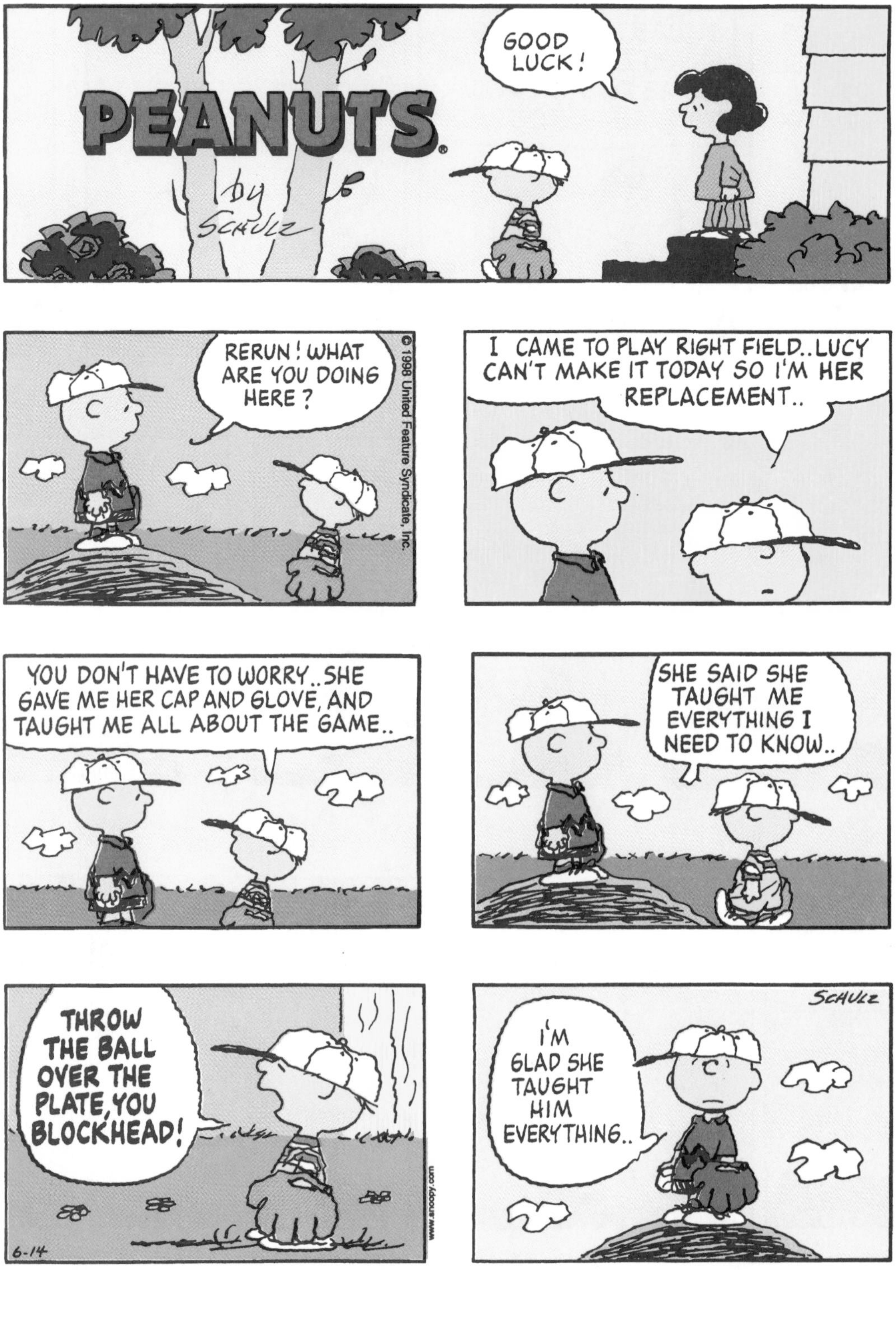
PEANUTS
by SCHULZ
GOOD LUCK!
RERUN! WHAT ARE YOU DOING HERE?
© 1998 United Feature Syndicate, Inc.
I CAME TO PLAY RIGHT FIELD..LUCY CAN'T MAKE IT TODAY SO I'M HER REPLACEMENT..
YOU DON'T HAVE TO WORRY..SHE GAVE ME HER CAP AND GLOVE, AND TAUGHT ME ALL ABOUT THE GAME..
SHE SAID SHE TAUGHT ME EVERYTHING I NEED TO KNOW..
THROW THE BALL OVER THE PLATE, YOU BLOCKHEAD!
www.snoopy.com
6-14
SCHULZ
I'M GLAD SHE TAUGHT HIM EVERYTHING..

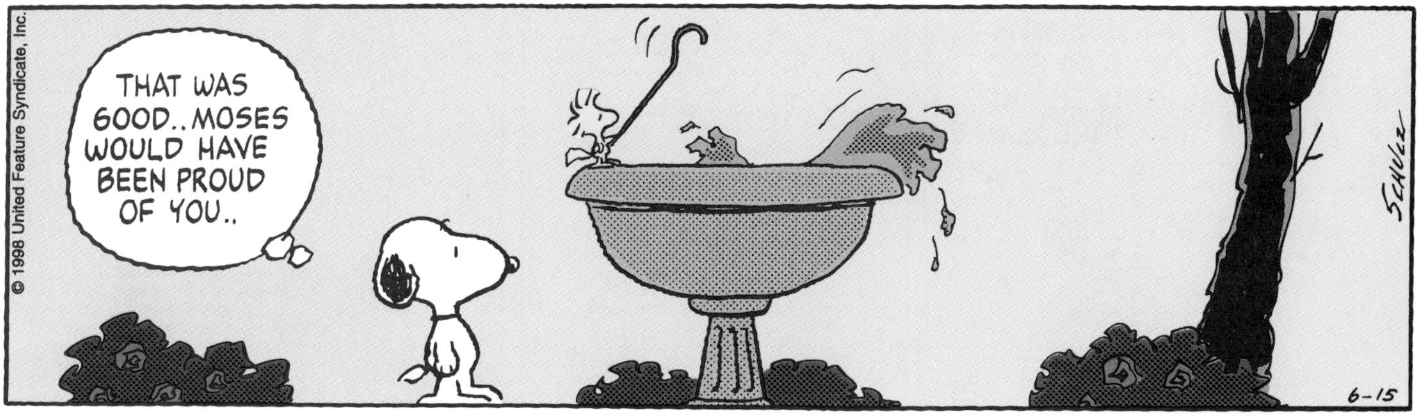
© 1998 United Feature Syndicate, Inc.
THAT WAS GOOD..MOSES WOULD HAVE BEEN PROUD OF YOU..
SCHULZ
6-15

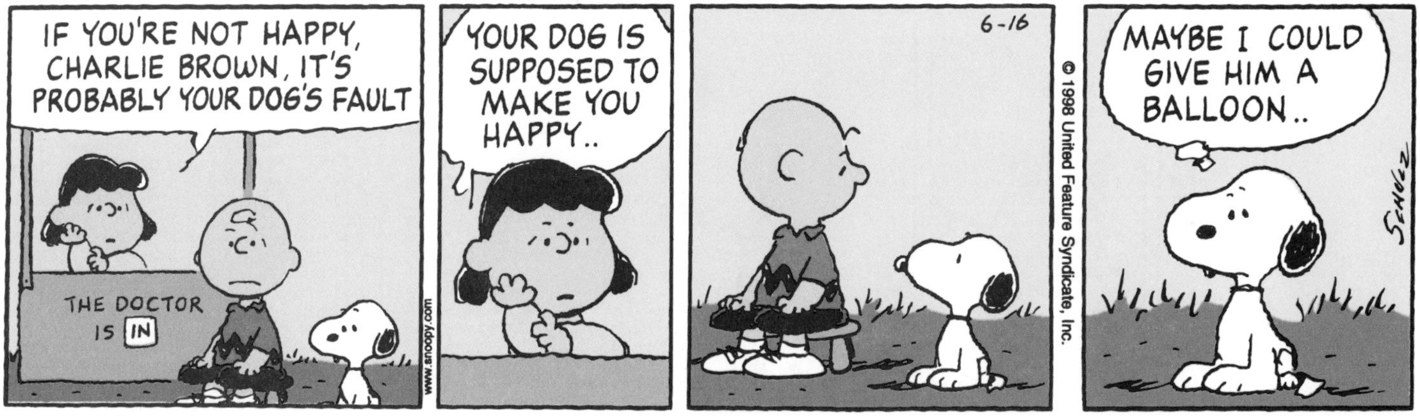
IF YOU'RE NOT HAPPY, CHARLIE BROWN, IT'S PROBABLY YOUR DOG'S FAULT
THE DOCTOR IS IN
www.snoopy.com
YOUR DOG IS SUPPOSED TO MAKE YOU HAPPY..
6-16
© 1998 United Feature Syndicate, Inc.
MAYBE I COULD GIVE HIM A BALLOON..
SCHULZ

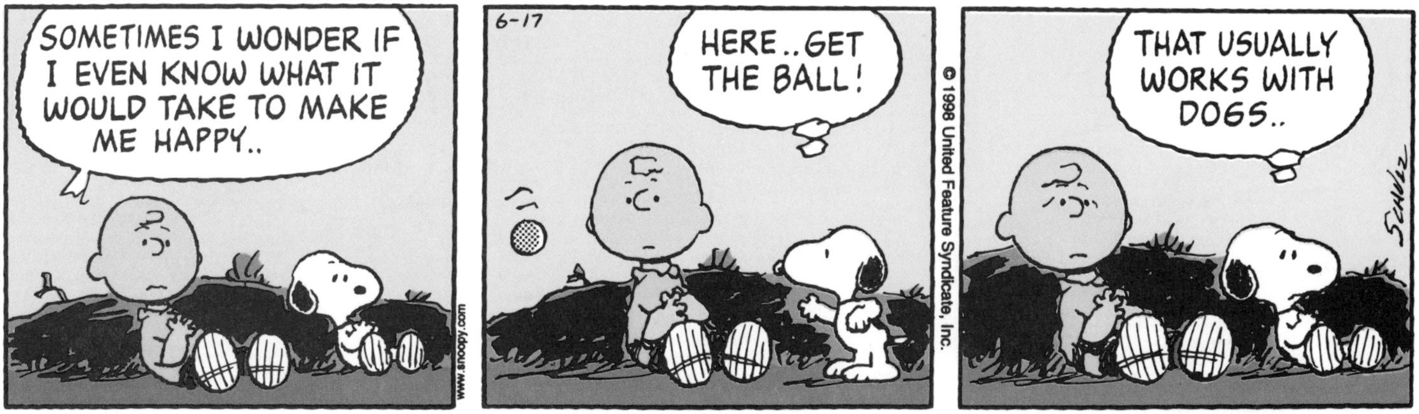
SOMETIMES I WONDER IF I EVEN KNOW WHAT IT WOULD TAKE TO MAKE ME HAPPY..
www.snoopy.com
6-17
HERE..GET THE BALL!
© 1998 United Feature Syndicate, Inc.
THAT USUALLY WORKS WITH DOGS..
SCHULZ

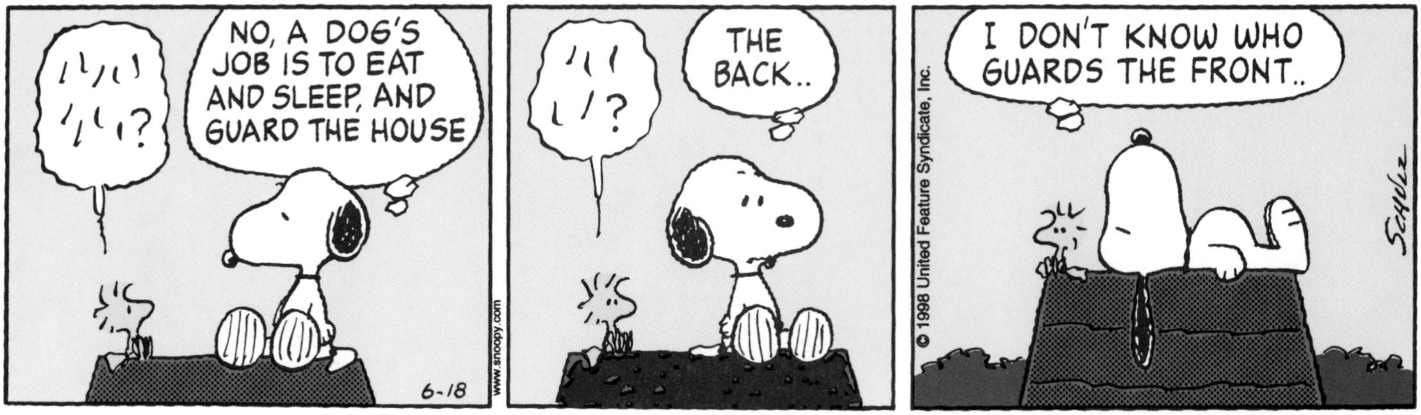
NO, A DOG'S JOB IS TO EAT AND SLEEP, AND GUARD THE HOUSE
6-18
www.snoopy.com
THE BACK..
© 1998 United Feature Syndicate, Inc.
I DON'T KNOW WHO GUARDS THE FRONT..
SCHULZ

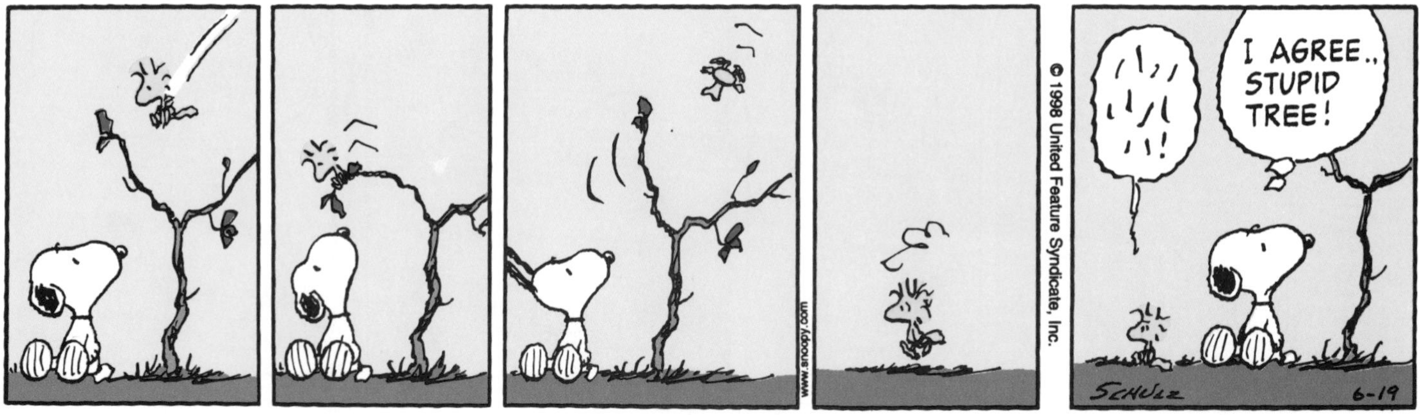
www.snoopy.com
© 1998 United Feature Syndicate, Inc.
I AGREE.. STUPID TREE!
SCHULZ
6-19

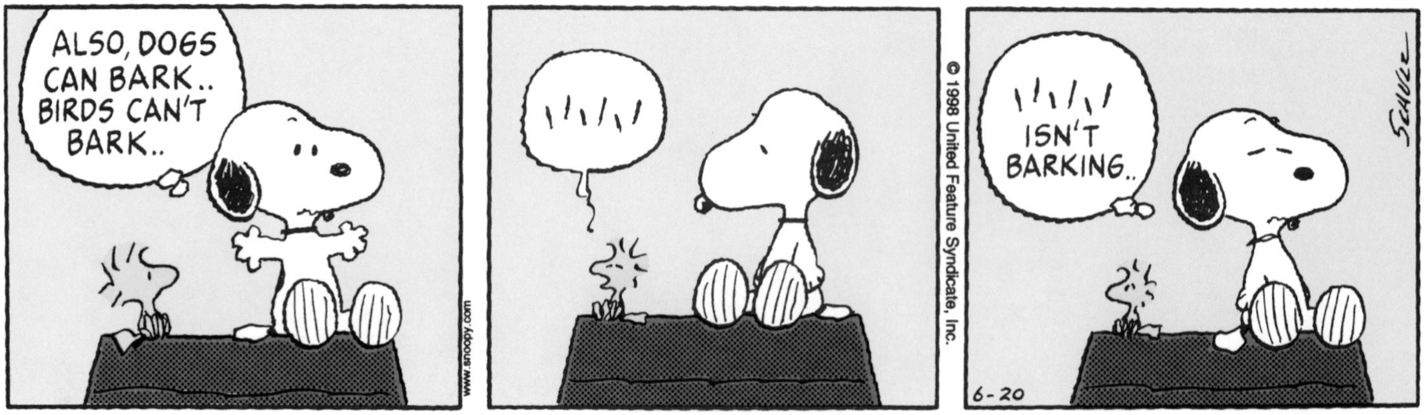
ALSO, DOGS CAN BARK.. BIRDS CAN'T BARK..
www.snoopy.com
© 1998 United Feature Syndicate, Inc.
ISN'T BARKING..
6-20
SCHULZ

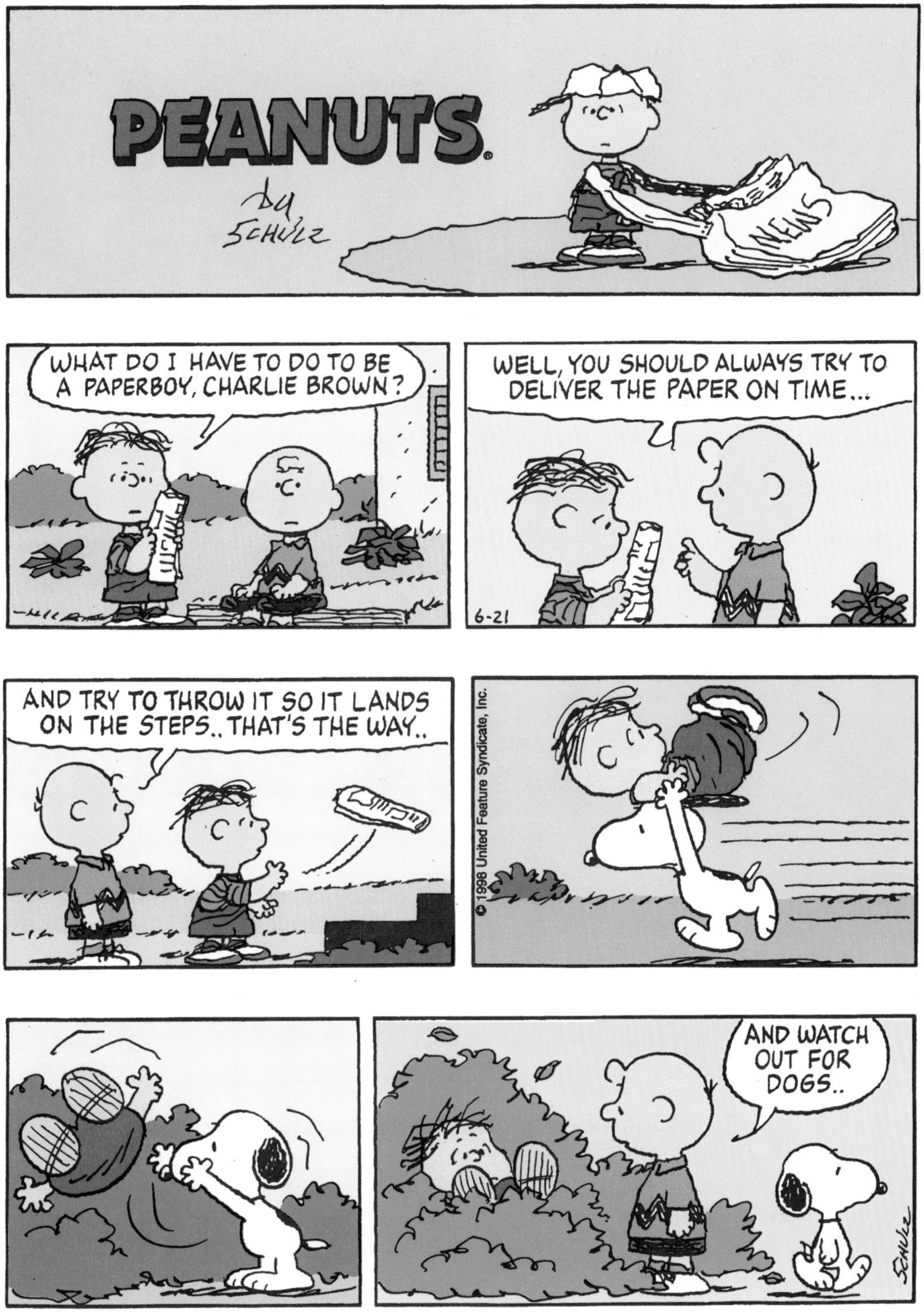
PEANUTS
SCHULZ
NEWS
WHAT DO I HAVE TO DO TO BE A PAPERBOY, CHARLIE BROWN?
WELL, YOU SHOULD ALWAYS TRY TO DELIVER THE PAPER ON TIME...
6-21
AND TRY TO THROW IT SO IT LANDS ON THE STEPS.. THAT'S THE WAY..
© 1998 United Feature Syndicate, Inc.
AND WATCH OUT FOR DOGS..
SCHULZ

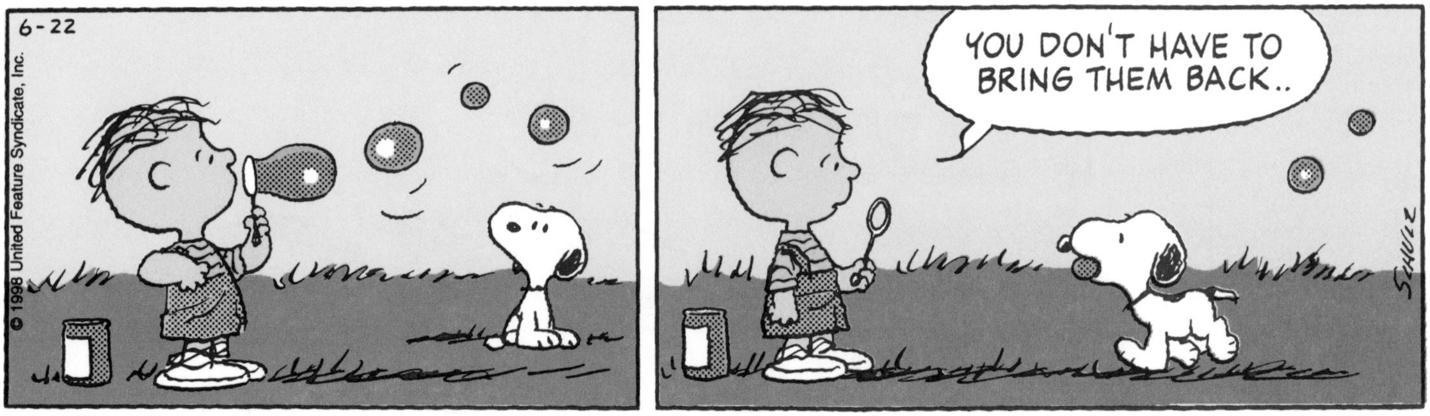
6-22
© 1998 United Feature Syndicate, Inc.
YOU DON'T HAVE TO BRING THEM BACK..
SCHULZ

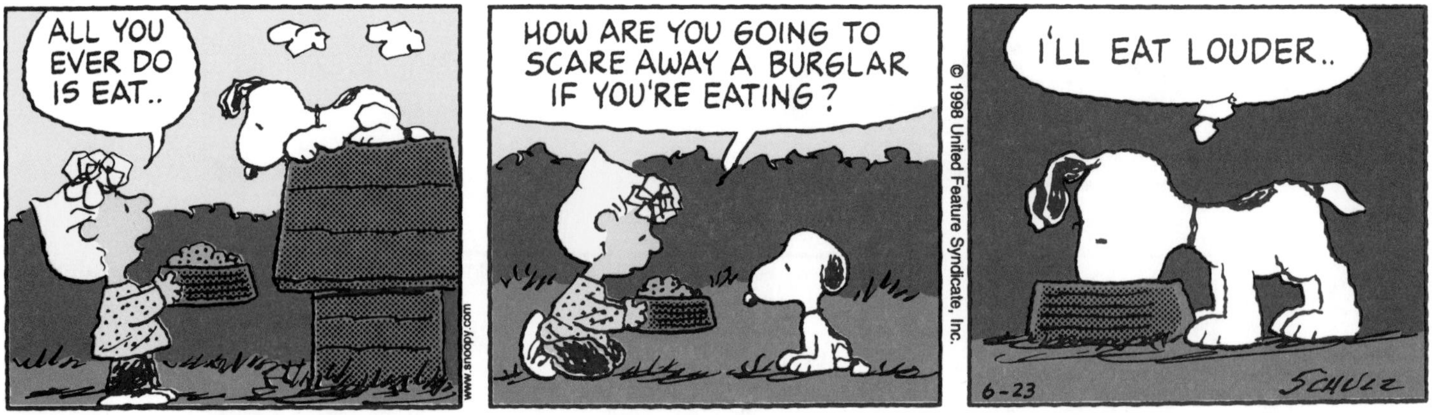
ALL YOU EVER DO IS EAT..
www.snoopy.com
HOW ARE YOU GOING TO SCARE AWAY A BURGLAR IF YOU'RE EATING?
© 1998 United Feature Syndicate, Inc.
I'LL EAT LOUDER..
6-23
SCHULZ

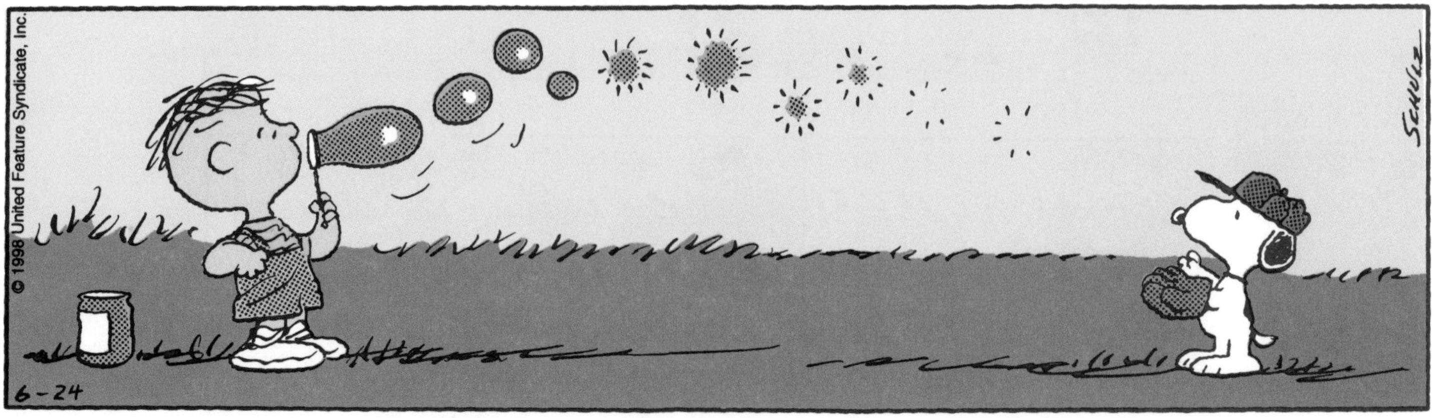
© 1998 United Feature Syndicate, Inc.
SCHULZ
6-24

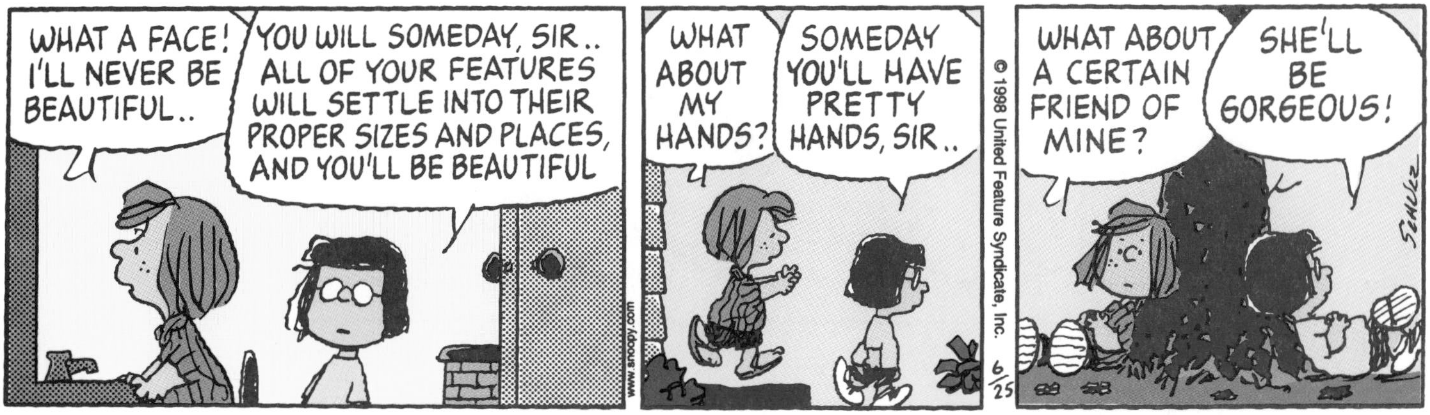
WHAT A FACE! I'LL NEVER BE BEAUTIFUL..
YOU WILL SOMEDAY, SIR.. ALL OF YOUR FEATURES WILL SETTLE INTO THEIR PROPER SIZES AND PLACES, AND YOU'LL BE BEAUTIFUL
www.snoopy.com
WHAT ABOUT MY HANDS?
SOMEDAY YOU'LL HAVE PRETTY HANDS, SIR..
© 1998 United Feature Syndicate, Inc.
6/25
WHAT ABOUT A CERTAIN FRIEND OF MINE?
SHE'LL BE GORGEOUS!
SCHULZ

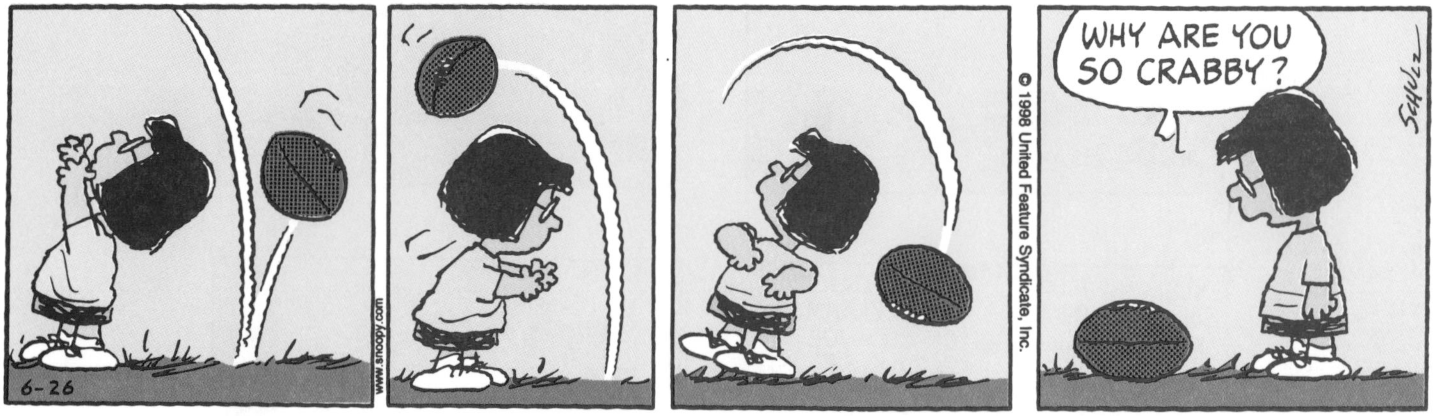
6-26
www.snoopy.com
© 1998 United Feature Syndicate, Inc.
WHY ARE YOU SO CRABBY?
SCHULZ

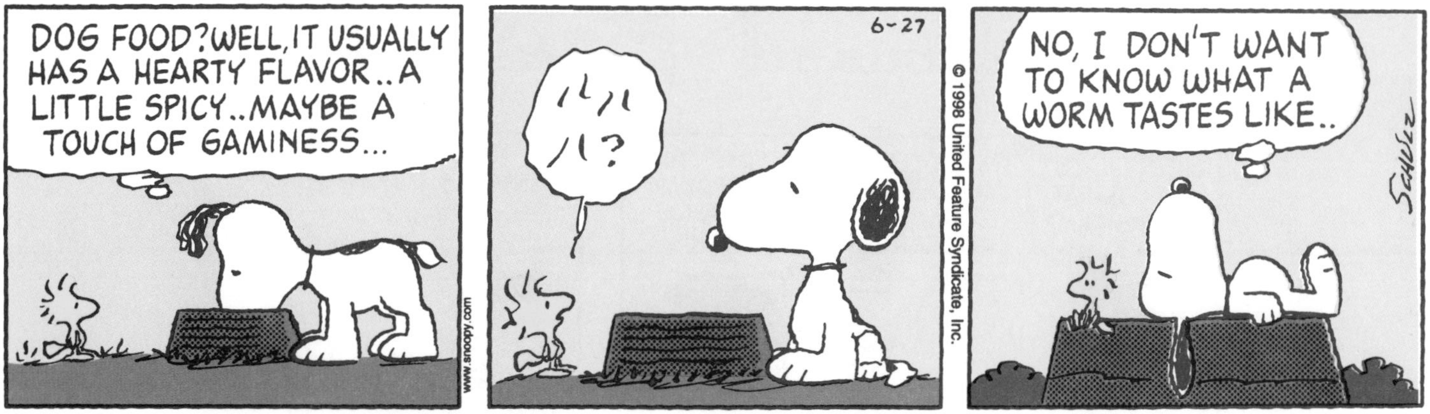
DOG FOOD? WELL, IT USUALLY HAS A HEARTY FLAVOR.. A LITTLE SPICY.. MAYBE A TOUCH OF GAMINESS...
www.snoopy.com
6-27
© 1998 United Feature Syndicate, Inc.
NO, I DON'T WANT TO KNOW WHAT A WORM TASTES LIKE..
SCHULZ

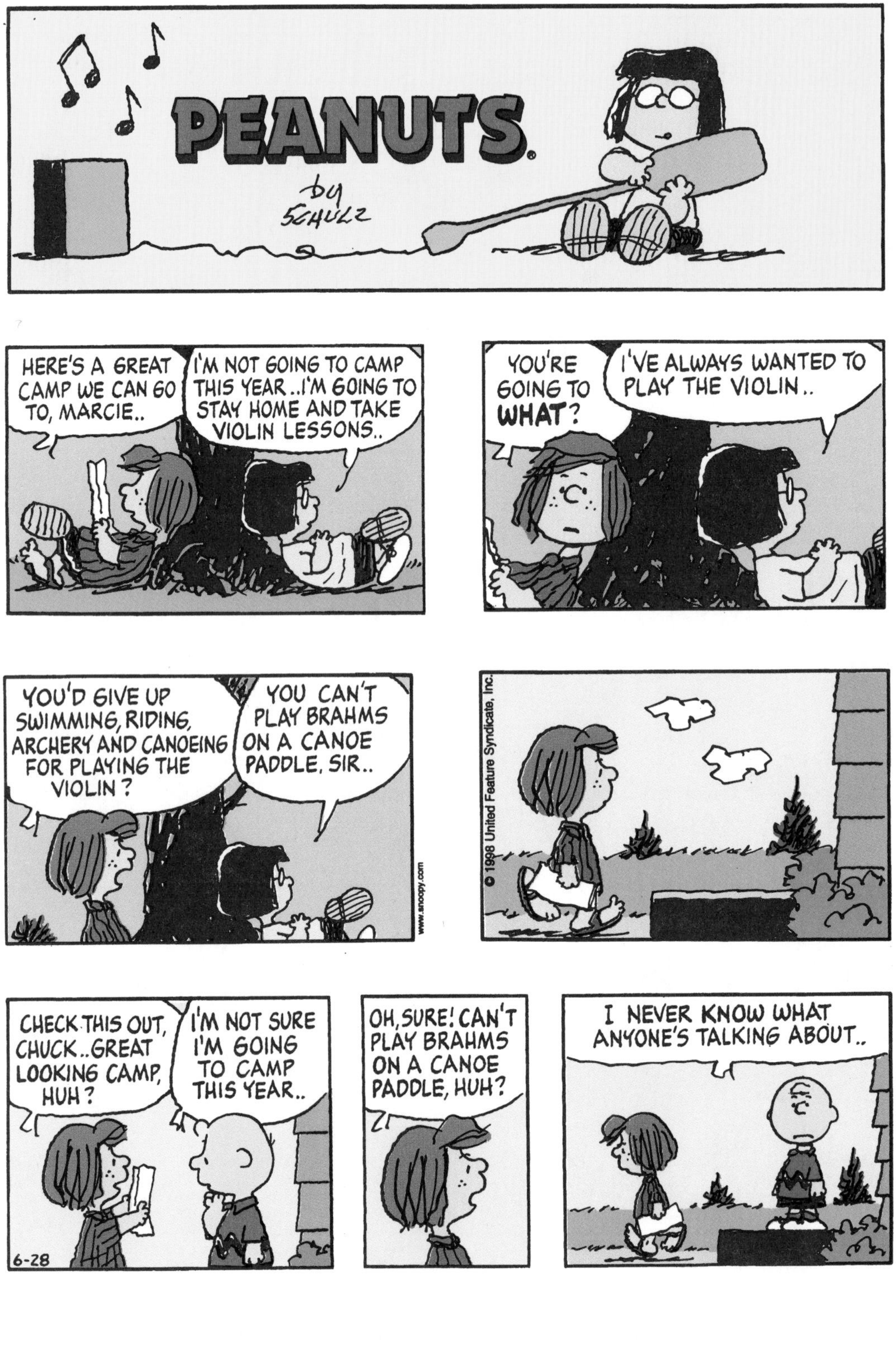
PEANUTS
by SCHULZ
HERE'S A GREAT CAMP WE CAN GO TO, MARCIE..
I'M NOT GOING TO CAMP THIS YEAR..I'M GOING TO STAY HOME AND TAKE VIOLIN LESSONS..
YOU'RE GOING TO WHAT?
I'VE ALWAYS WANTED TO PLAY THE VIOLIN..
YOU'D GIVE UP SWIMMING, RIDING, ARCHERY AND CANOEING FOR PLAYING THE VIOLIN?
YOU CAN'T PLAY BRAHMS ON A CANOE PADDLE, SIR..
www.snoopy.com
© 1998 United Feature Syndicate, Inc.
CHECK THIS OUT, CHUCK..GREAT LOOKING CAMP, HUH?
I'M NOT SURE I'M GOING TO CAMP THIS YEAR..
6-28
OH, SURE! CAN'T PLAY BRAHMS ON A CANOE PADDLE, HUH?
I NEVER KNOW WHAT ANYONE'S TALKING ABOUT..

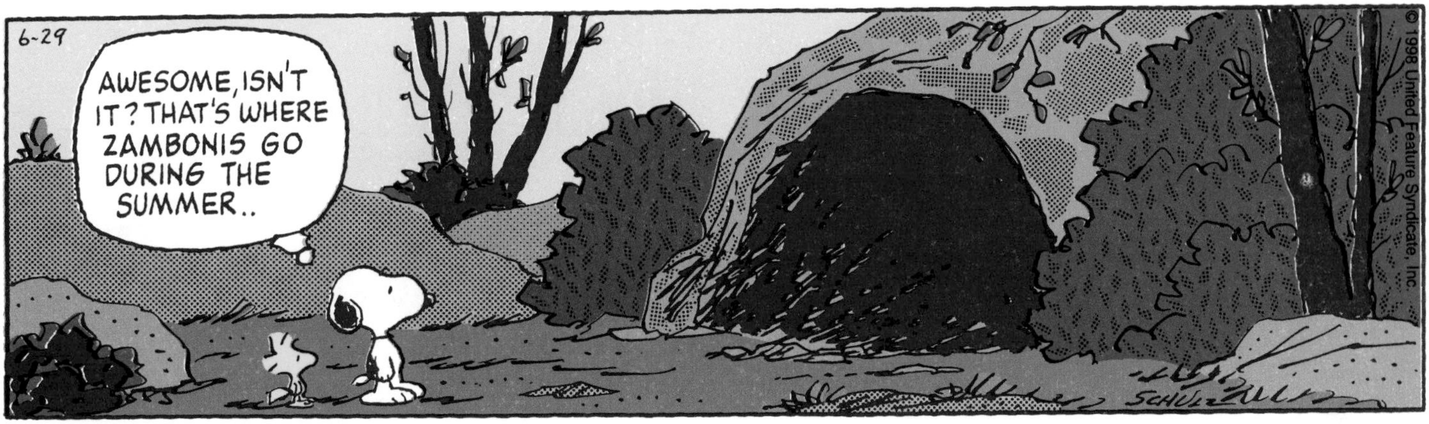
6-29
AWESOME, ISN'T IT? THAT'S WHERE ZAMBONIS GO DURING THE SUMMER..
© 1998 United Feature Syndicate, Inc.
SCHULZ

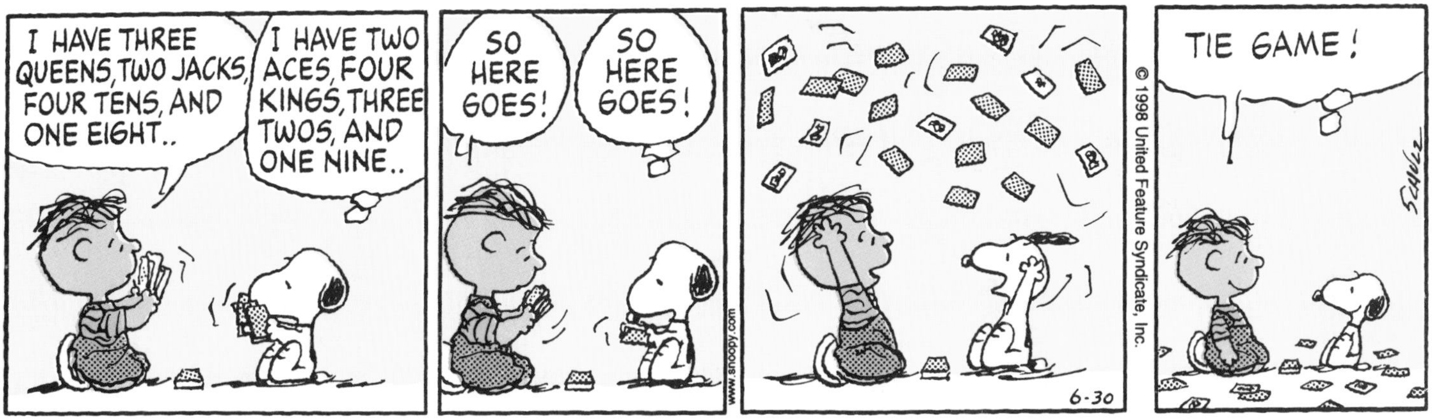
I HAVE THREE QUEENS, TWO JACKS, FOUR TENS, AND ONE EIGHT..
I HAVE TWO ACES, FOUR KINGS, THREE TWOS, AND ONE NINE..
SO HERE GOES!
SO HERE GOES!
www.snoopy.com
6-30
© 1998 United Feature Syndicate, Inc.
TIE GAME!
SCHULZ

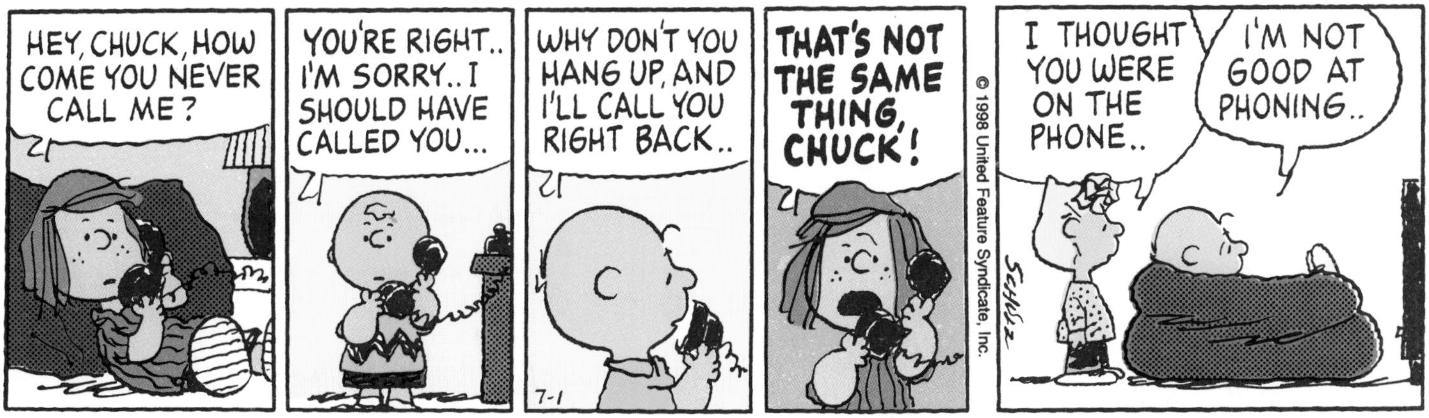
HEY, CHUCK, HOW COME YOU NEVER CALL ME?
YOU'RE RIGHT.. I'M SORRY.. I SHOULD HAVE CALLED YOU...
WHY DON'T YOU HANG UP, AND I'LL CALL YOU RIGHT BACK..
7-1
THAT'S NOT THE SAME THING, CHUCK!
© 1998 United Feature Syndicate, Inc.
SCHULZ
I THOUGHT YOU WERE ON THE PHONE..
I'M NOT GOOD AT PHONING..

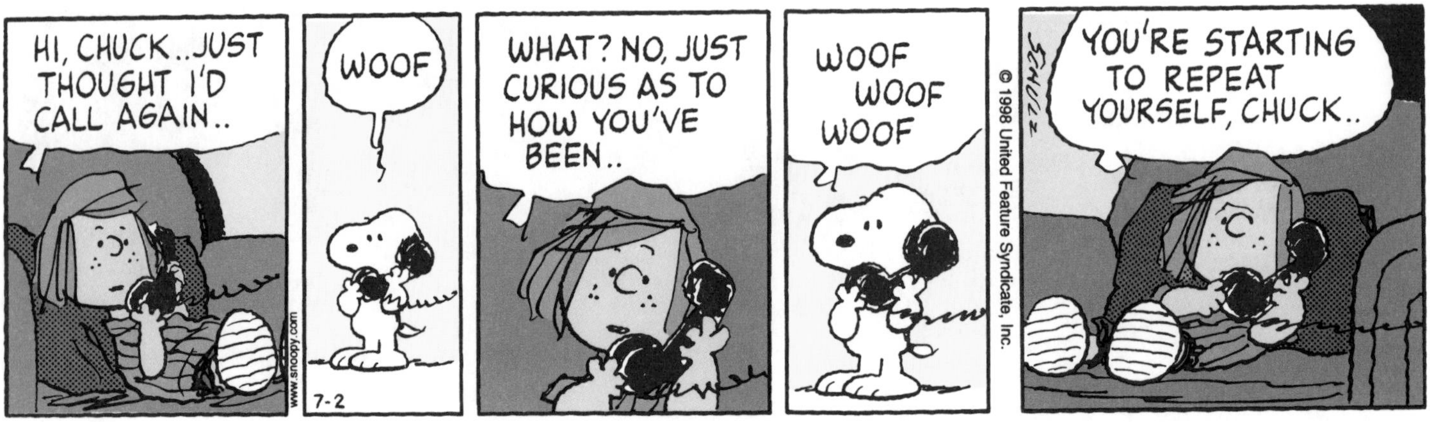
HI, CHUCK..JUST THOUGHT I'D CALL AGAIN..
www.snoopy.com
WOOF
7-2
WHAT? NO, JUST CURIOUS AS TO HOW YOU'VE BEEN..
WOOF WOOF WOOF
© 1998 United Feature Syndicate, Inc.
SCHULZ
YOU'RE STARTING TO REPEAT YOURSELF, CHUCK..

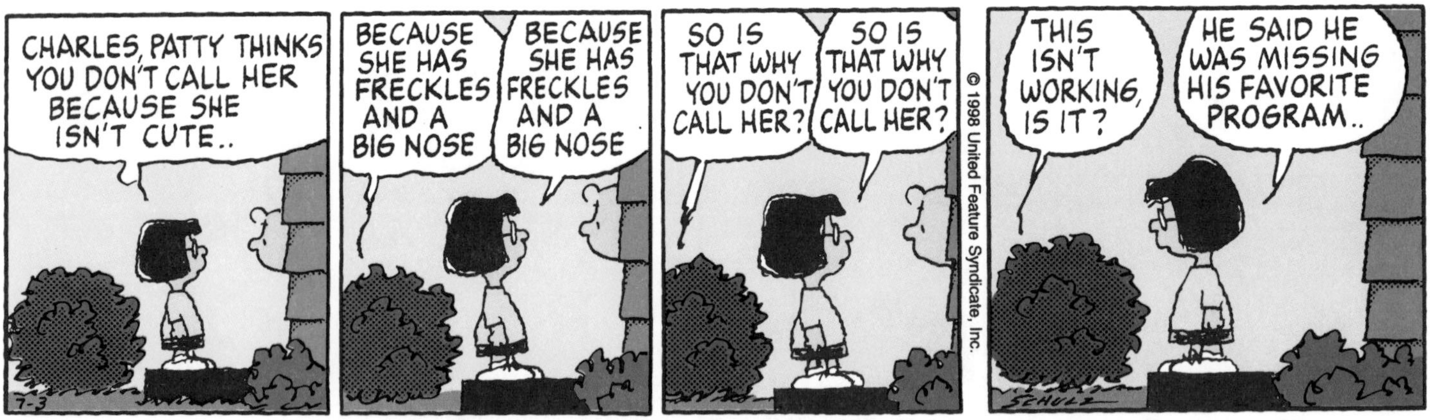
CHARLES, PATTY THINKS YOU DON'T CALL HER BECAUSE SHE ISN'T CUTE..
7-3
BECAUSE SHE HAS FRECKLES AND A BIG NOSE
BECAUSE SHE HAS FRECKLES AND A BIG NOSE
SO IS THAT WHY YOU DON'T CALL HER?
SO IS THAT WHY YOU DON'T CALL HER?
© 1998 United Feature Syndicate, Inc.
THIS ISN'T WORKING, IS IT?
HE SAID HE WAS MISSING HIS FAVORITE PROGRAM..
SCHULZ

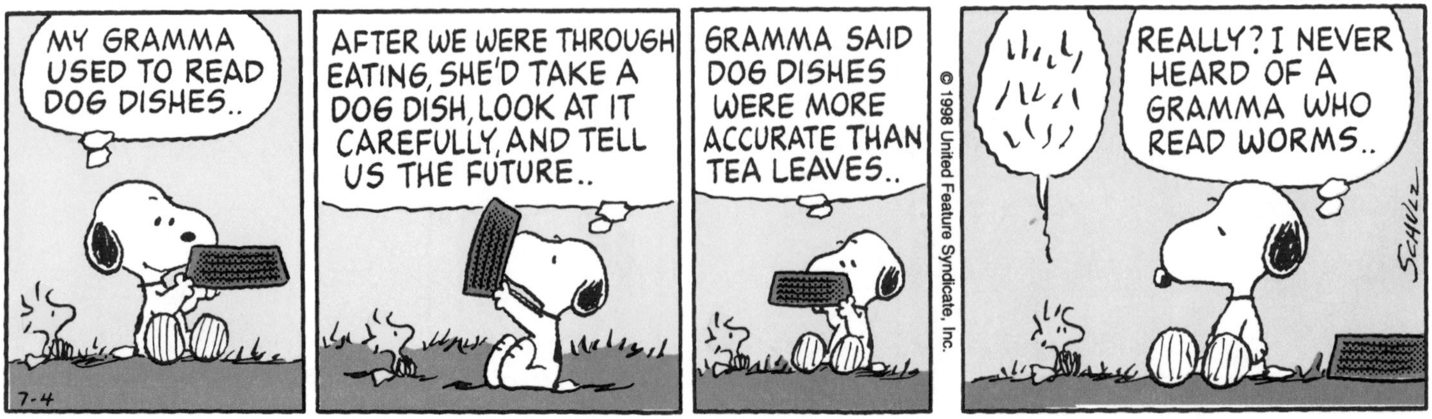
MY GRAMMA USED TO READ DOG DISHES..
7-4
AFTER WE WERE THROUGH EATING, SHE'D TAKE A DOG DISH, LOOK AT IT CAREFULLY, AND TELL US THE FUTURE..
GRAMMA SAID DOG DISHES WERE MORE ACCURATE THAN TEA LEAVES..
© 1998 United Feature Syndicate, Inc.
REALLY? I NEVER HEARD OF A GRAMMA WHO READ WORMS..
SCHULZ

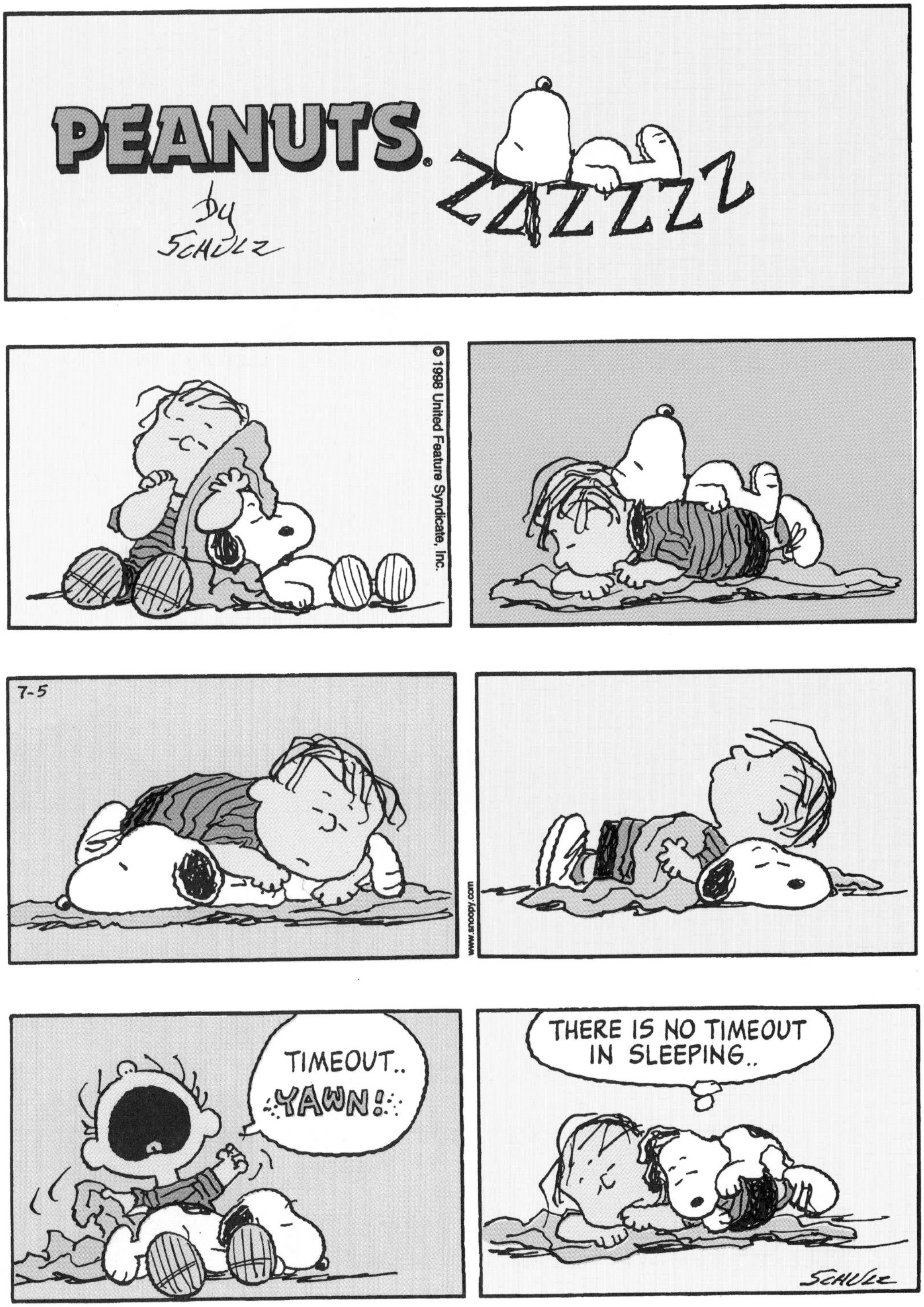
PEANUTS
by SCHULZ
ZZZZZZ
© 1998 United Feature Syndicate, Inc.
7-5
www.snoopy.com
TIMEOUT..
YAWN!
THERE IS NO TIMEOUT IN SLEEPING..
SCHULZ

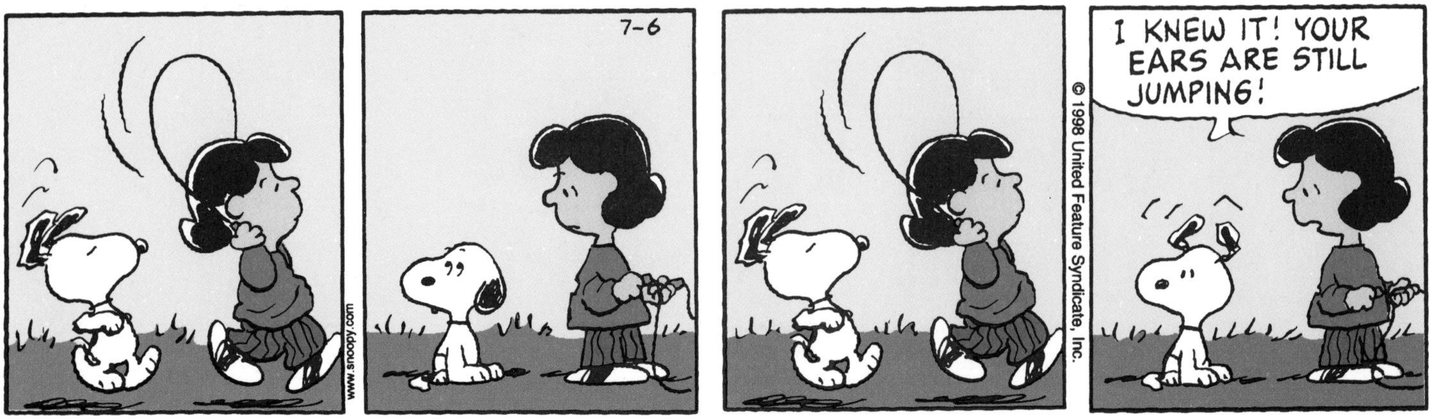
I KNEW IT! YOUR EARS ARE STILL JUMPING!

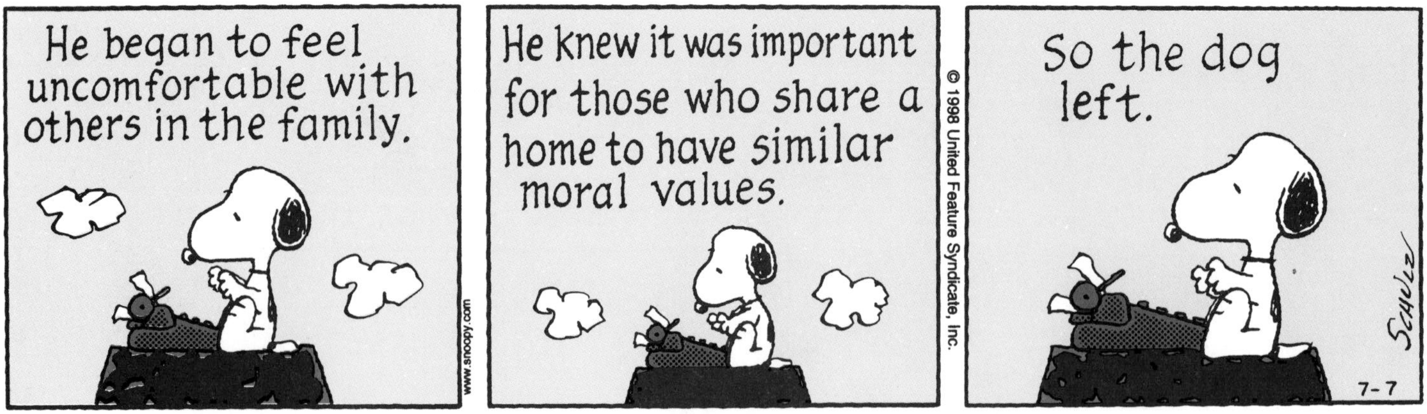
He began to feel uncomfortable with others in the family.
He knew it was important for those who share a home to have similar moral values.
So the dog left.

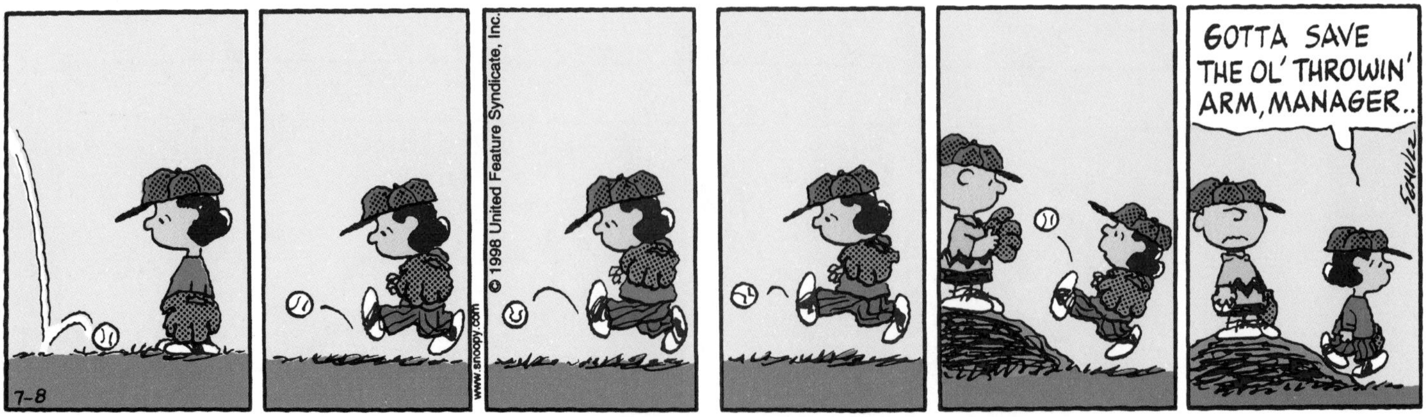
GOTTA SAVE THE OL' THROWIN' ARM, MANAGER..

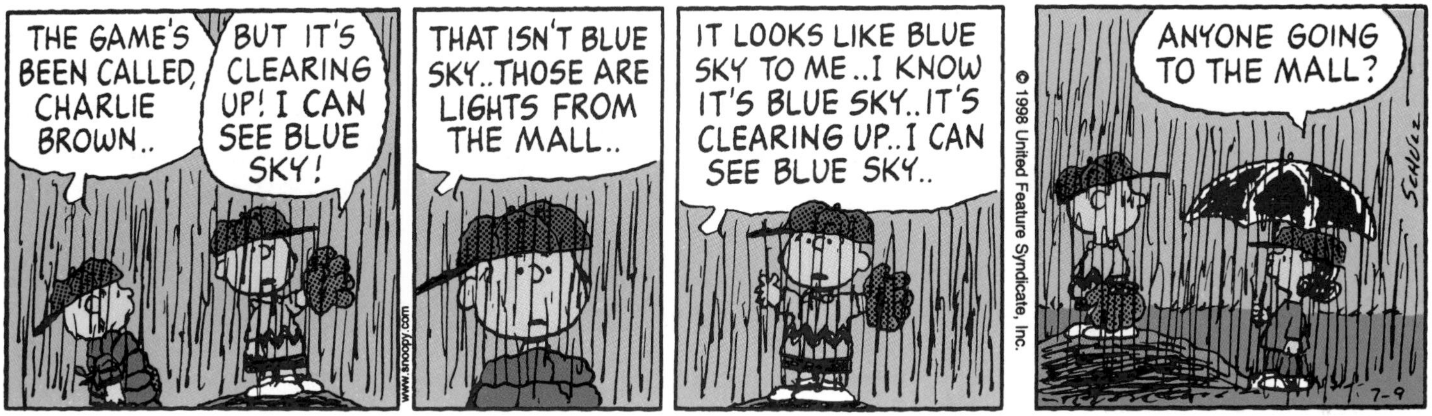
THE GAME'S BEEN CALLED, CHARLIE BROWN..
BUT IT'S CLEARING UP! I CAN SEE BLUE SKY!
www.snoopy.com
THAT ISN'T BLUE SKY..THOSE ARE LIGHTS FROM THE MALL..
IT LOOKS LIKE BLUE SKY TO ME..I KNOW IT'S BLUE SKY..IT'S CLEARING UP..I CAN SEE BLUE SKY..
© 1998 United Feature Syndicate, Inc.
ANYONE GOING TO THE MALL?
SCHULZ
7-9

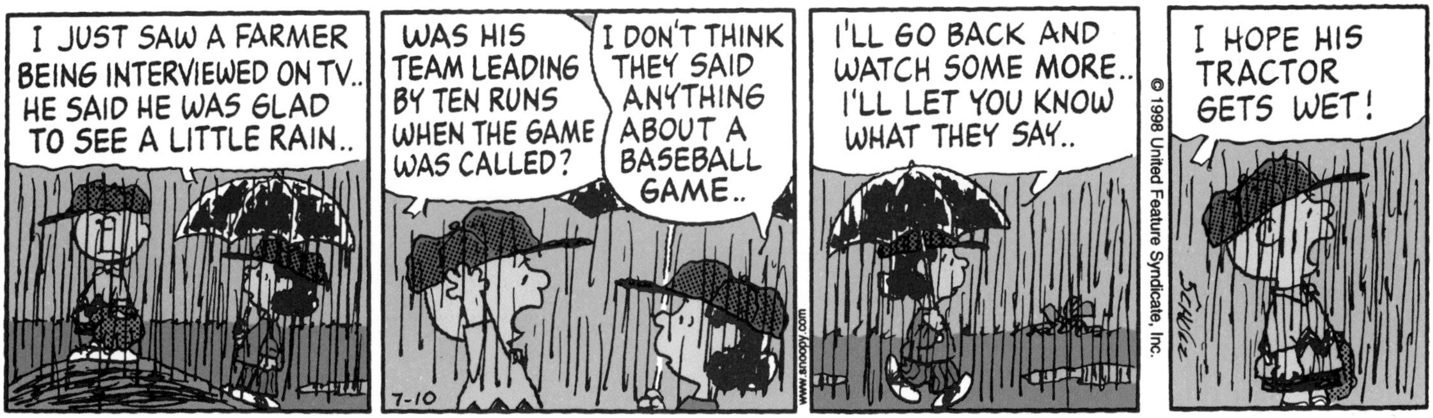
I JUST SAW A FARMER BEING INTERVIEWED ON TV.. HE SAID HE WAS GLAD TO SEE A LITTLE RAIN..
WAS HIS TEAM LEADING BY TEN RUNS WHEN THE GAME WAS CALLED?
I DON'T THINK THEY SAID ANYTHING ABOUT A BASEBALL GAME..
7-10
www.snoopy.com
I'LL GO BACK AND WATCH SOME MORE.. I'LL LET YOU KNOW WHAT THEY SAY..
© 1998 United Feature Syndicate, Inc.
SCHULZ
I HOPE HIS TRACTOR GETS WET!

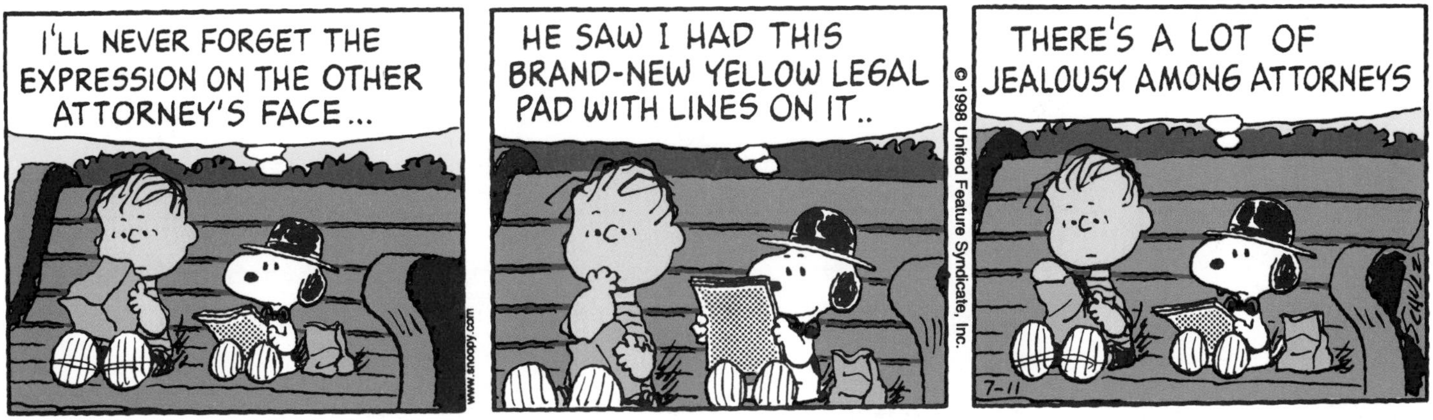
I'LL NEVER FORGET THE EXPRESSION ON THE OTHER ATTORNEY'S FACE...
www.snoopy.com
HE SAW I HAD THIS BRAND-NEW YELLOW LEGAL PAD WITH LINES ON IT..
© 1998 United Feature Syndicate, Inc.
THERE'S A LOT OF JEALOUSY AMONG ATTORNEYS
7-11
SCHULZ

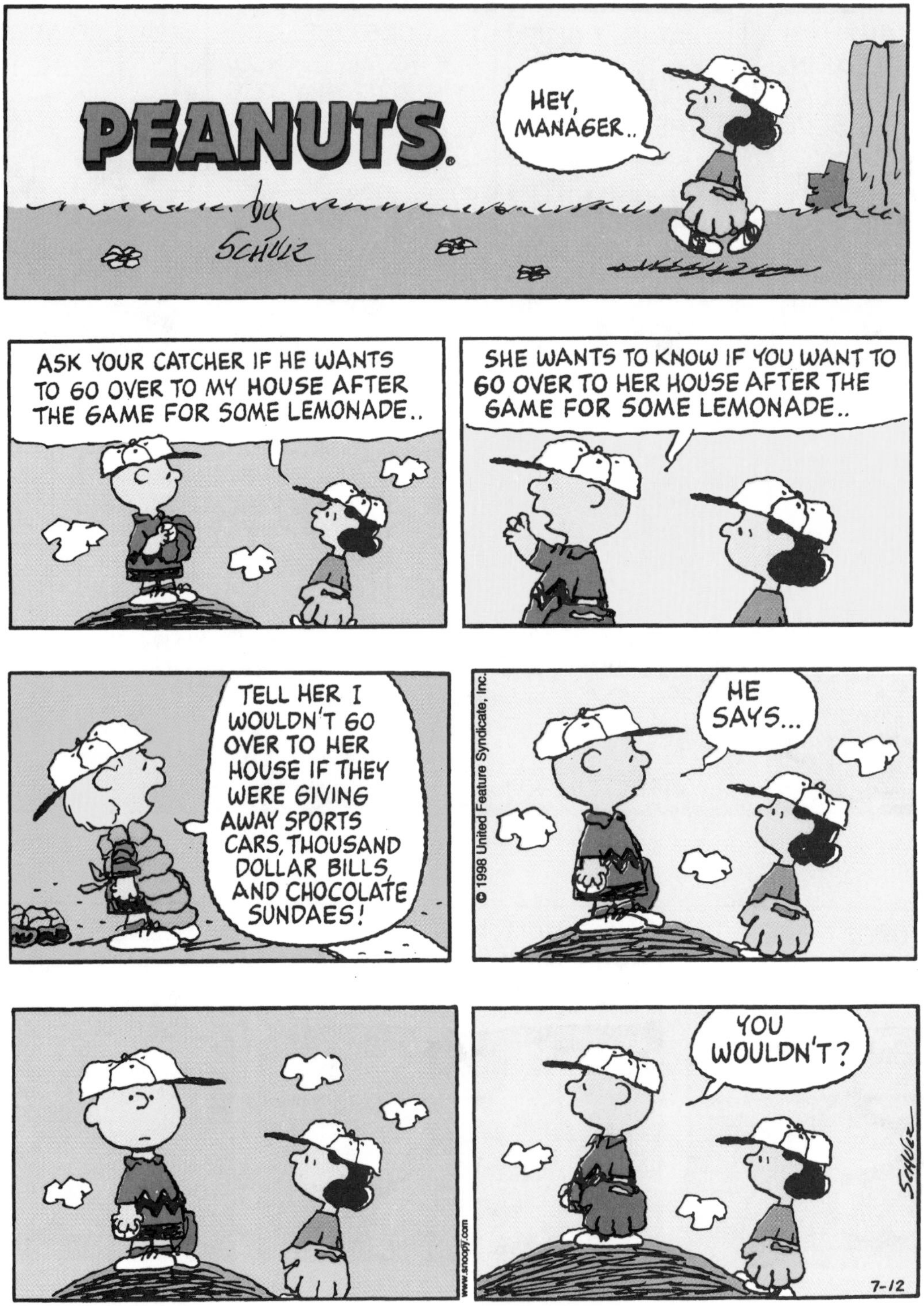
PEANUTS
by SCHULZ
HEY, MANAGER..
ASK YOUR CATCHER IF HE WANTS TO GO OVER TO MY HOUSE AFTER THE GAME FOR SOME LEMONADE..
SHE WANTS TO KNOW IF YOU WANT TO GO OVER TO HER HOUSE AFTER THE GAME FOR SOME LEMONADE..
TELL HER I WOULDN'T GO OVER TO HER HOUSE IF THEY WERE GIVING AWAY SPORTS CARS, THOUSAND DOLLAR BILLS, AND CHOCOLATE SUNDAES!
© 1998 United Feature Syndicate, Inc.
HE SAYS...
www.snoopy.com
YOU WOULDN'T?
SCHULZ
7-12

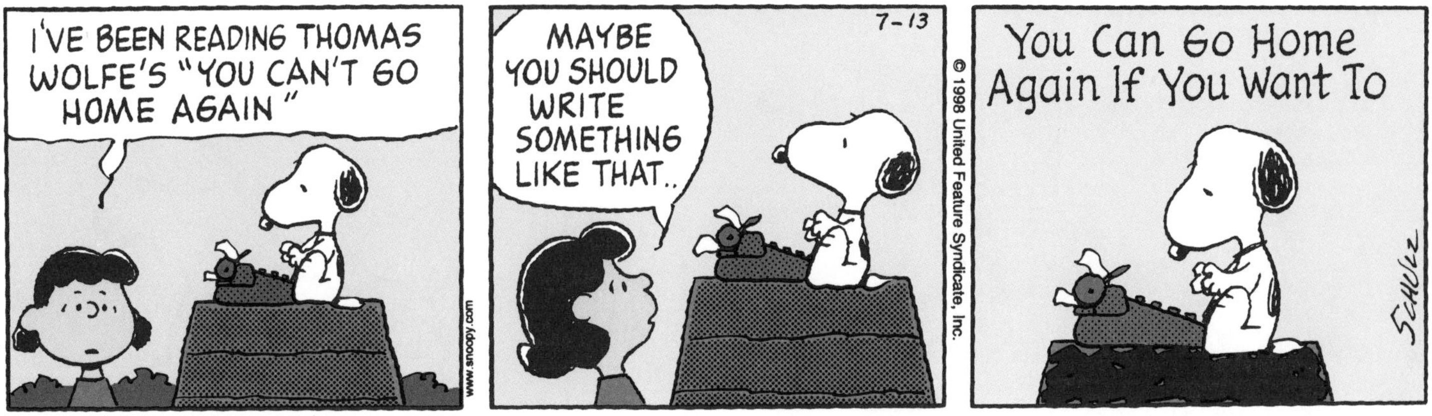
I'VE BEEN READING THOMAS WOLFE'S "YOU CAN'T GO HOME AGAIN"
www.snoopy.com
7-13
MAYBE YOU SHOULD WRITE SOMETHING LIKE THAT..
© 1998 United Feature Syndicate, Inc.
You Can Go Home Again If You Want To
SCHULZ

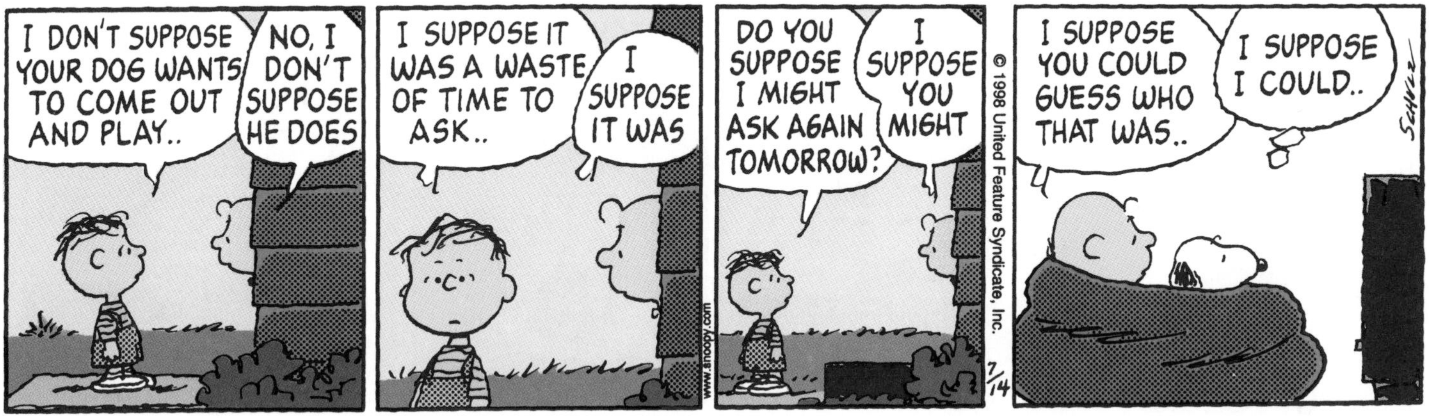
I DON'T SUPPOSE YOUR DOG WANTS TO COME OUT AND PLAY..
NO, I DON'T SUPPOSE HE DOES
I SUPPOSE IT WAS A WASTE OF TIME TO ASK..
I SUPPOSE IT WAS
www.snoopy.com
DO YOU SUPPOSE I MIGHT ASK AGAIN TOMORROW?
I SUPPOSE YOU MIGHT
7/14
© 1998 United Feature Syndicate, Inc.
I SUPPOSE YOU COULD GUESS WHO THAT WAS..
I SUPPOSE I COULD..
SCHULZ

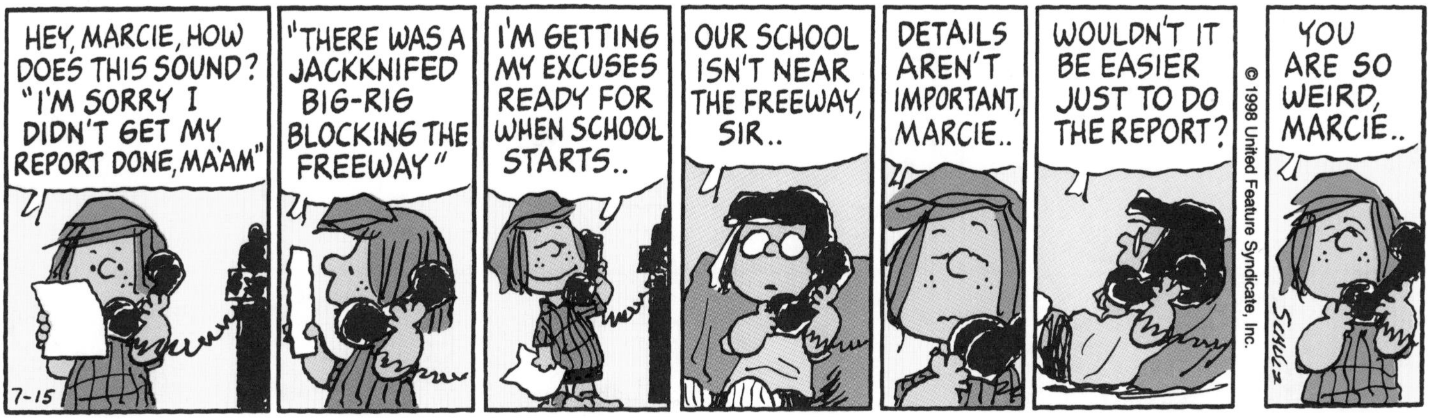
HEY, MARCIE, HOW DOES THIS SOUND? "I'M SORRY I DIDN'T GET MY REPORT DONE, MA'AM"
7-15
"THERE WAS A JACKKNIFED BIG-RIG BLOCKING THE FREEWAY"
I'M GETTING MY EXCUSES READY FOR WHEN SCHOOL STARTS..
OUR SCHOOL ISN'T NEAR THE FREEWAY, SIR..
DETAILS AREN'T IMPORTANT, MARCIE..
WOULDN'T IT BE EASIER JUST TO DO THE REPORT?
© 1998 United Feature Syndicate, Inc.
YOU ARE SO WEIRD, MARCIE..
SCHULZ

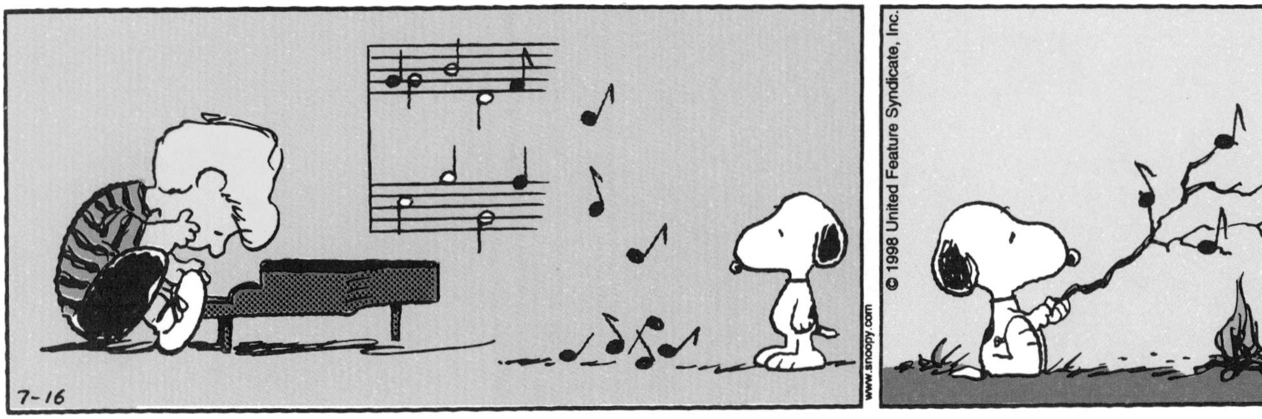
7-16
www.snoopy.com
© 1998 United Feature Syndicate, Inc.
SCHULZ

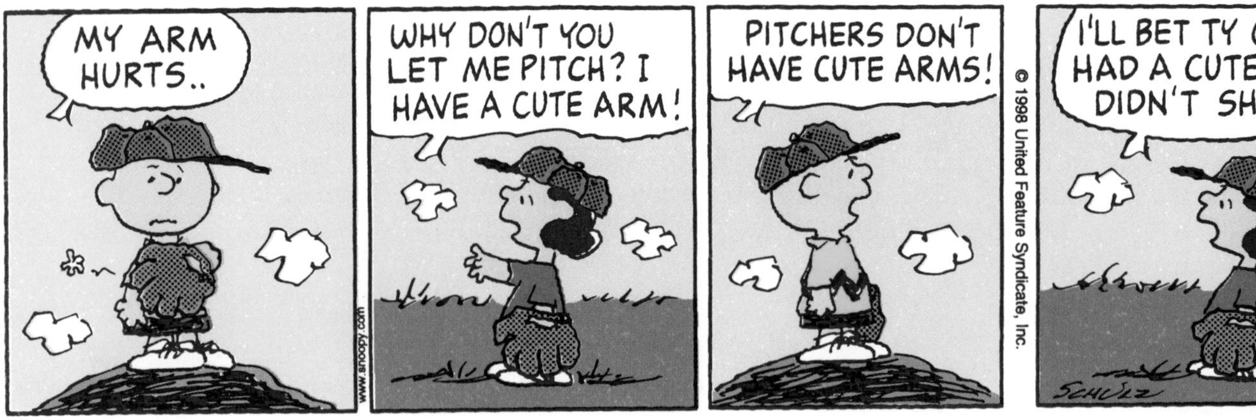
MY ARM HURTS..
www.snoopy.com
WHY DON'T YOU LET ME PITCH? I HAVE A CUTE ARM!
PITCHERS DON'T HAVE CUTE ARMS!
© 1998 United Feature Syndicate, Inc.
I'LL BET TY COBB HAD A CUTE ARM, DIDN'T SHE?
SCHULZ
7-17

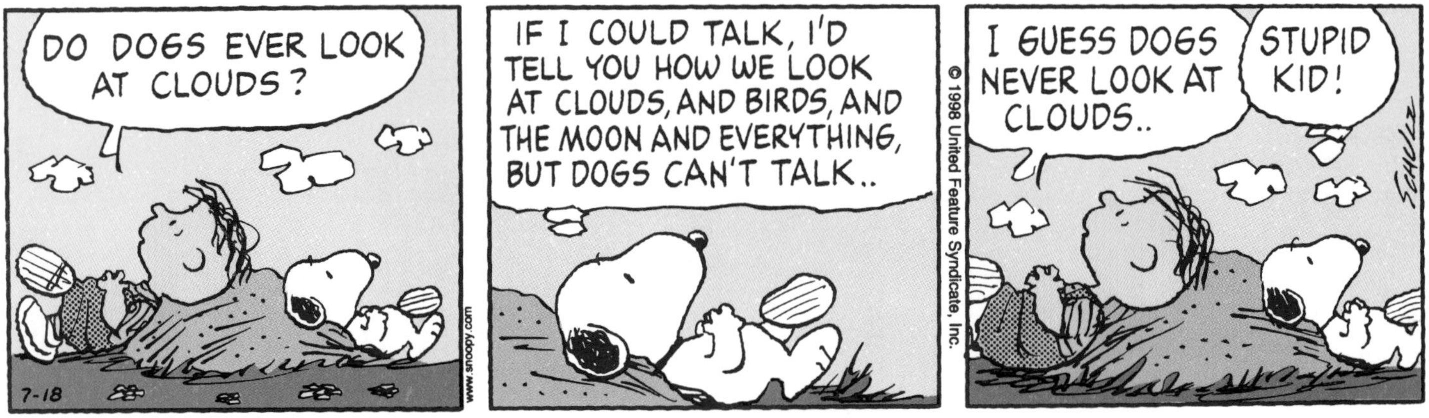
DO DOGS EVER LOOK AT CLOUDS?
7-18
www.snoopy.com
IF I COULD TALK, I'D TELL YOU HOW WE LOOK AT CLOUDS, AND BIRDS, AND THE MOON AND EVERYTHING, BUT DOGS CAN'T TALK..
© 1998 United Feature Syndicate, Inc.
I GUESS DOGS NEVER LOOK AT CLOUDS..
STUPID KID!
SCHULZ

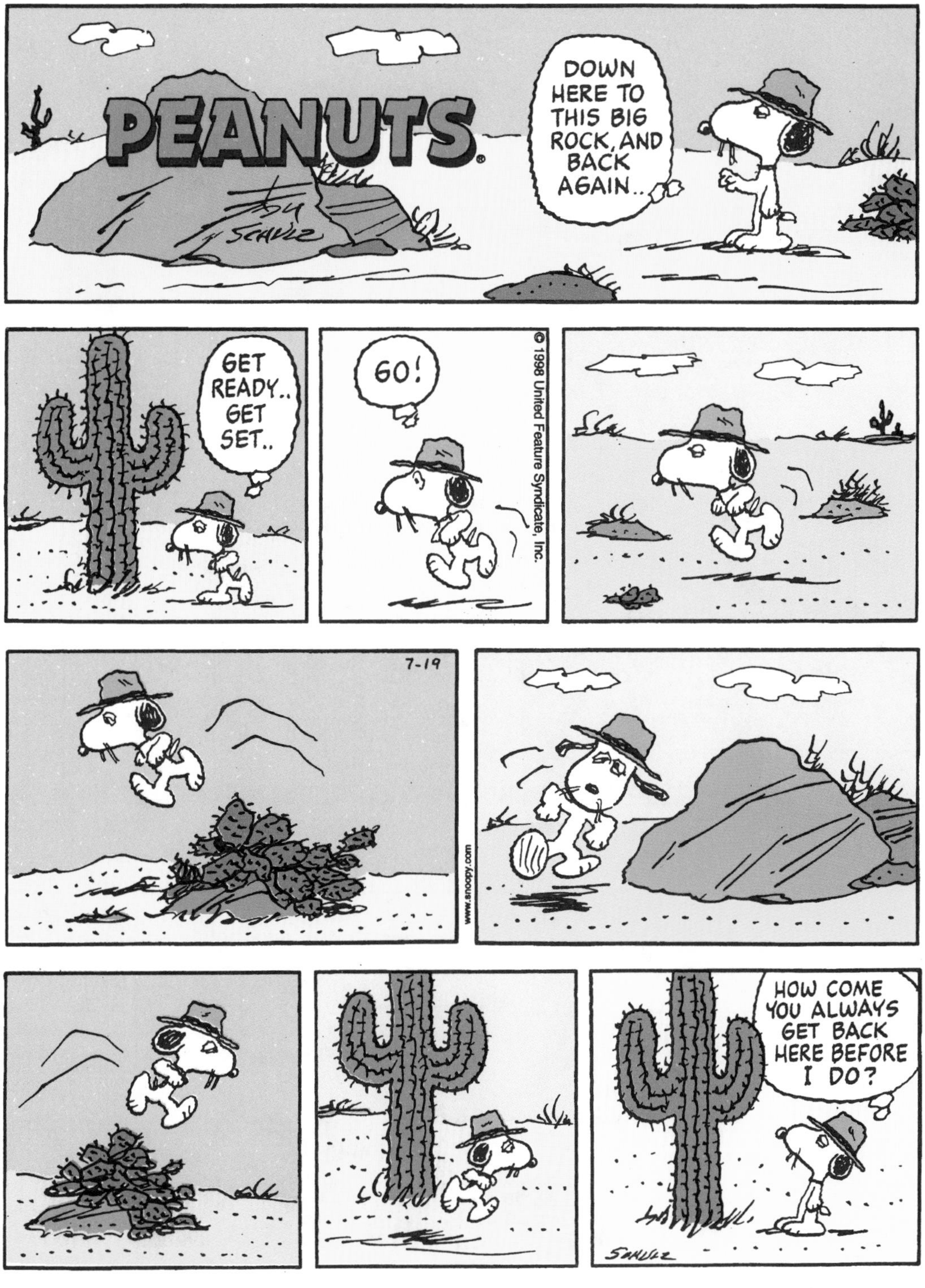
PEANUTS
DOWN HERE TO THIS BIG ROCK, AND BACK AGAIN..
GET READY.. GET SET..
GO!
© 1998 United Feature Syndicate, Inc.
7-19
www.snoopy.com
HOW COME YOU ALWAYS GET BACK HERE BEFORE I DO?
SCHULZ

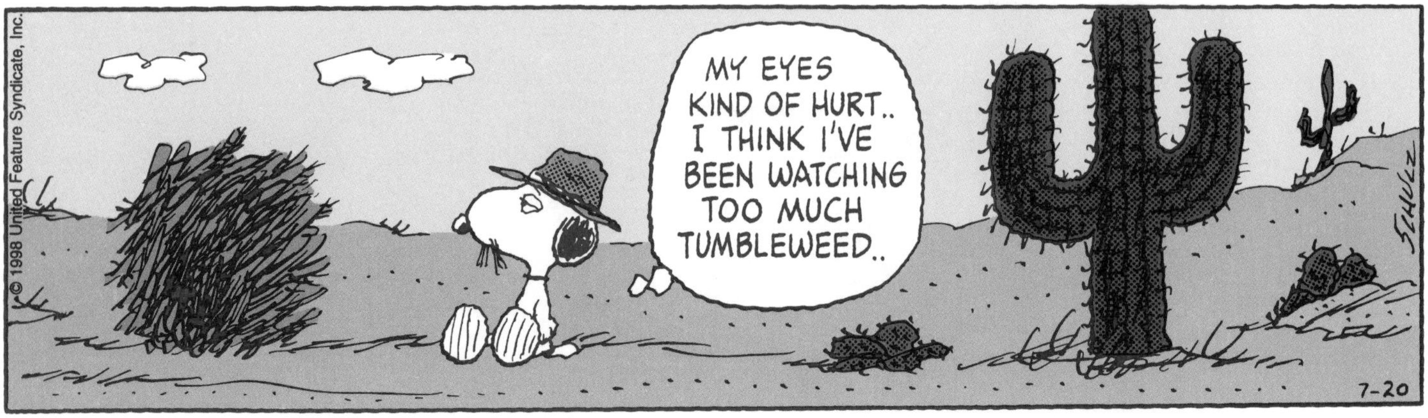
© 1998 United Feature Syndicate, Inc.
MY EYES KIND OF HURT.. I THINK I'VE BEEN WATCHING TOO MUCH TUMBLEWEED..
SCHULZ
7-20

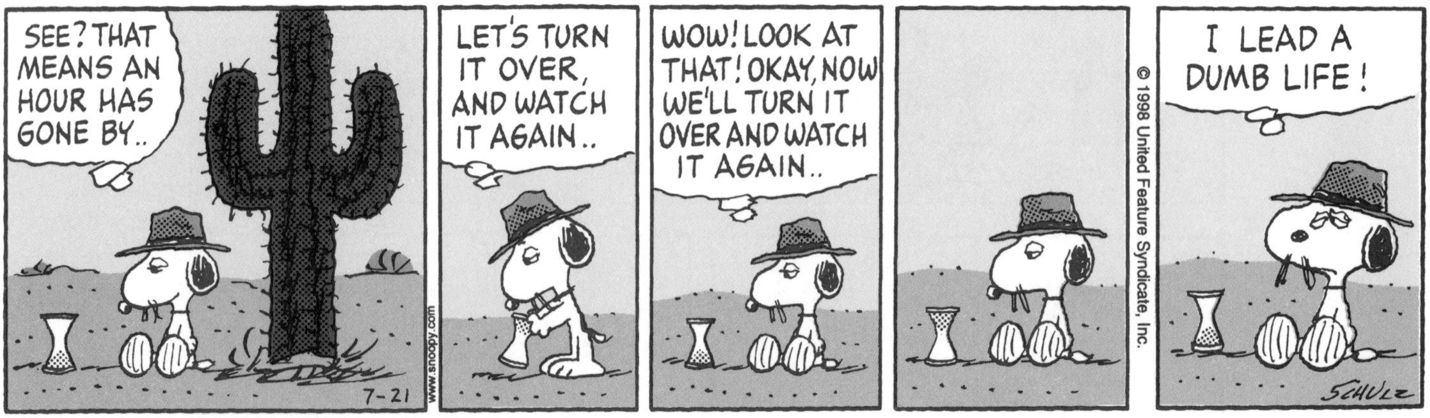
SEE? THAT MEANS AN HOUR HAS GONE BY..
7-21
www.snoopy.com
LET'S TURN IT OVER, AND WATCH IT AGAIN..
WOW! LOOK AT THAT! OKAY, NOW WE'LL TURN IT OVER AND WATCH IT AGAIN..
© 1998 United Feature Syndicate, Inc.
I LEAD A DUMB LIFE!
SCHULZ

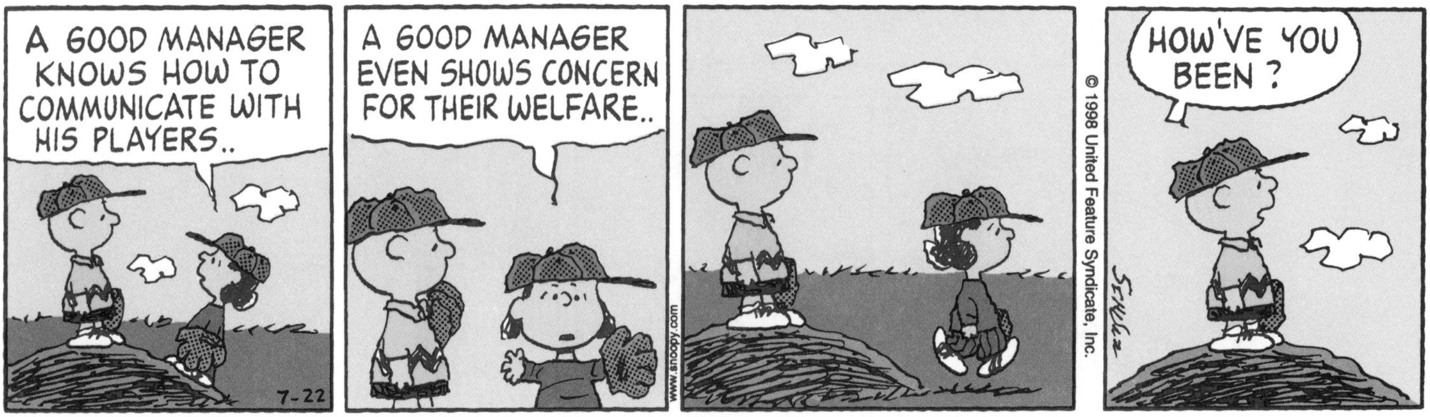
A GOOD MANAGER KNOWS HOW TO COMMUNICATE WITH HIS PLAYERS..
7-22
A GOOD MANAGER EVEN SHOWS CONCERN FOR THEIR WELFARE..
www.snoopy.com
SCHULZ
© 1998 United Feature Syndicate, Inc.
HOW'VE YOU BEEN ?

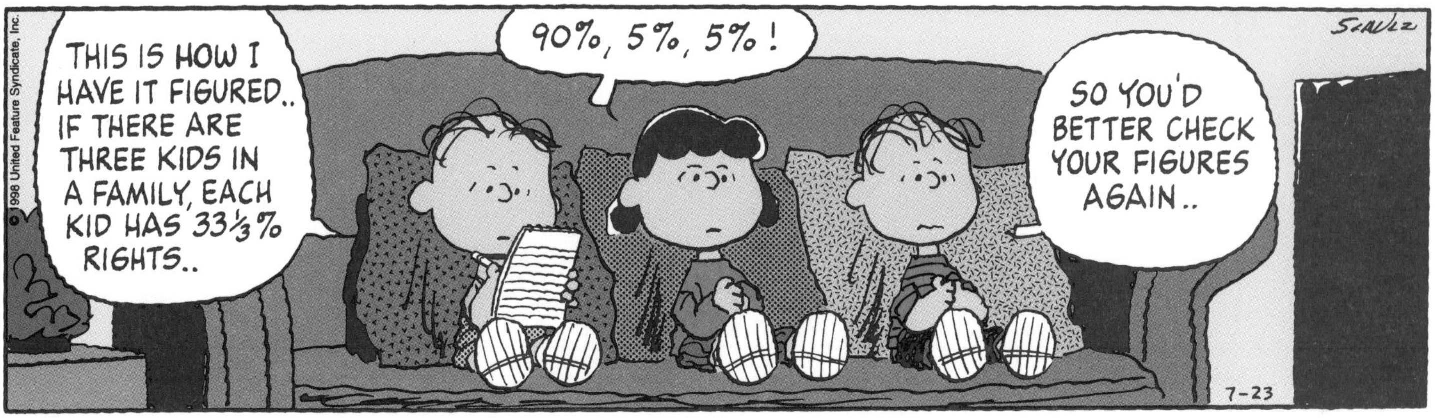
© 1998 United Feature Syndicate, Inc.
THIS IS HOW I HAVE IT FIGURED.. IF THERE ARE THREE KIDS IN A FAMILY, EACH KID HAS 33⅓% RIGHTS..
90%, 5%, 5%!
SO YOU'D BETTER CHECK YOUR FIGURES AGAIN..
SCHULZ
7-23

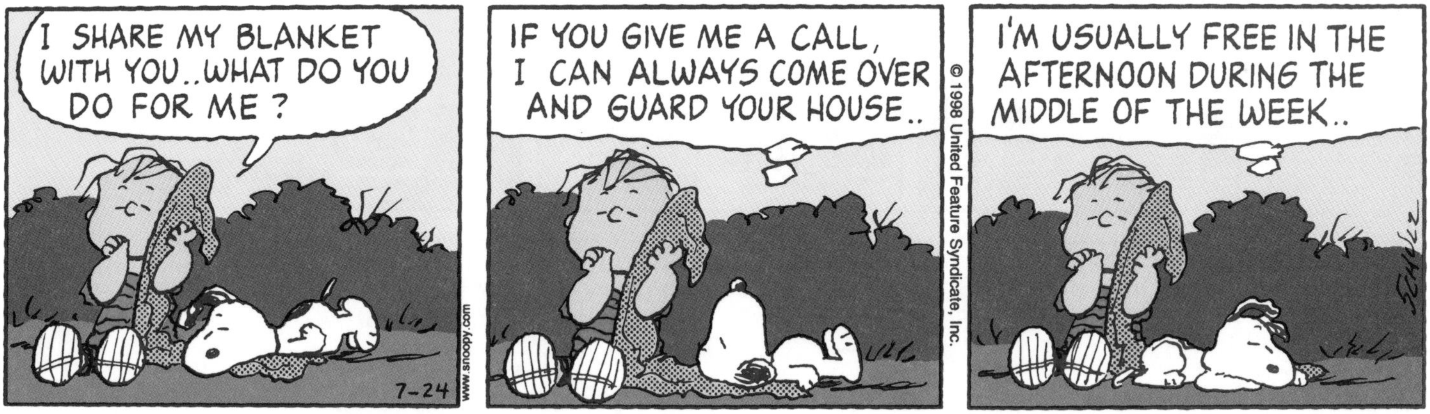
I SHARE MY BLANKET WITH YOU..WHAT DO YOU DO FOR ME ?
7-24
www.snoopy.com
IF YOU GIVE ME A CALL, I CAN ALWAYS COME OVER AND GUARD YOUR HOUSE..
© 1998 United Feature Syndicate, Inc.
I'M USUALLY FREE IN THE AFTERNOON DURING THE MIDDLE OF THE WEEK..
SCHULZ

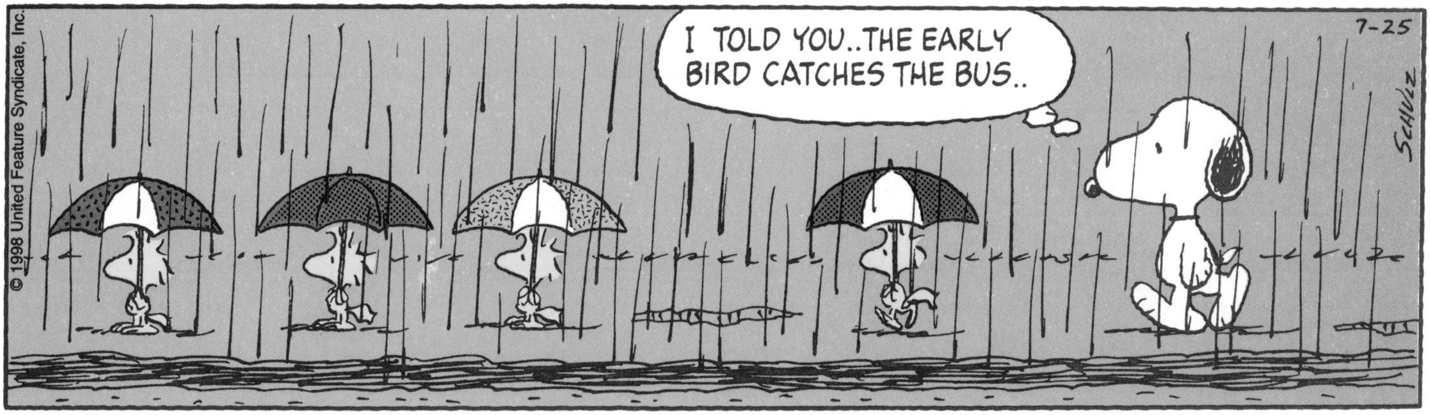
© 1998 United Feature Syndicate, Inc.
I TOLD YOU..THE EARLY BIRD CATCHES THE BUS..
7-25
SCHULZ

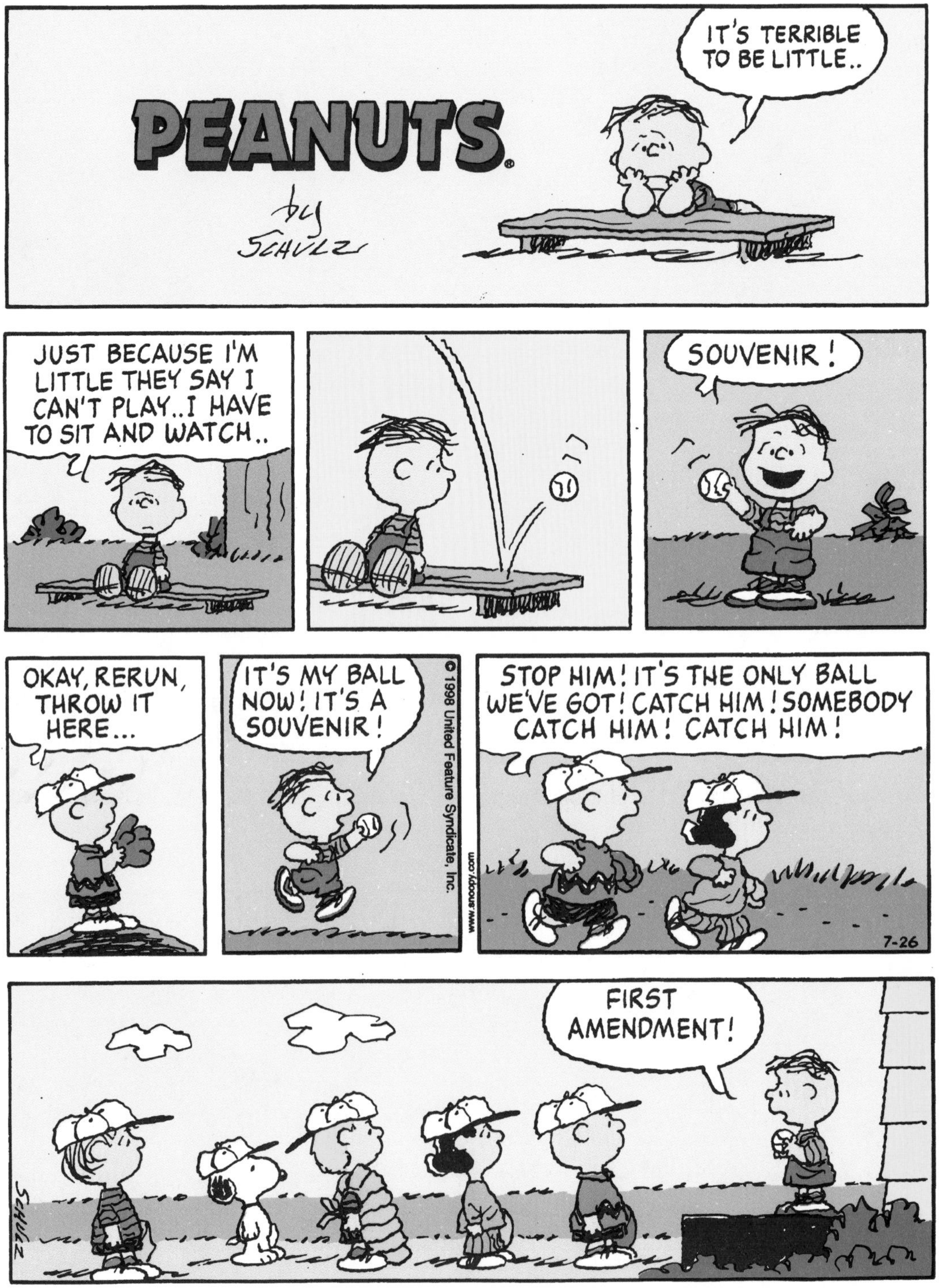
IT'S TERRIBLE TO BE LITTLE..
PEANUTS
by SCHULZ
JUST BECAUSE I'M LITTLE THEY SAY I CAN'T PLAY..I HAVE TO SIT AND WATCH..
SOUVENIR!
OKAY, RERUN, THROW IT HERE...
IT'S MY BALL NOW! IT'S A SOUVENIR!
© 1998 United Feature Syndicate, Inc.
www.snoopy.com
STOP HIM! IT'S THE ONLY BALL WE'VE GOT! CATCH HIM! SOMEBODY CATCH HIM! CATCH HIM!
7-26
FIRST AMENDMENT!
SCHULZ

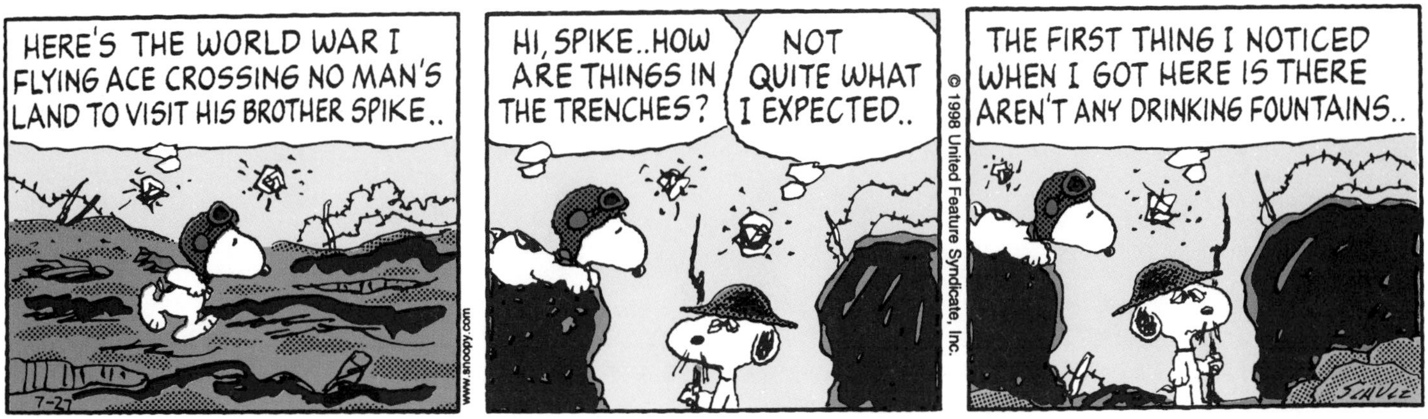
HERE'S THE WORLD WAR I FLYING ACE CROSSING NO MAN'S LAND TO VISIT HIS BROTHER SPIKE..
HI, SPIKE..HOW ARE THINGS IN THE TRENCHES?
NOT QUITE WHAT I EXPECTED..
THE FIRST THING I NOTICED WHEN I GOT HERE IS THERE AREN'T ANY DRINKING FOUNTAINS..
7-27
www.snoopy.com
© 1998 United Feature Syndicate, Inc.
SCHULZ

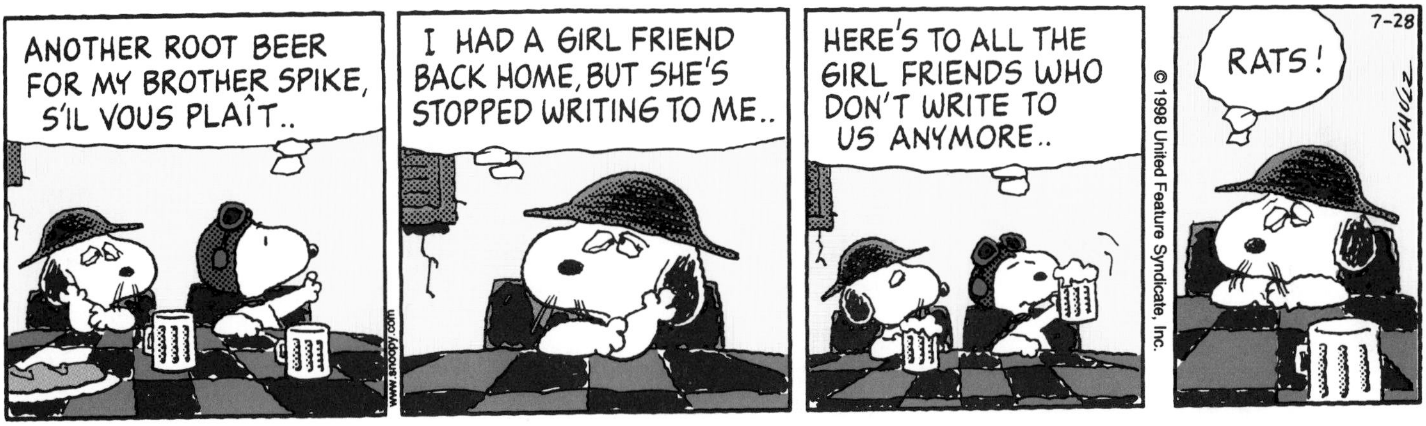
ANOTHER ROOT BEER FOR MY BROTHER SPIKE, S'IL VOUS PLAÎT..
I HAD A GIRL FRIEND BACK HOME, BUT SHE'S STOPPED WRITING TO ME..
HERE'S TO ALL THE GIRL FRIENDS WHO DON'T WRITE TO US ANYMORE..
RATS!
7-28
www.snoopy.com
© 1998 United Feature Syndicate, Inc.
SCHULZ

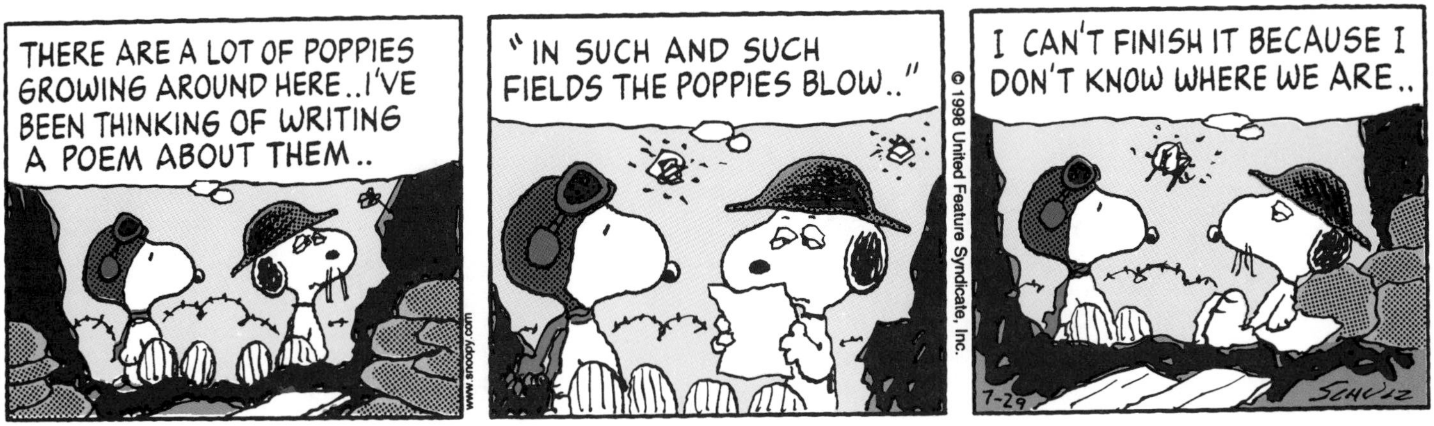
THERE ARE A LOT OF POPPIES GROWING AROUND HERE..I'VE BEEN THINKING OF WRITING A POEM ABOUT THEM..
"IN SUCH AND SUCH FIELDS THE POPPIES BLOW.."
I CAN'T FINISH IT BECAUSE I DON'T KNOW WHERE WE ARE..
7-29
www.snoopy.com
© 1998 United Feature Syndicate, Inc.
SCHULZ

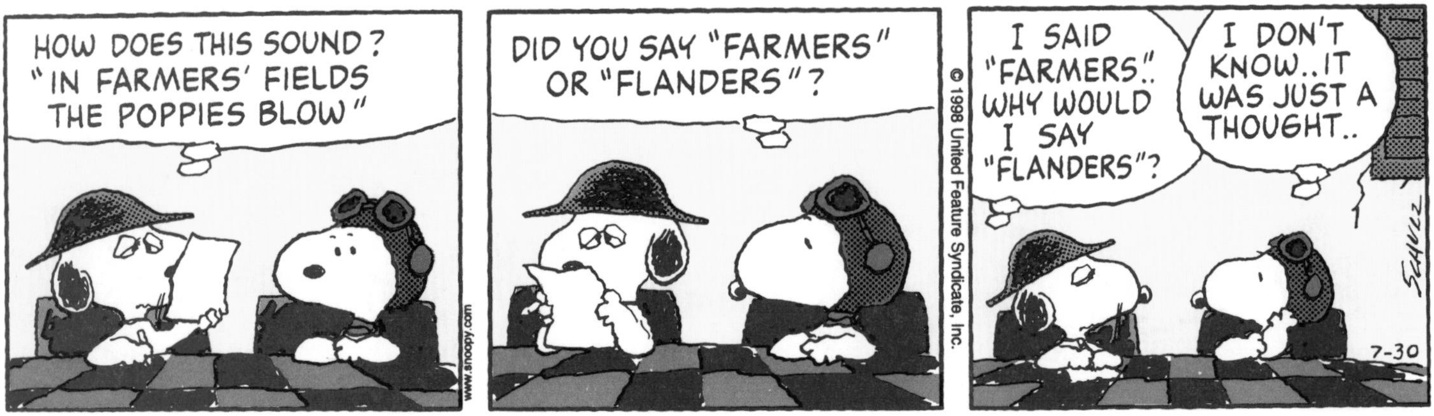
HOW DOES THIS SOUND? "IN FARMERS' FIELDS THE POPPIES BLOW"
DID YOU SAY "FARMERS" OR "FLANDERS"?
I SAID "FARMERS".. WHY WOULD I SAY "FLANDERS"?
I DON'T KNOW..IT WAS JUST A THOUGHT..
www.snoopy.com
© 1998 United Feature Syndicate, Inc.
SCHULZ
7-30

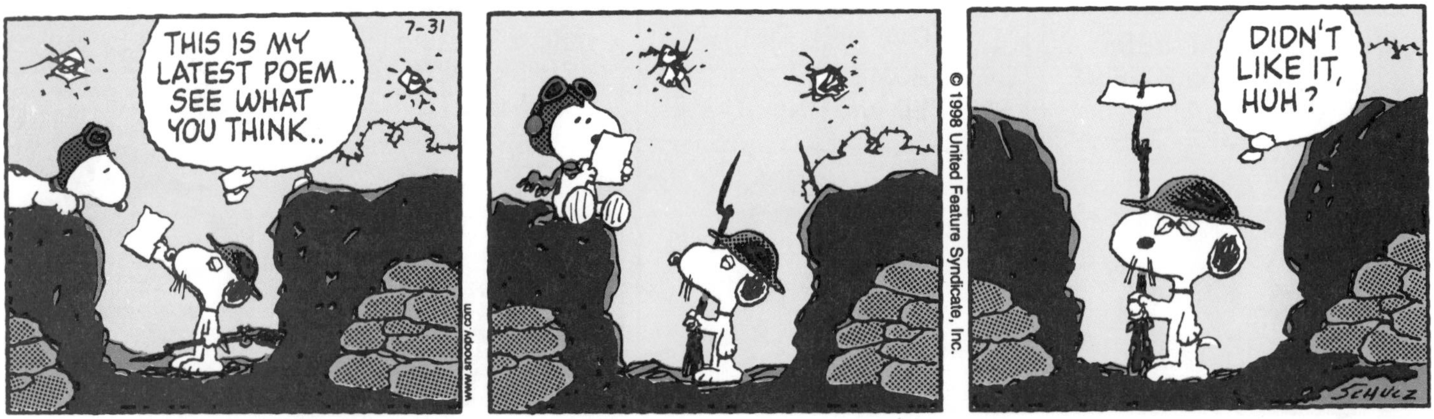
7-31
THIS IS MY LATEST POEM.. SEE WHAT YOU THINK..
DIDN'T LIKE IT, HUH?
www.snoopy.com
© 1998 United Feature Syndicate, Inc.
SCHULZ

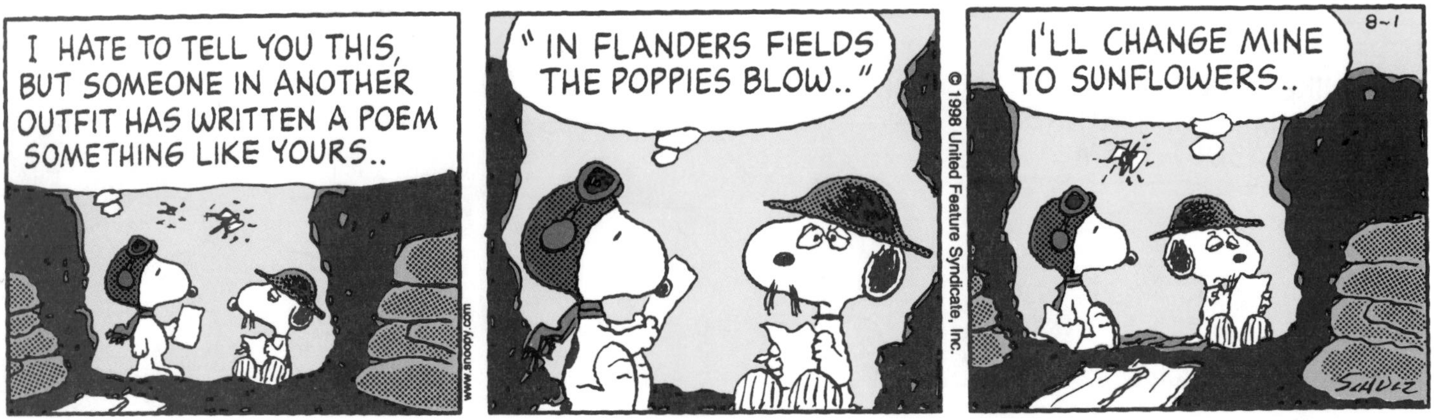
I HATE TO TELL YOU THIS, BUT SOMEONE IN ANOTHER OUTFIT HAS WRITTEN A POEM SOMETHING LIKE YOURS..
"IN FLANDERS FIELDS THE POPPIES BLOW.."
8-1
I'LL CHANGE MINE TO SUNFLOWERS..
www.snoopy.com
© 1998 United Feature Syndicate, Inc.
SCHULZ

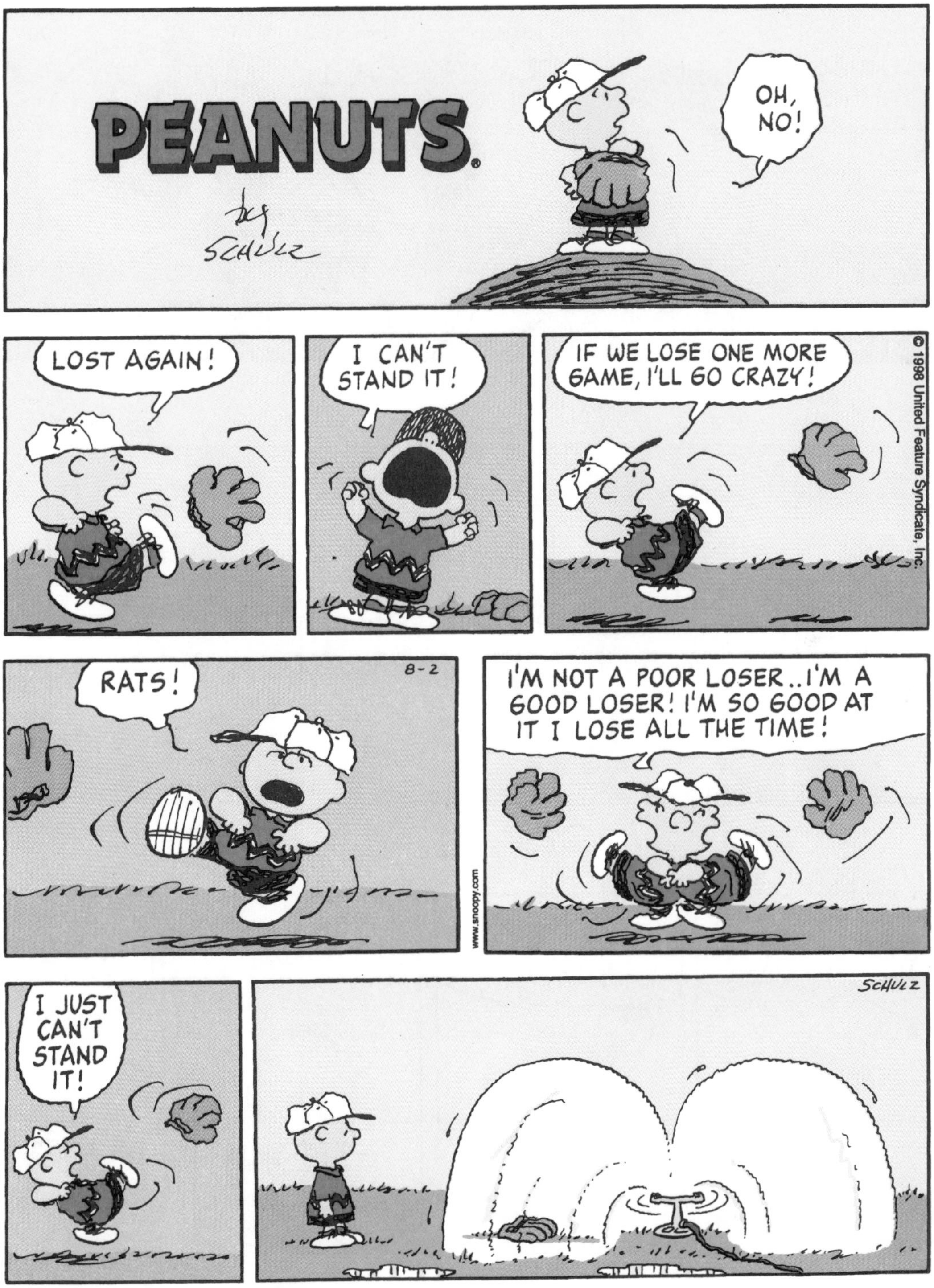
PEANUTS
by SCHULZ
OH, NO!
LOST AGAIN!
I CAN'T STAND IT!
IF WE LOSE ONE MORE GAME, I'LL GO CRAZY!
© 1998 United Feature Syndicate, Inc.
RATS!
8-2
www.snoopy.com
I'M NOT A POOR LOSER..I'M A GOOD LOSER! I'M SO GOOD AT IT I LOSE ALL THE TIME!
I JUST CAN'T STAND IT!
SCHULZ

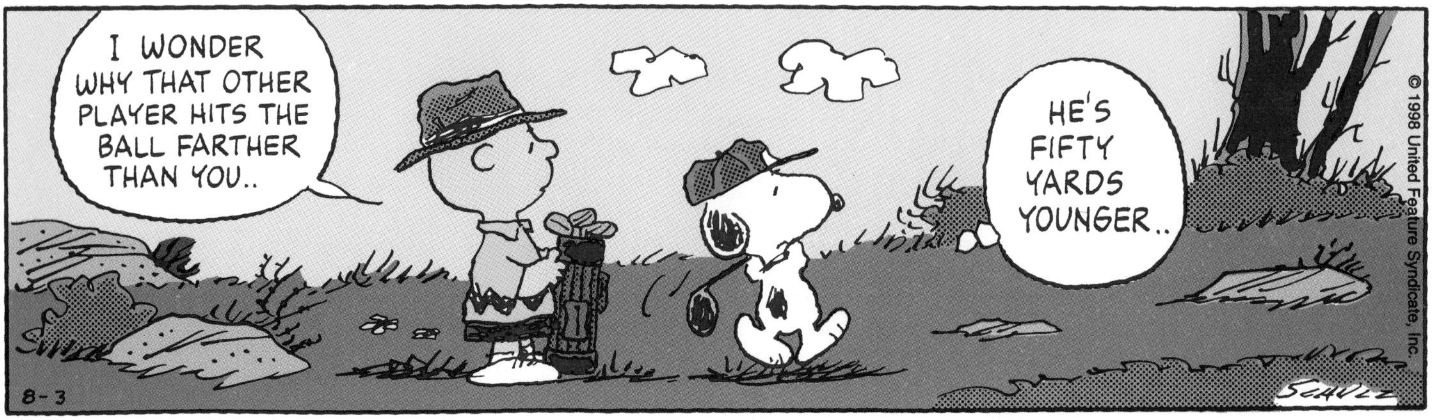
I WONDER WHY THAT OTHER PLAYER HITS THE BALL FARTHER THAN YOU..
HE'S FIFTY YARDS YOUNGER..
8-3
© 1998 United Feature Syndicate, Inc.
SCHULZ

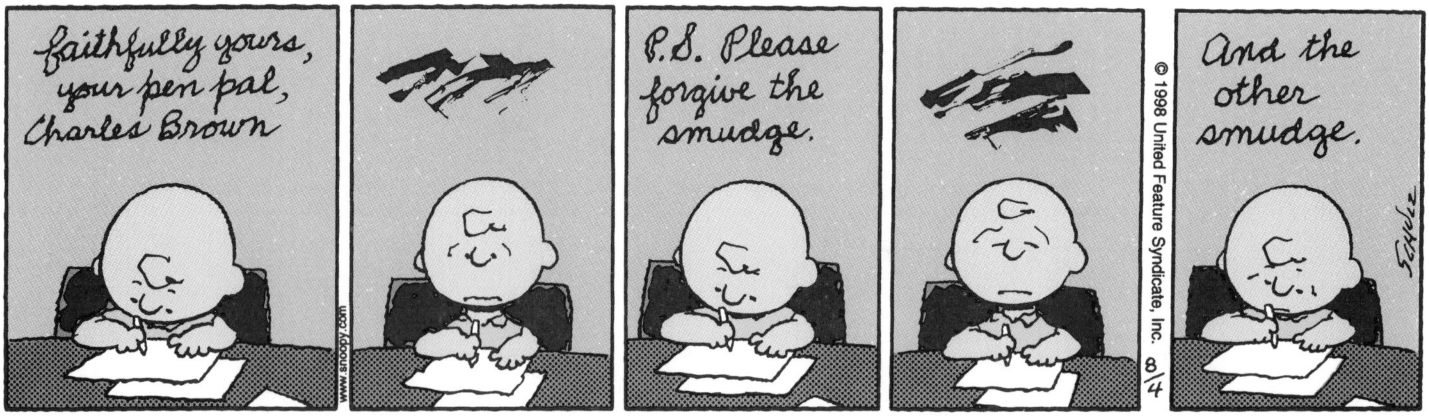
faithfully yours, your pen pal, Charles Brown
P.S. Please forgive the smudge.
And the other smudge.
www.snoopy.com
© 1998 United Feature Syndicate, Inc.
8/4
SCHULZ

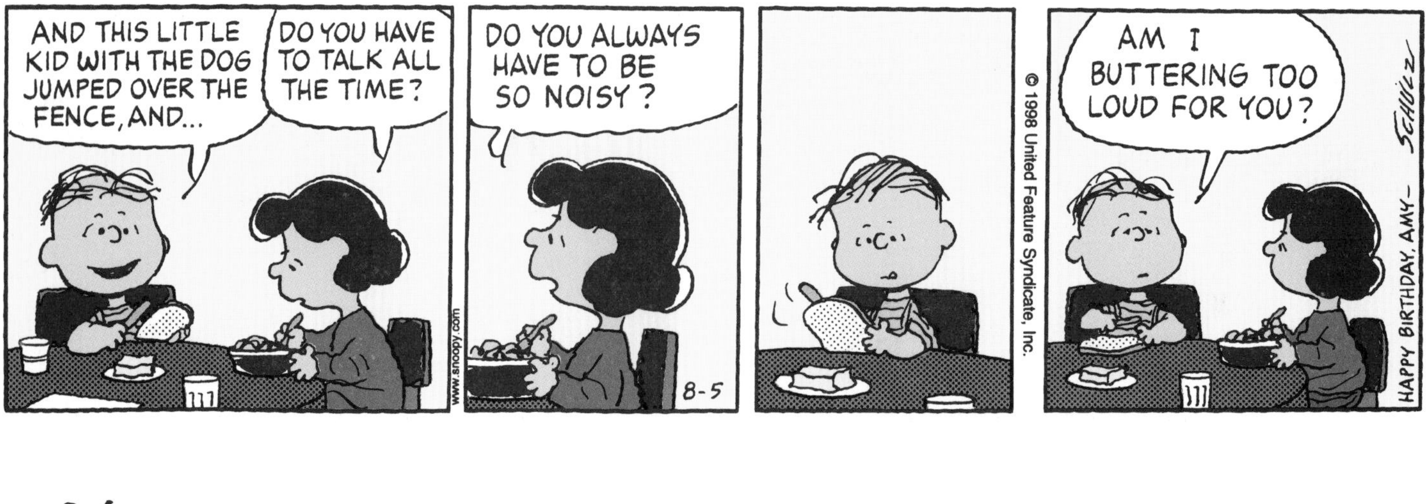
AND THIS LITTLE KID WITH THE DOG JUMPED OVER THE FENCE, AND...
DO YOU HAVE TO TALK ALL THE TIME?
DO YOU ALWAYS HAVE TO BE SO NOISY?
AM I BUTTERING TOO LOUD FOR YOU?
www.snoopy.com
8-5
© 1998 United Feature Syndicate, Inc.
HAPPY BIRTHDAY, AMY–
SCHULZ

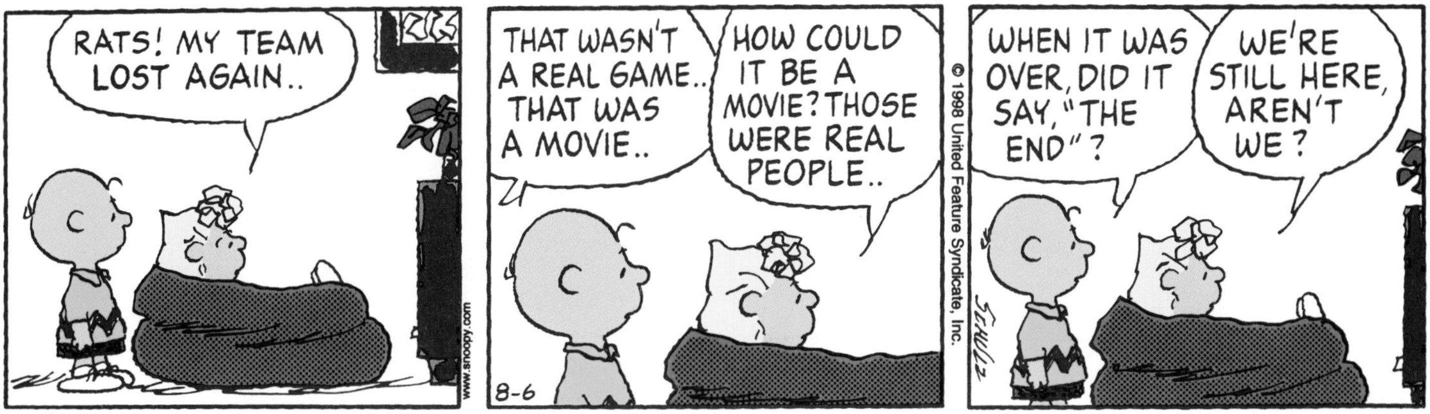
RATS! MY TEAM LOST AGAIN..
www.snoopy.com
8-6
THAT WASN'T A REAL GAME.. THAT WAS A MOVIE..
HOW COULD IT BE A MOVIE? THOSE WERE REAL PEOPLE..
© 1998 United Feature Syndicate, Inc.
WHEN IT WAS OVER, DID IT SAY, "THE END"?
WE'RE STILL HERE, AREN'T WE?
SCHULZ

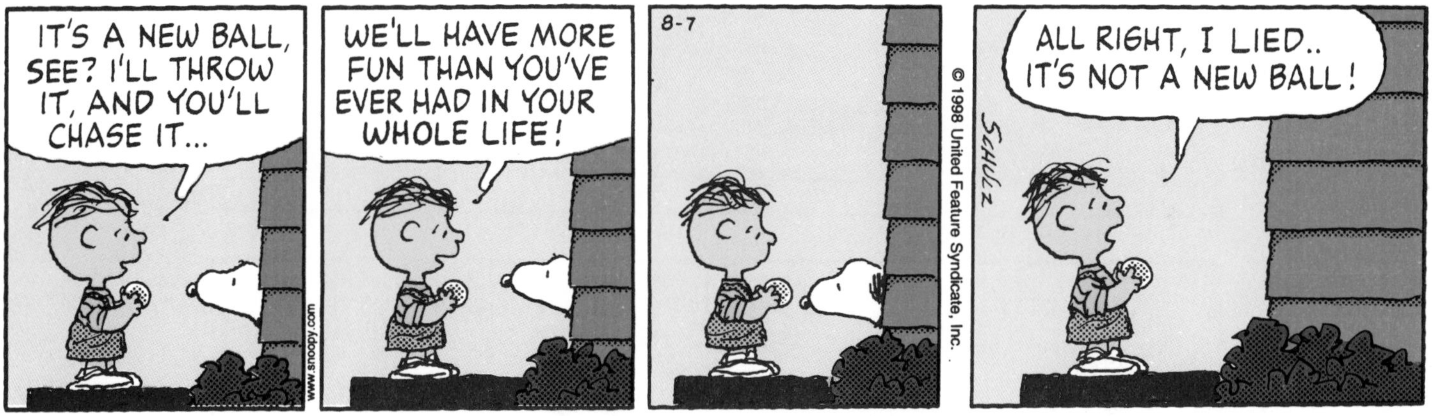
IT'S A NEW BALL, SEE? I'LL THROW IT, AND YOU'LL CHASE IT...
www.snoopy.com
WE'LL HAVE MORE FUN THAN YOU'VE EVER HAD IN YOUR WHOLE LIFE!
8-7
© 1998 United Feature Syndicate, Inc.
SCHULZ
ALL RIGHT, I LIED.. IT'S NOT A NEW BALL!

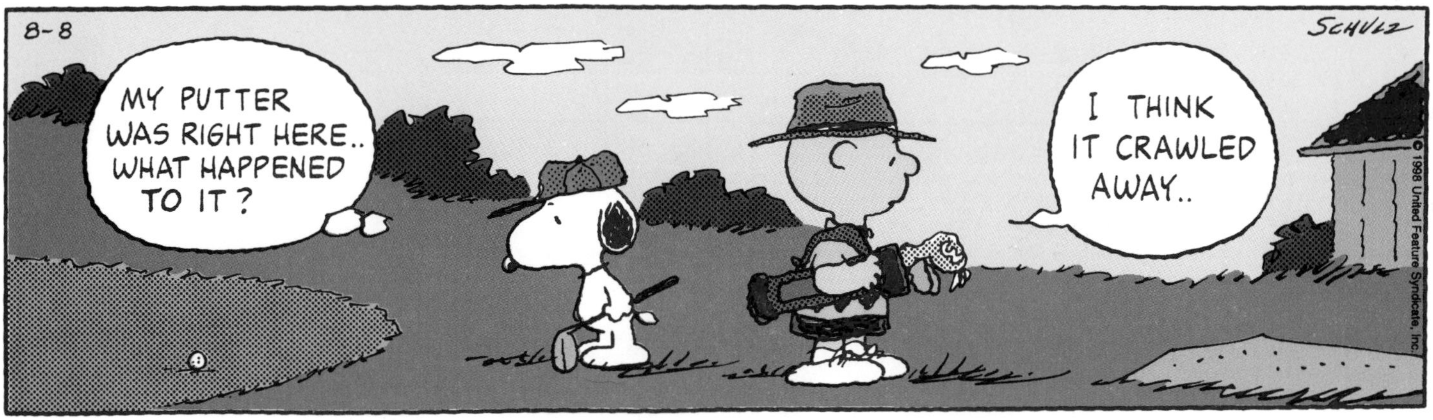
8-8
SCHULZ
MY PUTTER WAS RIGHT HERE.. WHAT HAPPENED TO IT?
I THINK IT CRAWLED AWAY..
© 1998 United Feature Syndicate, Inc.

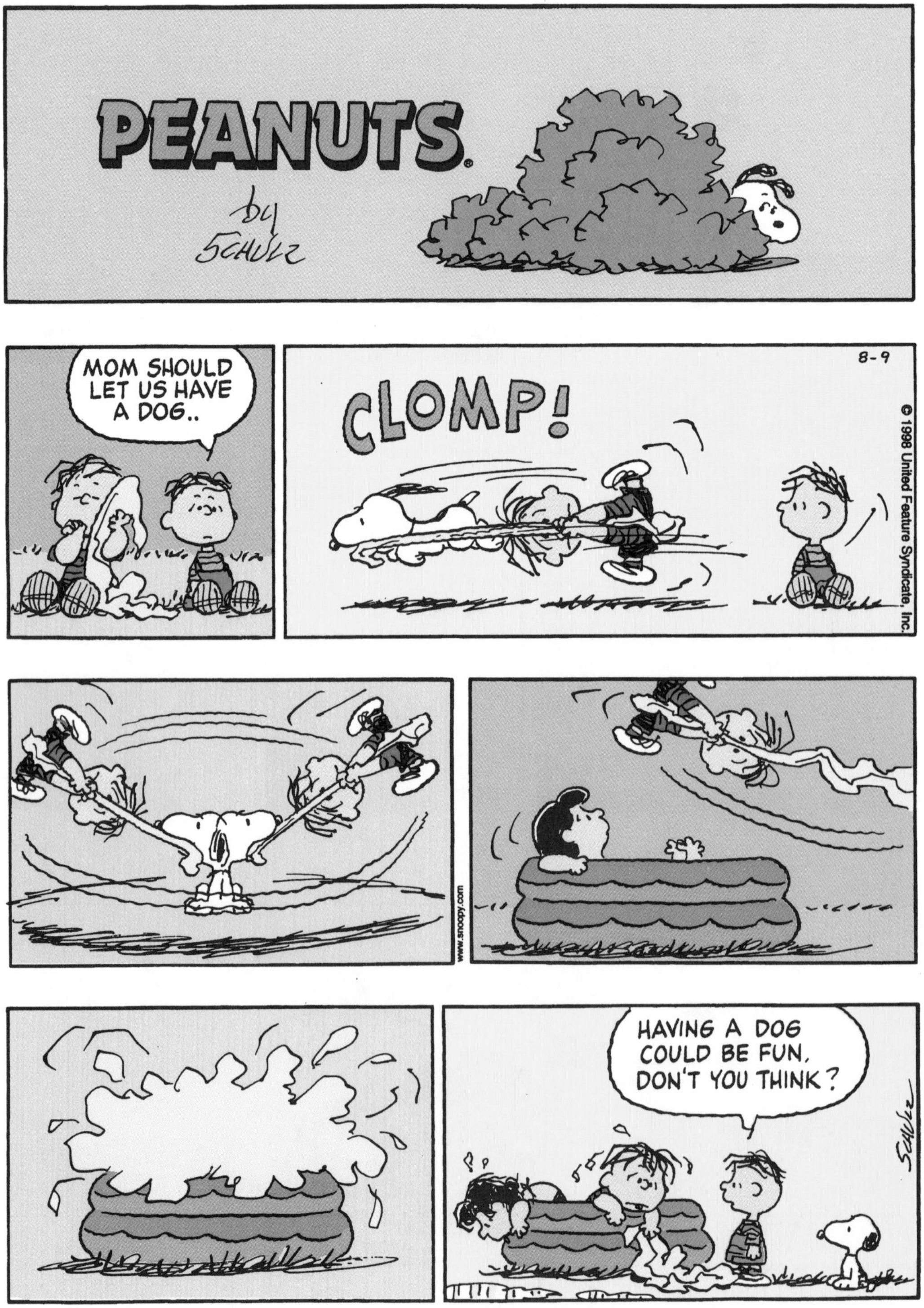
PEANUTS
by SCHULZ
MOM SHOULD LET US HAVE A DOG..
8-9
CLOMP!
© 1998 United Feature Syndicate, Inc.
www.snoopy.com
HAVING A DOG COULD BE FUN, DON'T YOU THINK?
SCHULZ

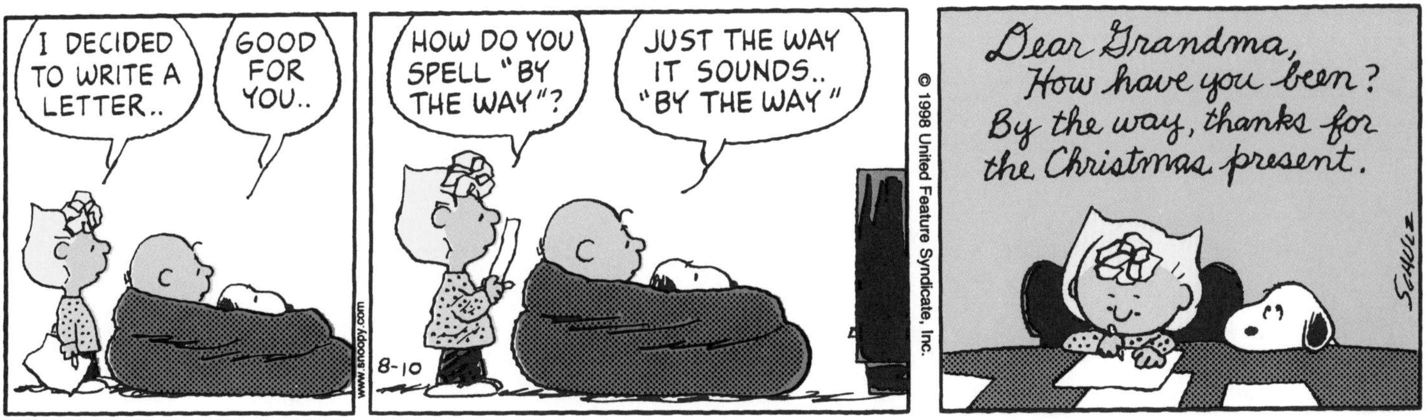
I DECIDED TO WRITE A LETTER..
GOOD FOR YOU..
HOW DO YOU SPELL "BY THE WAY"?
JUST THE WAY IT SOUNDS.. "BY THE WAY"
8-10
www.snoopy.com
© 1998 United Feature Syndicate, Inc.
Dear Grandma,
How have you been?
By the way, thanks for the Christmas present.
SCHULZ

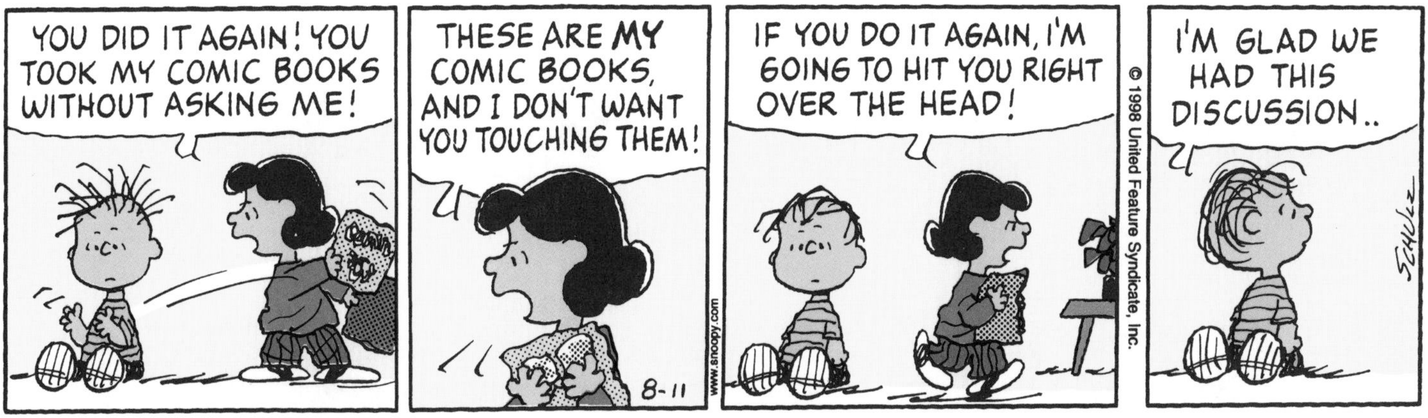
YOU DID IT AGAIN! YOU TOOK MY COMIC BOOKS WITHOUT ASKING ME!
THESE ARE MY COMIC BOOKS, AND I DON'T WANT YOU TOUCHING THEM!
8-11
www.snoopy.com
IF YOU DO IT AGAIN, I'M GOING TO HIT YOU RIGHT OVER THE HEAD!
© 1998 United Feature Syndicate, Inc.
I'M GLAD WE HAD THIS DISCUSSION..
SCHULZ

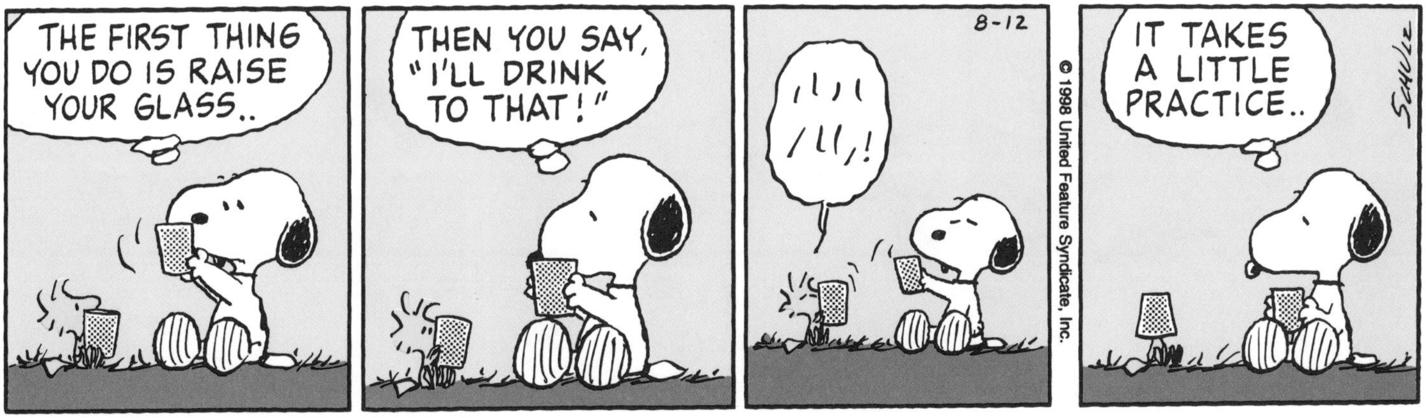
THE FIRST THING YOU DO IS RAISE YOUR GLASS..
THEN YOU SAY, "I'LL DRINK TO THAT!"
8-12
© 1998 United Feature Syndicate, Inc.
IT TAKES A LITTLE PRACTICE..
SCHULZ

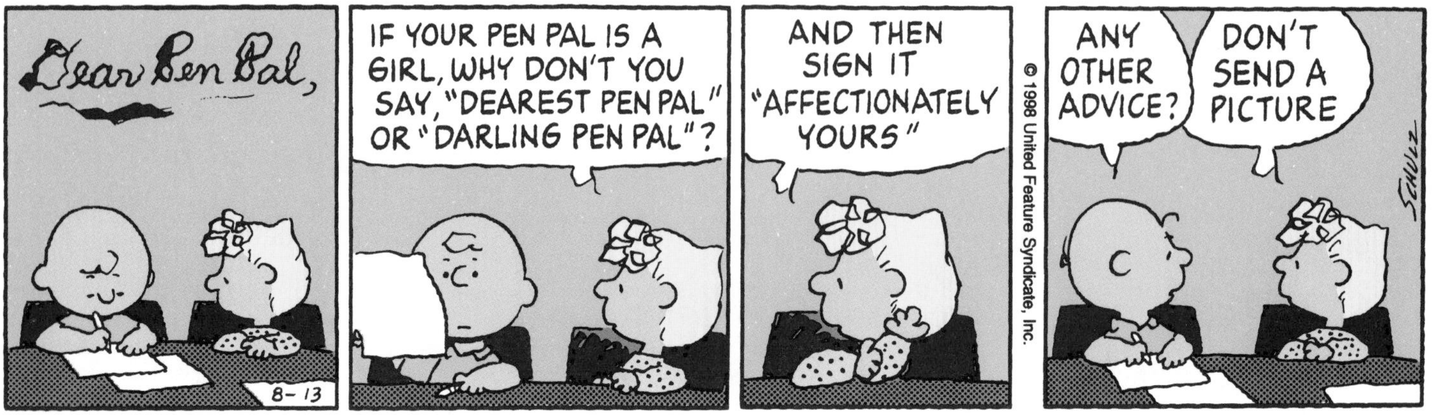
Dear Pen Pal,
8-13
IF YOUR PEN PAL IS A GIRL, WHY DON'T YOU SAY, "DEAREST PEN PAL" OR "DARLING PEN PAL"?
AND THEN SIGN IT "AFFECTIONATELY YOURS"
© 1998 United Feature Syndicate, Inc.
ANY OTHER ADVICE?
DON'T SEND A PICTURE
SCHULZ

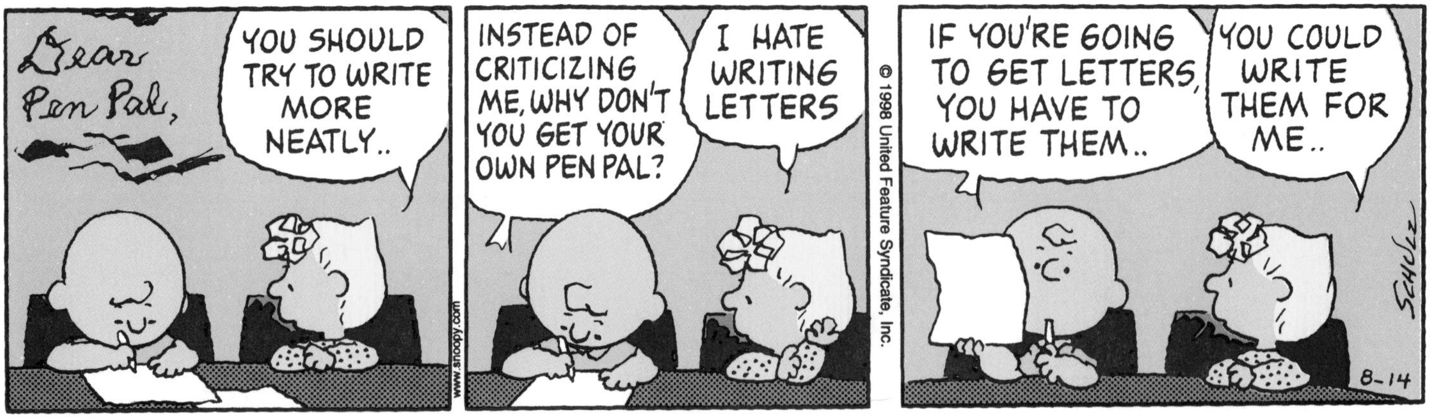
Dear Pen Pal,
YOU SHOULD TRY TO WRITE MORE NEATLY..
www.snoopy.com
INSTEAD OF CRITICIZING ME, WHY DON'T YOU GET YOUR OWN PEN PAL?
I HATE WRITING LETTERS
© 1998 United Feature Syndicate, Inc.
IF YOU'RE GOING TO GET LETTERS, YOU HAVE TO WRITE THEM..
YOU COULD WRITE THEM FOR ME..
SCHULZ
8-14

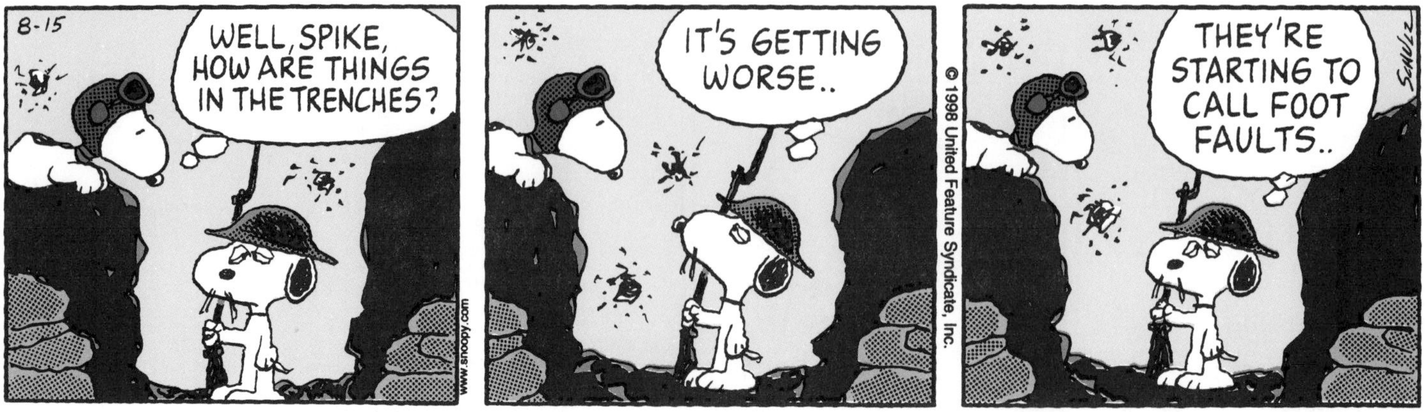
8-15
WELL, SPIKE, HOW ARE THINGS IN THE TRENCHES?
www.snoopy.com
IT'S GETTING WORSE..
© 1998 United Feature Syndicate, Inc.
THEY'RE STARTING TO CALL FOOT FAULTS..
SCHULZ

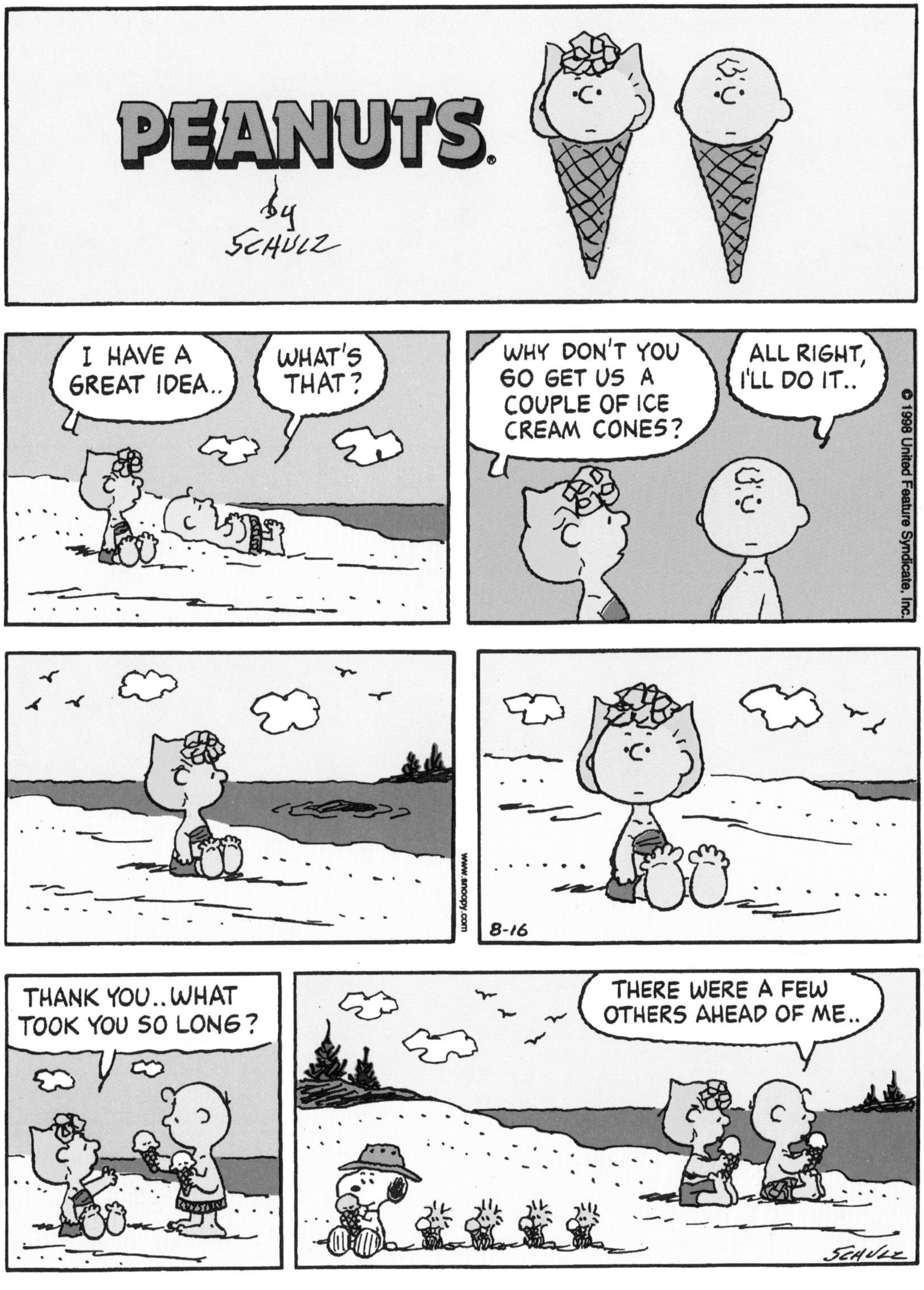
PEANUTS
by SCHULZ
I HAVE A GREAT IDEA..
WHAT'S THAT?
WHY DON'T YOU GO GET US A COUPLE OF ICE CREAM CONES?
ALL RIGHT, I'LL DO IT..
© 1998 United Feature Syndicate, Inc.
www.snoopy.com
8-16
THANK YOU.. WHAT TOOK YOU SO LONG?
THERE WERE A FEW OTHERS AHEAD OF ME..
SCHULZ

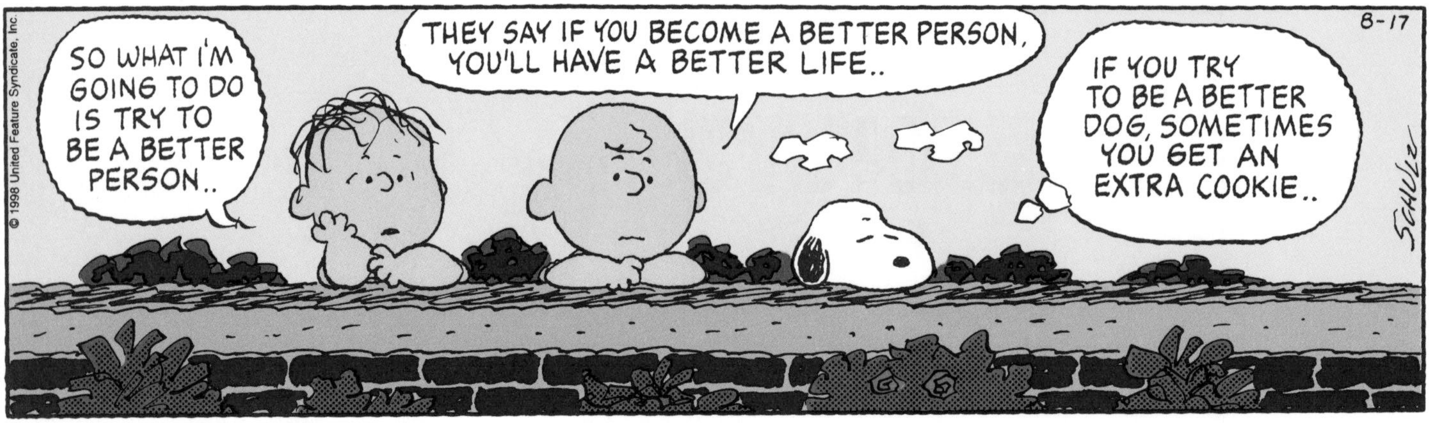
© 1998 United Feature Syndicate, Inc.
SO WHAT I'M GOING TO DO IS TRY TO BE A BETTER PERSON..
THEY SAY IF YOU BECOME A BETTER PERSON, YOU'LL HAVE A BETTER LIFE..
8-17
IF YOU TRY TO BE A BETTER DOG, SOMETIMES YOU GET AN EXTRA COOKIE..
SCHULZ

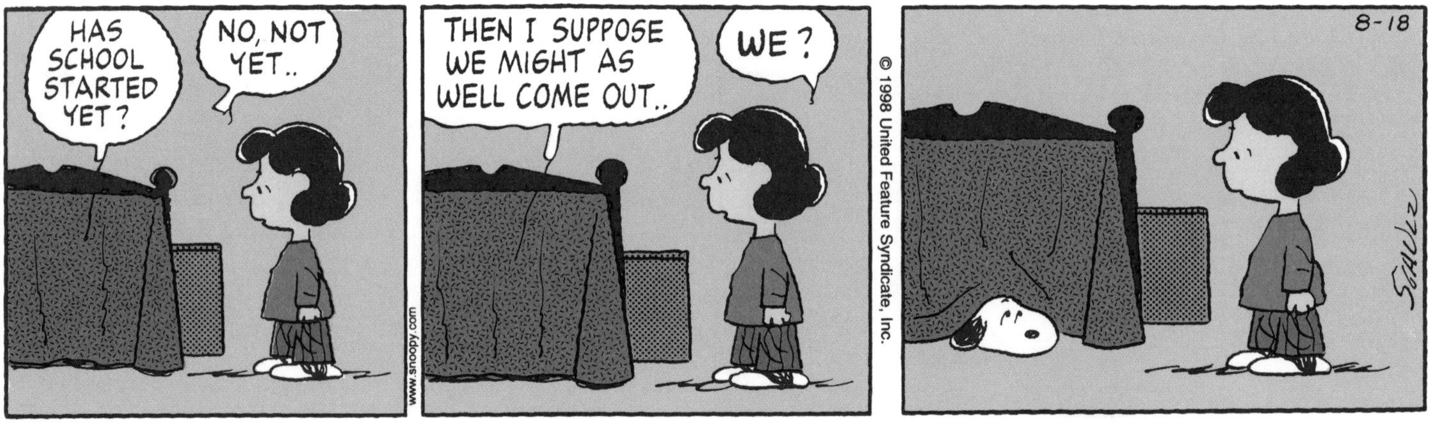
HAS SCHOOL STARTED YET?
NO, NOT YET..
www.snoopy.com
THEN I SUPPOSE WE MIGHT AS WELL COME OUT..
WE?
© 1998 United Feature Syndicate, Inc.
8-18
SCHULZ

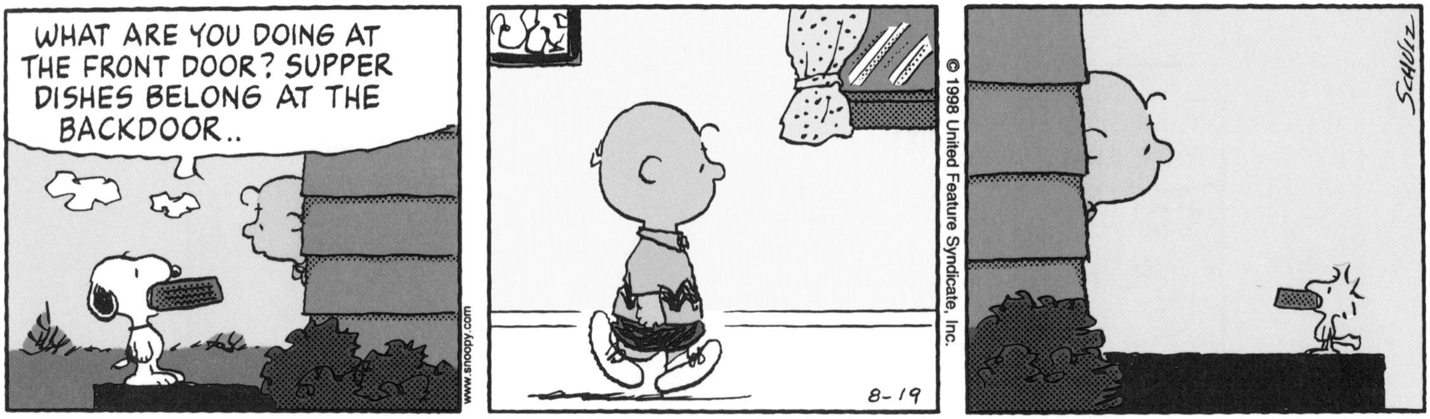
WHAT ARE YOU DOING AT THE FRONT DOOR? SUPPER DISHES BELONG AT THE BACKDOOR..
www.snoopy.com
8-19
© 1998 United Feature Syndicate, Inc.
SCHULZ

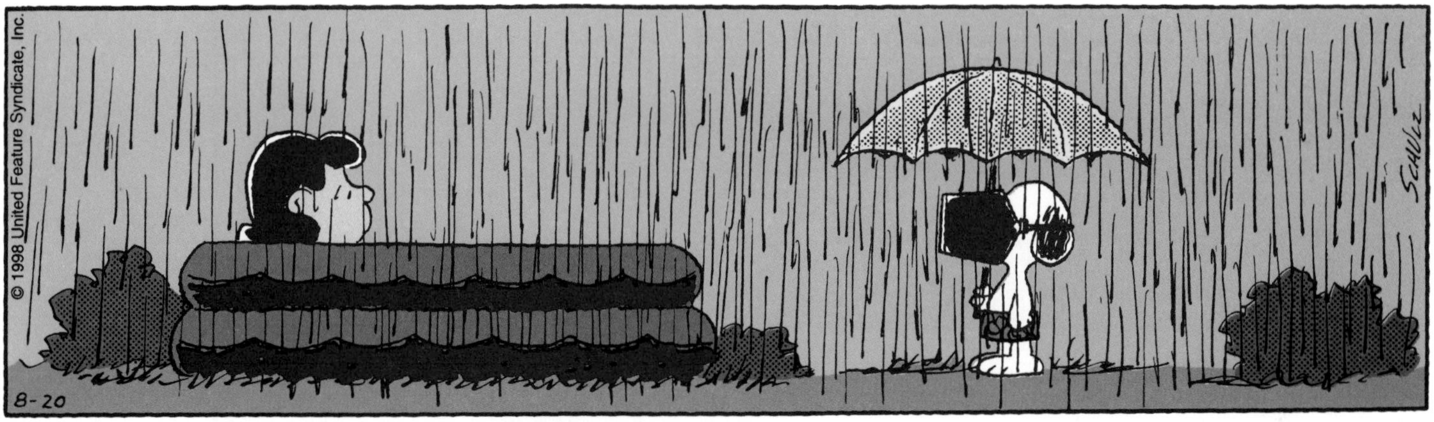
© 1998 United Feature Syndicate, Inc.
SCHULZ
8-20

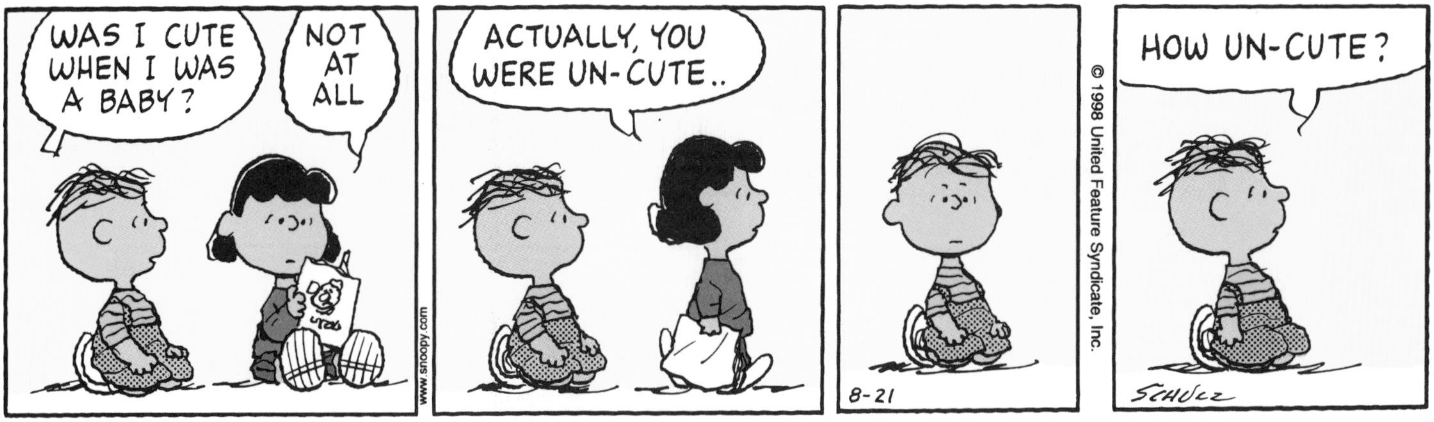
WAS I CUTE WHEN I WAS A BABY?
NOT AT ALL
www.snoopy.com
ACTUALLY, YOU WERE UN-CUTE..
© 1998 United Feature Syndicate, Inc.
8-21
HOW UN-CUTE?
SCHULZ

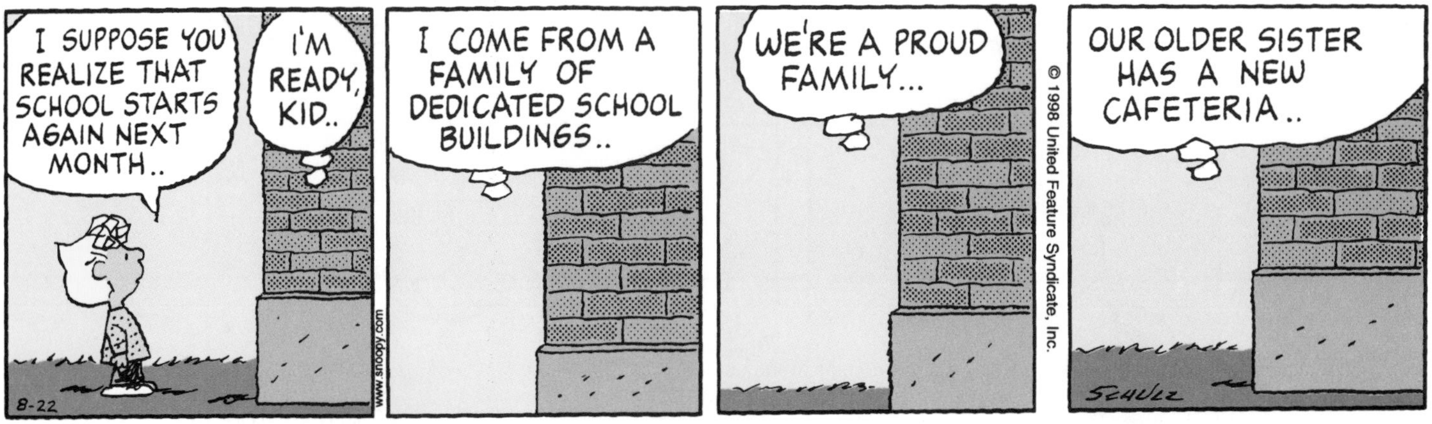
I SUPPOSE YOU REALIZE THAT SCHOOL STARTS AGAIN NEXT MONTH..
I'M READY, KID..
8-22
www.snoopy.com
I COME FROM A FAMILY OF DEDICATED SCHOOL BUILDINGS..
WE'RE A PROUD FAMILY...
© 1998 United Feature Syndicate, Inc.
OUR OLDER SISTER HAS A NEW CAFETERIA..
SCHULZ

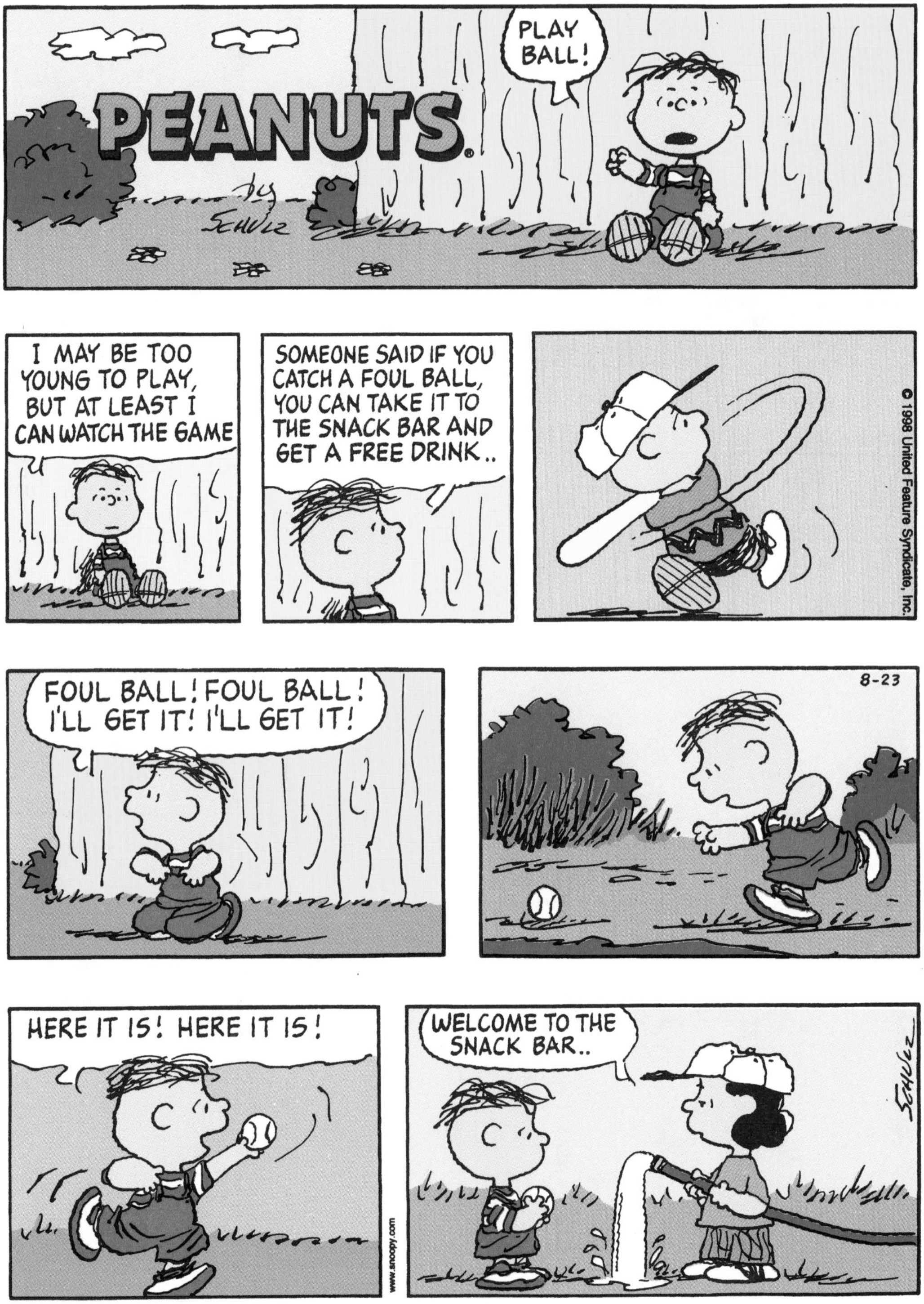
PEANUTS
by SCHULZ
PLAY BALL!
I MAY BE TOO YOUNG TO PLAY, BUT AT LEAST I CAN WATCH THE GAME
SOMEONE SAID IF YOU CATCH A FOUL BALL, YOU CAN TAKE IT TO THE SNACK BAR AND GET A FREE DRINK..
© 1998 United Feature Syndicate, Inc.
FOUL BALL! FOUL BALL! I'LL GET IT! I'LL GET IT!
8-23
HERE IT IS! HERE IT IS!
www.snoopy.com
WELCOME TO THE SNACK BAR..
SCHULZ

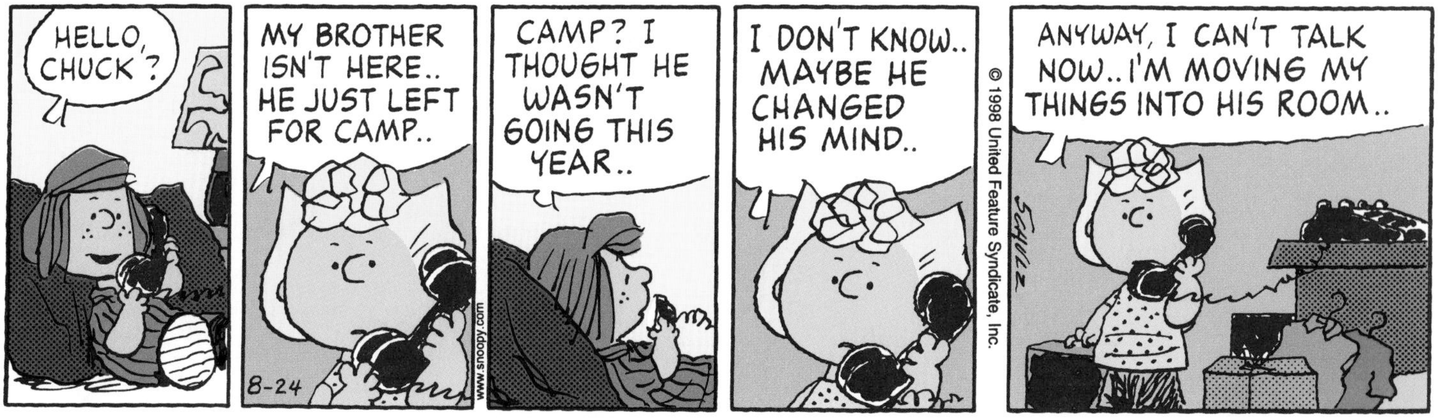
HELLO, CHUCK?
MY BROTHER ISN'T HERE.. HE JUST LEFT FOR CAMP..
CAMP? I THOUGHT HE WASN'T GOING THIS YEAR..
I DON'T KNOW.. MAYBE HE CHANGED HIS MIND..
ANYWAY, I CAN'T TALK NOW.. I'M MOVING MY THINGS INTO HIS ROOM..
8-24
www.snoopy.com
© 1998 United Feature Syndicate, Inc.
SCHULZ

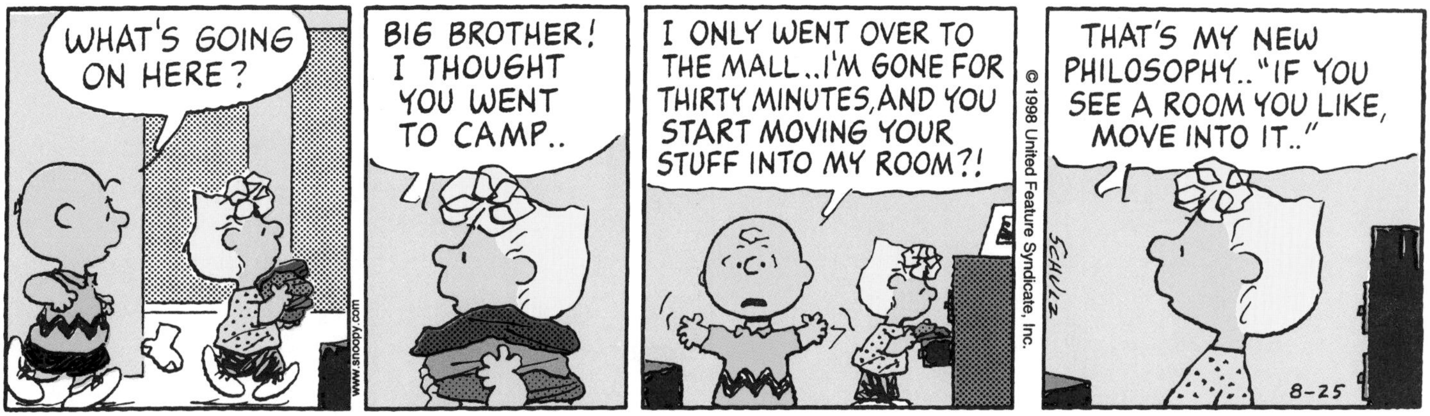
WHAT'S GOING ON HERE?
BIG BROTHER! I THOUGHT YOU WENT TO CAMP..
I ONLY WENT OVER TO THE MALL.. I'M GONE FOR THIRTY MINUTES, AND YOU START MOVING YOUR STUFF INTO MY ROOM?!
THAT'S MY NEW PHILOSOPHY.. "IF YOU SEE A ROOM YOU LIKE, MOVE INTO IT.."
8-25
www.snoopy.com
© 1998 United Feature Syndicate, Inc.
SCHULZ

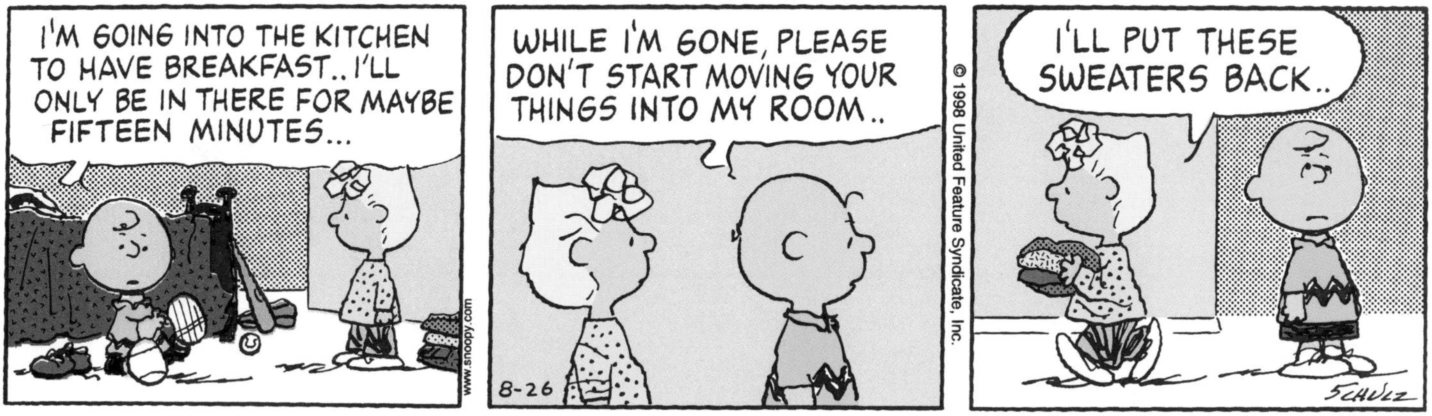
I'M GOING INTO THE KITCHEN TO HAVE BREAKFAST.. I'LL ONLY BE IN THERE FOR MAYBE FIFTEEN MINUTES...
WHILE I'M GONE, PLEASE DON'T START MOVING YOUR THINGS INTO MY ROOM..
I'LL PUT THESE SWEATERS BACK..
8-26
www.snoopy.com
© 1998 United Feature Syndicate, Inc.
SCHULZ

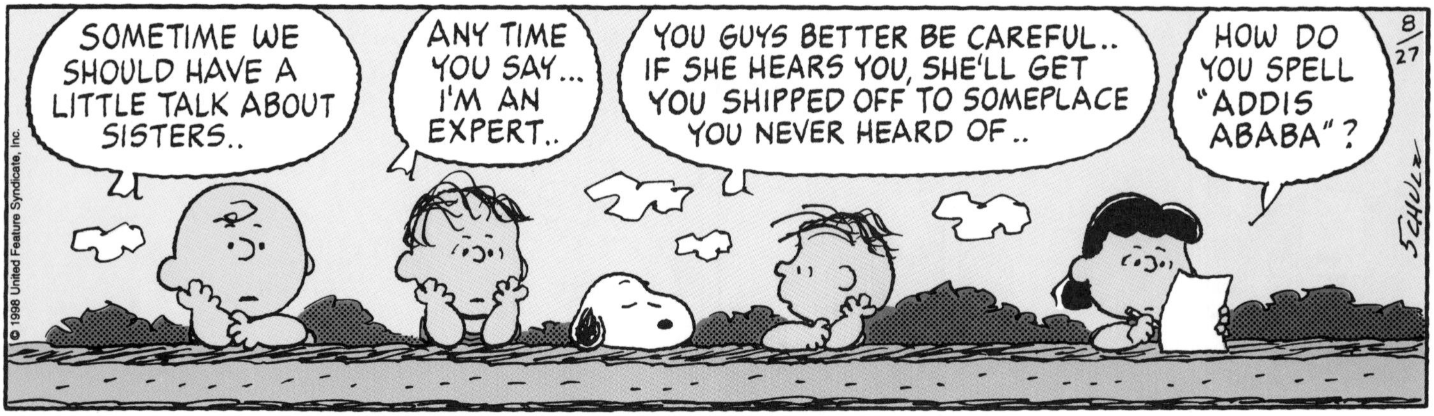
8/27
© 1998 United Feature Syndicate, Inc.
SOMETIME WE SHOULD HAVE A LITTLE TALK ABOUT SISTERS..
ANY TIME YOU SAY... I'M AN EXPERT..
YOU GUYS BETTER BE CAREFUL.. IF SHE HEARS YOU, SHE'LL GET YOU SHIPPED OFF TO SOMEPLACE YOU NEVER HEARD OF..
HOW DO YOU SPELL "ADDIS ABABA"?
SCHULZ

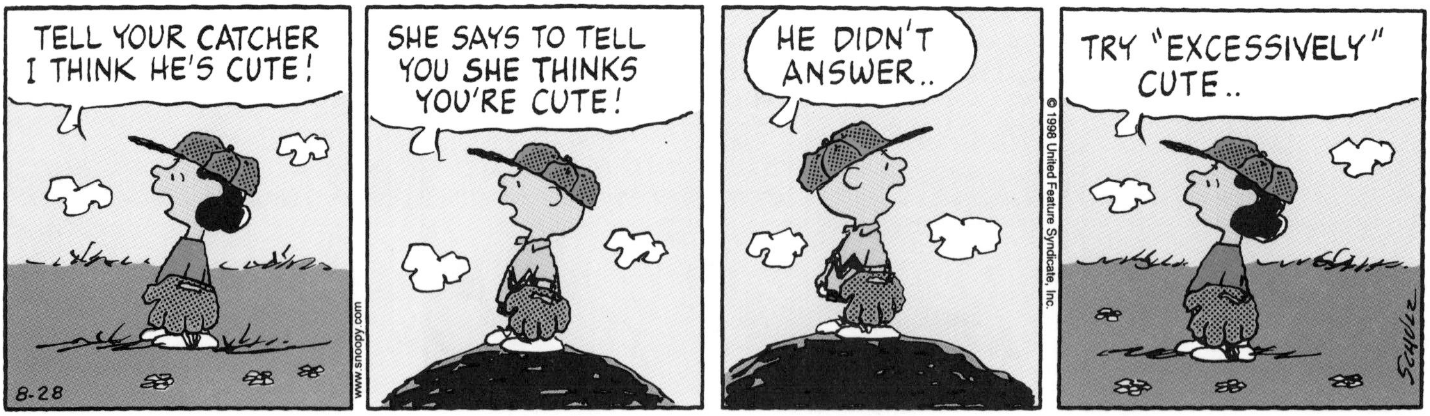
TELL YOUR CATCHER I THINK HE'S CUTE!
8-28
www.snoopy.com
SHE SAYS TO TELL YOU SHE THINKS YOU'RE CUTE!
HE DIDN'T ANSWER..
© 1998 United Feature Syndicate, Inc.
TRY "EXCESSIVELY" CUTE..
SCHULZ

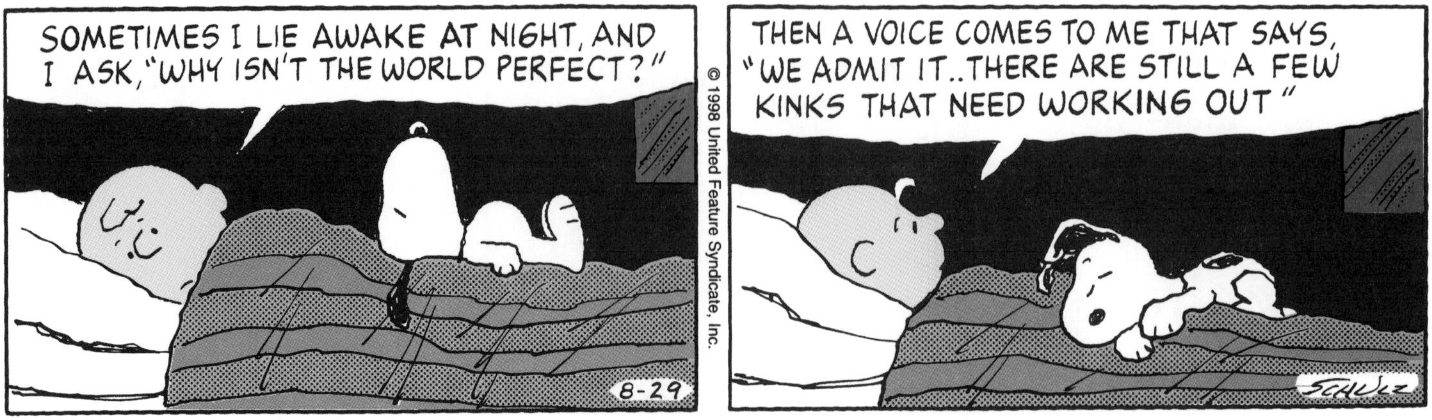
SOMETIMES I LIE AWAKE AT NIGHT, AND I ASK, "WHY ISN'T THE WORLD PERFECT?"
8-29
© 1998 United Feature Syndicate, Inc.
THEN A VOICE COMES TO ME THAT SAYS, "WE ADMIT IT..THERE ARE STILL A FEW KINKS THAT NEED WORKING OUT"
SCHULZ

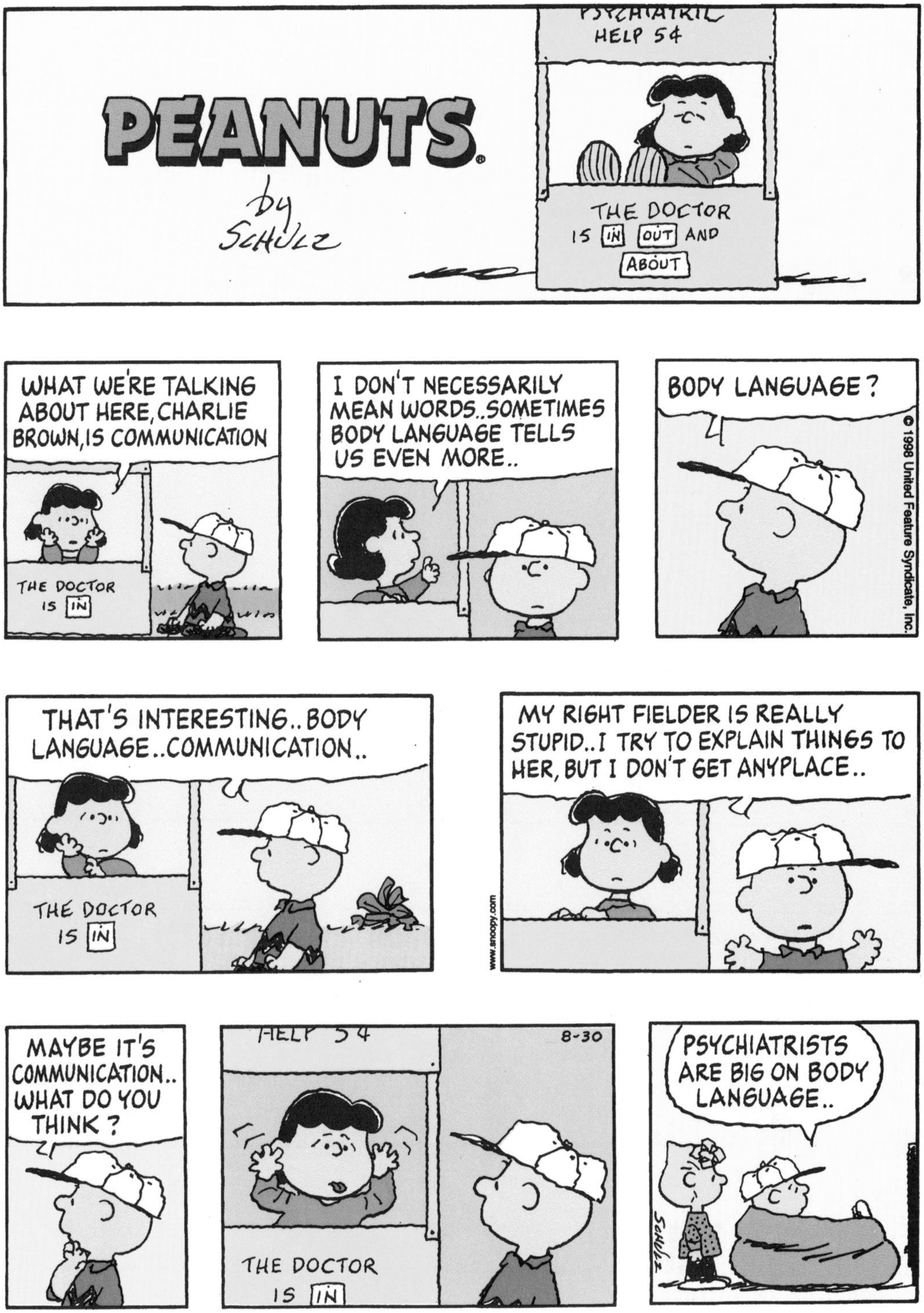
PEANUTS
by SCHULZ
HELP 5¢
THE DOCTOR IS IN OUT AND ABOUT
WHAT WE'RE TALKING ABOUT HERE, CHARLIE BROWN, IS COMMUNICATION
THE DOCTOR IS IN
I DON'T NECESSARILY MEAN WORDS..SOMETIMES BODY LANGUAGE TELLS US EVEN MORE..
BODY LANGUAGE?
© 1996 United Feature Syndicate, Inc.
THAT'S INTERESTING..BODY LANGUAGE..COMMUNICATION..
THE DOCTOR IS IN
www.snoopy.com
MY RIGHT FIELDER IS REALLY STUPID..I TRY TO EXPLAIN THINGS TO HER, BUT I DON'T GET ANYPLACE..
MAYBE IT'S COMMUNICATION.. WHAT DO YOU THINK?
8-30
THE DOCTOR IS IN
PSYCHIATRISTS ARE BIG ON BODY LANGUAGE..
SCHULZ

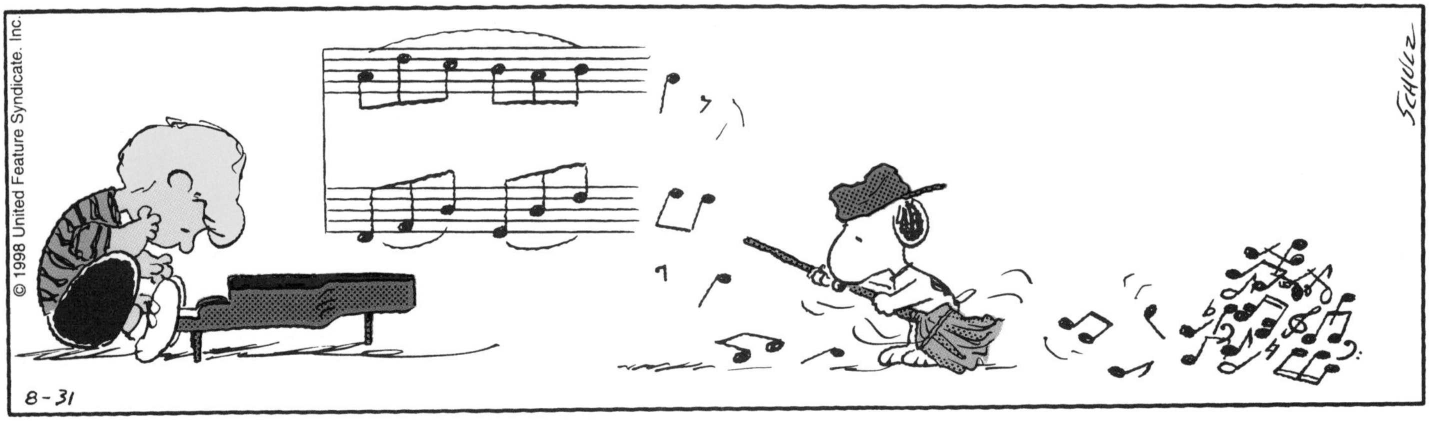
© 1998 United Feature Syndicate, Inc.
SCHULZ
8-31

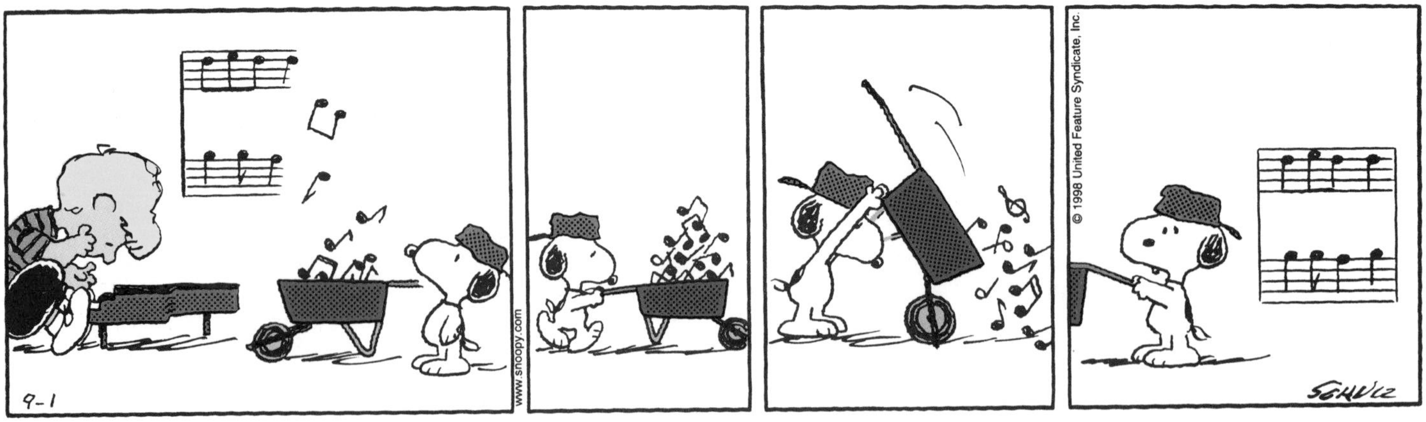
9-1
www.snoopy.com
© 1998 United Feature Syndicate, Inc.
SCHULZ

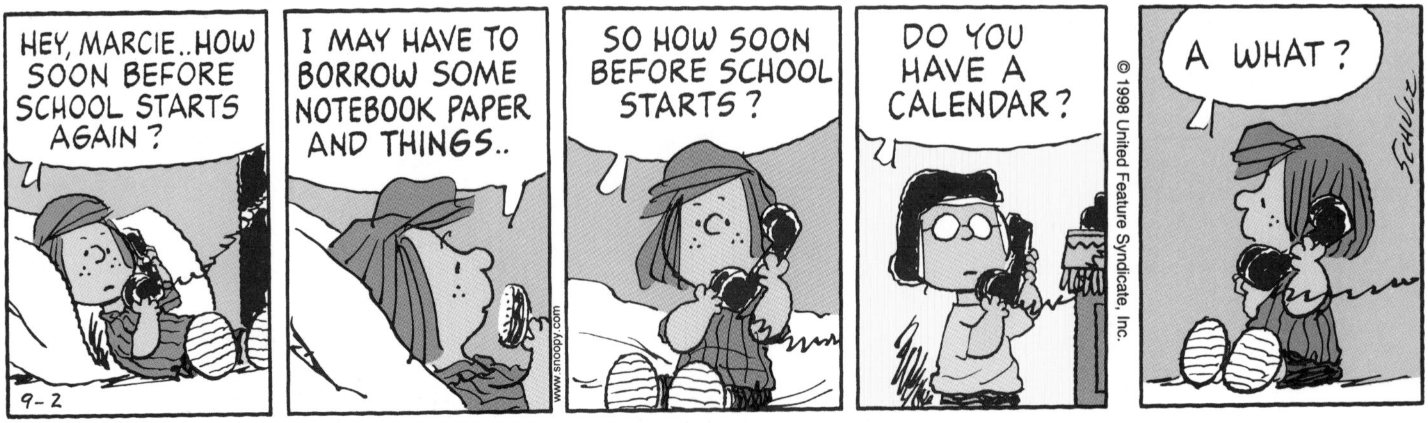
HEY, MARCIE..HOW SOON BEFORE SCHOOL STARTS AGAIN?
I MAY HAVE TO BORROW SOME NOTEBOOK PAPER AND THINGS..
SO HOW SOON BEFORE SCHOOL STARTS?
DO YOU HAVE A CALENDAR?
A WHAT?
9-2
www.snoopy.com
© 1998 United Feature Syndicate, Inc.
SCHULZ

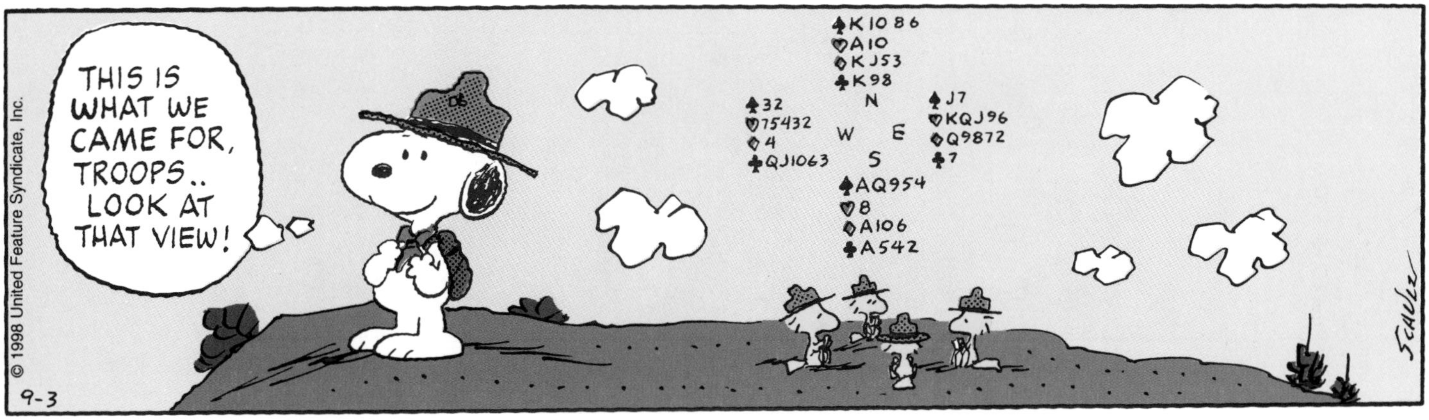
THIS IS WHAT WE CAME FOR, TROOPS.. LOOK AT THAT VIEW!
♠K1086
♡A10
◊KJ53
♣K98
N
♠32
♡75432
◊4
♣QJ1063
W
E
♠J7
♡KQJ96
◊Q9872
♣7
S
♠AQ954
♡8
◊A106
♣A542
© 1998 United Feature Syndicate, Inc.
9-3
SCHULZ

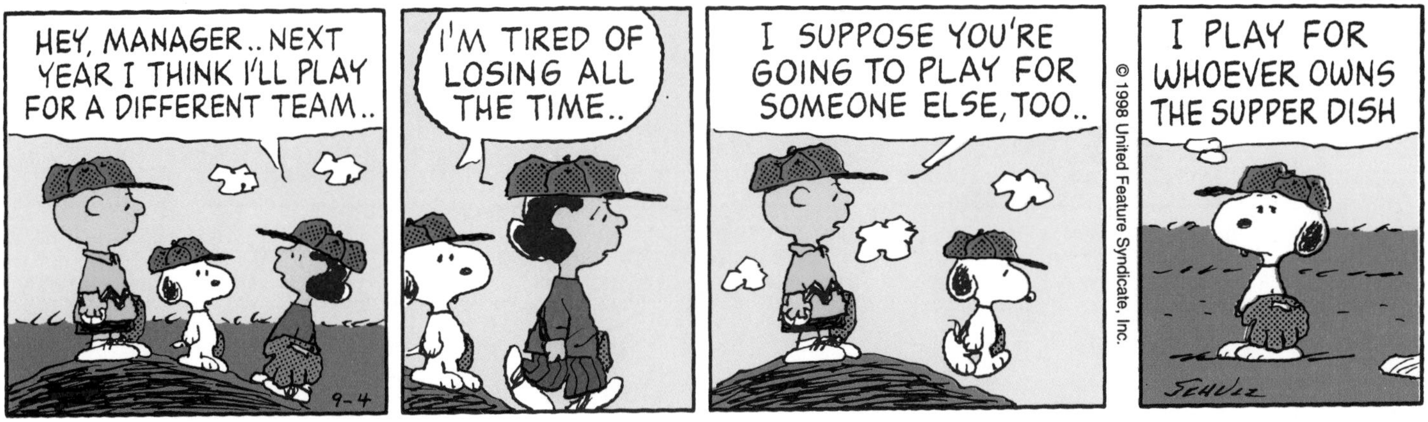
HEY, MANAGER.. NEXT YEAR I THINK I'LL PLAY FOR A DIFFERENT TEAM..
9-4
I'M TIRED OF LOSING ALL THE TIME..
I SUPPOSE YOU'RE GOING TO PLAY FOR SOMEONE ELSE, TOO..
© 1998 United Feature Syndicate, Inc.
I PLAY FOR WHOEVER OWNS THE SUPPER DISH
SCHULZ

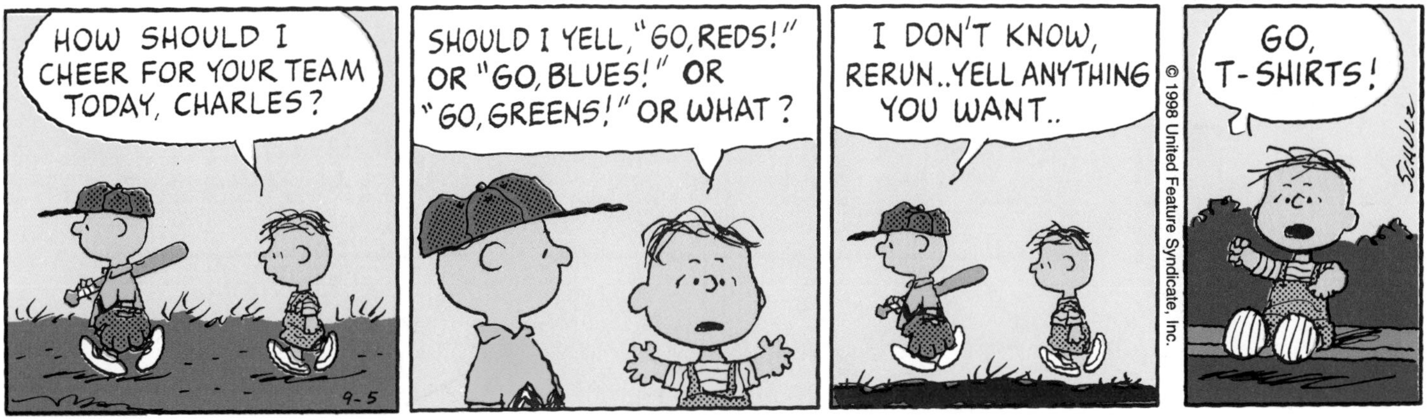
HOW SHOULD I CHEER FOR YOUR TEAM TODAY, CHARLES?
9-5
SHOULD I YELL, "GO, REDS!" OR "GO, BLUES!" OR "GO, GREENS!" OR WHAT?
I DON'T KNOW, RERUN.. YELL ANYTHING YOU WANT..
© 1998 United Feature Syndicate, Inc.
GO, T-SHIRTS!
SCHULZ

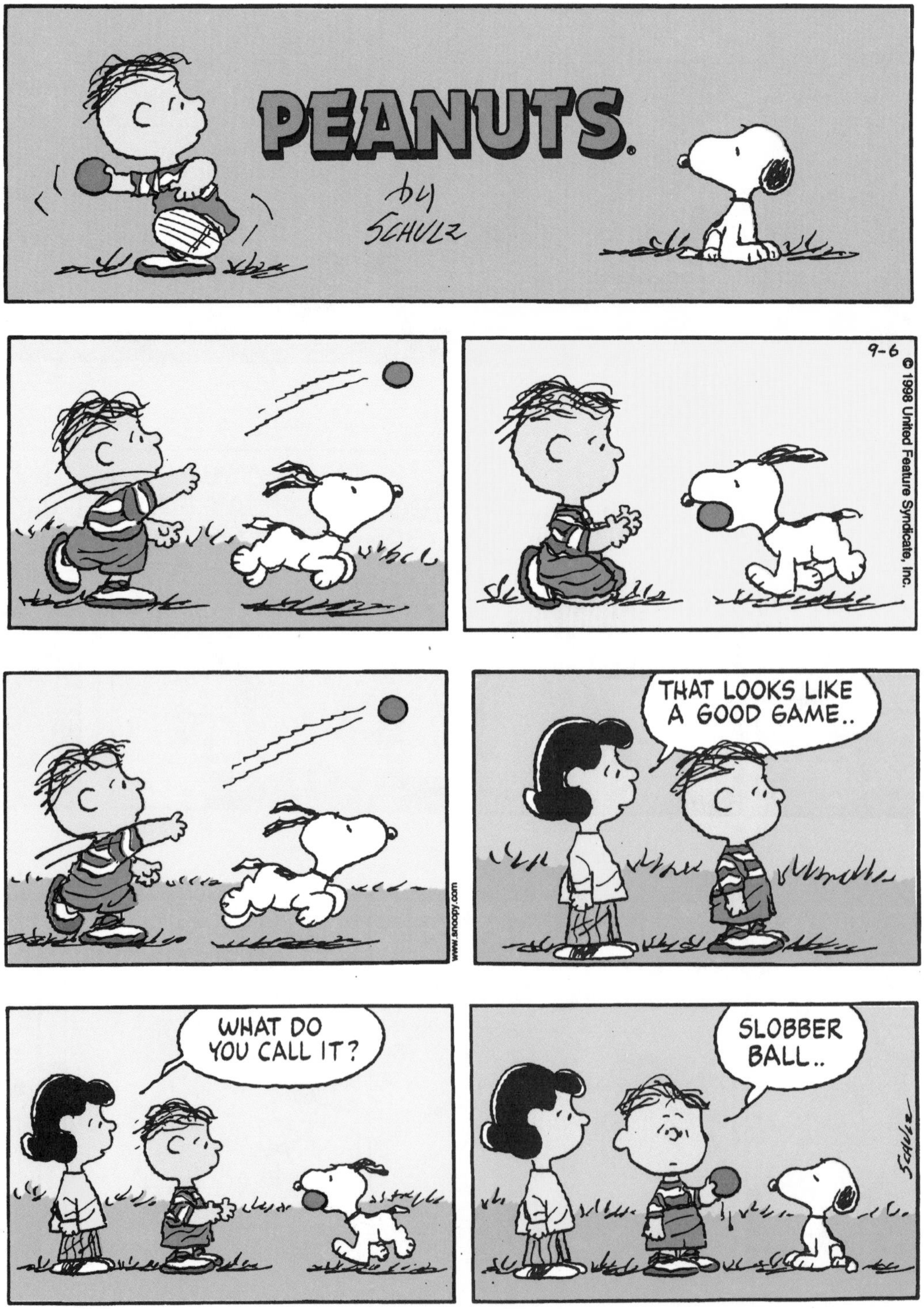
PEANUTS
by SCHULZ
9-6
© 1998 United Feature Syndicate, Inc.
www.snoopy.com
THAT LOOKS LIKE A GOOD GAME..
WHAT DO YOU CALL IT?
SLOBBER BALL..
SCHULZ

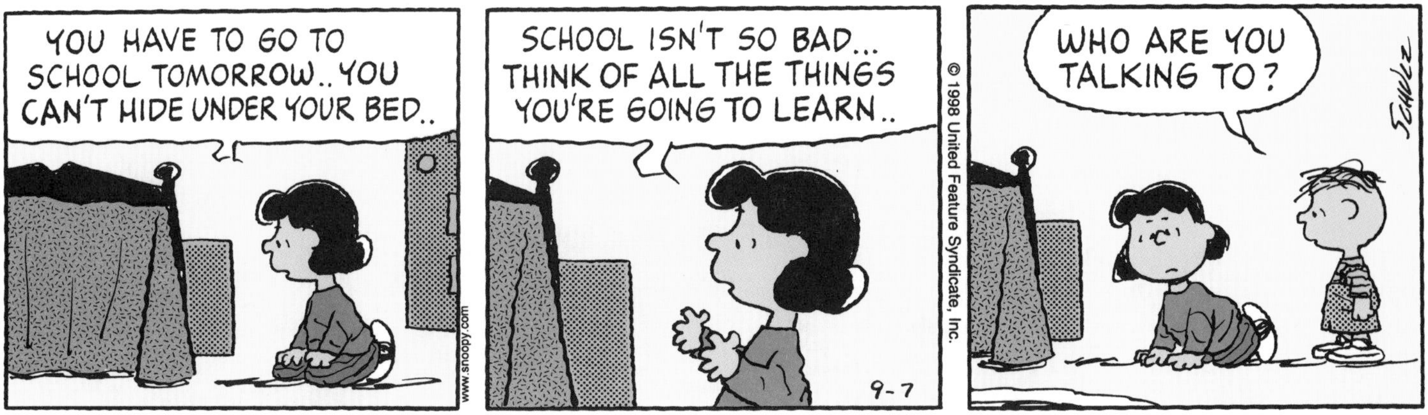
YOU HAVE TO GO TO SCHOOL TOMORROW.. YOU CAN'T HIDE UNDER YOUR BED..
www.snoopy.com
SCHOOL ISN'T SO BAD... THINK OF ALL THE THINGS YOU'RE GOING TO LEARN..
9-7
© 1998 United Feature Syndicate, Inc.
WHO ARE YOU TALKING TO?
SCHULZ

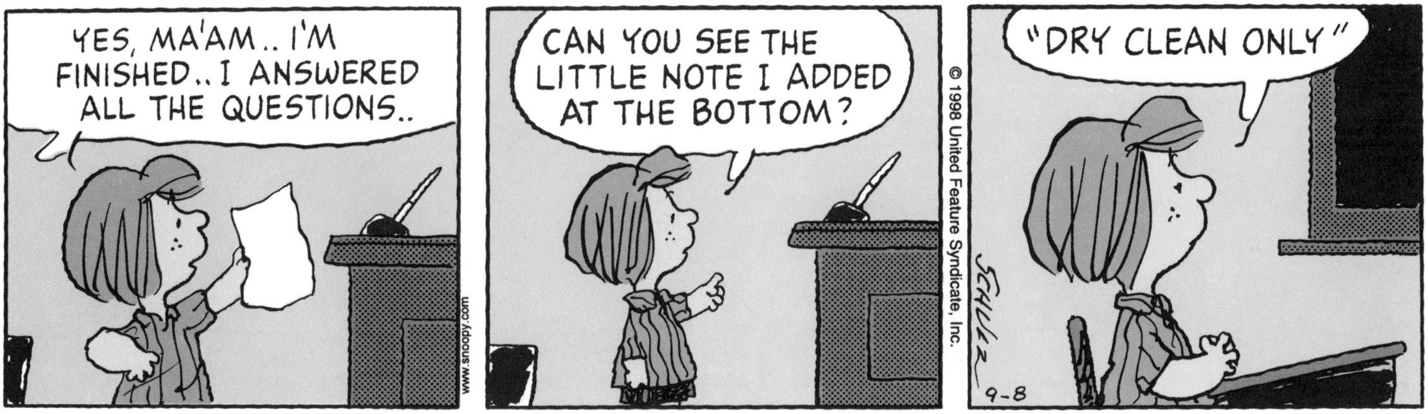
YES, MA'AM.. I'M FINISHED.. I ANSWERED ALL THE QUESTIONS..
www.snoopy.com
CAN YOU SEE THE LITTLE NOTE I ADDED AT THE BOTTOM?
© 1998 United Feature Syndicate, Inc.
"DRY CLEAN ONLY"
SCHULZ
9-8

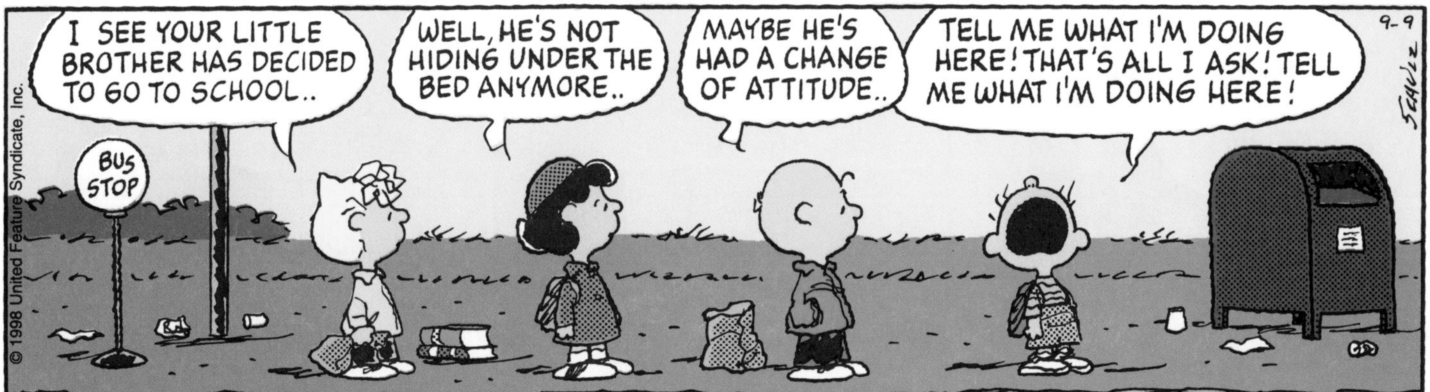
© 1998 United Feature Syndicate, Inc.
I SEE YOUR LITTLE BROTHER HAS DECIDED TO GO TO SCHOOL..
BUS STOP
WELL, HE'S NOT HIDING UNDER THE BED ANYMORE..
MAYBE HE'S HAD A CHANGE OF ATTITUDE..
TELL ME WHAT I'M DOING HERE! THAT'S ALL I ASK! TELL ME WHAT I'M DOING HERE!
9-9
SCHULZ

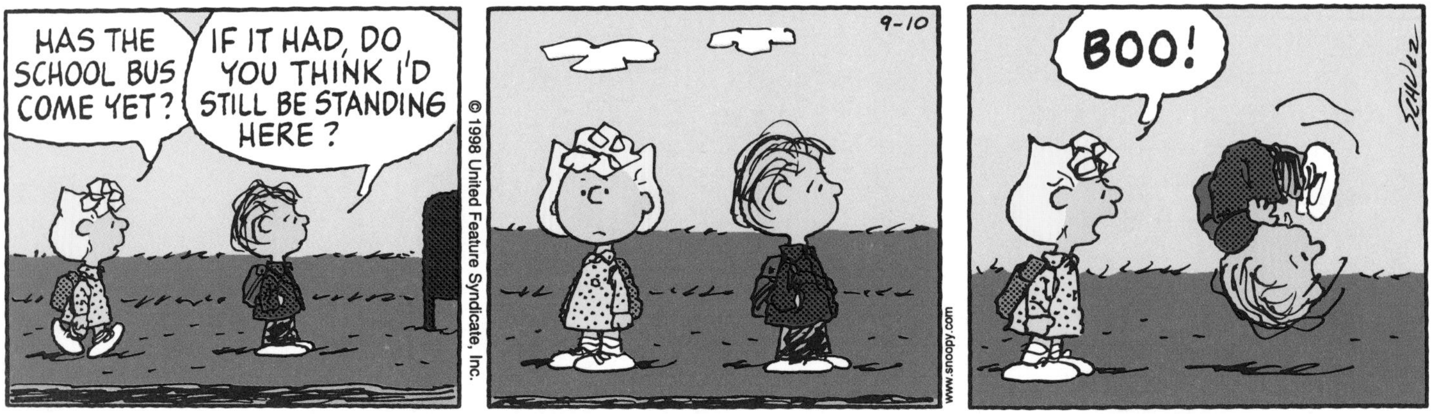
HAS THE SCHOOL BUS COME YET?
IF IT HAD, DO YOU THINK I'D STILL BE STANDING HERE?
© 1998 United Feature Syndicate, Inc.
9-10
www.snoopy.com
BOO!
SCHULZ

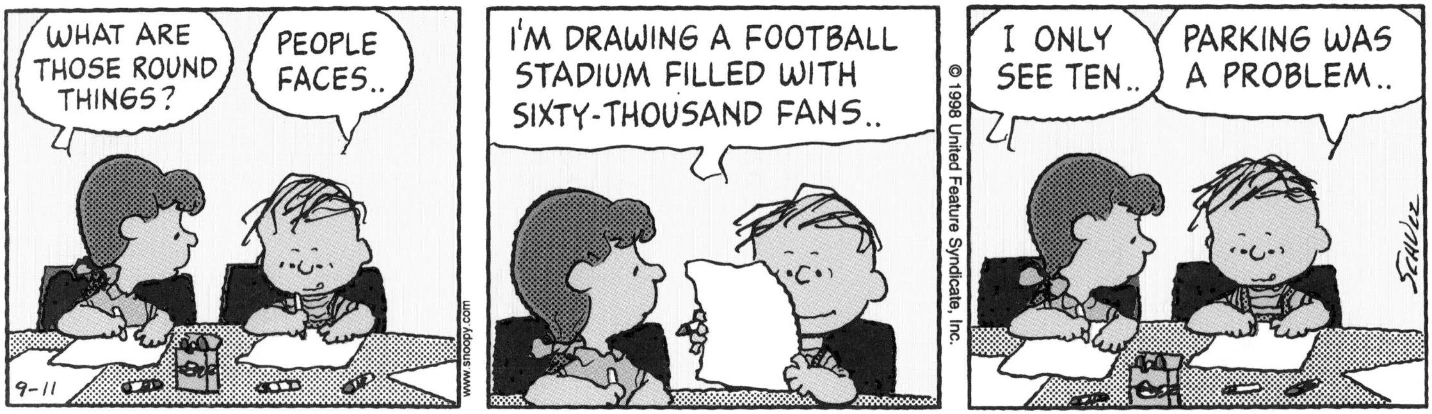
WHAT ARE THOSE ROUND THINGS?
PEOPLE FACES..
9-11
www.snoopy.com
I'M DRAWING A FOOTBALL STADIUM FILLED WITH SIXTY-THOUSAND FANS..
© 1998 United Feature Syndicate, Inc.
I ONLY SEE TEN..
PARKING WAS A PROBLEM..
SCHULZ

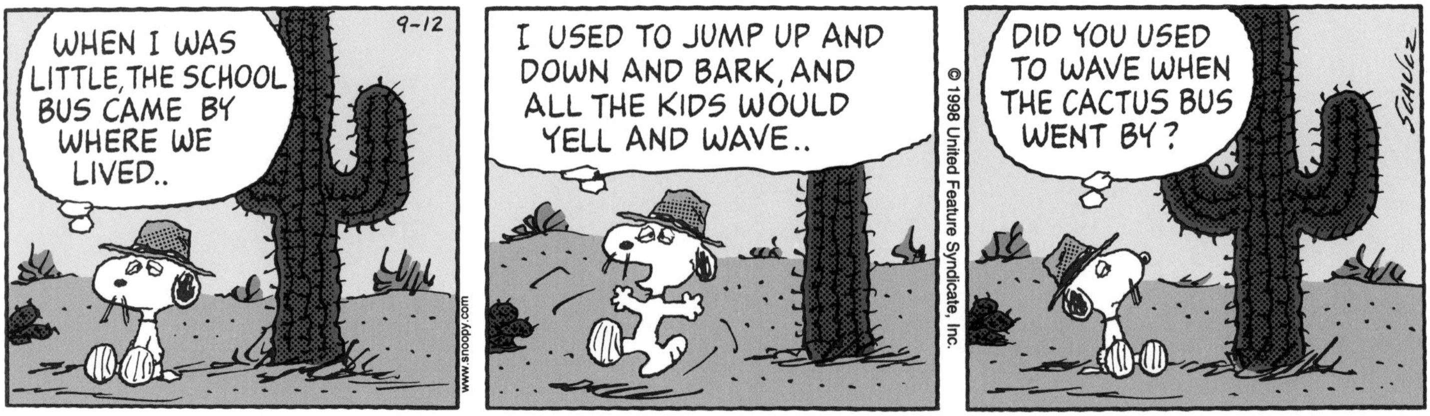
9-12
WHEN I WAS LITTLE, THE SCHOOL BUS CAME BY WHERE WE LIVED..
www.snoopy.com
I USED TO JUMP UP AND DOWN AND BARK, AND ALL THE KIDS WOULD YELL AND WAVE..
© 1998 United Feature Syndicate, Inc.
DID YOU USED TO WAVE WHEN THE CACTUS BUS WENT BY?
SCHULZ

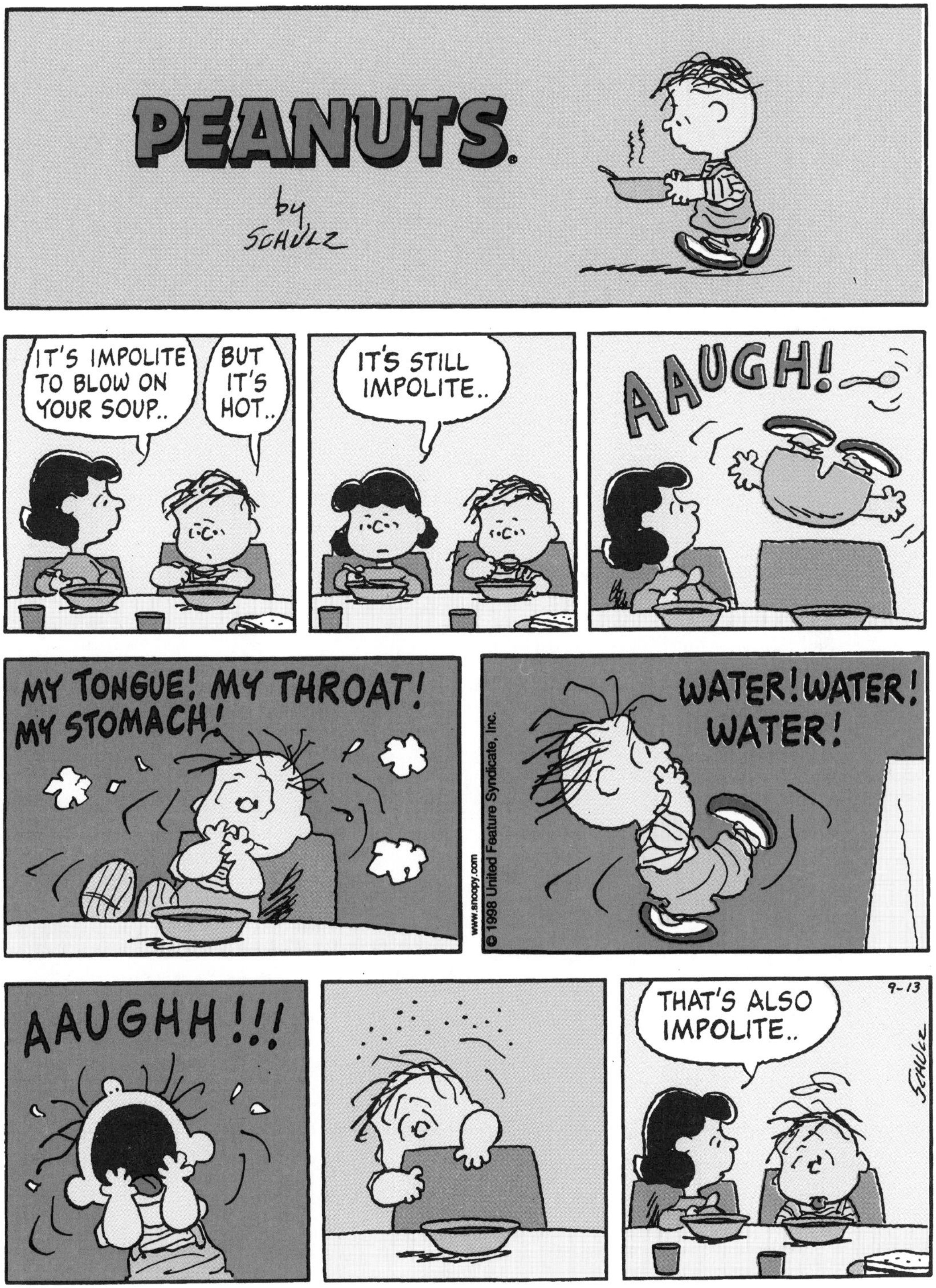
PEANUTS
by SCHULZ
IT'S IMPOLITE TO BLOW ON YOUR SOUP..
BUT IT'S HOT..
IT'S STILL IMPOLITE..
AAUGH!
MY TONGUE! MY THROAT! MY STOMACH!
© 1998 United Feature Syndicate, Inc.
www.snoopy.com
WATER! WATER! WATER!
AAUGHH!!!
THAT'S ALSO IMPOLITE..
9-13
SCHULZ

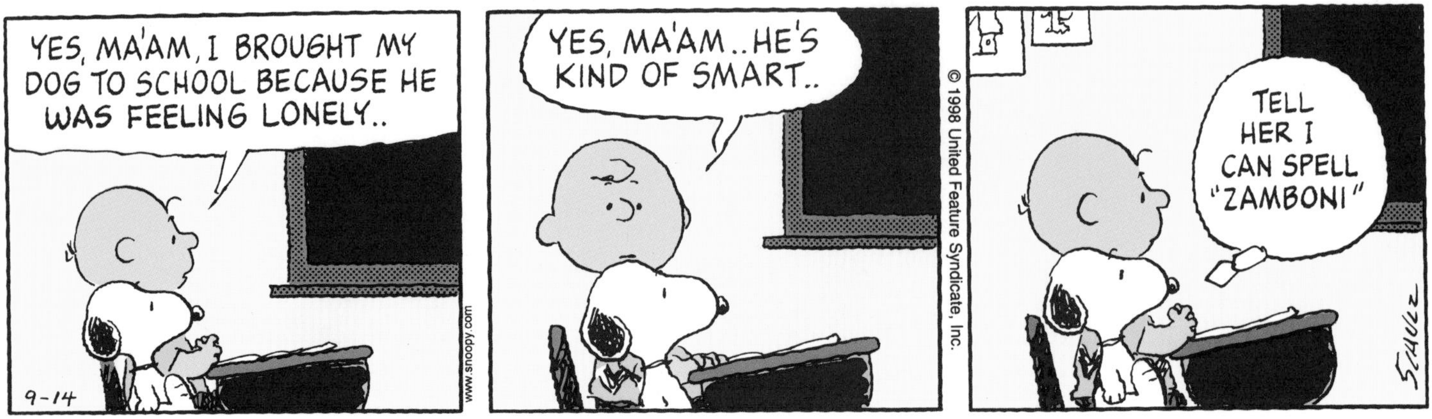
9-14
YES, MA'AM, I BROUGHT MY DOG TO SCHOOL BECAUSE HE WAS FEELING LONELY..
www.snoopy.com
YES, MA'AM..HE'S KIND OF SMART..
© 1998 United Feature Syndicate, Inc.
TELL HER I CAN SPELL "ZAMBONI"
SCHULZ

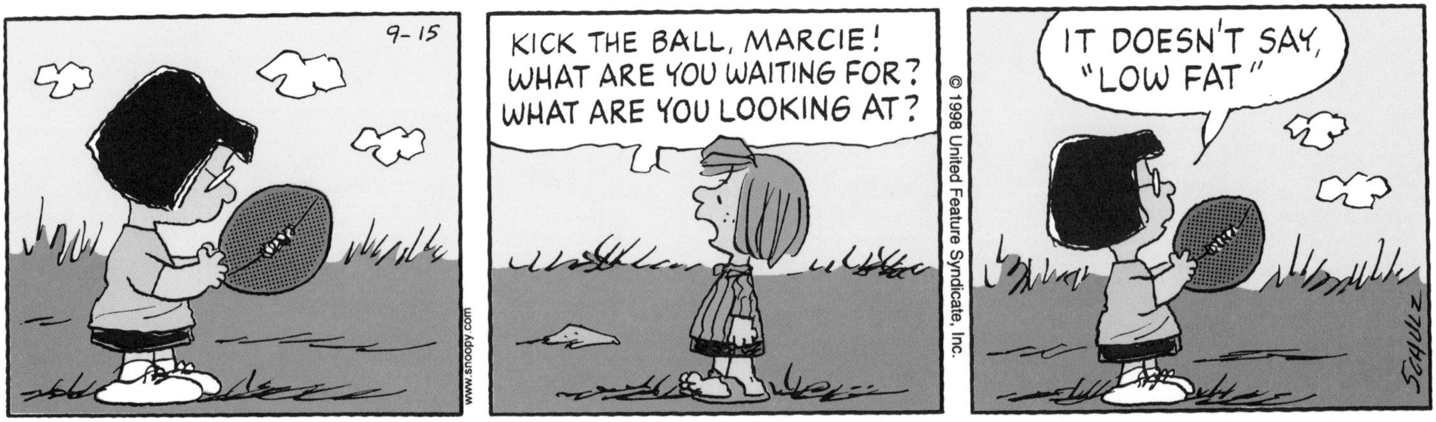
9-15
www.snoopy.com
KICK THE BALL, MARCIE! WHAT ARE YOU WAITING FOR? WHAT ARE YOU LOOKING AT?
© 1998 United Feature Syndicate, Inc.
IT DOESN'T SAY, "LOW FAT"
SCHULZ

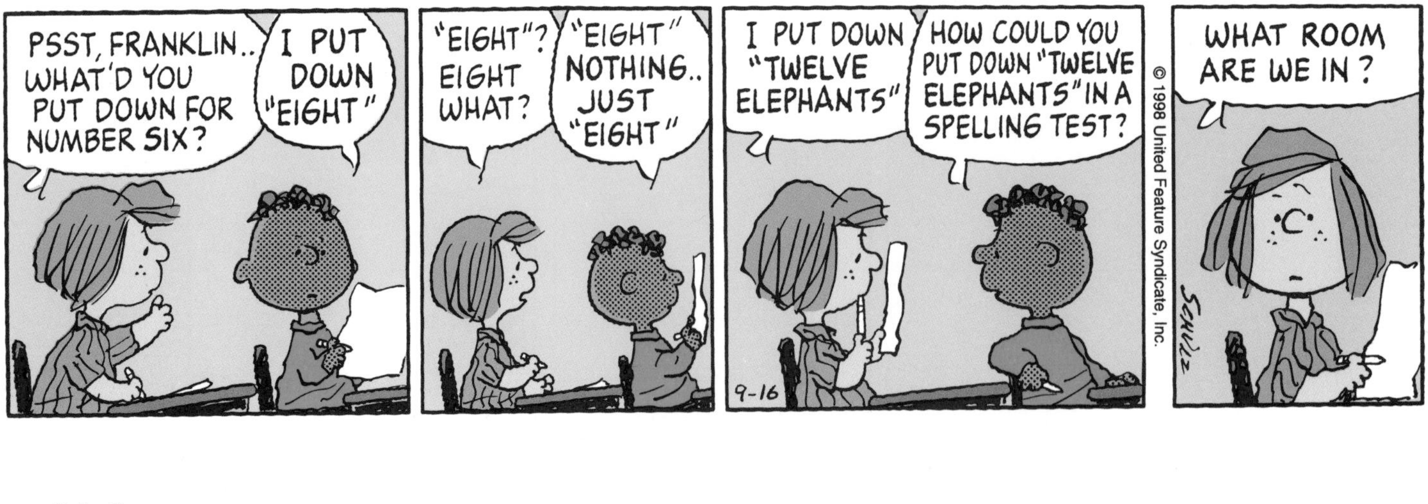
PSST, FRANKLIN.. WHAT'D YOU PUT DOWN FOR NUMBER SIX?
I PUT DOWN "EIGHT"
"EIGHT"? EIGHT WHAT?
"EIGHT" NOTHING.. JUST "EIGHT"
9-16
I PUT DOWN "TWELVE ELEPHANTS"
HOW COULD YOU PUT DOWN "TWELVE ELEPHANTS" IN A SPELLING TEST?
© 1998 United Feature Syndicate, Inc.
WHAT ROOM ARE WE IN?
SCHULZ

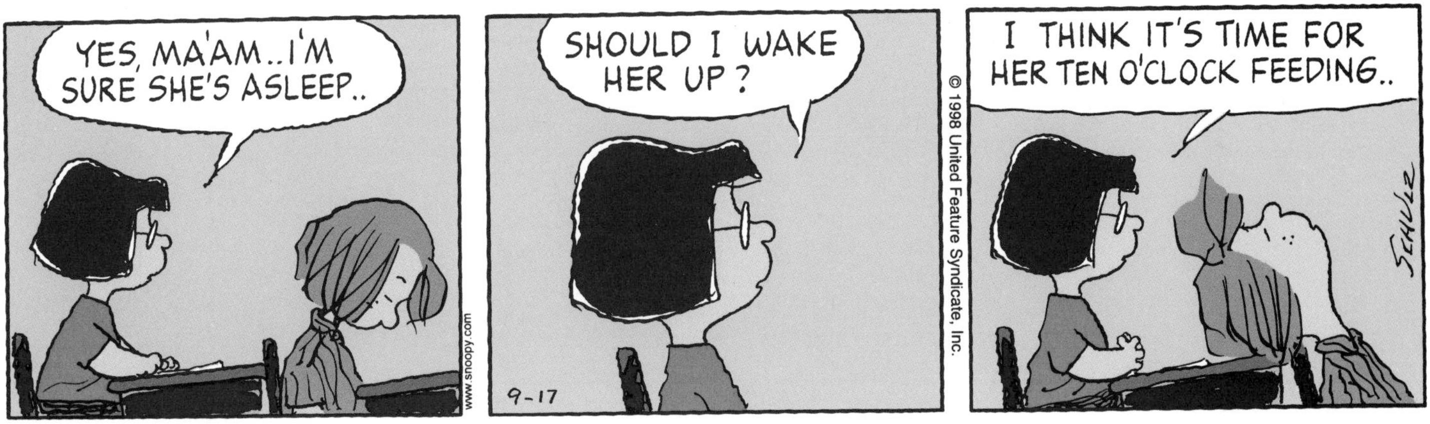
YES, MA'AM..I'M SURE SHE'S ASLEEP..
SHOULD I WAKE HER UP?
9-17
I THINK IT'S TIME FOR HER TEN O'CLOCK FEEDING..
© 1998 United Feature Syndicate, Inc.
www.snoopy.com
SCHULZ

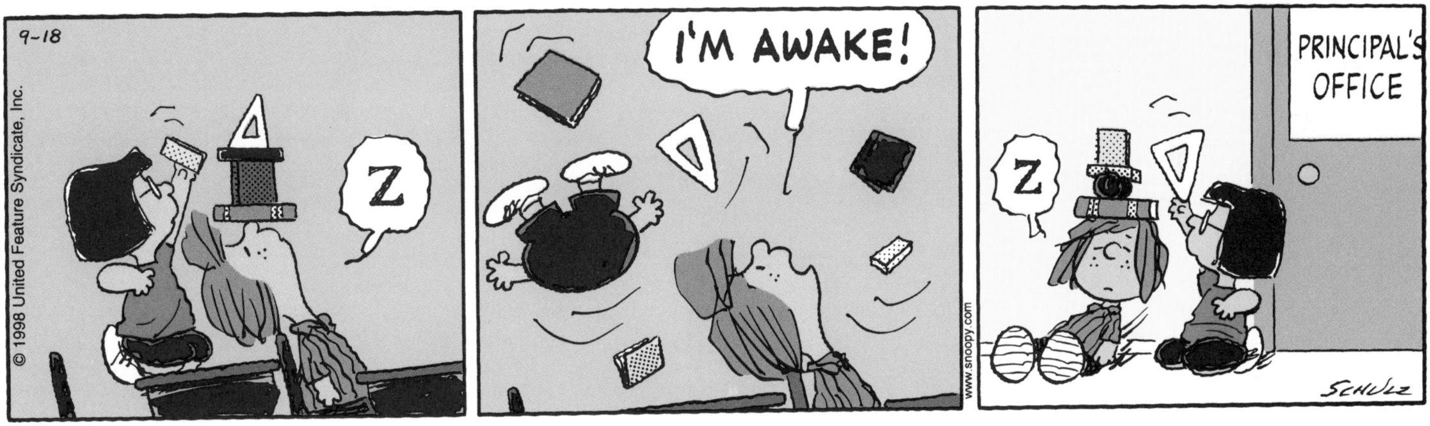
9-18
© 1998 United Feature Syndicate, Inc.
Z
I'M AWAKE!
www.snoopy.com
PRINCIPAL'S OFFICE
Z
SCHULZ

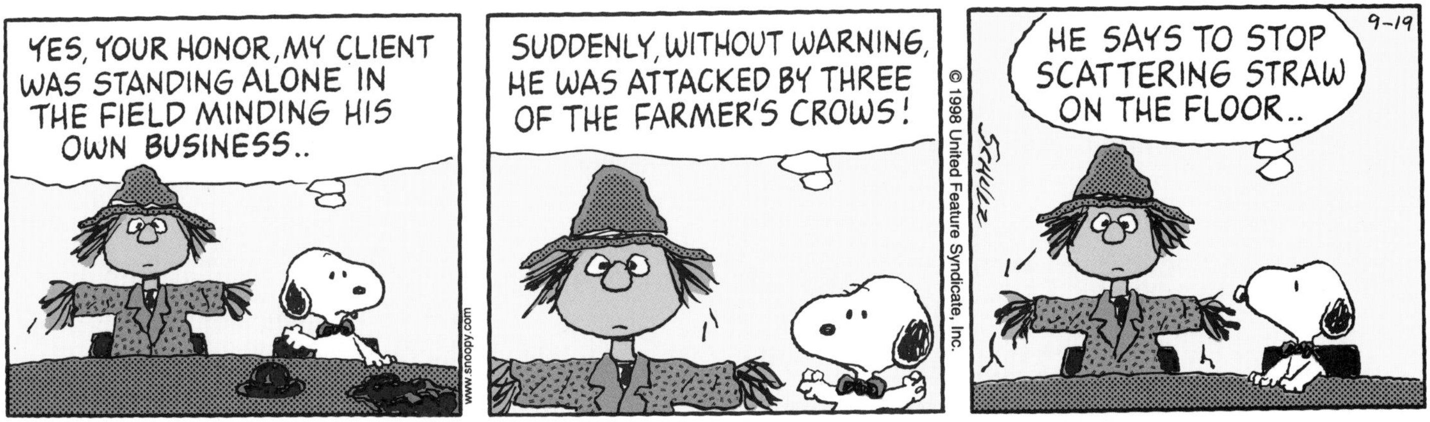
YES, YOUR HONOR, MY CLIENT WAS STANDING ALONE IN THE FIELD MINDING HIS OWN BUSINESS..
www.snoopy.com
SUDDENLY, WITHOUT WARNING, HE WAS ATTACKED BY THREE OF THE FARMER'S CROWS!
© 1998 United Feature Syndicate, Inc.
SCHULZ
9-19
HE SAYS TO STOP SCATTERING STRAW ON THE FLOOR..

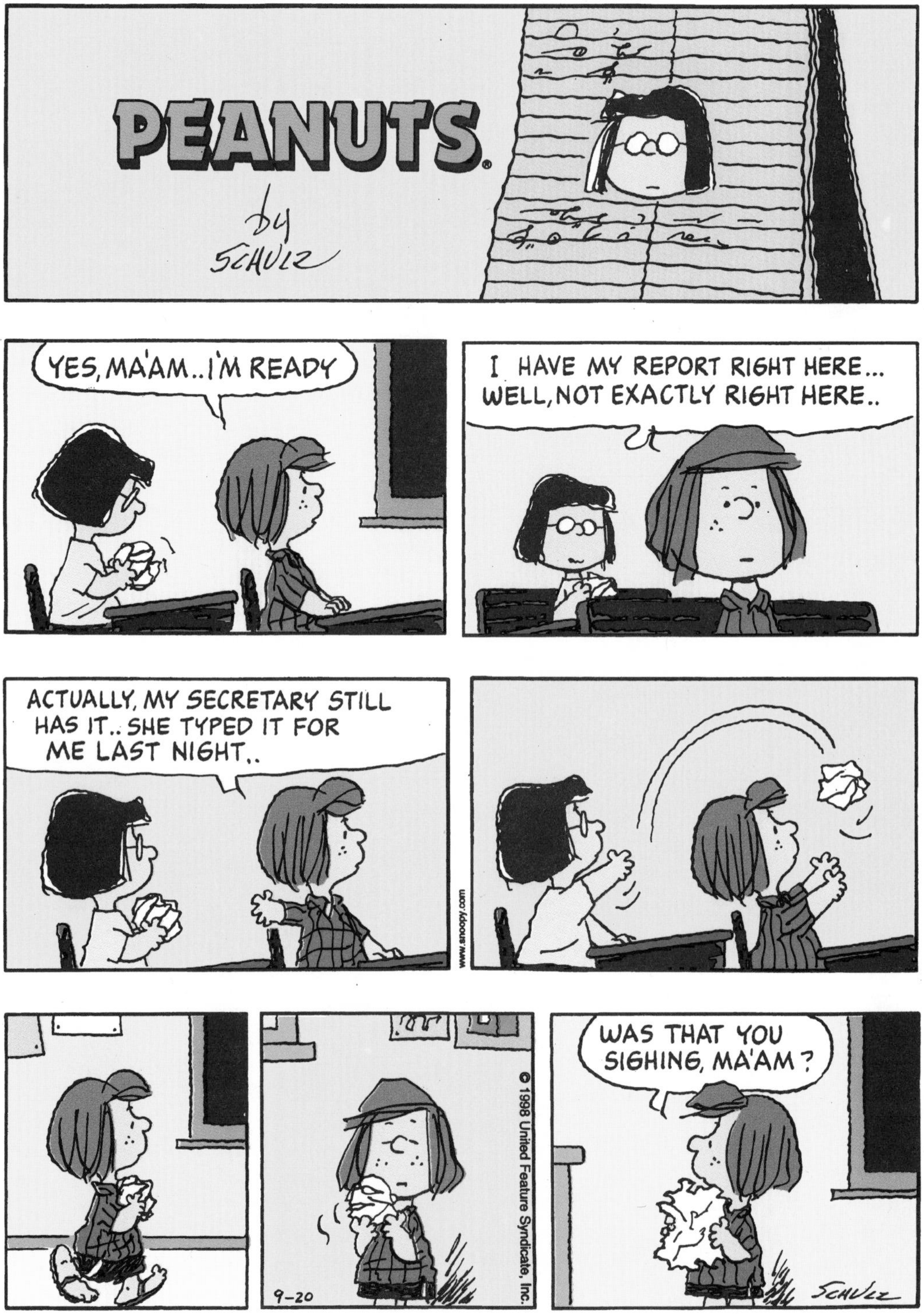
PEANUTS
by SCHULZ
YES, MA'AM.. I'M READY
I HAVE MY REPORT RIGHT HERE... WELL, NOT EXACTLY RIGHT HERE..
ACTUALLY, MY SECRETARY STILL HAS IT.. SHE TYPED IT FOR ME LAST NIGHT..
www.snoopy.com
© 1998 United Feature Syndicate, Inc.
9-20
WAS THAT YOU SIGHING, MA'AM ?
SCHULZ

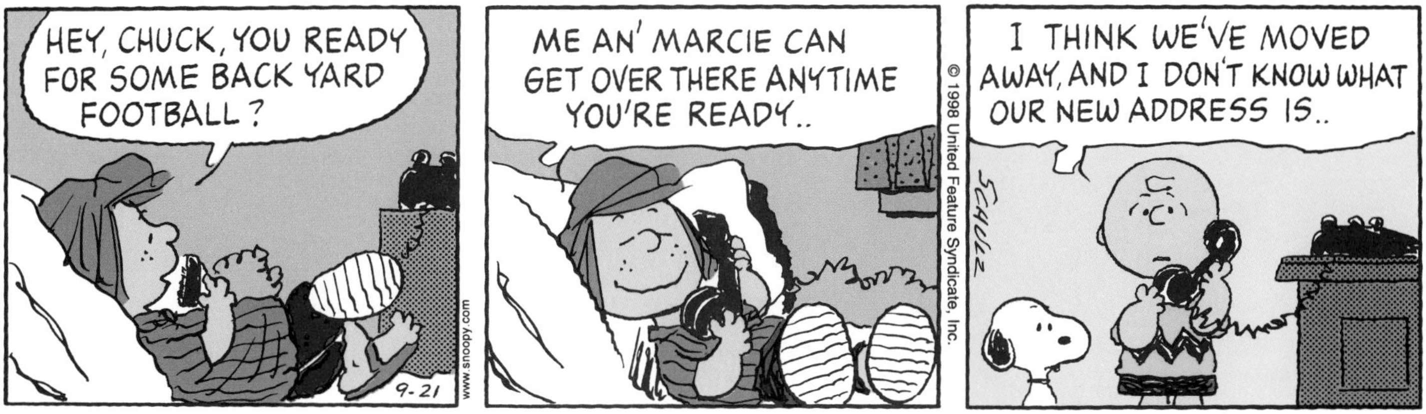
HEY, CHUCK, YOU READY FOR SOME BACK YARD FOOTBALL?
9-21
www.snoopy.com
ME AN' MARCIE CAN GET OVER THERE ANYTIME YOU'RE READY..
© 1998 United Feature Syndicate, Inc.
I THINK WE'VE MOVED AWAY, AND I DON'T KNOW WHAT OUR NEW ADDRESS IS..
SCHULZ

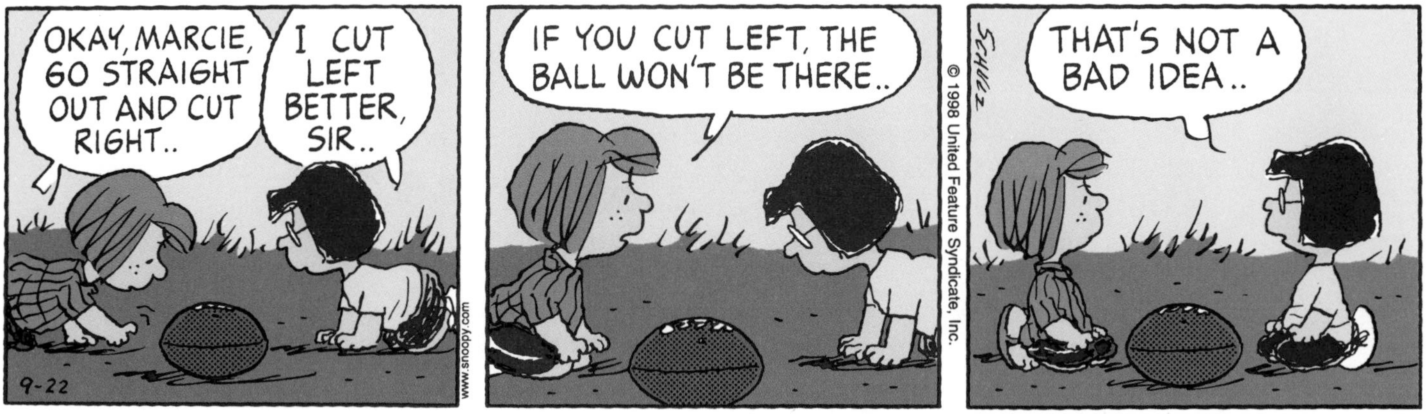
OKAY, MARCIE, GO STRAIGHT OUT AND CUT RIGHT..
I CUT LEFT BETTER, SIR..
9-22
www.snoopy.com
IF YOU CUT LEFT, THE BALL WON'T BE THERE..
© 1998 United Feature Syndicate, Inc.
SCHULZ
THAT'S NOT A BAD IDEA..

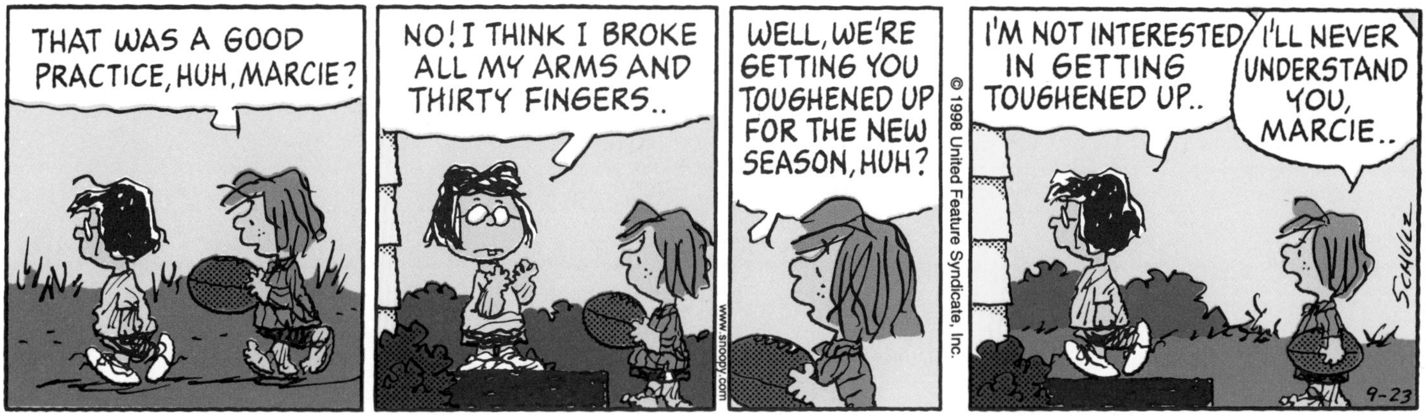
THAT WAS A GOOD PRACTICE, HUH, MARCIE?
NO! I THINK I BROKE ALL MY ARMS AND THIRTY FINGERS..
www.snoopy.com
WELL, WE'RE GETTING YOU TOUGHENED UP FOR THE NEW SEASON, HUH?
© 1998 United Feature Syndicate, Inc.
I'M NOT INTERESTED IN GETTING TOUGHENED UP..
I'LL NEVER UNDERSTAND YOU, MARCIE..
SCHULZ
9-23

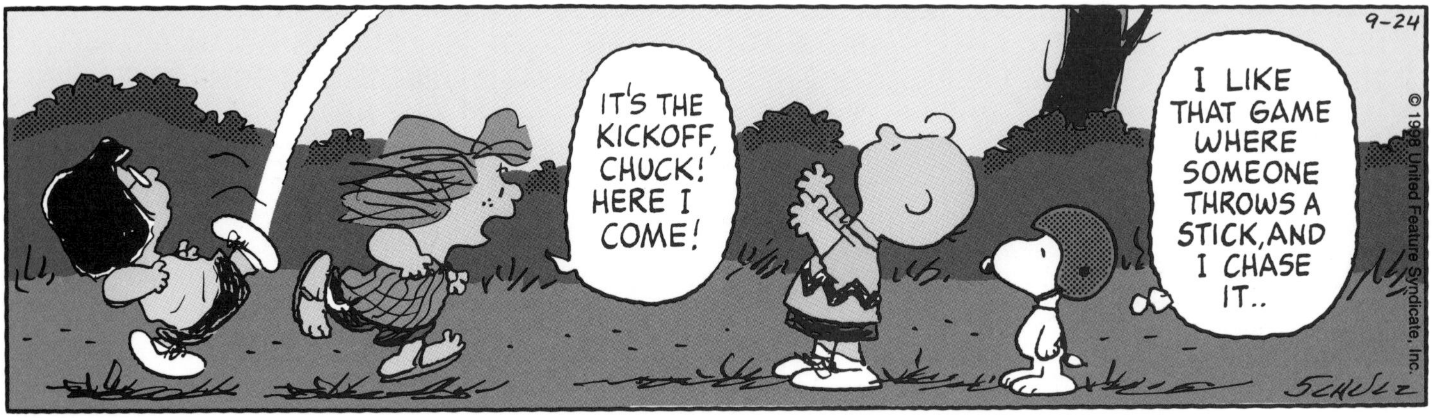
9-24
IT'S THE KICKOFF, CHUCK! HERE I COME!
I LIKE THAT GAME WHERE SOMEONE THROWS A STICK, AND I CHASE IT..
SCHULZ
© 1998 United Feature Syndicate, Inc.

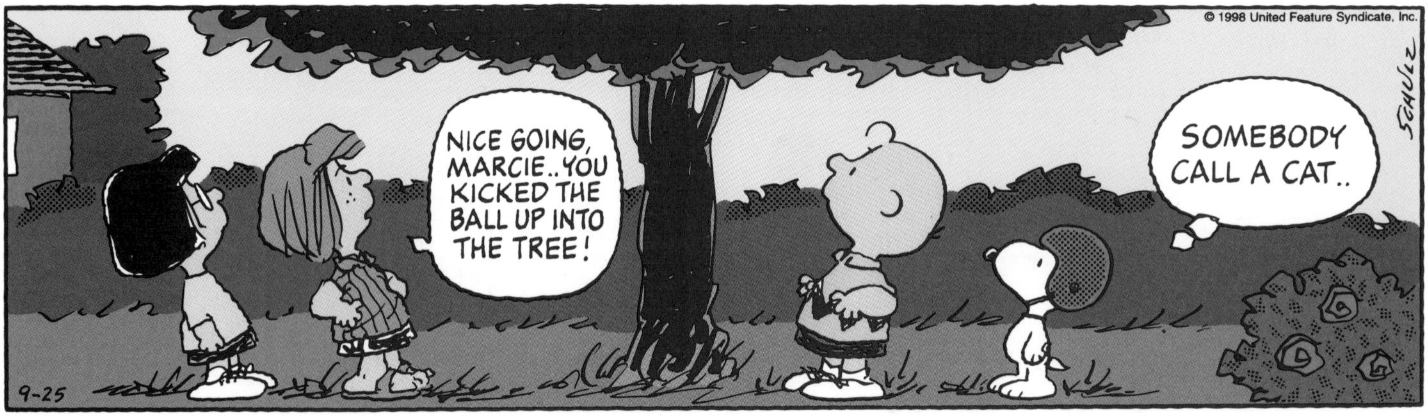
© 1998 United Feature Syndicate, Inc.
NICE GOING, MARCIE.. YOU KICKED THE BALL UP INTO THE TREE!
SOMEBODY CALL A CAT..
SCHULZ
9-25

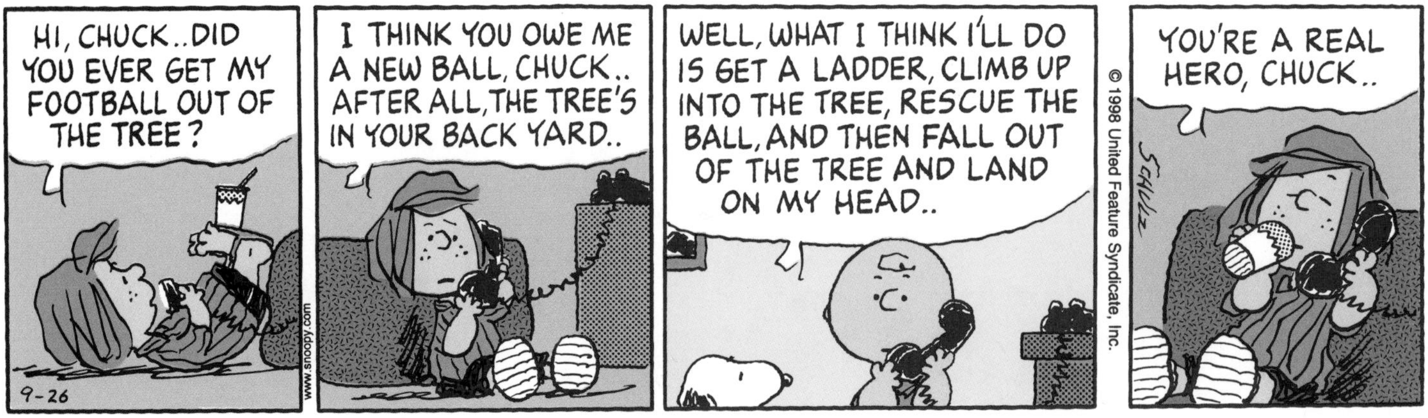
HI, CHUCK.. DID YOU EVER GET MY FOOTBALL OUT OF THE TREE?
9-26
www.snoopy.com
I THINK YOU OWE ME A NEW BALL, CHUCK.. AFTER ALL, THE TREE'S IN YOUR BACK YARD..
WELL, WHAT I THINK I'LL DO IS GET A LADDER, CLIMB UP INTO THE TREE, RESCUE THE BALL, AND THEN FALL OUT OF THE TREE AND LAND ON MY HEAD..
© 1998 United Feature Syndicate, Inc.
YOU'RE A REAL HERO, CHUCK..
SCHULZ

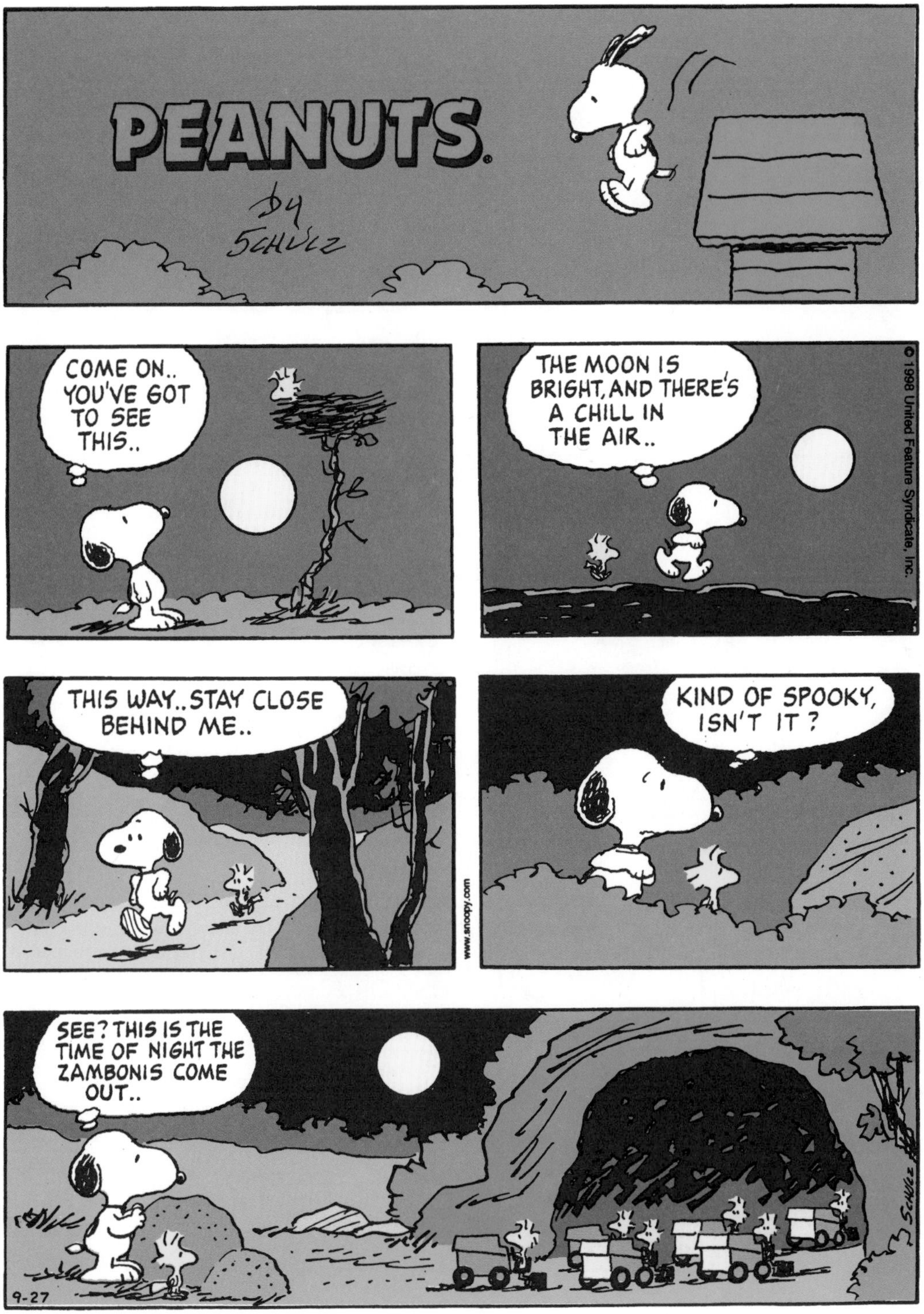
PEANUTS
by SCHULZ
COME ON.. YOU'VE GOT TO SEE THIS..
THE MOON IS BRIGHT, AND THERE'S A CHILL IN THE AIR..
© 1998 United Feature Syndicate, Inc.
THIS WAY..STAY CLOSE BEHIND ME..
www.snoopy.com
KIND OF SPOOKY, ISN'T IT?
SEE? THIS IS THE TIME OF NIGHT THE ZAMBONIS COME OUT..
9-27
SCHULZ

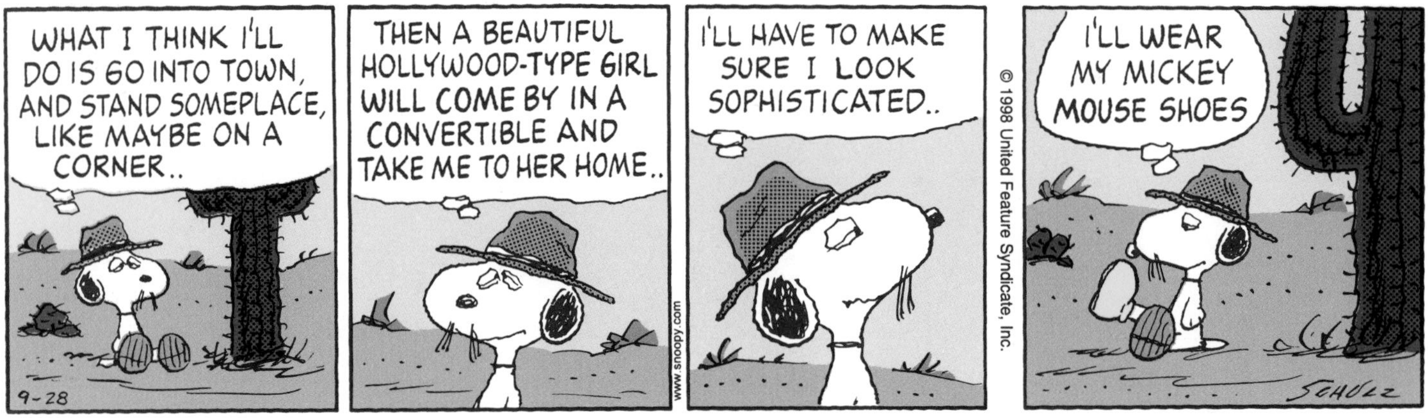
WHAT I THINK I'LL DO IS GO INTO TOWN, AND STAND SOMEPLACE, LIKE MAYBE ON A CORNER..
9-28
THEN A BEAUTIFUL HOLLYWOOD-TYPE GIRL WILL COME BY IN A CONVERTIBLE AND TAKE ME TO HER HOME..
www.snoopy.com
I'LL HAVE TO MAKE SURE I LOOK SOPHISTICATED..
© 1998 United Feature Syndicate, Inc.
I'LL WEAR MY MICKEY MOUSE SHOES
SCHULZ

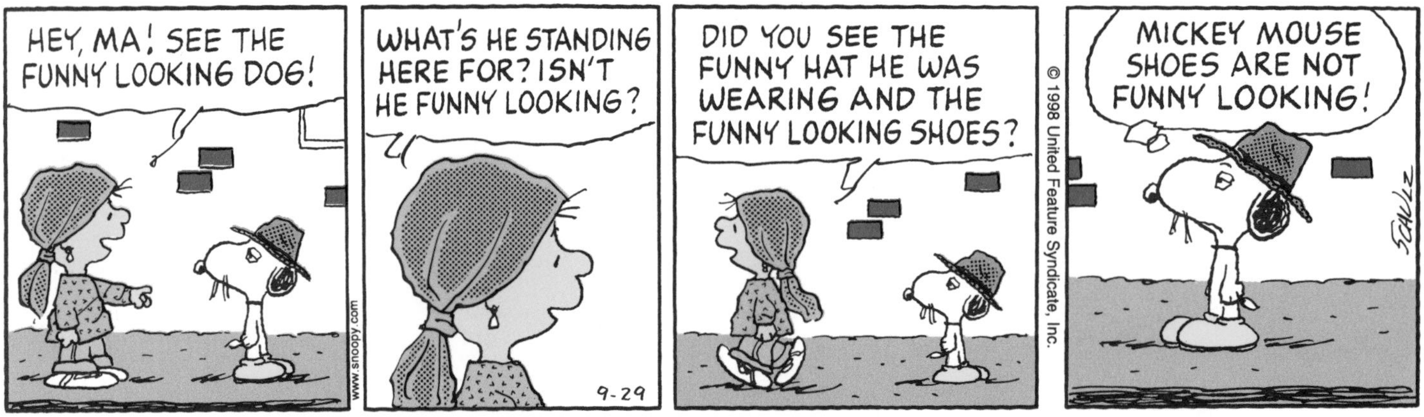
HEY, MA! SEE THE FUNNY LOOKING DOG!
www.snoopy.com
WHAT'S HE STANDING HERE FOR? ISN'T HE FUNNY LOOKING?
9-29
DID YOU SEE THE FUNNY HAT HE WAS WEARING AND THE FUNNY LOOKING SHOES?
© 1998 United Feature Syndicate, Inc.
MICKEY MOUSE SHOES ARE NOT FUNNY LOOKING!
SCHULZ

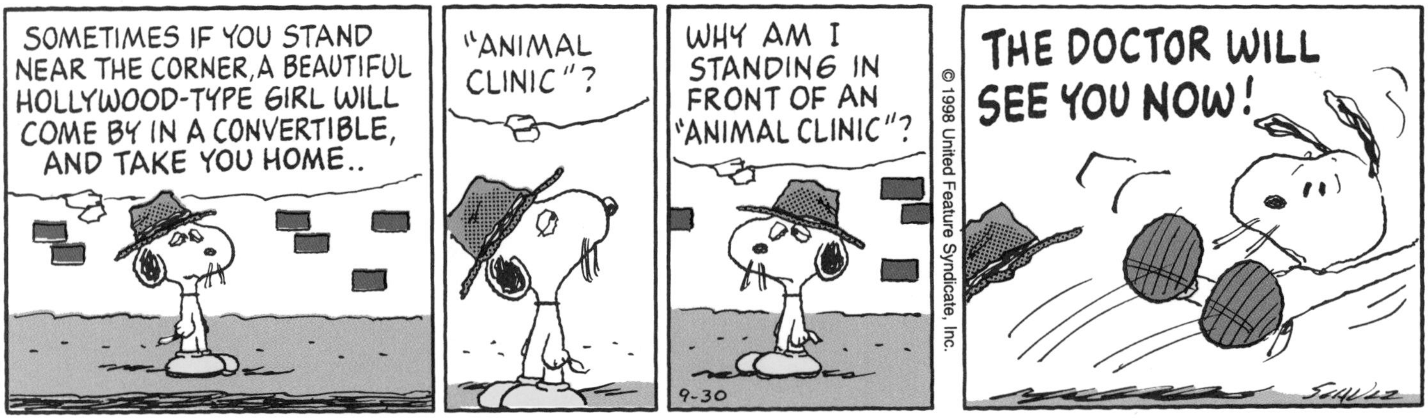
SOMETIMES IF YOU STAND NEAR THE CORNER, A BEAUTIFUL HOLLYWOOD-TYPE GIRL WILL COME BY IN A CONVERTIBLE, AND TAKE YOU HOME..
"ANIMAL CLINIC"?
WHY AM I STANDING IN FRONT OF AN "ANIMAL CLINIC"?
9-30
© 1998 United Feature Syndicate, Inc.
THE DOCTOR WILL SEE YOU NOW!
SCHULZ

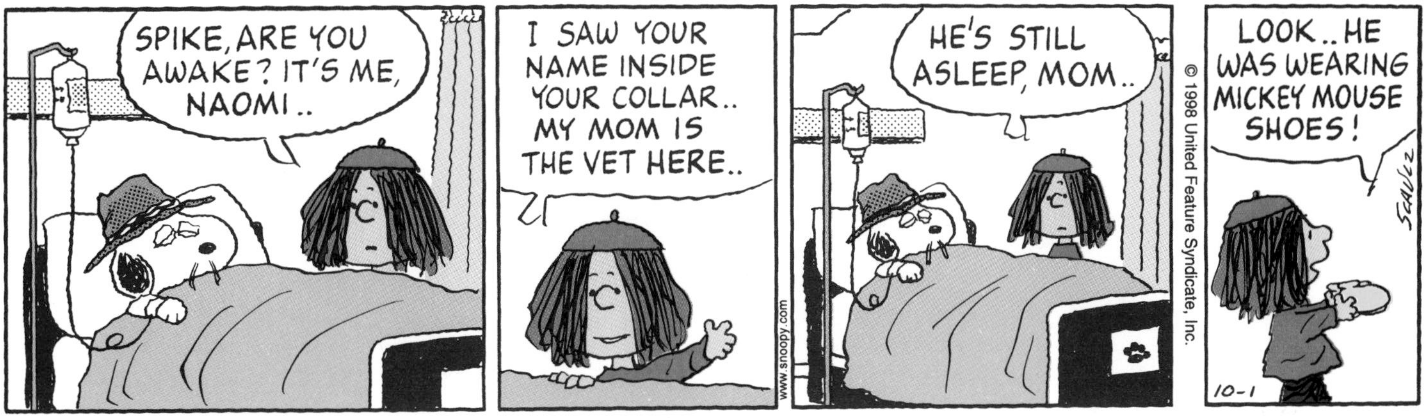
SPIKE, ARE YOU AWAKE? IT'S ME, NAOMI..
I SAW YOUR NAME INSIDE YOUR COLLAR.. MY MOM IS THE VET HERE..
www.snoopy.com
HE'S STILL ASLEEP, MOM..
© 1998 United Feature Syndicate, Inc.
LOOK.. HE WAS WEARING MICKEY MOUSE SHOES!
SCHULZ
10-1

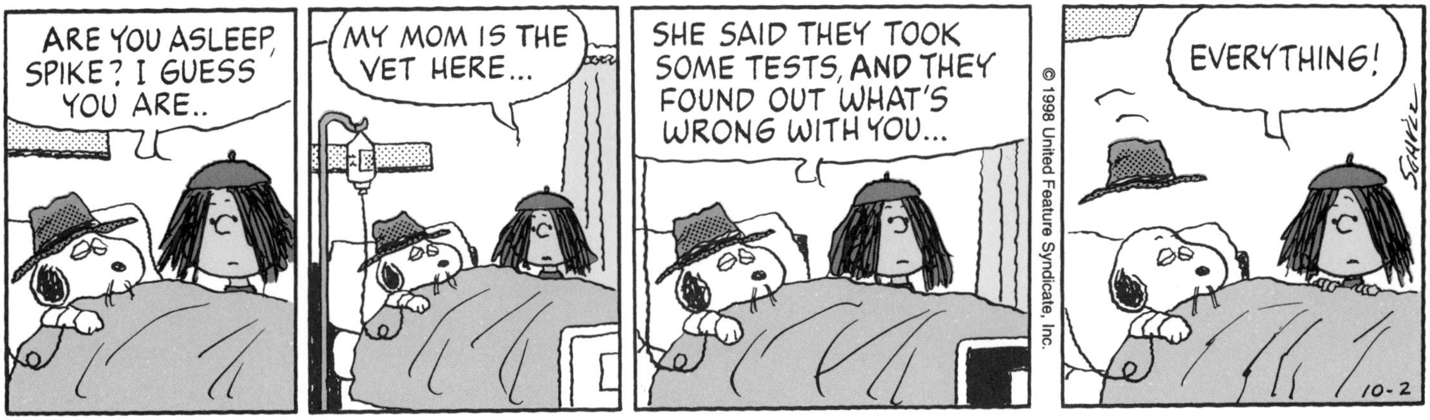
ARE YOU ASLEEP, SPIKE? I GUESS YOU ARE..
MY MOM IS THE VET HERE...
SHE SAID THEY TOOK SOME TESTS, AND THEY FOUND OUT WHAT'S WRONG WITH YOU...
© 1998 United Feature Syndicate, Inc.
EVERYTHING!
SCHULZ
10-2

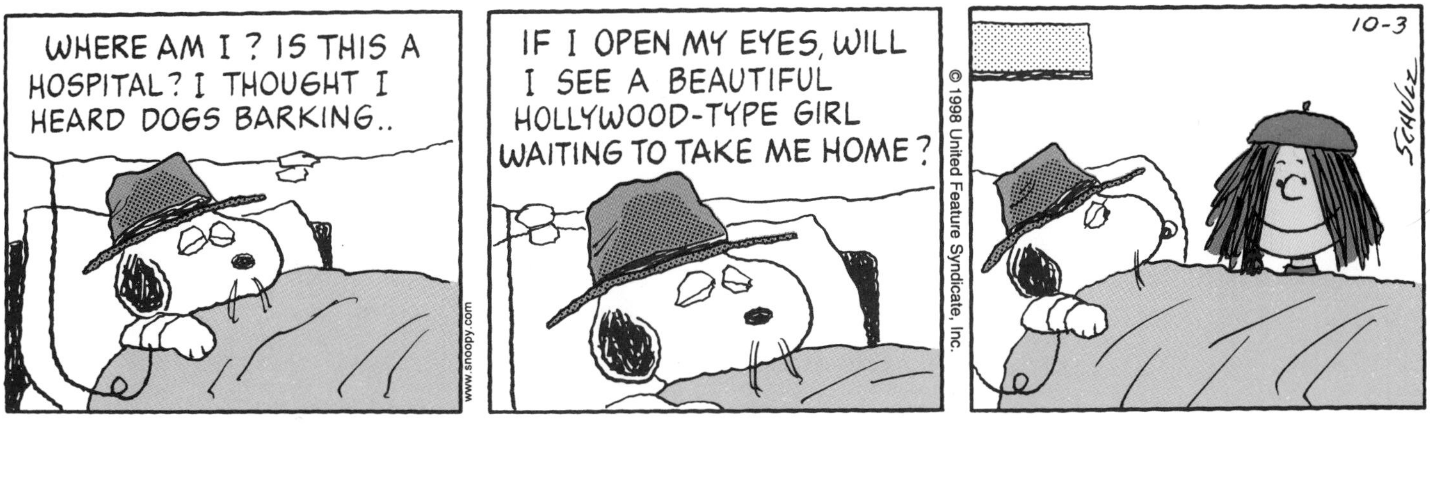
WHERE AM I? IS THIS A HOSPITAL? I THOUGHT I HEARD DOGS BARKING..
www.snoopy.com
IF I OPEN MY EYES, WILL I SEE A BEAUTIFUL HOLLYWOOD-TYPE GIRL WAITING TO TAKE ME HOME?
© 1998 United Feature Syndicate, Inc.
10-3
SCHULZ

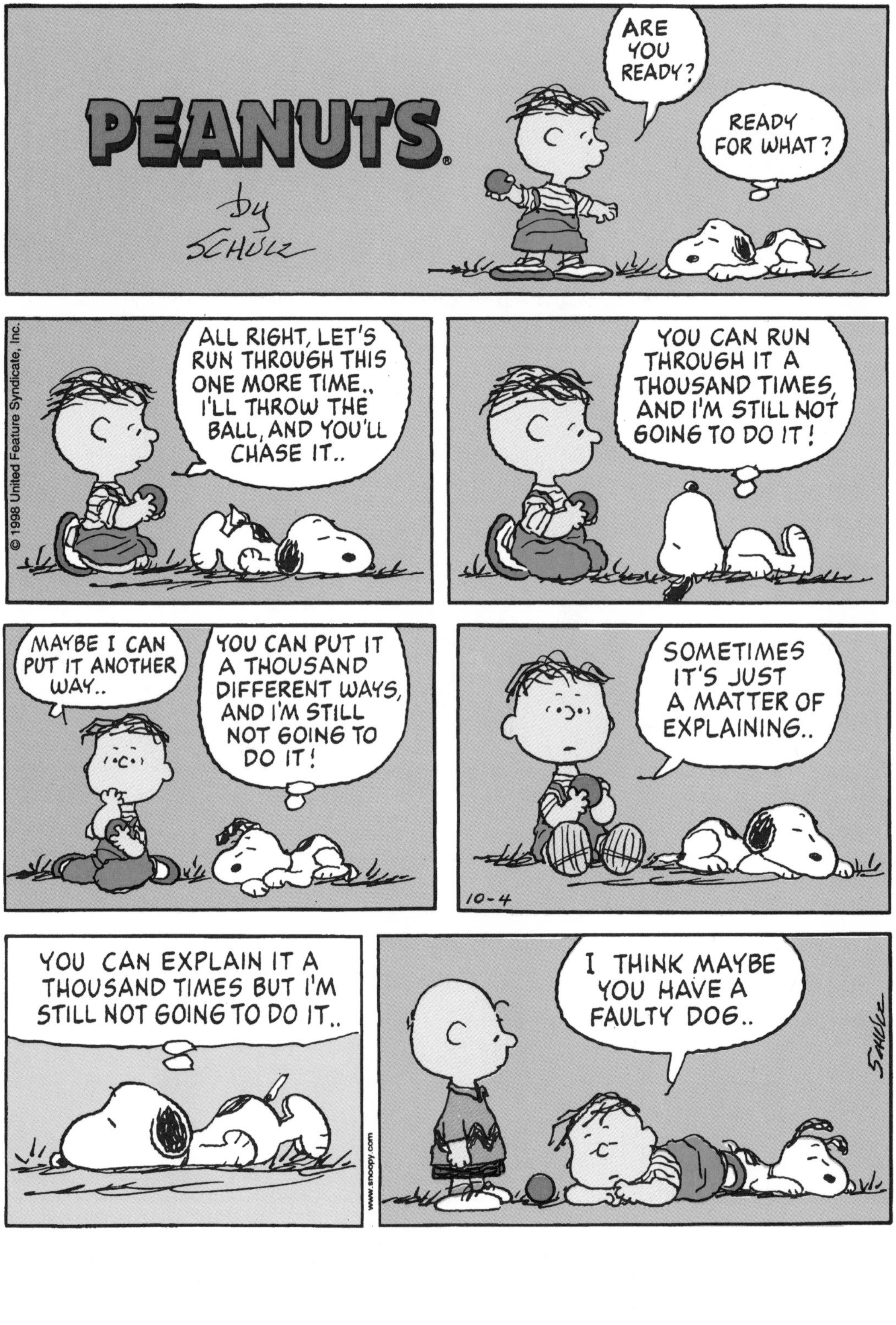
PEANUTS
by SCHULZ
ARE YOU READY?
READY FOR WHAT?
© 1998 United Feature Syndicate, Inc.
ALL RIGHT, LET'S RUN THROUGH THIS ONE MORE TIME.. I'LL THROW THE BALL, AND YOU'LL CHASE IT..
YOU CAN RUN THROUGH IT A THOUSAND TIMES, AND I'M STILL NOT GOING TO DO IT!
MAYBE I CAN PUT IT ANOTHER WAY..
YOU CAN PUT IT A THOUSAND DIFFERENT WAYS, AND I'M STILL NOT GOING TO DO IT!
SOMETIMES IT'S JUST A MATTER OF EXPLAINING..
10-4
YOU CAN EXPLAIN IT A THOUSAND TIMES BUT I'M STILL NOT GOING TO DO IT..
www.snoopy.com
I THINK MAYBE YOU HAVE A FAULTY DOG..
SCHULZ

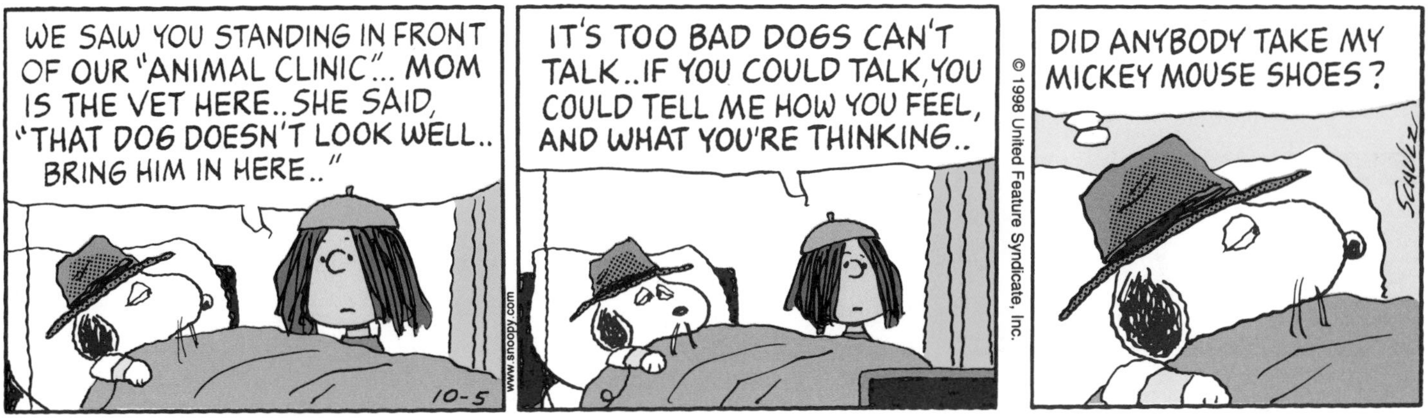
WE SAW YOU STANDING IN FRONT OF OUR "ANIMAL CLINIC"... MOM IS THE VET HERE..SHE SAID, "THAT DOG DOESN'T LOOK WELL.. BRING HIM IN HERE.."
10-5
www.snoopy.com
IT'S TOO BAD DOGS CAN'T TALK..IF YOU COULD TALK, YOU COULD TELL ME HOW YOU FEEL, AND WHAT YOU'RE THINKING..
© 1998 United Feature Syndicate, Inc.
DID ANYBODY TAKE MY MICKEY MOUSE SHOES?
SCHULZ

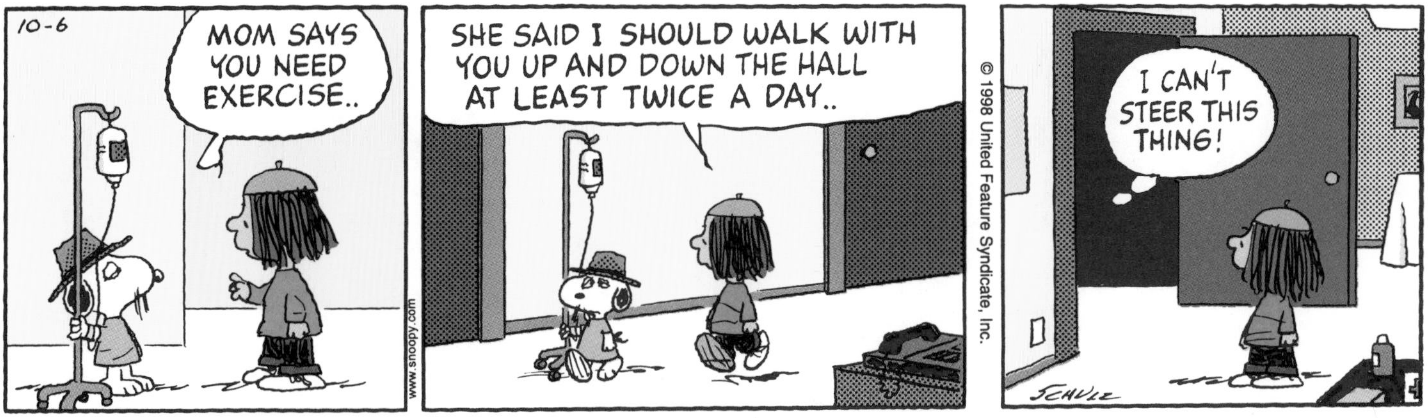
10-6
MOM SAYS YOU NEED EXERCISE..
www.snoopy.com
SHE SAID I SHOULD WALK WITH YOU UP AND DOWN THE HALL AT LEAST TWICE A DAY..
© 1998 United Feature Syndicate, Inc.
I CAN'T STEER THIS THING!
SCHULZ

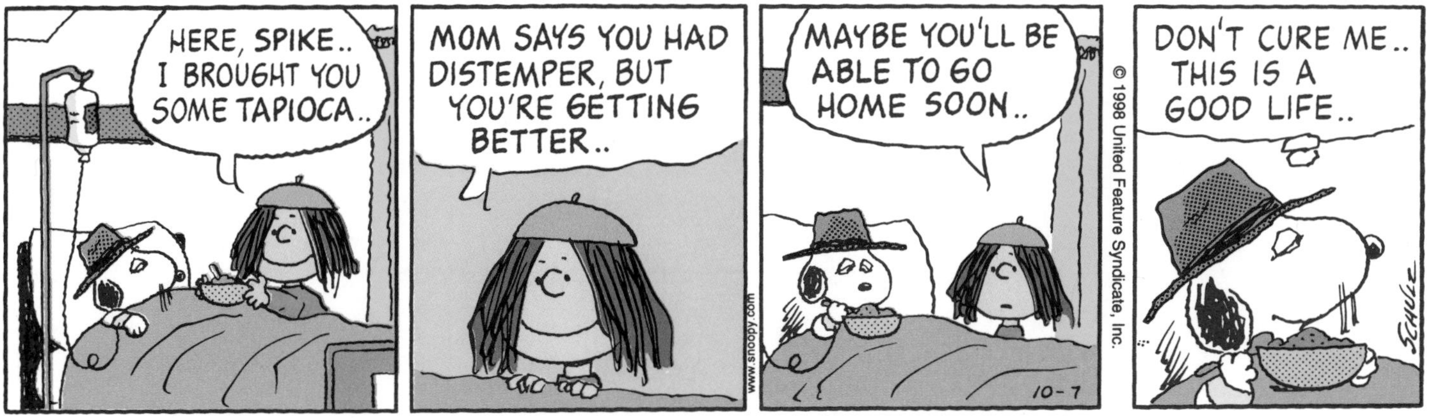
HERE, SPIKE.. I BROUGHT YOU SOME TAPIOCA..
MOM SAYS YOU HAD DISTEMPER, BUT YOU'RE GETTING BETTER..
www.snoopy.com
MAYBE YOU'LL BE ABLE TO GO HOME SOON..
10-7
© 1998 United Feature Syndicate, Inc.
DON'T CURE ME.. THIS IS A GOOD LIFE..
SCHULZ

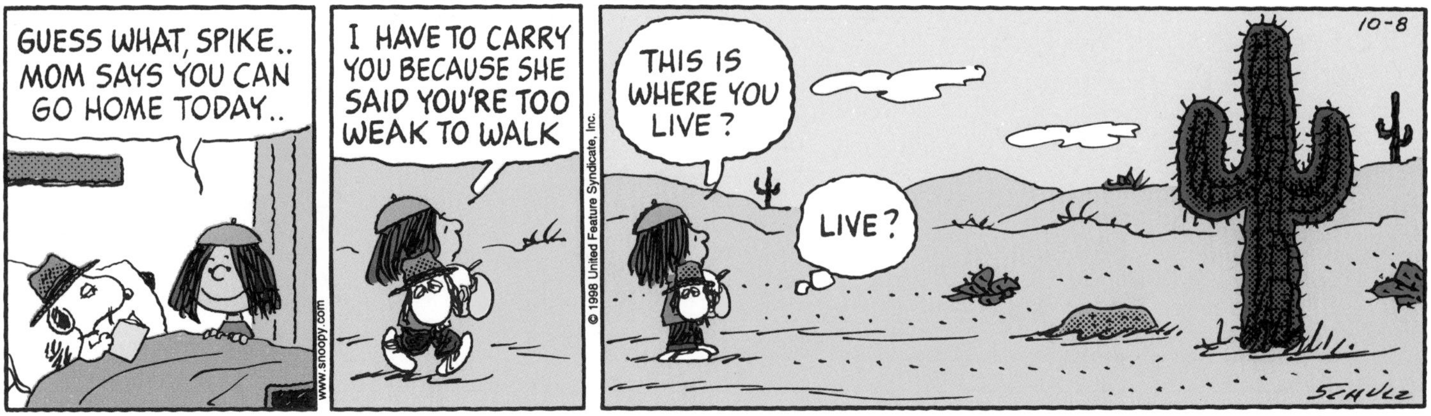
GUESS WHAT, SPIKE.. MOM SAYS YOU CAN GO HOME TODAY..
www.snoopy.com
I HAVE TO CARRY YOU BECAUSE SHE SAID YOU'RE TOO WEAK TO WALK
© 1998 United Feature Syndicate, Inc.
10-8
THIS IS WHERE YOU LIVE ?
LIVE ?
SCHULZ

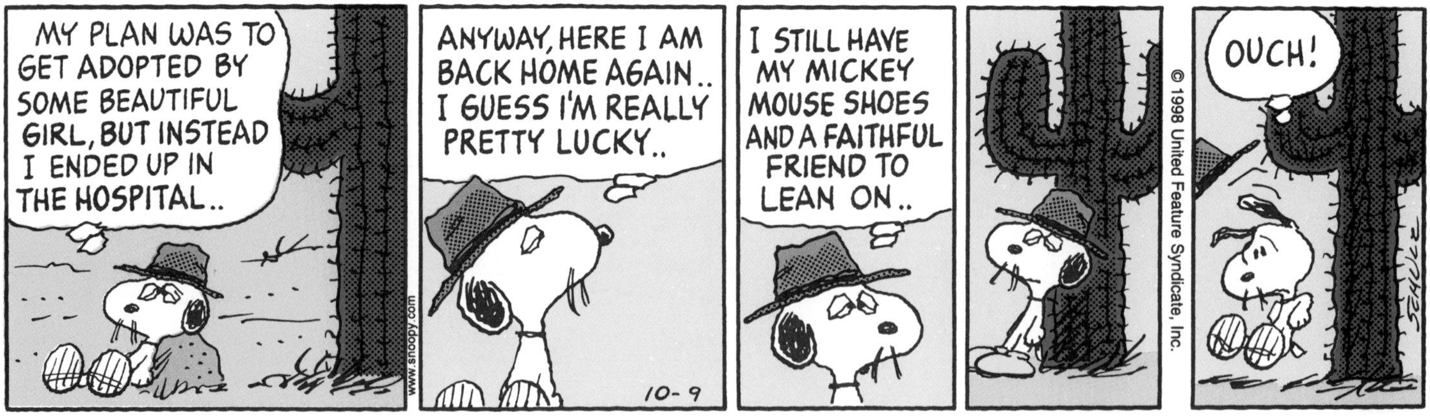
MY PLAN WAS TO GET ADOPTED BY SOME BEAUTIFUL GIRL, BUT INSTEAD I ENDED UP IN THE HOSPITAL..
www.snoopy.com
ANYWAY, HERE I AM BACK HOME AGAIN.. I GUESS I'M REALLY PRETTY LUCKY..
10-9
I STILL HAVE MY MICKEY MOUSE SHOES AND A FAITHFUL FRIEND TO LEAN ON..
© 1998 United Feature Syndicate, Inc.
OUCH!
SCHULZ

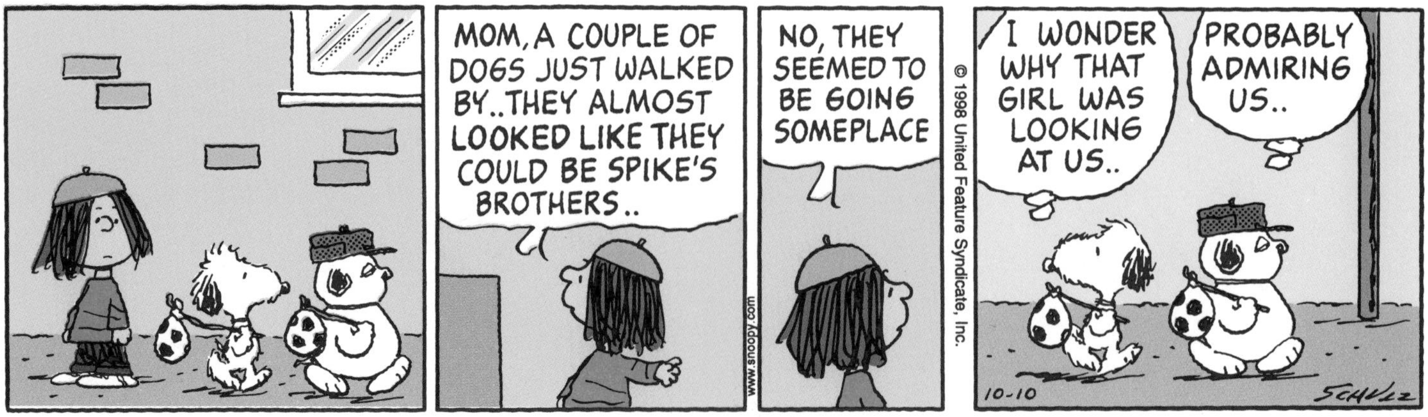
MOM, A COUPLE OF DOGS JUST WALKED BY.. THEY ALMOST LOOKED LIKE THEY COULD BE SPIKE'S BROTHERS..
www.snoopy.com
NO, THEY SEEMED TO BE GOING SOMEPLACE
© 1998 United Feature Syndicate, Inc.
I WONDER WHY THAT GIRL WAS LOOKING AT US..
PROBABLY ADMIRING US..
10-10
SCHULZ

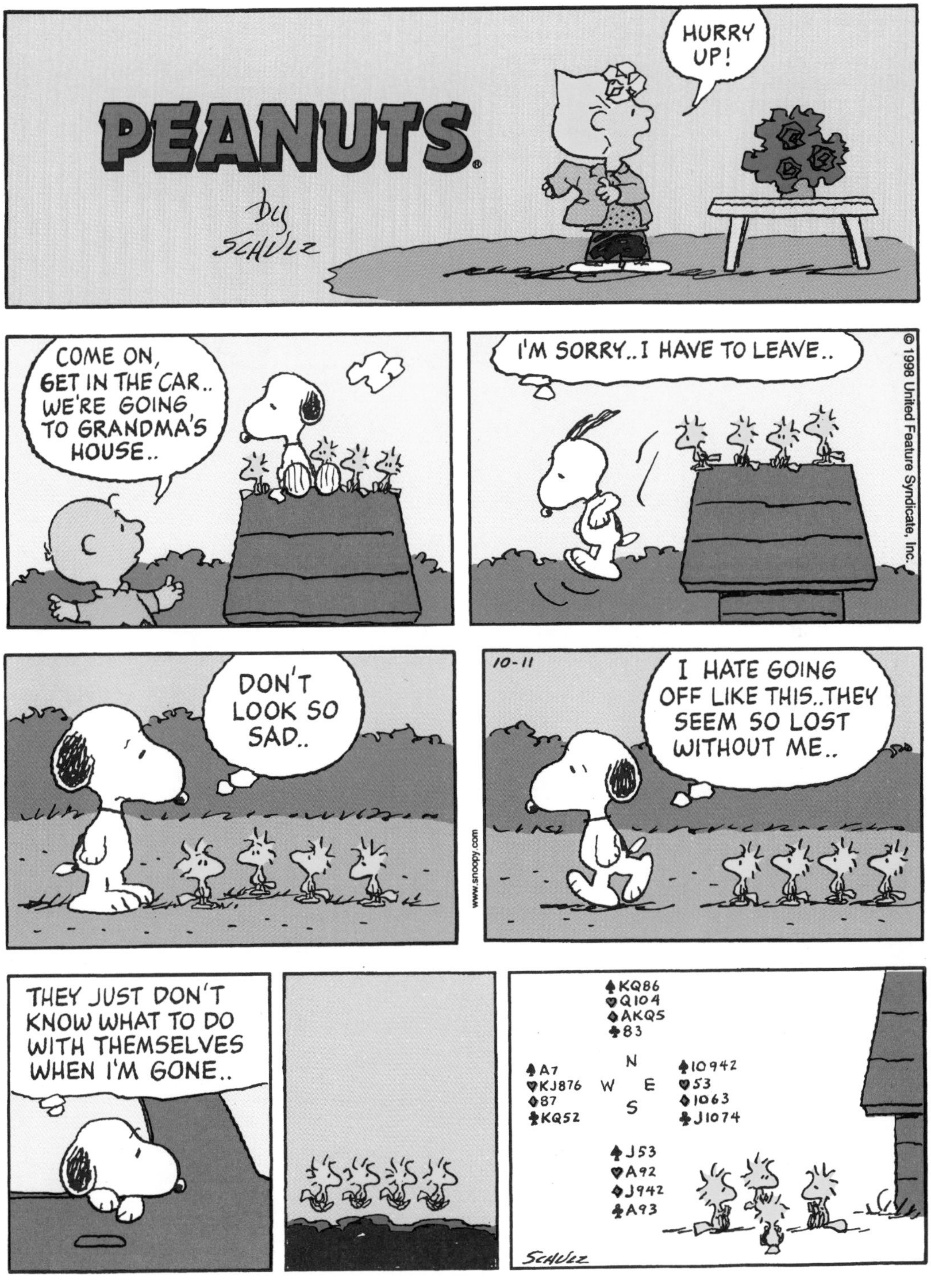

PEANUTS
by SCHULZ
HURRY UP!
COME ON, GET IN THE CAR.. WE'RE GOING TO GRANDMA'S HOUSE..
I'M SORRY.. I HAVE TO LEAVE..
© 1998 United Feature Syndicate, Inc.
DON'T LOOK SO SAD..
www.snoopy.com
10-11
I HATE GOING OFF LIKE THIS..THEY SEEM SO LOST WITHOUT ME..
THEY JUST DON'T KNOW WHAT TO DO WITH THEMSELVES WHEN I'M GONE..
♠KQ86
♥Q104
♦AKQ5
♣83
N
W E
S
♠A7
♥KJ876
♦87
♣KQ52
♠10942
♥53
♦1063
♣J1074
♠J53
♥A92
♦J942
♣A93
SCHULZ

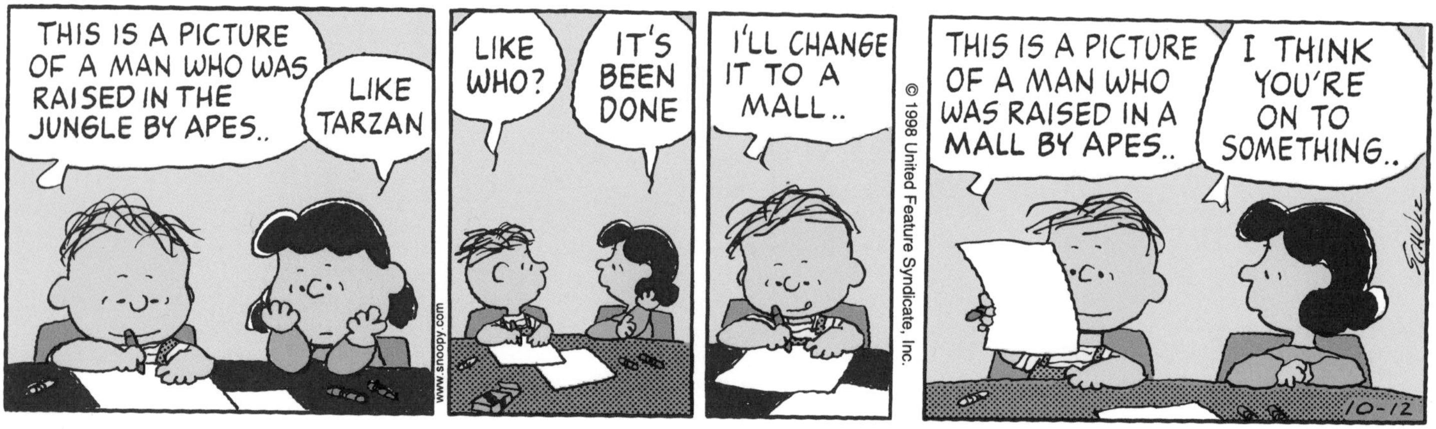
THIS IS A PICTURE OF A MAN WHO WAS RAISED IN THE JUNGLE BY APES..
LIKE TARZAN
LIKE WHO?
IT'S BEEN DONE
I'LL CHANGE IT TO A MALL..
THIS IS A PICTURE OF A MAN WHO WAS RAISED IN A MALL BY APES..
I THINK YOU'RE ON TO SOMETHING..
www.snoopy.com
© 1998 United Feature Syndicate, Inc.
SCHULZ
10-12

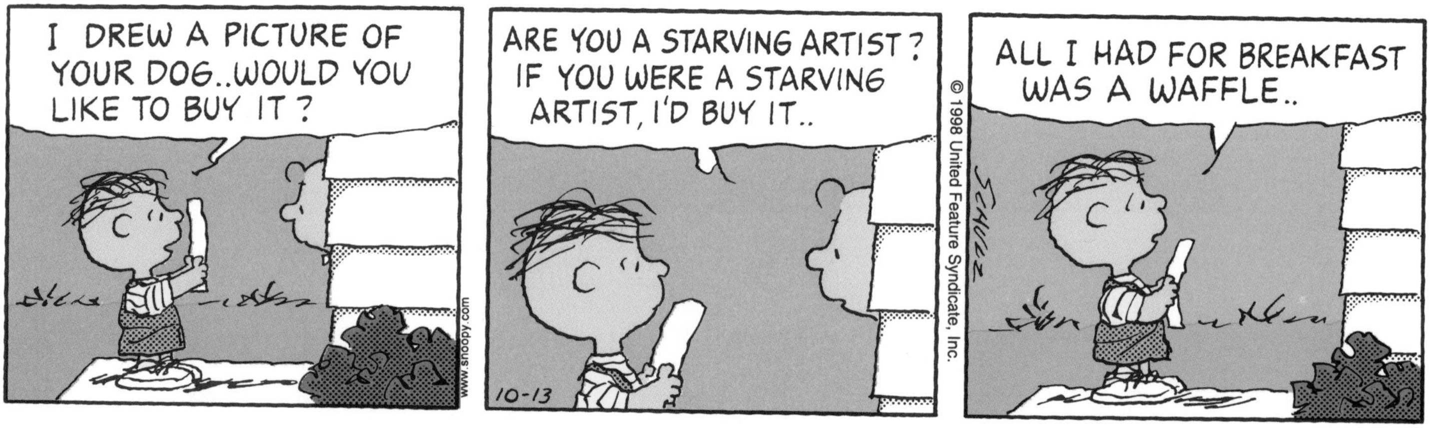
I DREW A PICTURE OF YOUR DOG..WOULD YOU LIKE TO BUY IT?
ARE YOU A STARVING ARTIST? IF YOU WERE A STARVING ARTIST, I'D BUY IT..
ALL I HAD FOR BREAKFAST WAS A WAFFLE..
www.snoopy.com
10-13
© 1998 United Feature Syndicate, Inc.
SCHULZ

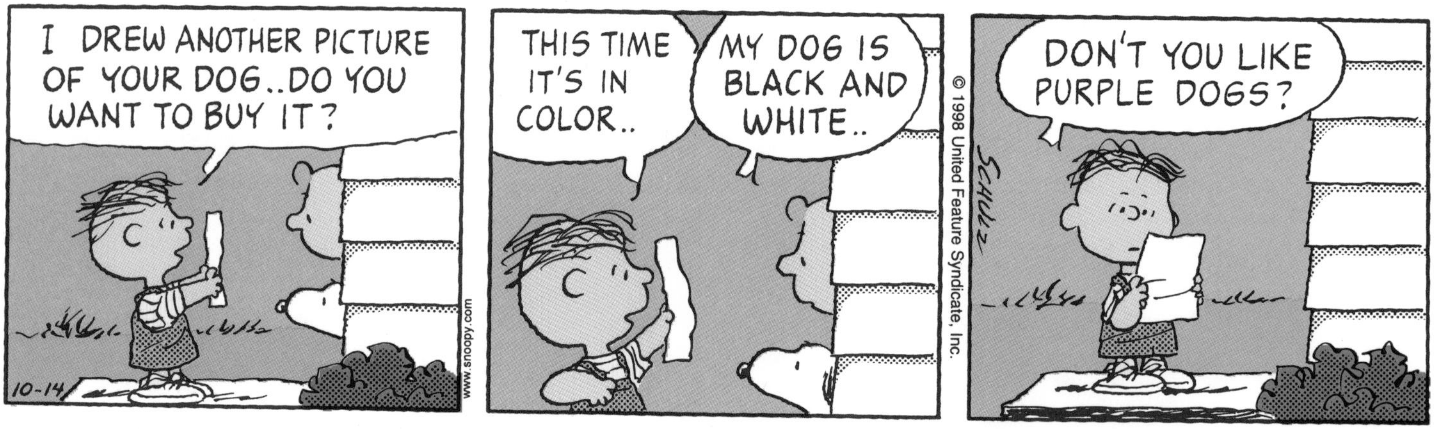
I DREW ANOTHER PICTURE OF YOUR DOG..DO YOU WANT TO BUY IT?
THIS TIME IT'S IN COLOR..
MY DOG IS BLACK AND WHITE..
DON'T YOU LIKE PURPLE DOGS?
10-14
www.snoopy.com
© 1998 United Feature Syndicate, Inc.
SCHULZ

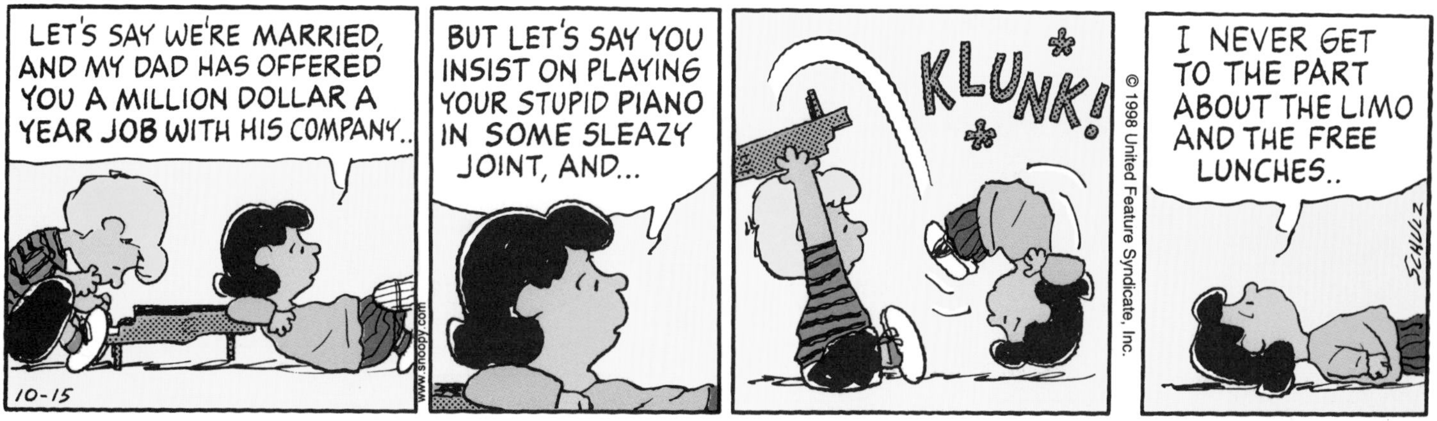
LET'S SAY WE'RE MARRIED, AND MY DAD HAS OFFERED YOU A MILLION DOLLAR A YEAR JOB WITH HIS COMPANY..
10-15
www.snoopy.com
BUT LET'S SAY YOU INSIST ON PLAYING YOUR STUPID PIANO IN SOME SLEAZY JOINT, AND...
KLUNK!
© 1998 United Feature Syndicate, Inc.
I NEVER GET TO THE PART ABOUT THE LIMO AND THE FREE LUNCHES..
SCHULZ

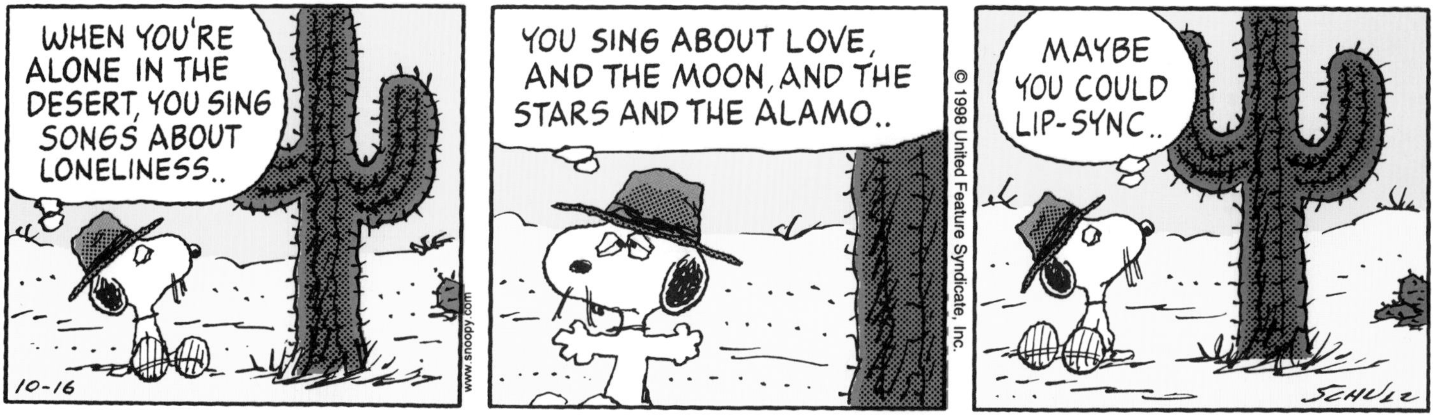
WHEN YOU'RE ALONE IN THE DESERT, YOU SING SONGS ABOUT LONELINESS..
10-16
www.snoopy.com
YOU SING ABOUT LOVE, AND THE MOON, AND THE STARS AND THE ALAMO..
© 1998 United Feature Syndicate, Inc.
MAYBE YOU COULD LIP-SYNC..
SCHULZ

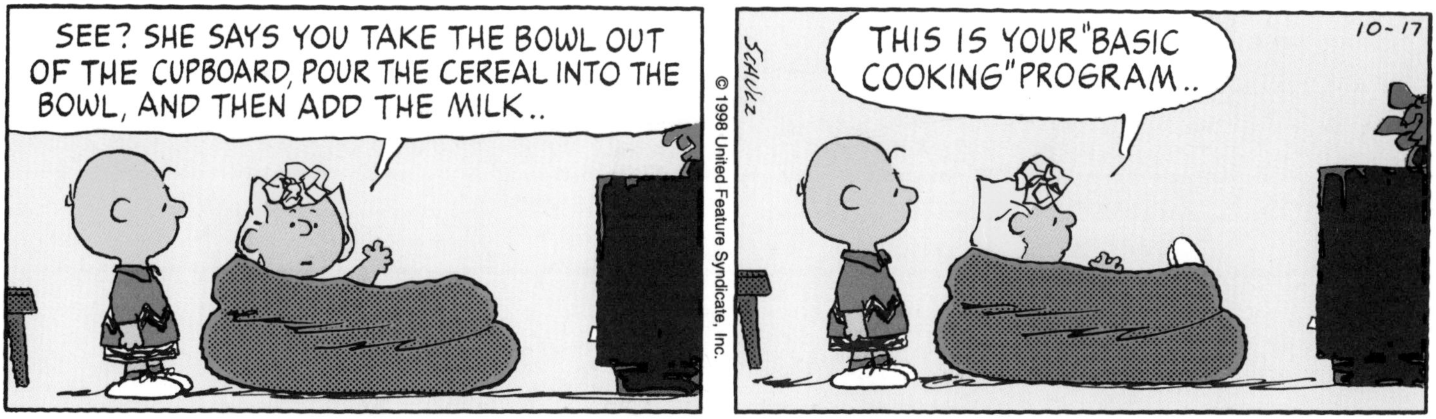
SEE? SHE SAYS YOU TAKE THE BOWL OUT OF THE CUPBOARD, POUR THE CEREAL INTO THE BOWL, AND THEN ADD THE MILK..
© 1998 United Feature Syndicate, Inc.
SCHULZ
THIS IS YOUR "BASIC COOKING" PROGRAM..
10-17

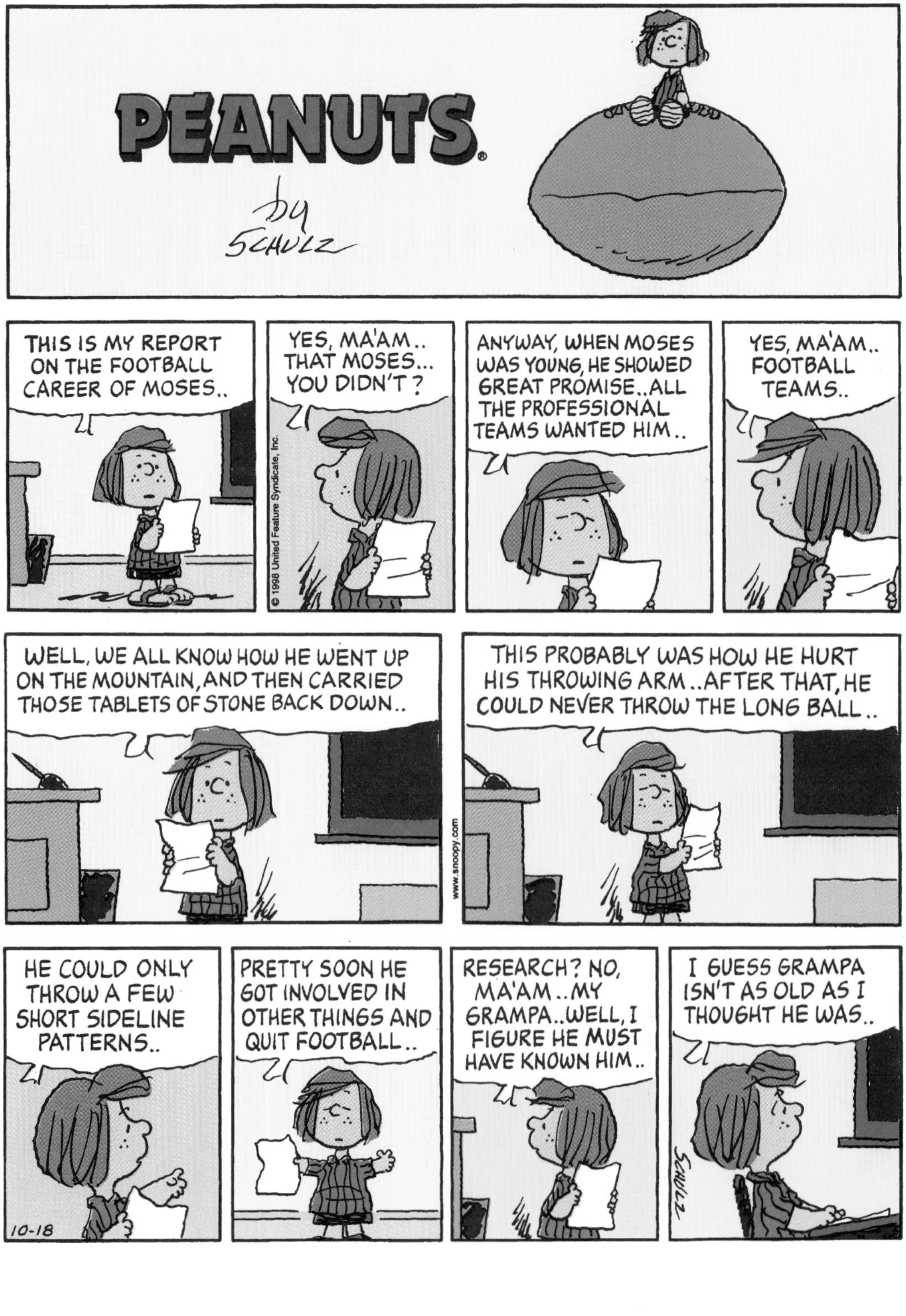

PEANUTS
by SCHULZ
THIS IS MY REPORT ON THE FOOTBALL CAREER OF MOSES..
YES, MA'AM.. THAT MOSES... YOU DIDN'T ?
ANYWAY, WHEN MOSES WAS YOUNG, HE SHOWED GREAT PROMISE..ALL THE PROFESSIONAL TEAMS WANTED HIM..
YES, MA'AM.. FOOTBALL TEAMS..
WELL, WE ALL KNOW HOW HE WENT UP ON THE MOUNTAIN, AND THEN CARRIED THOSE TABLETS OF STONE BACK DOWN..
THIS PROBABLY WAS HOW HE HURT HIS THROWING ARM..AFTER THAT, HE COULD NEVER THROW THE LONG BALL..
HE COULD ONLY THROW A FEW SHORT SIDELINE PATTERNS..
PRETTY SOON HE GOT INVOLVED IN OTHER THINGS AND QUIT FOOTBALL..
RESEARCH? NO, MA'AM..MY GRAMPA..WELL, I FIGURE HE MUST HAVE KNOWN HIM..
I GUESS GRAMPA ISN'T AS OLD AS I THOUGHT HE WAS..
© 1998 United Feature Syndicate, Inc.
www.snoopy.com
10-18
SCHULZ

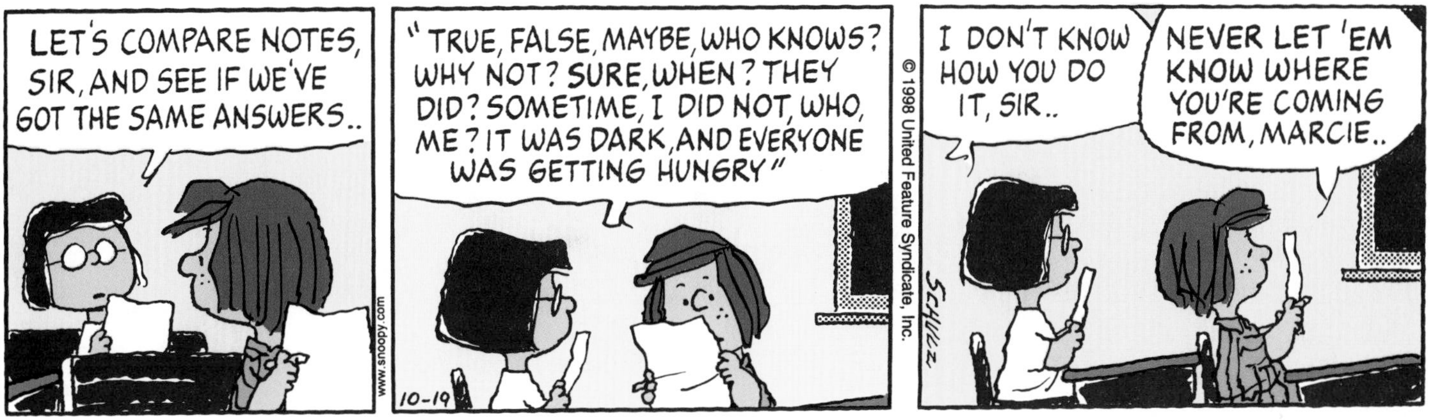
LET'S COMPARE NOTES, SIR, AND SEE IF WE'VE GOT THE SAME ANSWERS..
"TRUE, FALSE, MAYBE, WHO KNOWS? WHY NOT? SURE, WHEN? THEY DID? SOMETIME, I DID NOT, WHO, ME? IT WAS DARK, AND EVERYONE WAS GETTING HUNGRY"
I DON'T KNOW HOW YOU DO IT, SIR..
NEVER LET 'EM KNOW WHERE YOU'RE COMING FROM, MARCIE..
www.snoopy.com
10-19
© 1998 United Feature Syndicate, Inc.
SCHULZ

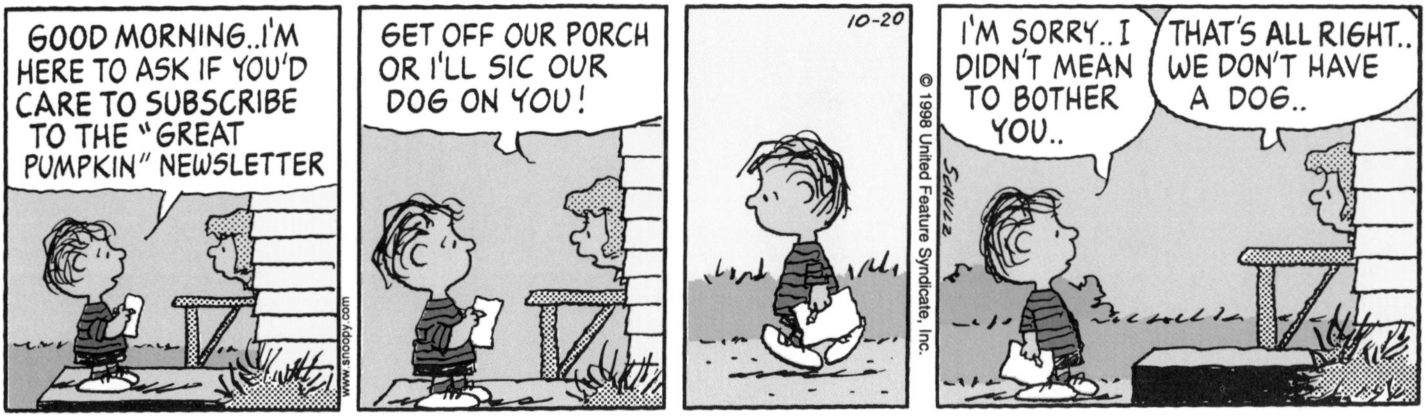
GOOD MORNING..I'M HERE TO ASK IF YOU'D CARE TO SUBSCRIBE TO THE "GREAT PUMPKIN" NEWSLETTER
GET OFF OUR PORCH OR I'LL SIC OUR DOG ON YOU!
I'M SORRY.. I DIDN'T MEAN TO BOTHER YOU..
THAT'S ALL RIGHT.. WE DON'T HAVE A DOG..
www.snoopy.com
10-20
© 1998 United Feature Syndicate, Inc.
SCHULZ

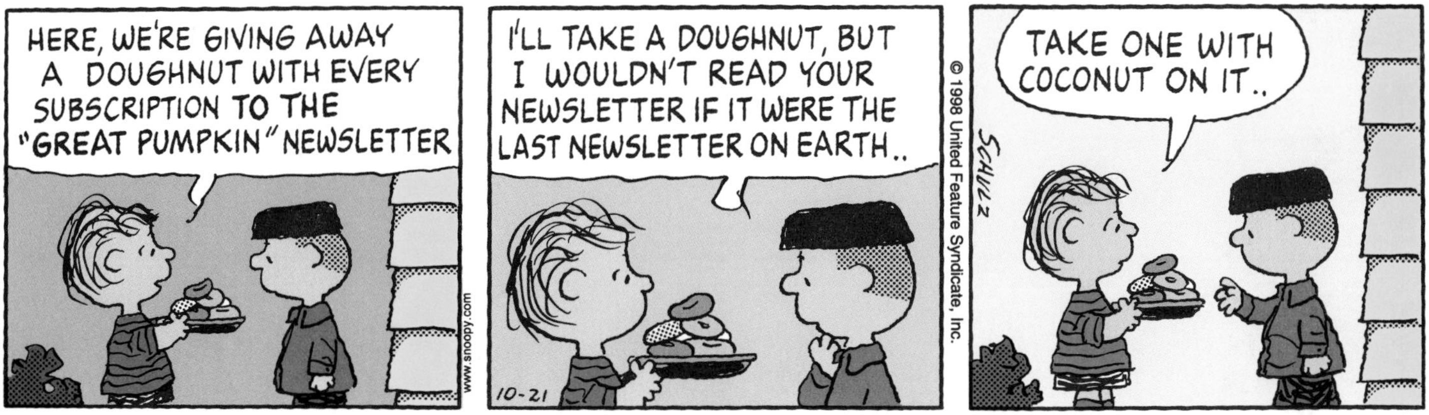
HERE, WE'RE GIVING AWAY A DOUGHNUT WITH EVERY SUBSCRIPTION TO THE "GREAT PUMPKIN" NEWSLETTER
I'LL TAKE A DOUGHNUT, BUT I WOULDN'T READ YOUR NEWSLETTER IF IT WERE THE LAST NEWSLETTER ON EARTH..
TAKE ONE WITH COCONUT ON IT..
www.snoopy.com
10-21
© 1998 United Feature Syndicate, Inc.
SCHULZ

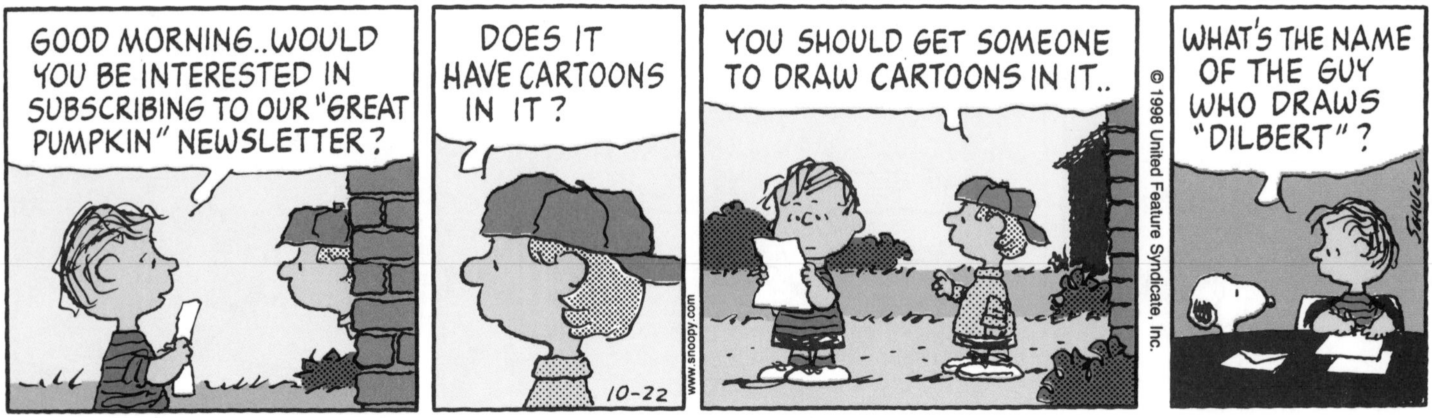
GOOD MORNING..WOULD YOU BE INTERESTED IN SUBSCRIBING TO OUR "GREAT PUMPKIN" NEWSLETTER?
DOES IT HAVE CARTOONS IN IT?
10-22
www.snoopy.com
YOU SHOULD GET SOMEONE TO DRAW CARTOONS IN IT..
© 1998 United Feature Syndicate, Inc.
WHAT'S THE NAME OF THE GUY WHO DRAWS "DILBERT"?
SCHULZ

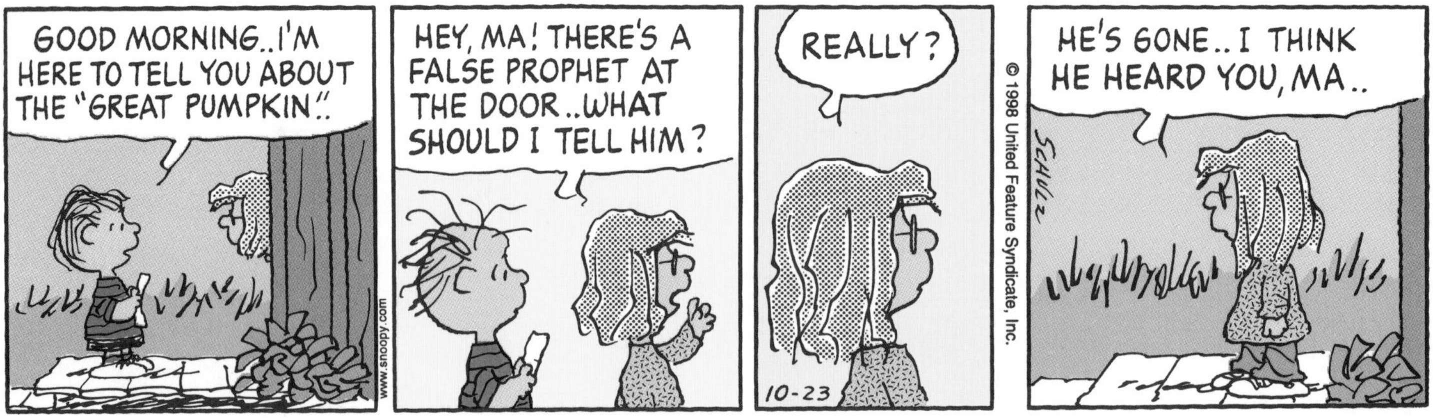
GOOD MORNING..I'M HERE TO TELL YOU ABOUT THE "GREAT PUMPKIN"..
www.snoopy.com
HEY, MA! THERE'S A FALSE PROPHET AT THE DOOR..WHAT SHOULD I TELL HIM?
REALLY?
SCHULZ
10-23
© 1998 United Feature Syndicate, Inc.
HE'S GONE..I THINK HE HEARD YOU, MA..

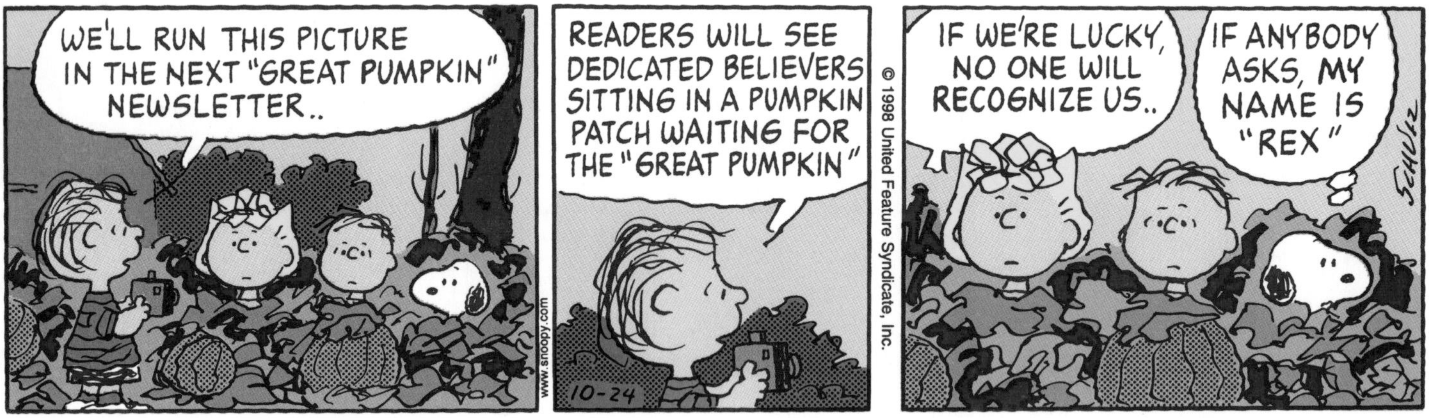
WE'LL RUN THIS PICTURE IN THE NEXT "GREAT PUMPKIN" NEWSLETTER..
www.snoopy.com
READERS WILL SEE DEDICATED BELIEVERS SITTING IN A PUMPKIN PATCH WAITING FOR THE "GREAT PUMPKIN"
10-24
© 1998 United Feature Syndicate, Inc.
IF WE'RE LUCKY, NO ONE WILL RECOGNIZE US..
IF ANYBODY ASKS, MY NAME IS "REX"
SCHULZ

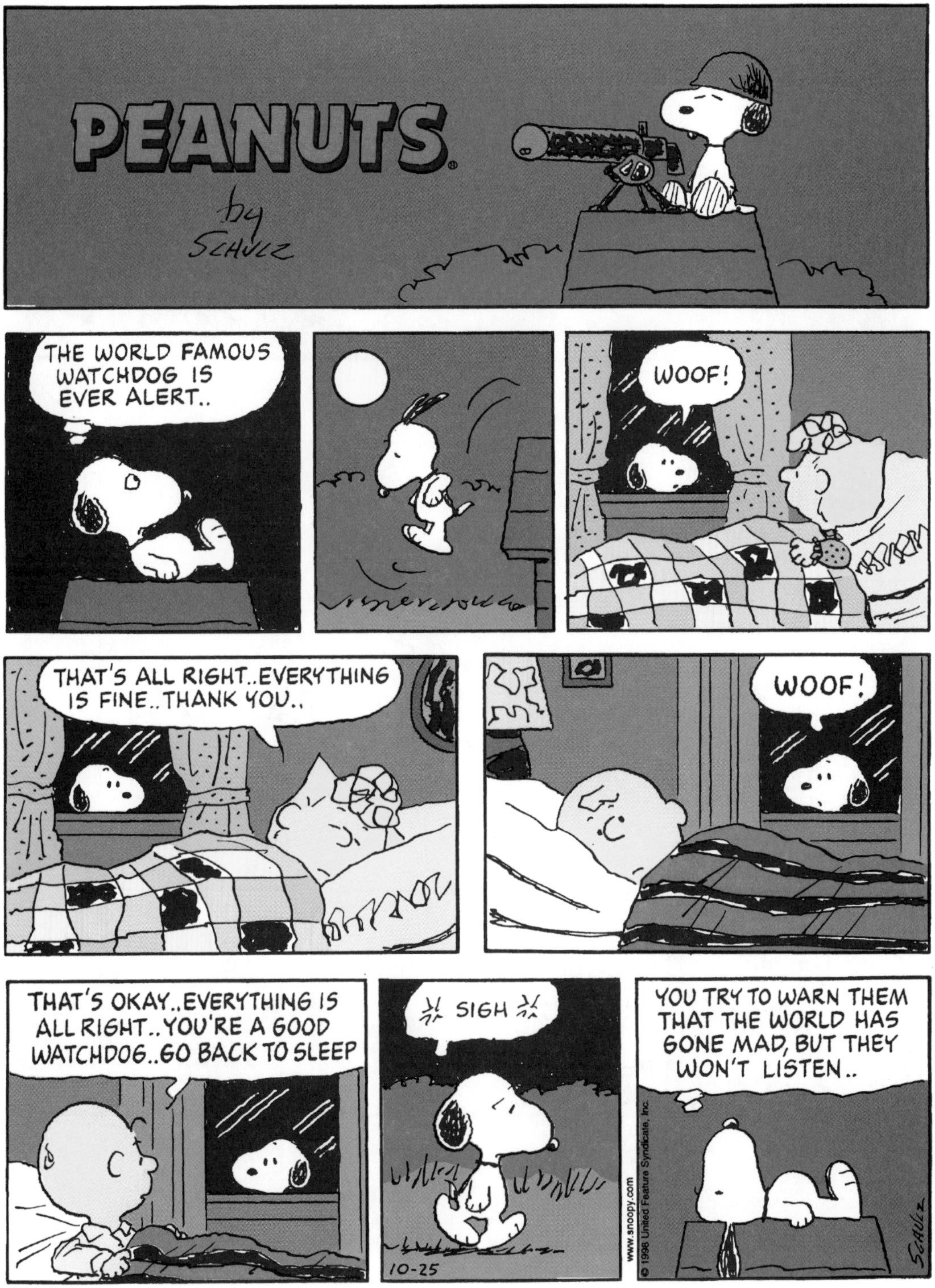
PEANUTS
by SCHULZ
THE WORLD FAMOUS WATCHDOG IS EVER ALERT..
WOOF!
THAT'S ALL RIGHT..EVERYTHING IS FINE..THANK YOU..
WOOF!
THAT'S OKAY..EVERYTHING IS ALL RIGHT..YOU'RE A GOOD WATCHDOG..GO BACK TO SLEEP
SIGH
10-25
YOU TRY TO WARN THEM THAT THE WORLD HAS GONE MAD, BUT THEY WON'T LISTEN..
© 1998 United Feature Syndicate, Inc.
www.snoopy.com
SCHULZ

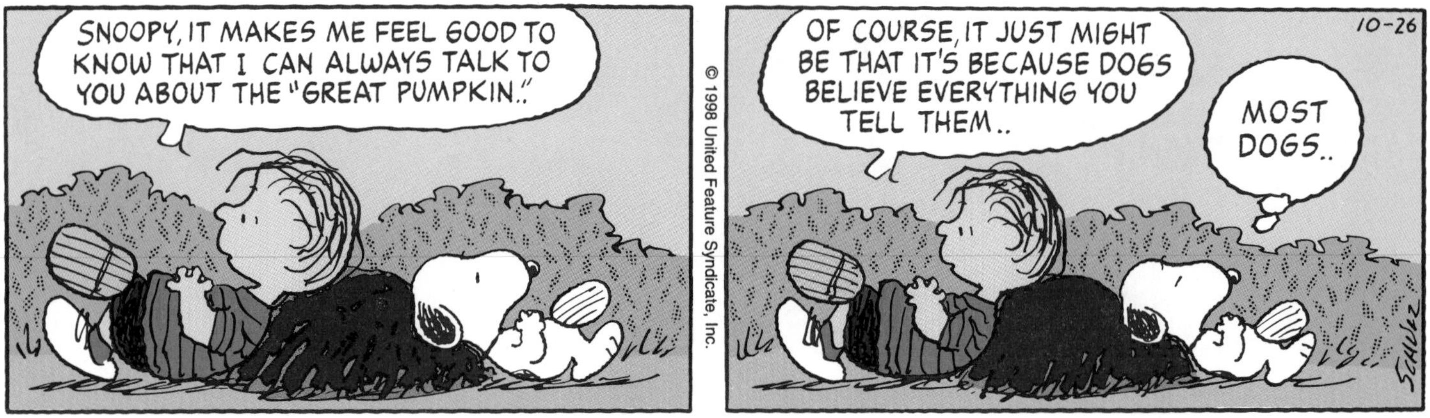
SNOOPY, IT MAKES ME FEEL GOOD TO KNOW THAT I CAN ALWAYS TALK TO YOU ABOUT THE "GREAT PUMPKIN."
© 1998 United Feature Syndicate, Inc.
10-26
OF COURSE, IT JUST MIGHT BE THAT IT'S BECAUSE DOGS BELIEVE EVERYTHING YOU TELL THEM..
MOST DOGS..
SCHULZ

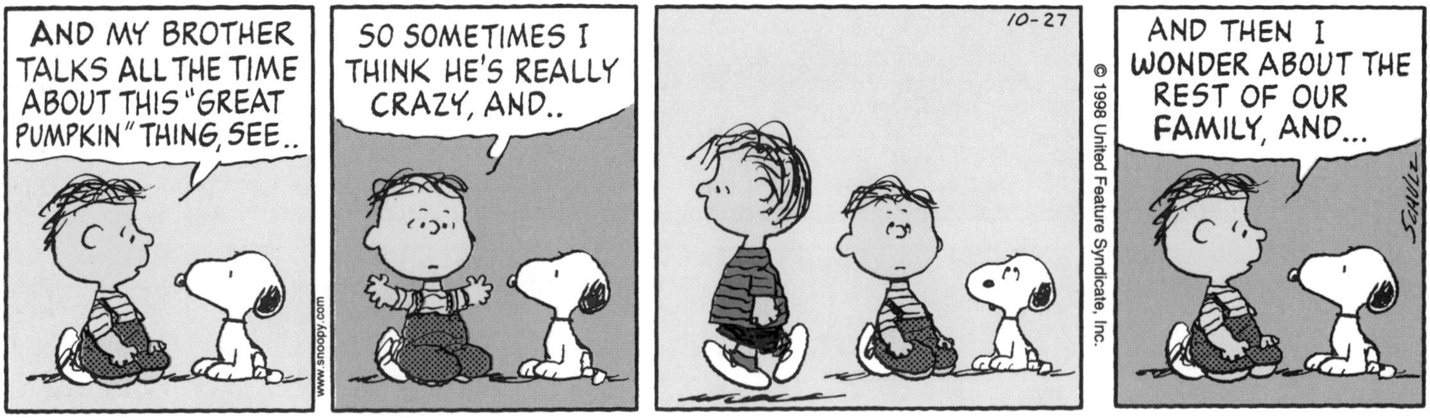
AND MY BROTHER TALKS ALL THE TIME ABOUT THIS "GREAT PUMPKIN" THING, SEE..
www.snoopy.com
SO SOMETIMES I THINK HE'S REALLY CRAZY, AND..
10-27
© 1998 United Feature Syndicate, Inc.
AND THEN I WONDER ABOUT THE REST OF OUR FAMILY, AND...
SCHULZ

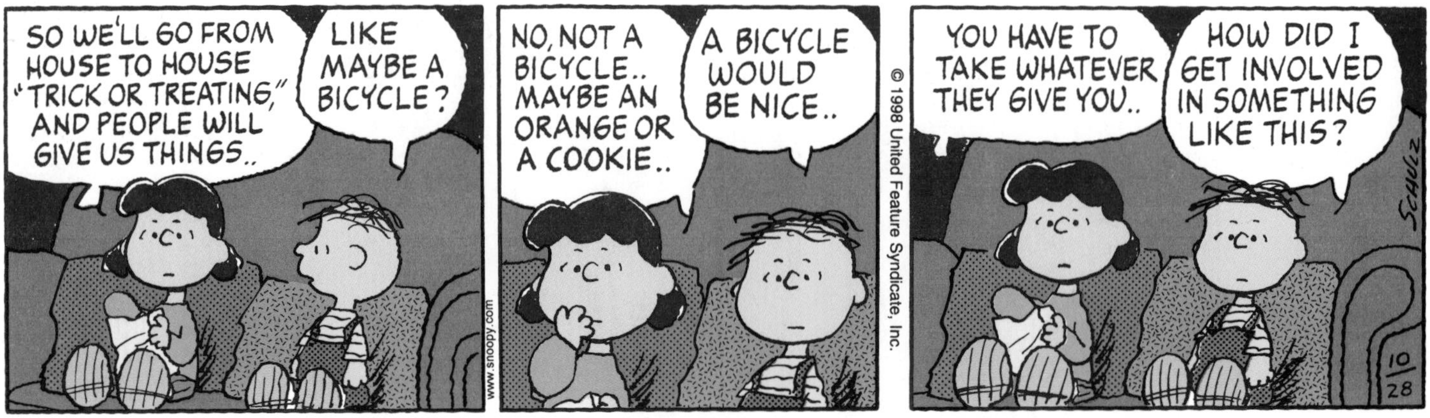
SO WE'LL GO FROM HOUSE TO HOUSE "TRICK OR TREATING," AND PEOPLE WILL GIVE US THINGS..
LIKE MAYBE A BICYCLE?
www.snoopy.com
NO, NOT A BICYCLE.. MAYBE AN ORANGE OR A COOKIE..
A BICYCLE WOULD BE NICE..
© 1998 United Feature Syndicate, Inc.
YOU HAVE TO TAKE WHATEVER THEY GIVE YOU..
HOW DID I GET INVOLVED IN SOMETHING LIKE THIS?
SCHULZ
10/28

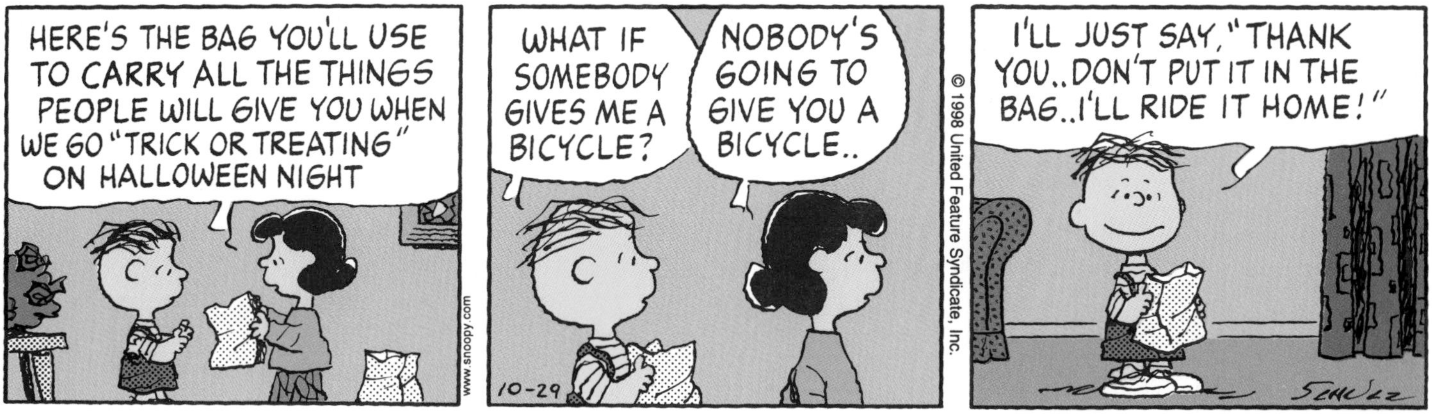
HERE'S THE BAG YOU'LL USE TO CARRY ALL THE THINGS PEOPLE WILL GIVE YOU WHEN WE GO "TRICK OR TREATING" ON HALLOWEEN NIGHT
WHAT IF SOMEBODY GIVES ME A BICYCLE?
NOBODY'S GOING TO GIVE YOU A BICYCLE..
I'LL JUST SAY, "THANK YOU..DON'T PUT IT IN THE BAG..I'LL RIDE IT HOME!"
10-29
www.snoopy.com
© 1998 United Feature Syndicate, Inc.
SCHULZ

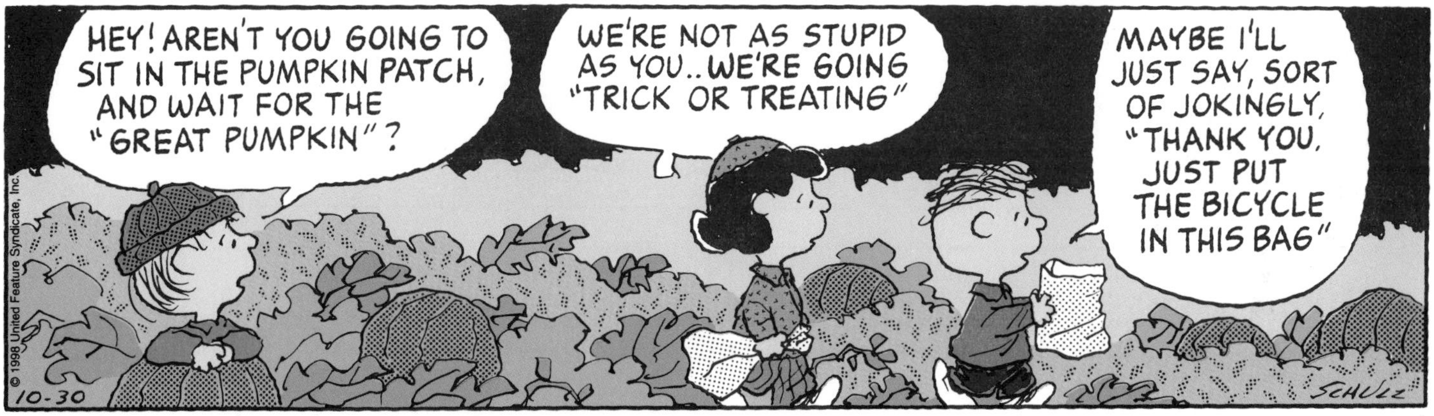
HEY! AREN'T YOU GOING TO SIT IN THE PUMPKIN PATCH, AND WAIT FOR THE "GREAT PUMPKIN"?
WE'RE NOT AS STUPID AS YOU..WE'RE GOING "TRICK OR TREATING"
MAYBE I'LL JUST SAY, SORT OF JOKINGLY, "THANK YOU. JUST PUT THE BICYCLE IN THIS BAG"
© 1998 United Feature Syndicate, Inc.
10-30
SCHULZ

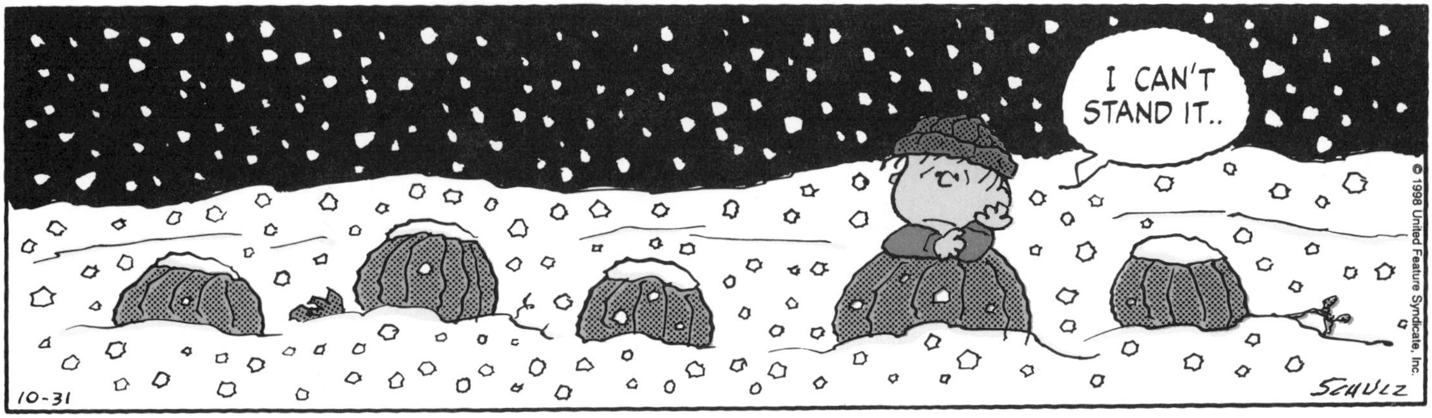
I CAN'T STAND IT..
© 1998 United Feature Syndicate, Inc.
10-31
SCHULZ

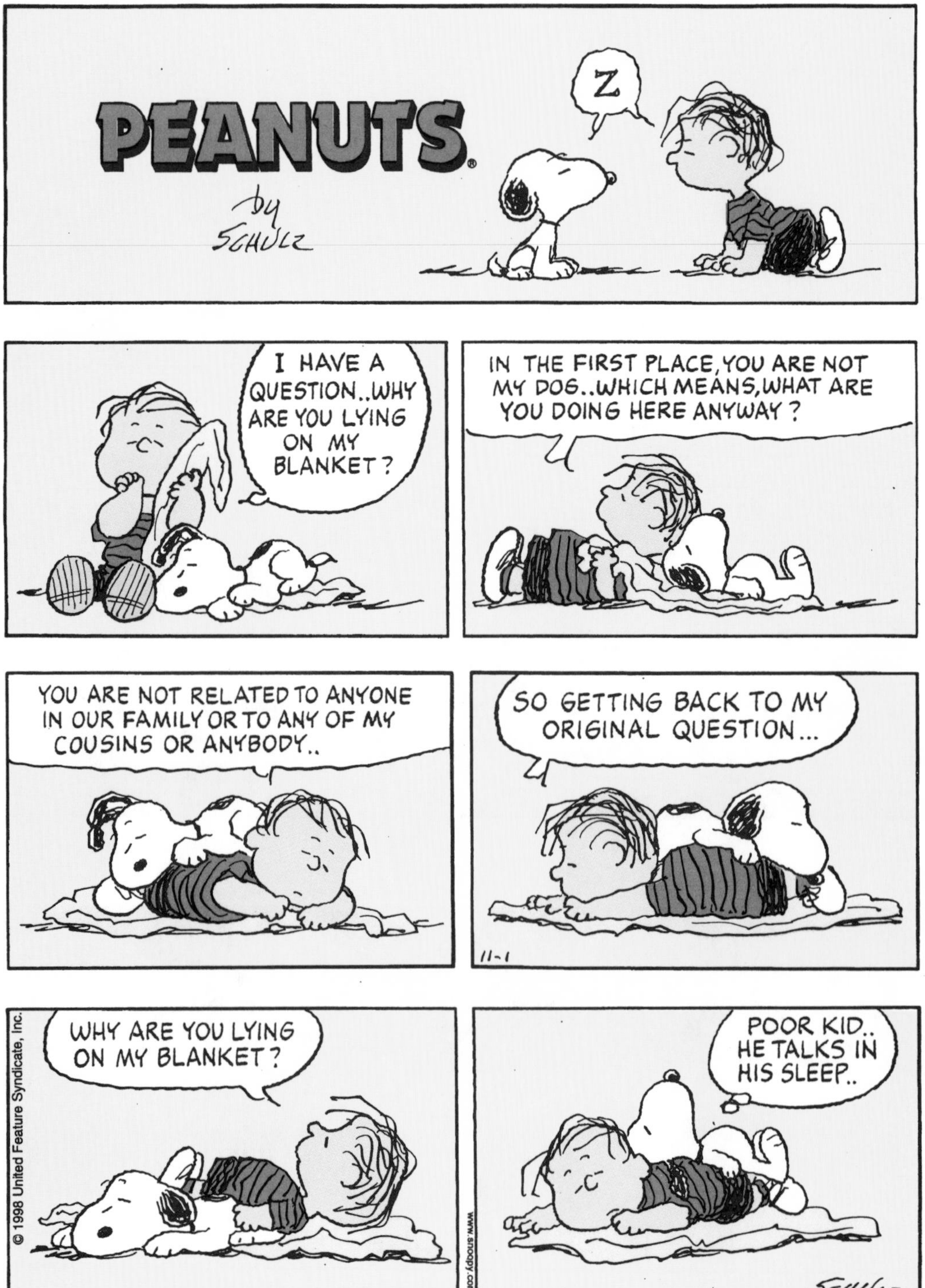
PEANUTS
by SCHULZ
Z
I HAVE A QUESTION..WHY ARE YOU LYING ON MY BLANKET?
IN THE FIRST PLACE, YOU ARE NOT MY DOG..WHICH MEANS, WHAT ARE YOU DOING HERE ANYWAY?
YOU ARE NOT RELATED TO ANYONE IN OUR FAMILY OR TO ANY OF MY COUSINS OR ANYBODY..
SO GETTING BACK TO MY ORIGINAL QUESTION...
11-1
WHY ARE YOU LYING ON MY BLANKET?
POOR KID.. HE TALKS IN HIS SLEEP..
© 1998 United Feature Syndicate, Inc.
www.snoopy.com
SCHULZ

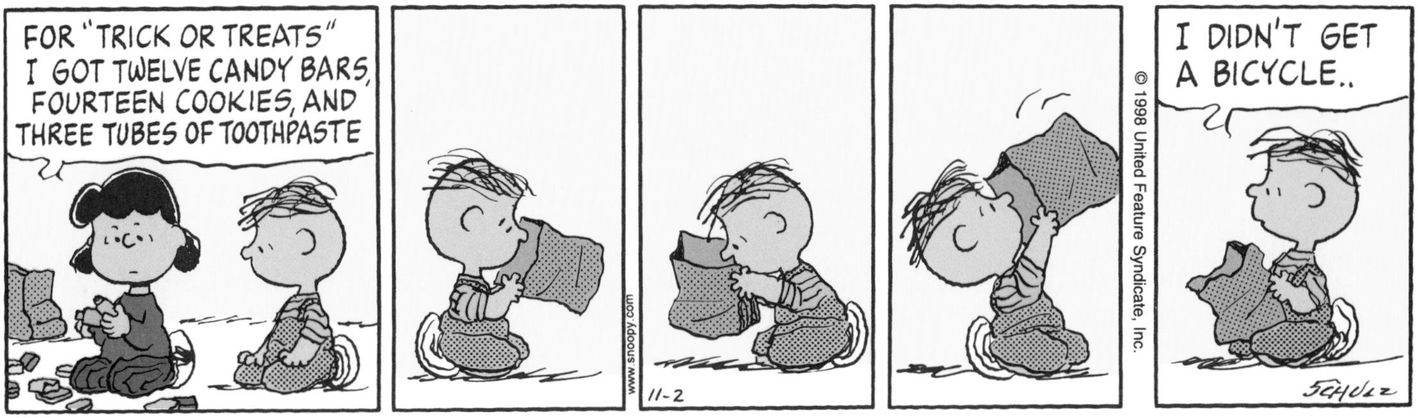
FOR "TRICK OR TREATS" I GOT TWELVE CANDY BARS, FOURTEEN COOKIES, AND THREE TUBES OF TOOTHPASTE
www.snoopy.com
11-2
© 1998 United Feature Syndicate, Inc.
I DIDN'T GET A BICYCLE..
SCHULZ

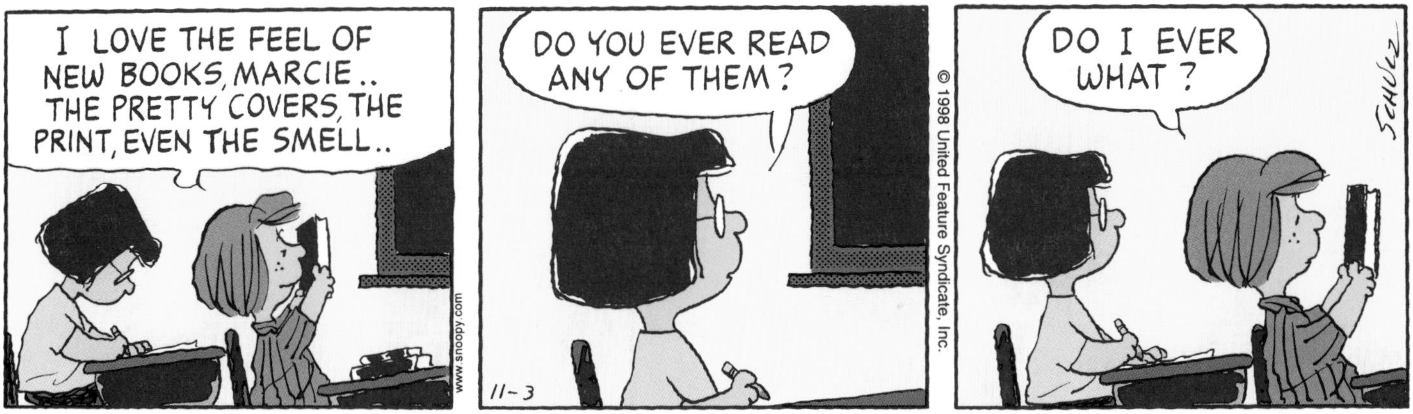
I LOVE THE FEEL OF NEW BOOKS, MARCIE.. THE PRETTY COVERS, THE PRINT, EVEN THE SMELL..
www.snoopy.com
DO YOU EVER READ ANY OF THEM?
11-3
© 1998 United Feature Syndicate, Inc.
DO I EVER WHAT?
SCHULZ

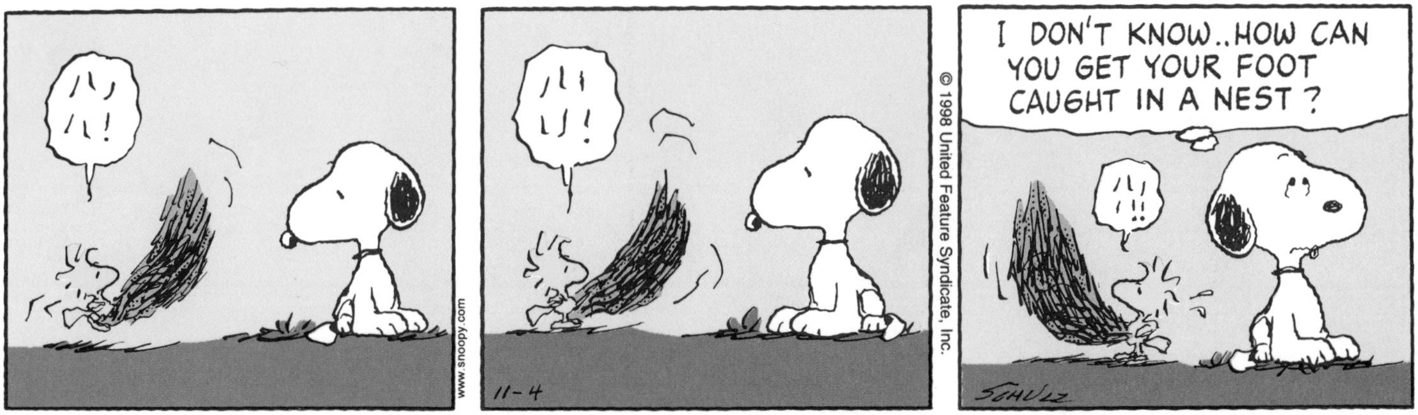
www.snoopy.com
11-4
© 1998 United Feature Syndicate, Inc.
I DON'T KNOW..HOW CAN YOU GET YOUR FOOT CAUGHT IN A NEST?
SCHULZ

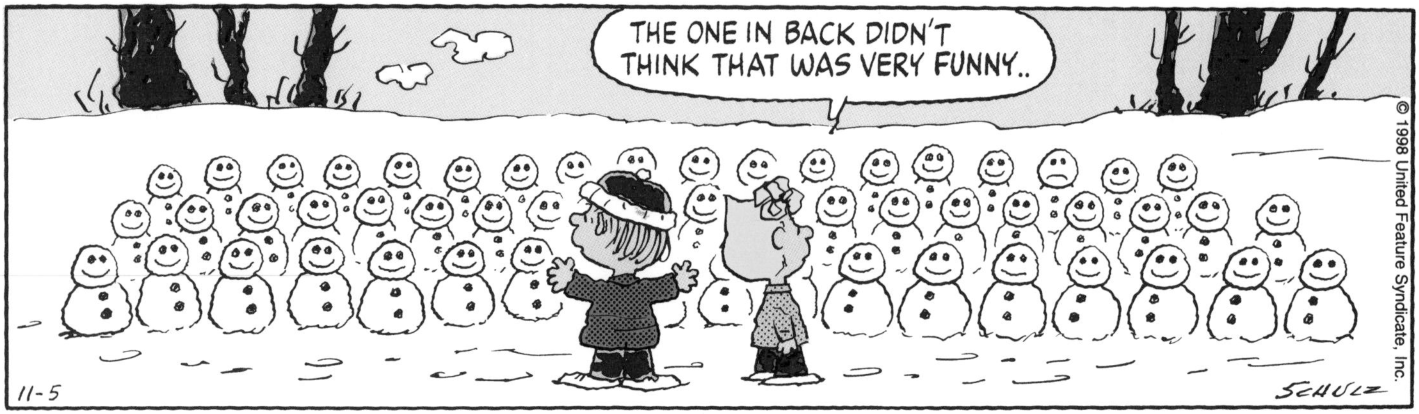
THE ONE IN BACK DIDN'T THINK THAT WAS VERY FUNNY..
© 1998 United Feature Syndicate, Inc.
11-5
SCHULZ

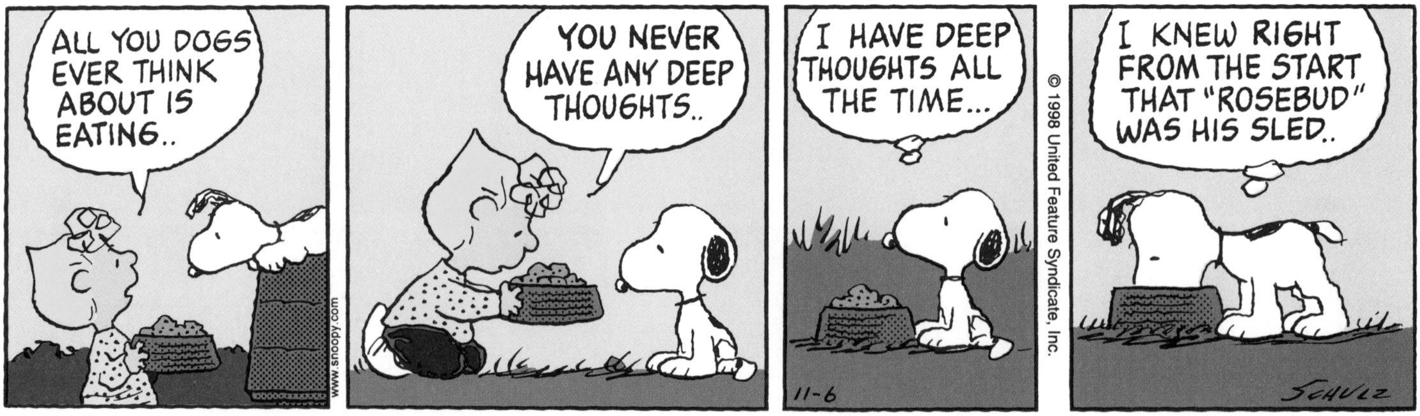
ALL YOU DOGS EVER THINK ABOUT IS EATING..
www.snoopy.com
YOU NEVER HAVE ANY DEEP THOUGHTS..
I HAVE DEEP THOUGHTS ALL THE TIME...
© 1998 United Feature Syndicate, Inc.
11-6
I KNEW RIGHT FROM THE START THAT "ROSEBUD" WAS HIS SLED..
SCHULZ

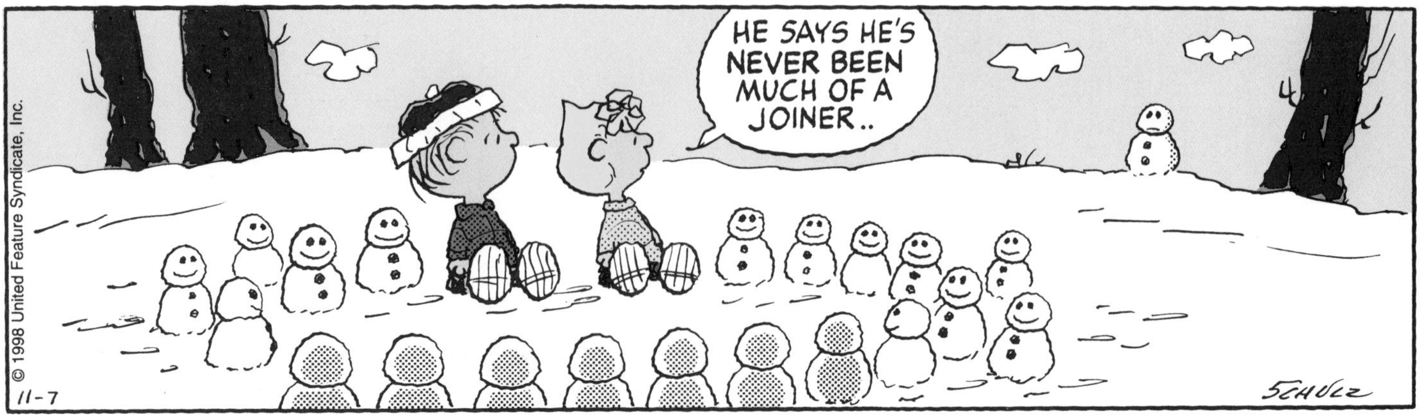
© 1998 United Feature Syndicate, Inc.
HE SAYS HE'S NEVER BEEN MUCH OF A JOINER..
11-7
SCHULZ

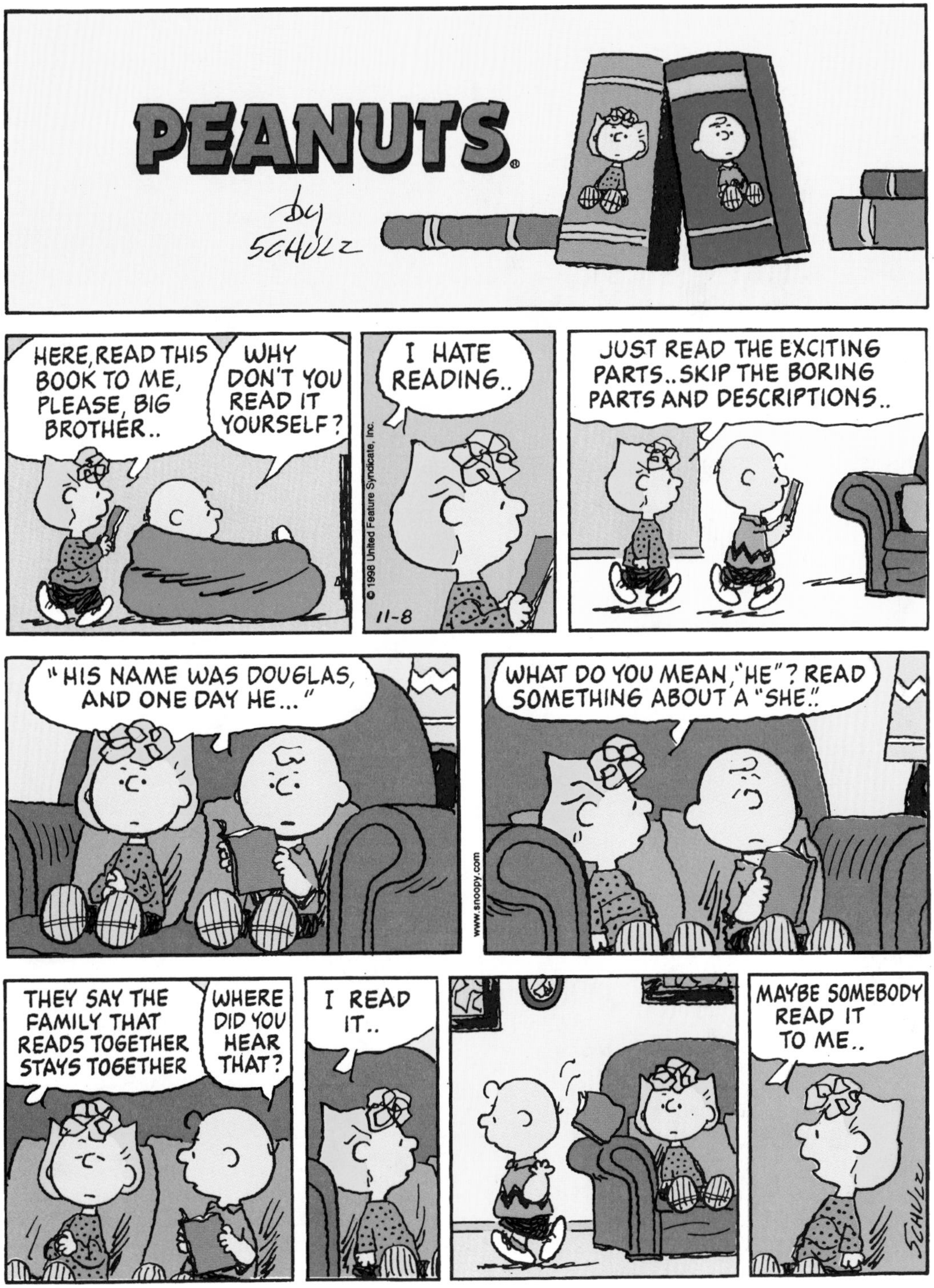
PEANUTS
by SCHULZ
HERE, READ THIS BOOK TO ME, PLEASE, BIG BROTHER..
WHY DON'T YOU READ IT YOURSELF?
© 1998 United Feature Syndicate, Inc.
I HATE READING..
11-8
JUST READ THE EXCITING PARTS..SKIP THE BORING PARTS AND DESCRIPTIONS..
"HIS NAME WAS DOUGLAS, AND ONE DAY HE..."
www.snoopy.com
WHAT DO YOU MEAN, "HE"? READ SOMETHING ABOUT A "SHE."
THEY SAY THE FAMILY THAT READS TOGETHER STAYS TOGETHER
WHERE DID YOU HEAR THAT?
I READ IT..
MAYBE SOMEBODY READ IT TO ME..
SCHULZ

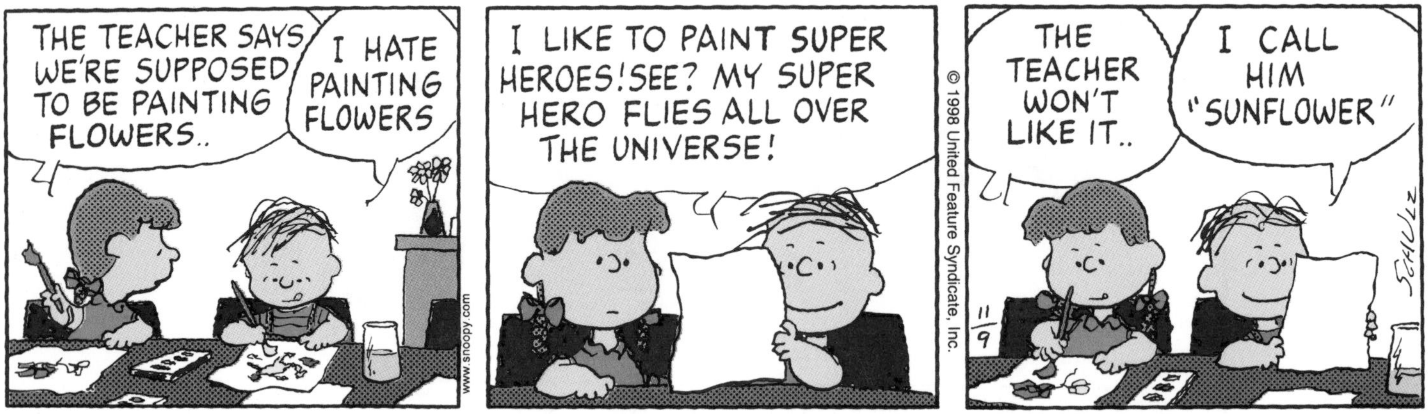
THE TEACHER SAYS WE'RE SUPPOSED TO BE PAINTING FLOWERS..
I HATE PAINTING FLOWERS
www.snoopy.com
I LIKE TO PAINT SUPER HEROES! SEE? MY SUPER HERO FLIES ALL OVER THE UNIVERSE!
© 1998 United Feature Syndicate, Inc.
THE TEACHER WON'T LIKE IT..
I CALL HIM "SUNFLOWER"
11/9
SCHULZ

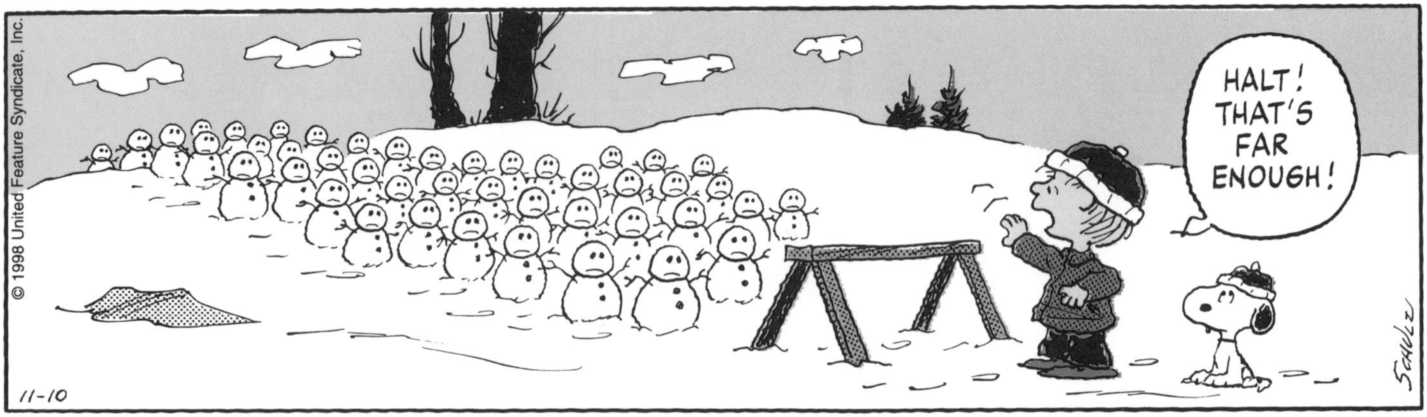
© 1998 United Feature Syndicate, Inc.
HALT! THAT'S FAR ENOUGH!
SCHULZ
11-10

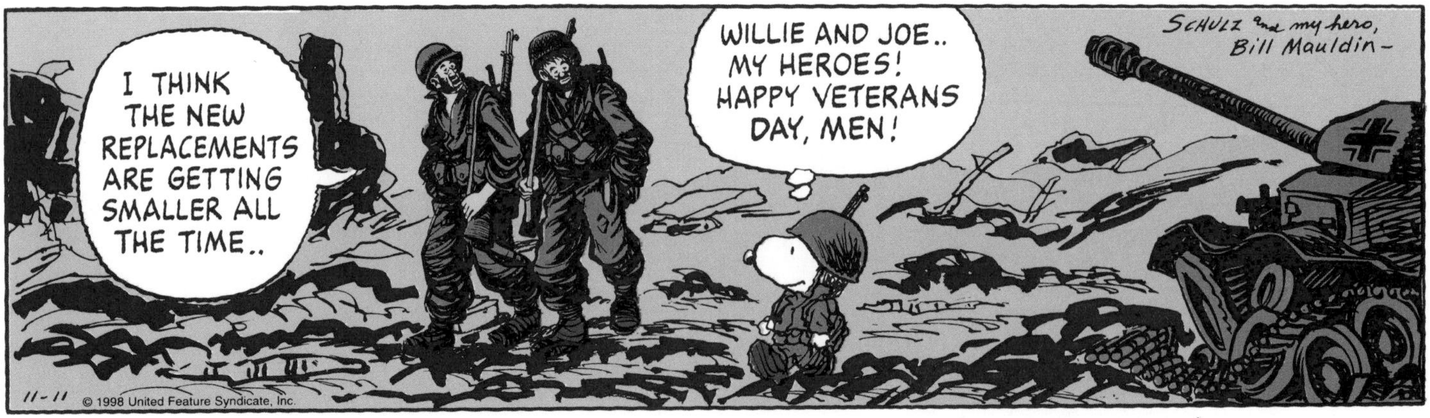
I THINK THE NEW REPLACEMENTS ARE GETTING SMALLER ALL THE TIME..
WILLIE AND JOE.. MY HEROES! HAPPY VETERANS DAY, MEN!
SCHULZ and my hero, Bill Mauldin-
11-11
© 1998 United Feature Syndicate, Inc.

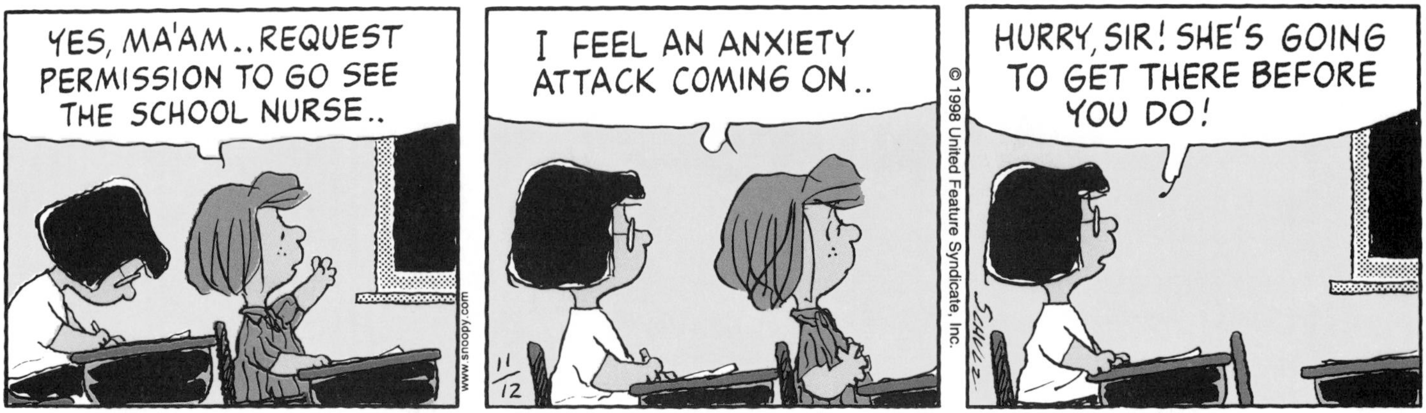
YES, MA'AM..REQUEST PERMISSION TO GO SEE THE SCHOOL NURSE..
I FEEL AN ANXIETY ATTACK COMING ON..
HURRY, SIR! SHE'S GOING TO GET THERE BEFORE YOU DO!
www.snoopy.com
11/12
© 1998 United Feature Syndicate, Inc.
SCHULZ

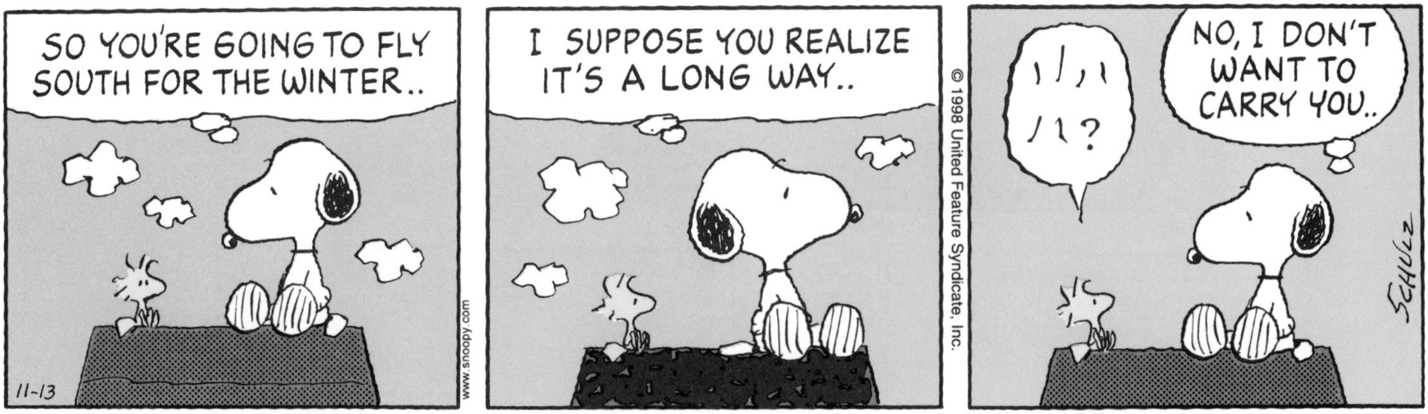
SO YOU'RE GOING TO FLY SOUTH FOR THE WINTER..
I SUPPOSE YOU REALIZE IT'S A LONG WAY..
NO, I DON'T WANT TO CARRY YOU..
11-13
www.snoopy.com
© 1998 United Feature Syndicate, Inc.
SCHULZ

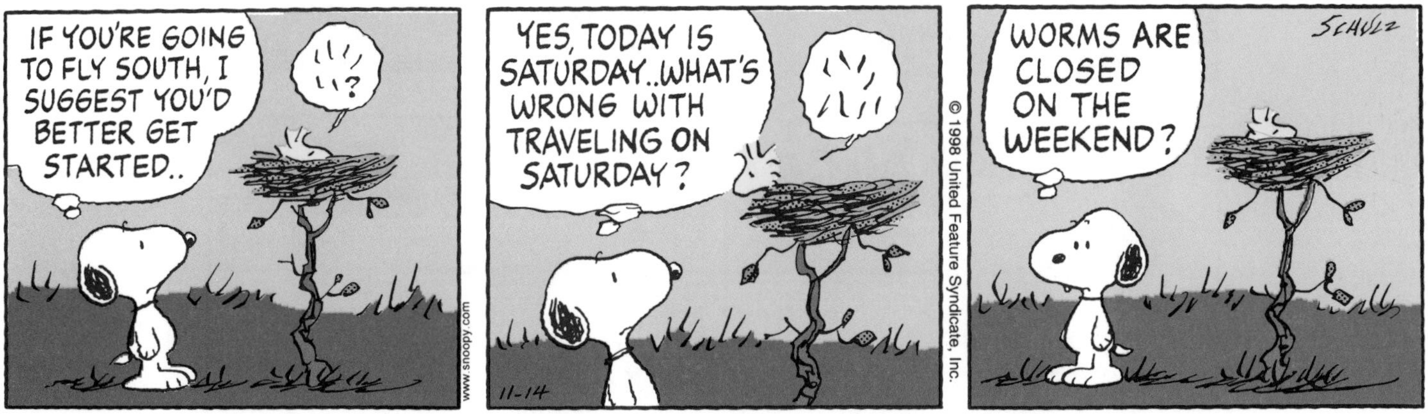
IF YOU'RE GOING TO FLY SOUTH, I SUGGEST YOU'D BETTER GET STARTED..
YES, TODAY IS SATURDAY..WHAT'S WRONG WITH TRAVELING ON SATURDAY?
WORMS ARE CLOSED ON THE WEEKEND?
SCHULZ
www.snoopy.com
11-14
© 1998 United Feature Syndicate, Inc.

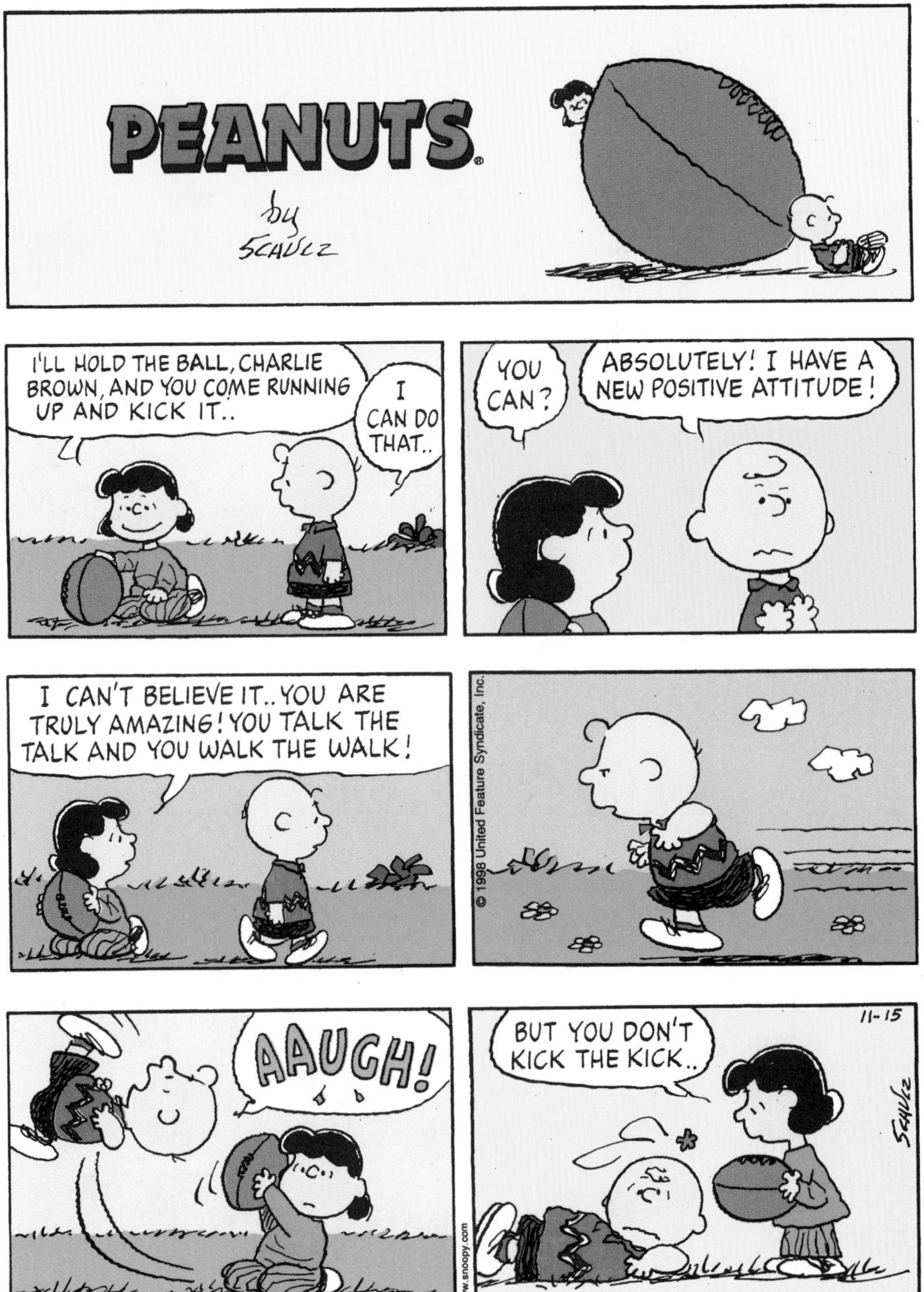
PEANUTS
by SCHULZ
I'LL HOLD THE BALL, CHARLIE BROWN, AND YOU COME RUNNING UP AND KICK IT..
I CAN DO THAT..
YOU CAN?
ABSOLUTELY! I HAVE A NEW POSITIVE ATTITUDE!
I CAN'T BELIEVE IT.. YOU ARE TRULY AMAZING! YOU TALK THE TALK AND YOU WALK THE WALK!
© 1998 United Feature Syndicate, Inc.
AAUGH!
www.snoopy.com
11-15
BUT YOU DON'T KICK THE KICK..
SCHULZ

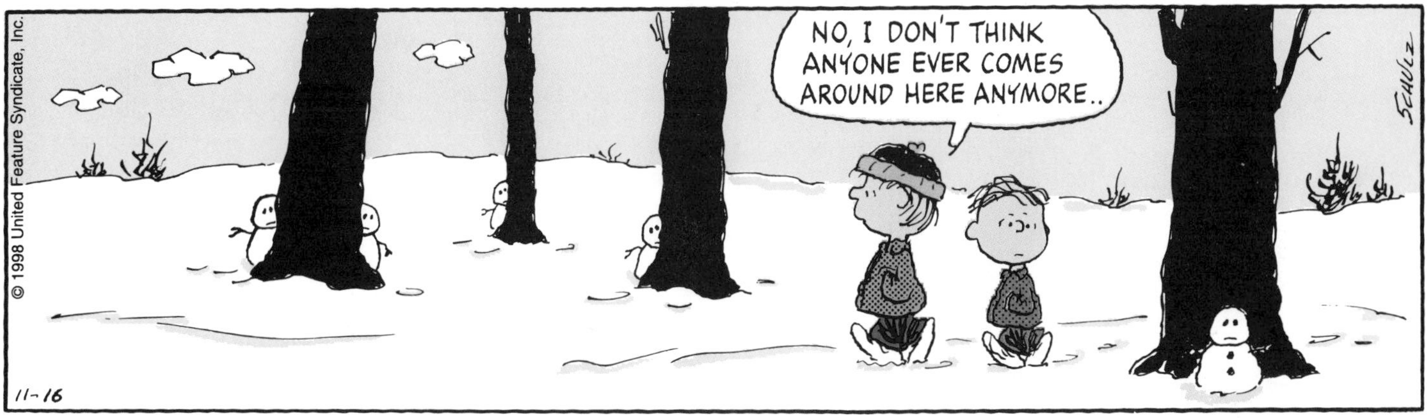
© 1998 United Feature Syndicate, Inc.
NO, I DON'T THINK ANYONE EVER COMES AROUND HERE ANYMORE..
SCHULZ
11-16

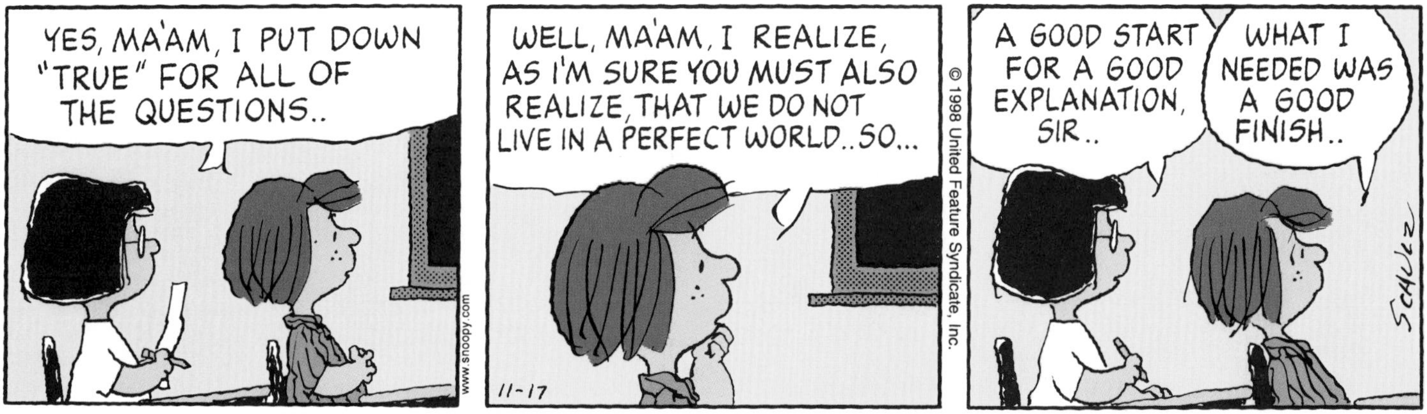
YES, MA'AM, I PUT DOWN "TRUE" FOR ALL OF THE QUESTIONS..
www.snoopy.com
WELL, MA'AM, I REALIZE, AS I'M SURE YOU MUST ALSO REALIZE, THAT WE DO NOT LIVE IN A PERFECT WORLD..SO...
11-17
© 1998 United Feature Syndicate, Inc.
A GOOD START FOR A GOOD EXPLANATION, SIR..
WHAT I NEEDED WAS A GOOD FINISH..
SCHULZ

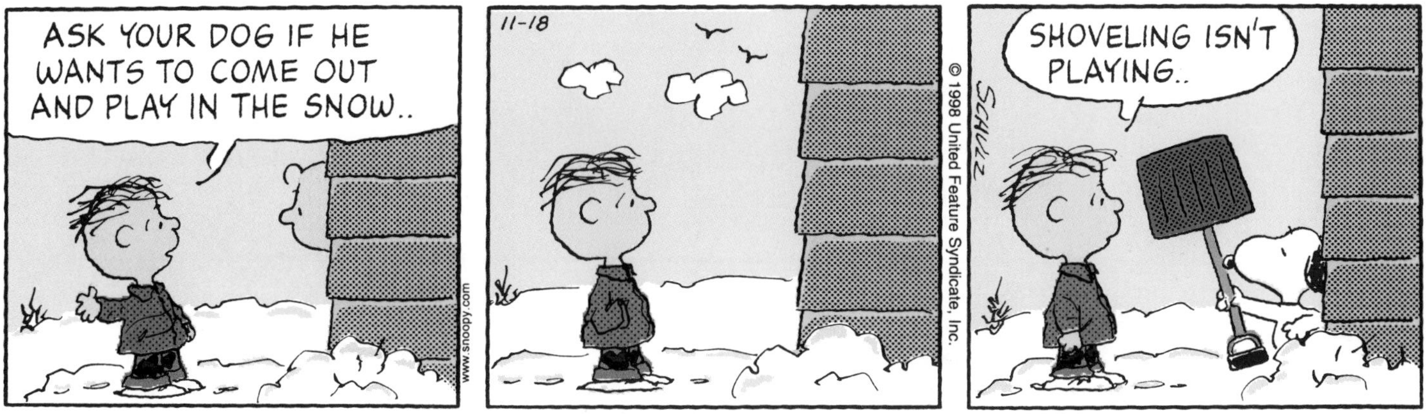
ASK YOUR DOG IF HE WANTS TO COME OUT AND PLAY IN THE SNOW..
www.snoopy.com
11-18
© 1998 United Feature Syndicate, Inc.
SCHULZ
SHOVELING ISN'T PLAYING..

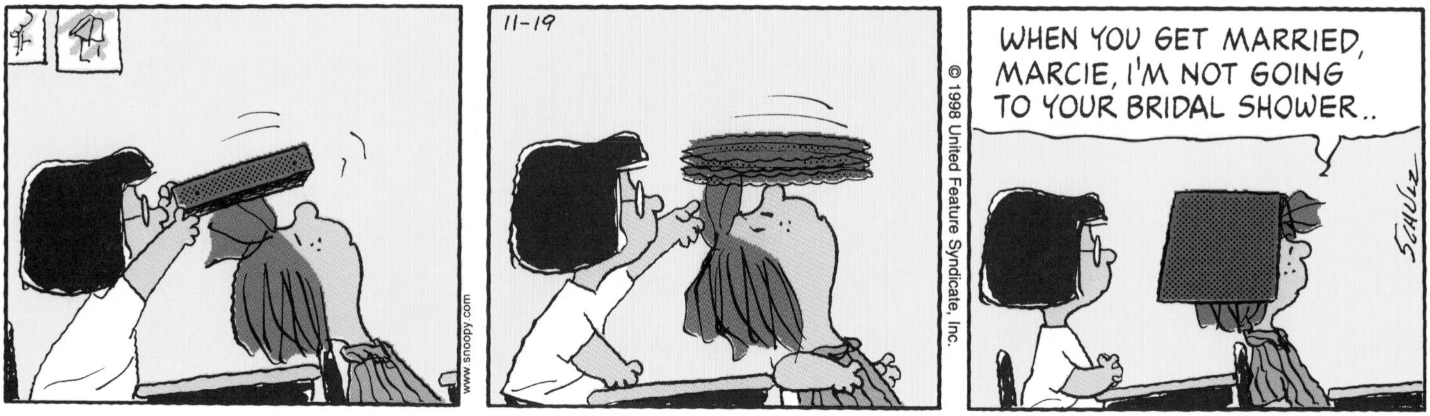
www.snoopy.com
11-19
© 1998 United Feature Syndicate, Inc.
WHEN YOU GET MARRIED, MARCIE, I'M NOT GOING TO YOUR BRIDAL SHOWER..
SCHULZ

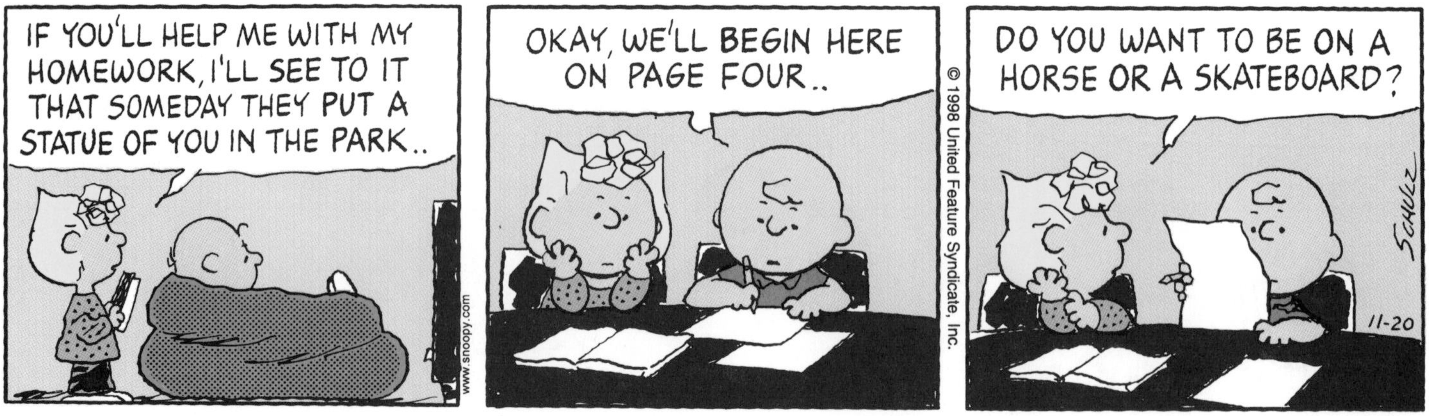
IF YOU'LL HELP ME WITH MY HOMEWORK, I'LL SEE TO IT THAT SOMEDAY THEY PUT A STATUE OF YOU IN THE PARK..
www.snoopy.com
OKAY, WE'LL BEGIN HERE ON PAGE FOUR..
© 1998 United Feature Syndicate, Inc.
DO YOU WANT TO BE ON A HORSE OR A SKATEBOARD?
SCHULZ
11-20

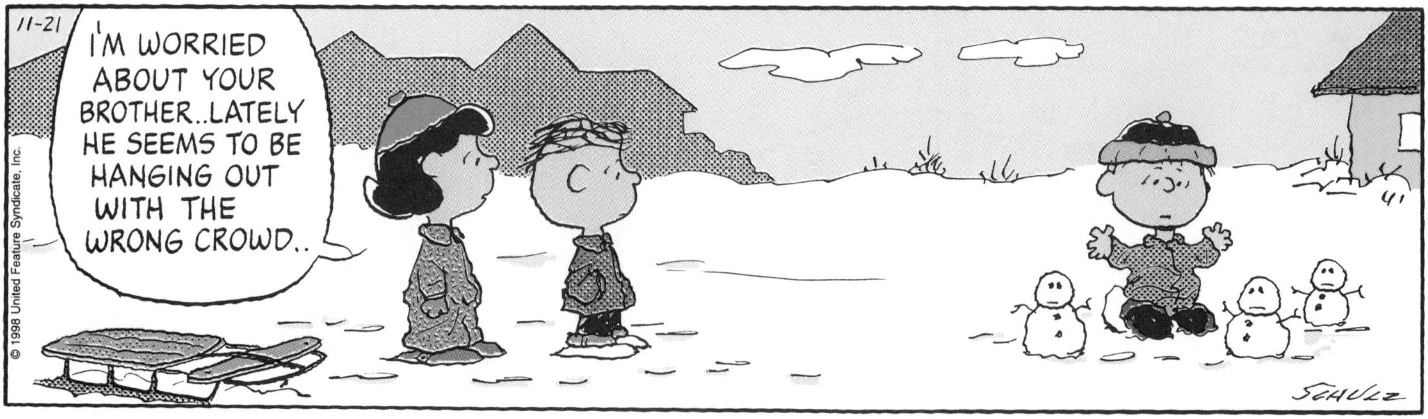
11-21
I'M WORRIED ABOUT YOUR BROTHER..LATELY HE SEEMS TO BE HANGING OUT WITH THE WRONG CROWD..
© 1998 United Feature Syndicate, Inc.
SCHULZ

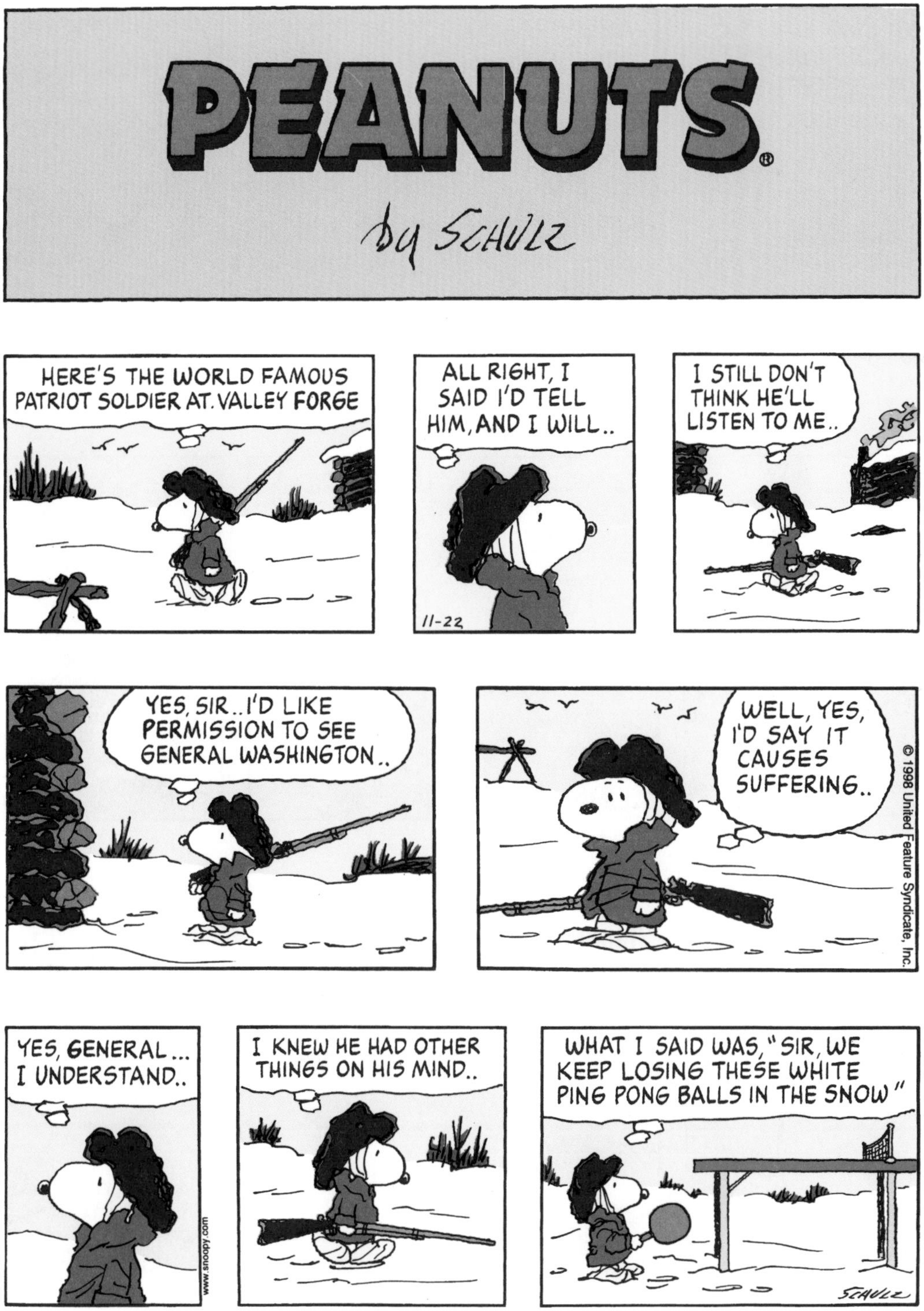
PEANUTS®
by SCHULZ
HERE'S THE WORLD FAMOUS PATRIOT SOLDIER AT VALLEY FORGE
ALL RIGHT, I SAID I'D TELL HIM, AND I WILL..
11-22
I STILL DON'T THINK HE'LL LISTEN TO ME..
YES, SIR..I'D LIKE PERMISSION TO SEE GENERAL WASHINGTON..
WELL, YES, I'D SAY IT CAUSES SUFFERING..
© 1998 United Feature Syndicate, Inc.
YES, GENERAL... I UNDERSTAND..
www.snoopy.com
I KNEW HE HAD OTHER THINGS ON HIS MIND..
WHAT I SAID WAS, "SIR, WE KEEP LOSING THESE WHITE PING PONG BALLS IN THE SNOW"
SCHULZ

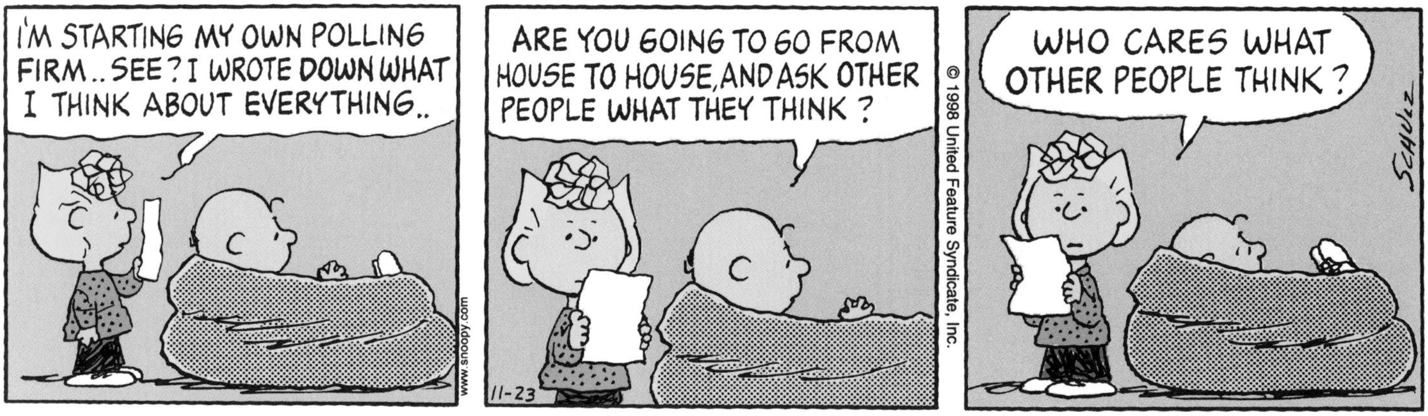
I'M STARTING MY OWN POLLING FIRM.. SEE? I WROTE DOWN WHAT I THINK ABOUT EVERYTHING..
ARE YOU GOING TO GO FROM HOUSE TO HOUSE, AND ASK OTHER PEOPLE WHAT THEY THINK?
WHO CARES WHAT OTHER PEOPLE THINK?
www.snoopy.com
11-23
© 1998 United Feature Syndicate, Inc.
SCHULZ

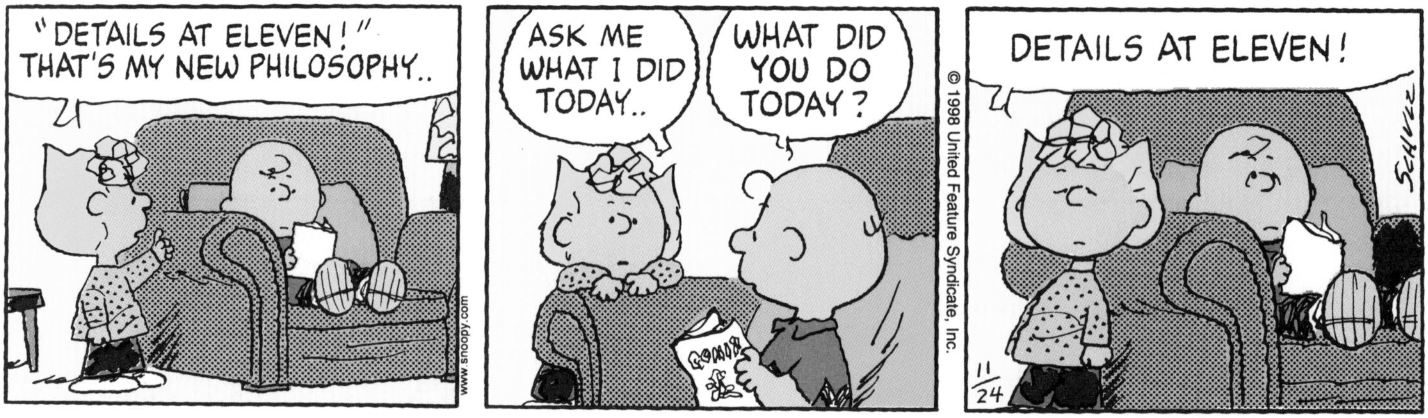
"DETAILS AT ELEVEN!" THAT'S MY NEW PHILOSOPHY..
ASK ME WHAT I DID TODAY..
WHAT DID YOU DO TODAY?
DETAILS AT ELEVEN!
www.snoopy.com
© 1998 United Feature Syndicate, Inc.
11/24
SCHULZ

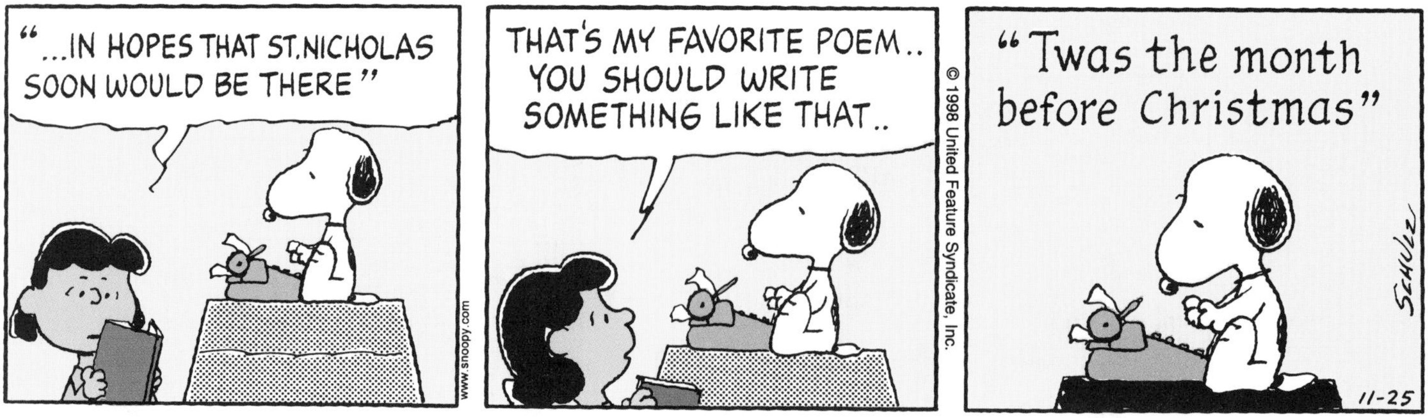
"...IN HOPES THAT ST. NICHOLAS SOON WOULD BE THERE"
THAT'S MY FAVORITE POEM.. YOU SHOULD WRITE SOMETHING LIKE THAT..
"Twas the month before Christmas"
www.snoopy.com
© 1998 United Feature Syndicate, Inc.
SCHULZ
11-25

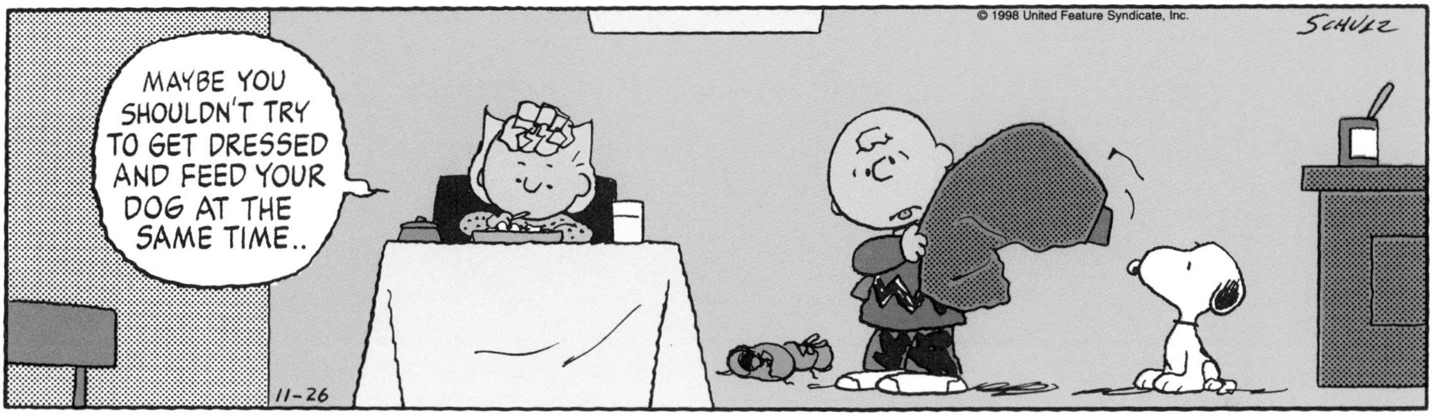
© 1998 United Feature Syndicate, Inc.
SCHULZ
MAYBE YOU SHOULDN'T TRY TO GET DRESSED AND FEED YOUR DOG AT THE SAME TIME..
11-26

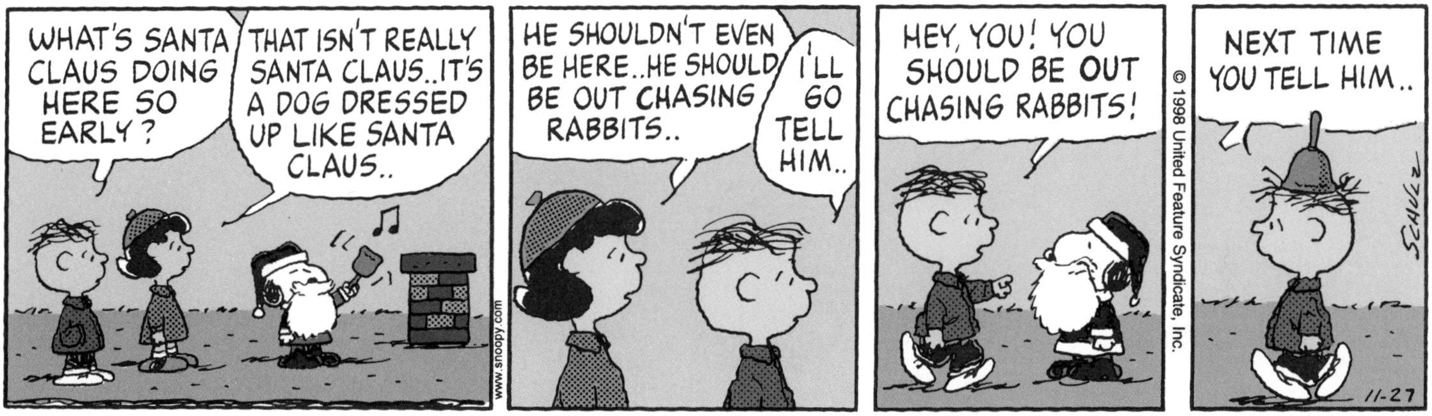
WHAT'S SANTA CLAUS DOING HERE SO EARLY?
THAT ISN'T REALLY SANTA CLAUS..IT'S A DOG DRESSED UP LIKE SANTA CLAUS..
www.snoopy.com
HE SHOULDN'T EVEN BE HERE..HE SHOULD BE OUT CHASING RABBITS..
I'LL GO TELL HIM..
HEY, YOU! YOU SHOULD BE OUT CHASING RABBITS!
© 1998 United Feature Syndicate, Inc.
NEXT TIME YOU TELL HIM..
SCHULZ
11-27

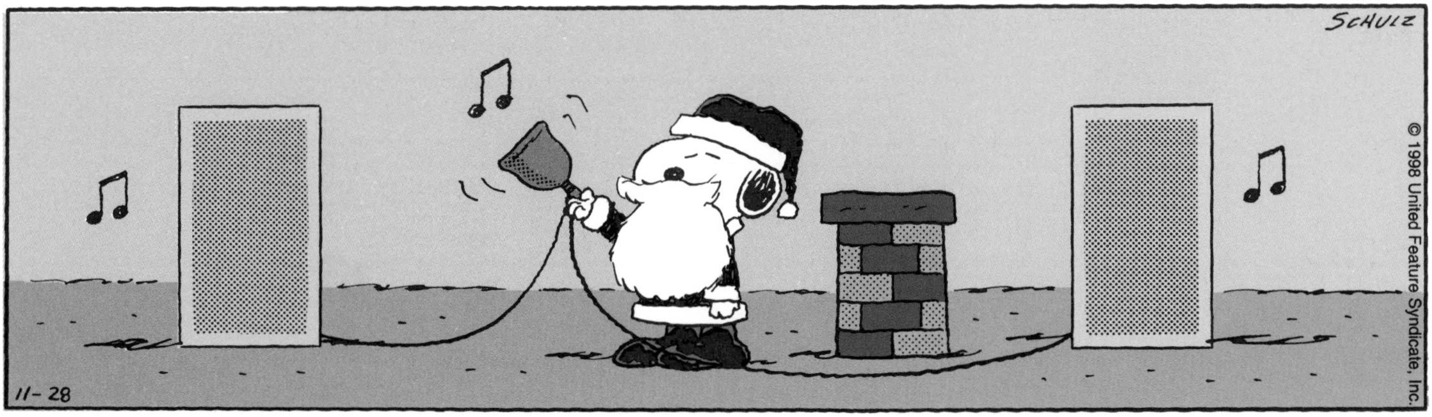
SCHULZ
© 1998 United Feature Syndicate, Inc.
11-28

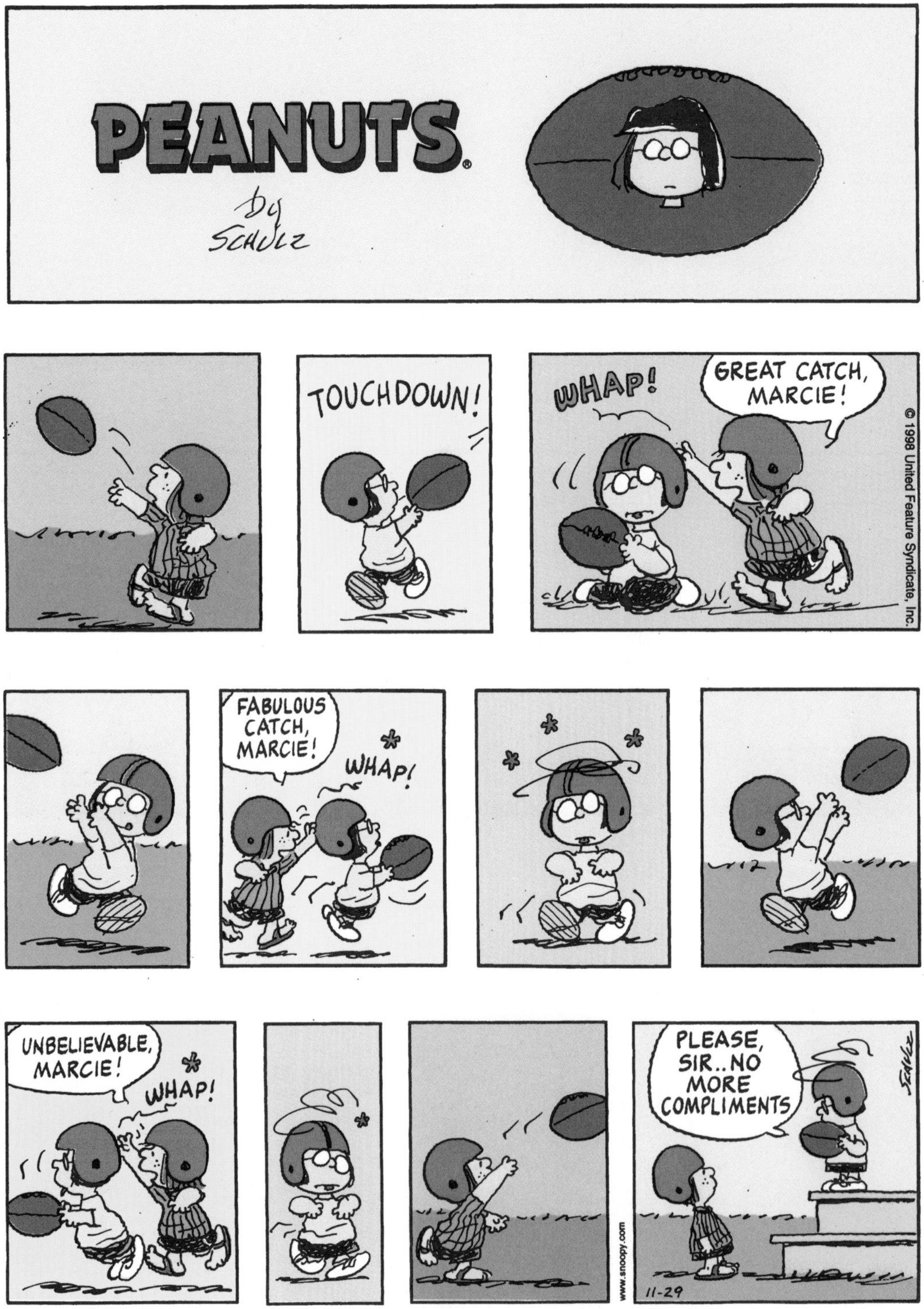
PEANUTS®
by SCHULZ
TOUCHDOWN!
WHAP!
GREAT CATCH, MARCIE!
© 1998 United Feature Syndicate, Inc.
FABULOUS CATCH, MARCIE!
WHAP!
UNBELIEVABLE, MARCIE!
WHAP!
www.snoopy.com
PLEASE, SIR..NO MORE COMPLIMENTS
SCHULZ
11-29

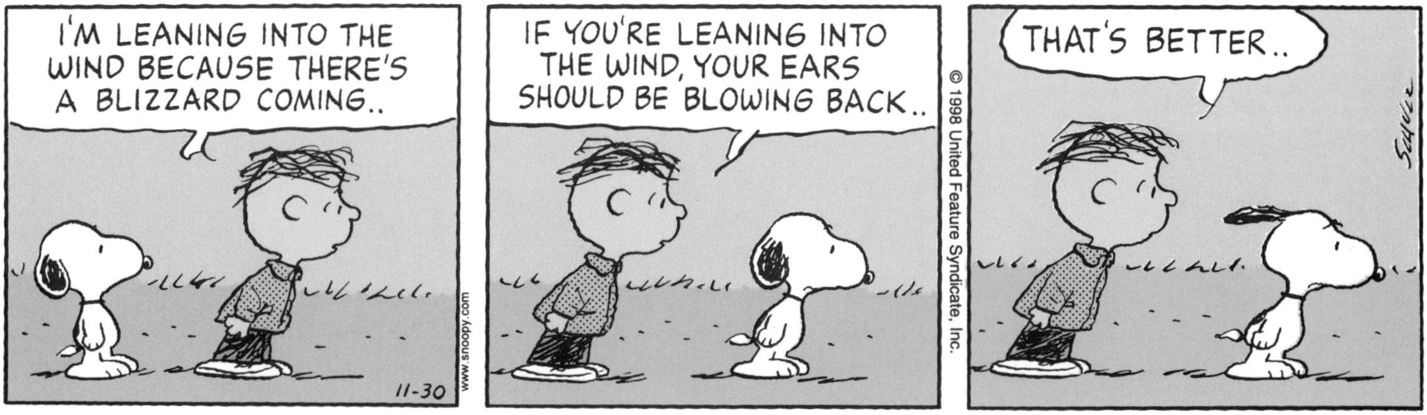
I'M LEANING INTO THE WIND BECAUSE THERE'S A BLIZZARD COMING..
11-30
www.snoopy.com
IF YOU'RE LEANING INTO THE WIND, YOUR EARS SHOULD BE BLOWING BACK..
© 1998 United Feature Syndicate, Inc.
THAT'S BETTER..
SCHULZ

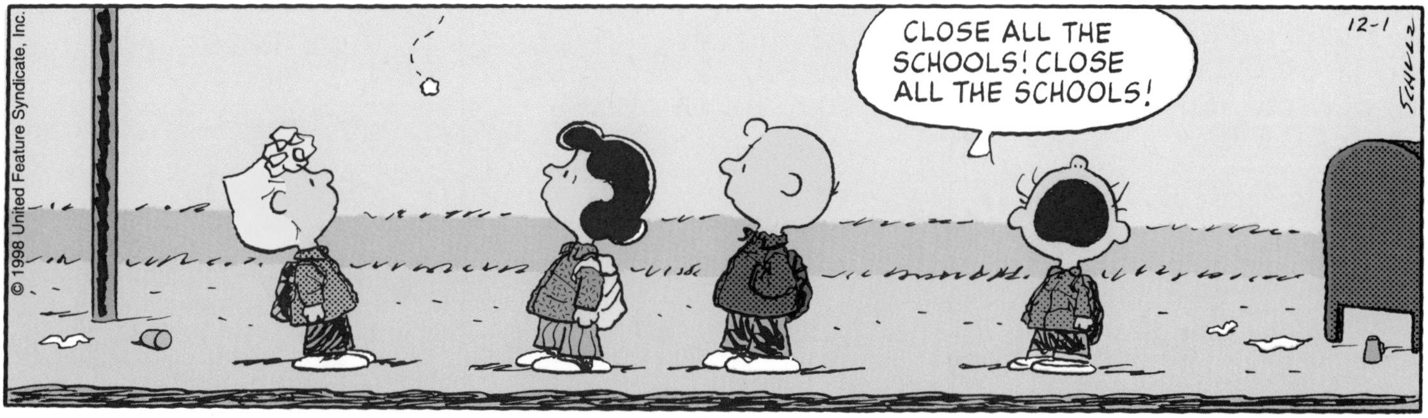
© 1998 United Feature Syndicate, Inc.
CLOSE ALL THE SCHOOLS! CLOSE ALL THE SCHOOLS!
12-1
SCHULZ

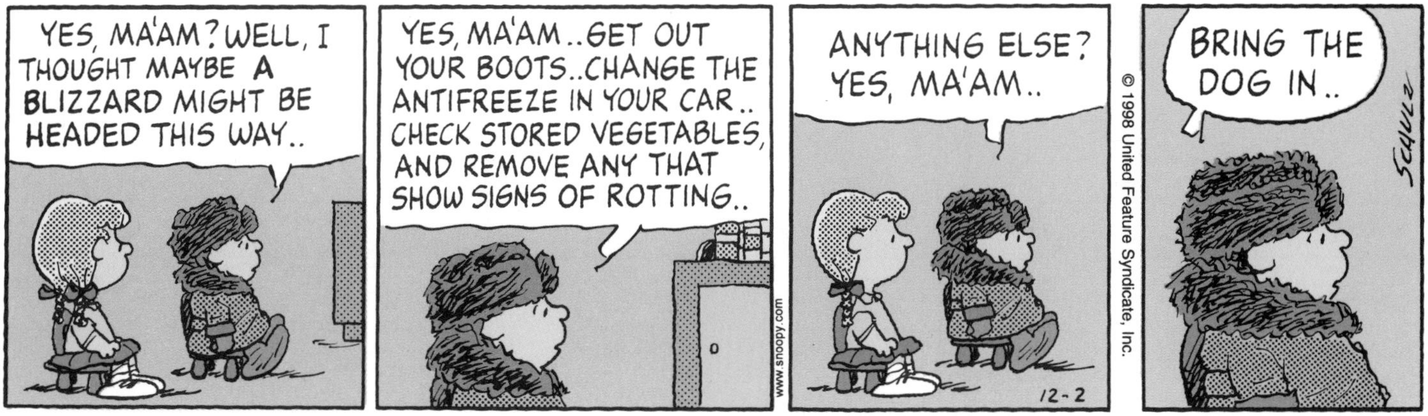
YES, MA'AM? WELL, I THOUGHT MAYBE A BLIZZARD MIGHT BE HEADED THIS WAY..
YES, MA'AM..GET OUT YOUR BOOTS..CHANGE THE ANTIFREEZE IN YOUR CAR.. CHECK STORED VEGETABLES, AND REMOVE ANY THAT SHOW SIGNS OF ROTTING..
www.snoopy.com
ANYTHING ELSE? YES, MA'AM..
12-2
© 1998 United Feature Syndicate, Inc.
BRING THE DOG IN..
SCHULZ

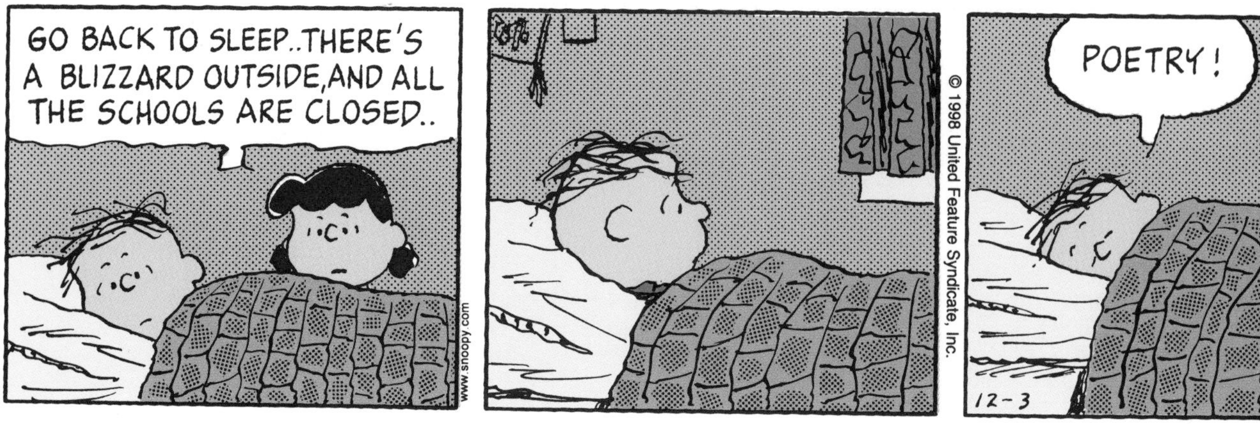
GO BACK TO SLEEP..THERE'S A BLIZZARD OUTSIDE, AND ALL THE SCHOOLS ARE CLOSED..
POETRY!
12-3

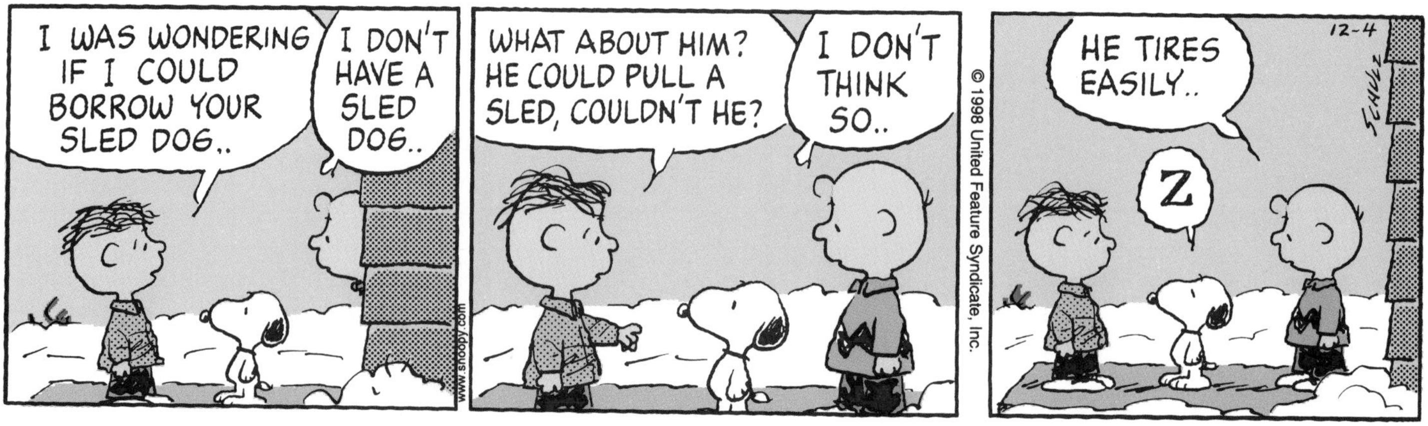
I WAS WONDERING IF I COULD BORROW YOUR SLED DOG..
I DON'T HAVE A SLED DOG..
WHAT ABOUT HIM? HE COULD PULL A SLED, COULDN'T HE?
I DON'T THINK SO..
12-4
HE TIRES EASILY..
Z
SCHULZ

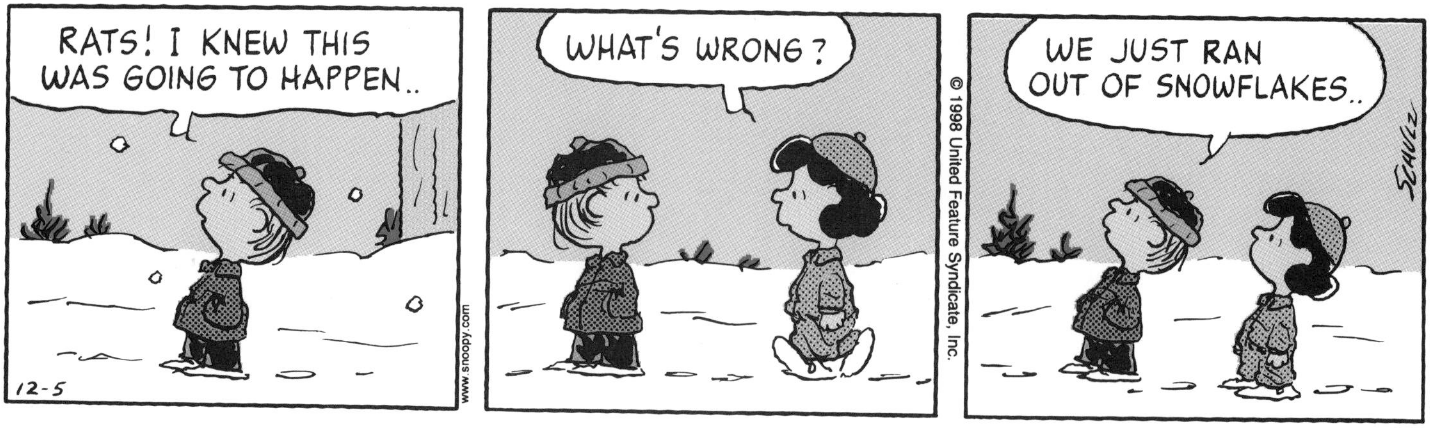
RATS! I KNEW THIS WAS GOING TO HAPPEN..
12-5
WHAT'S WRONG?
WE JUST RAN OUT OF SNOWFLAKES..
SCHULZ

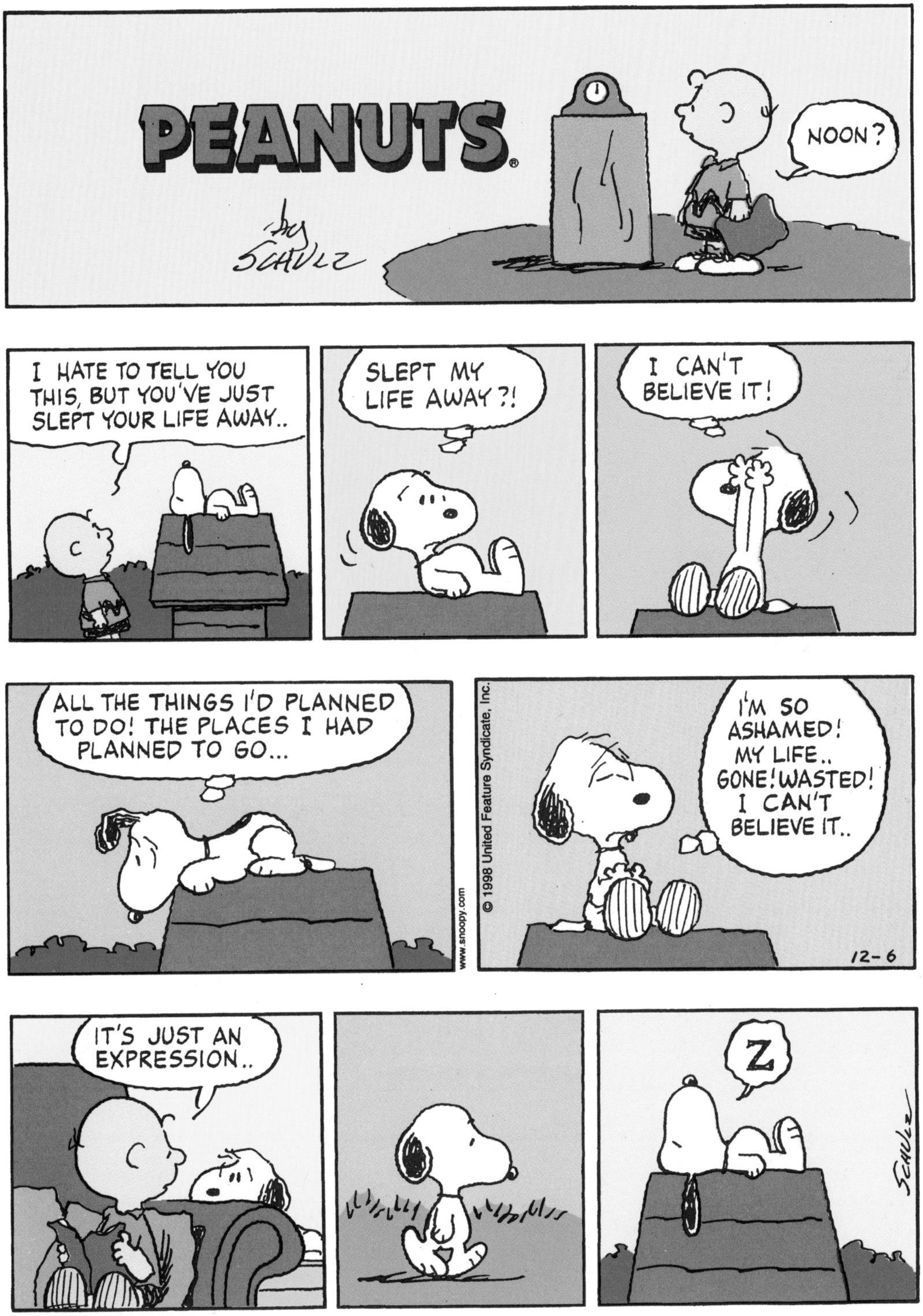
PEANUTS
by SCHULZ
NOON?
I HATE TO TELL YOU THIS, BUT YOU'VE JUST SLEPT YOUR LIFE AWAY..
SLEPT MY LIFE AWAY?!
I CAN'T BELIEVE IT!
ALL THE THINGS I'D PLANNED TO DO! THE PLACES I HAD PLANNED TO GO...
www.snoopy.com
© 1998 United Feature Syndicate, Inc.
I'M SO ASHAMED! MY LIFE.. GONE! WASTED! I CAN'T BELIEVE IT..
12-6
IT'S JUST AN EXPRESSION..
Z
SCHULZ

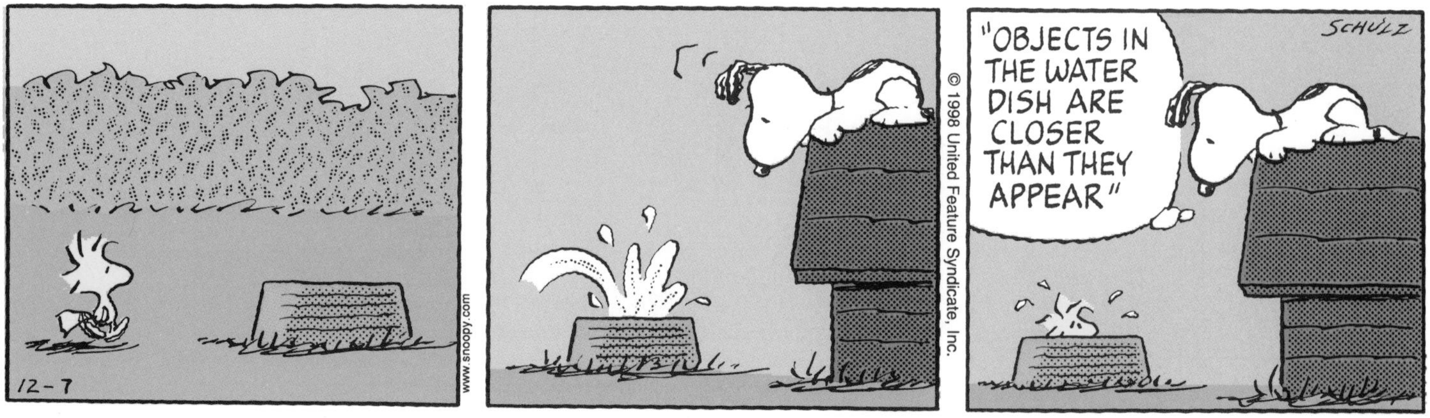
12-7
www.snoopy.com
© 1998 United Feature Syndicate, Inc.
"OBJECTS IN THE WATER DISH ARE CLOSER THAN THEY APPEAR"
SCHULZ

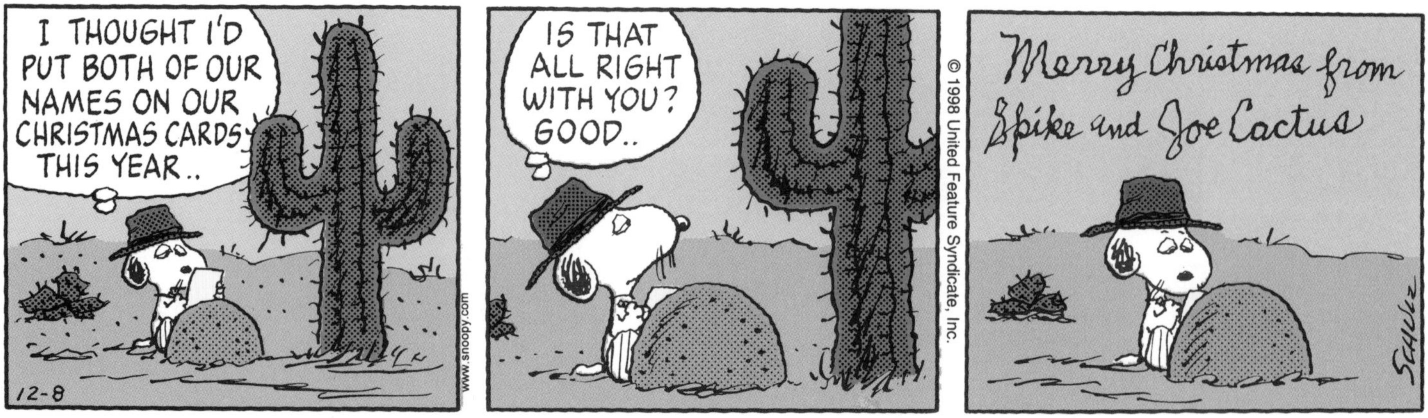
I THOUGHT I'D PUT BOTH OF OUR NAMES ON OUR CHRISTMAS CARDS THIS YEAR..
12-8
www.snoopy.com
IS THAT ALL RIGHT WITH YOU? GOOD..
© 1998 United Feature Syndicate, Inc.
Merry Christmas from Spike and Joe Cactus
SCHULZ

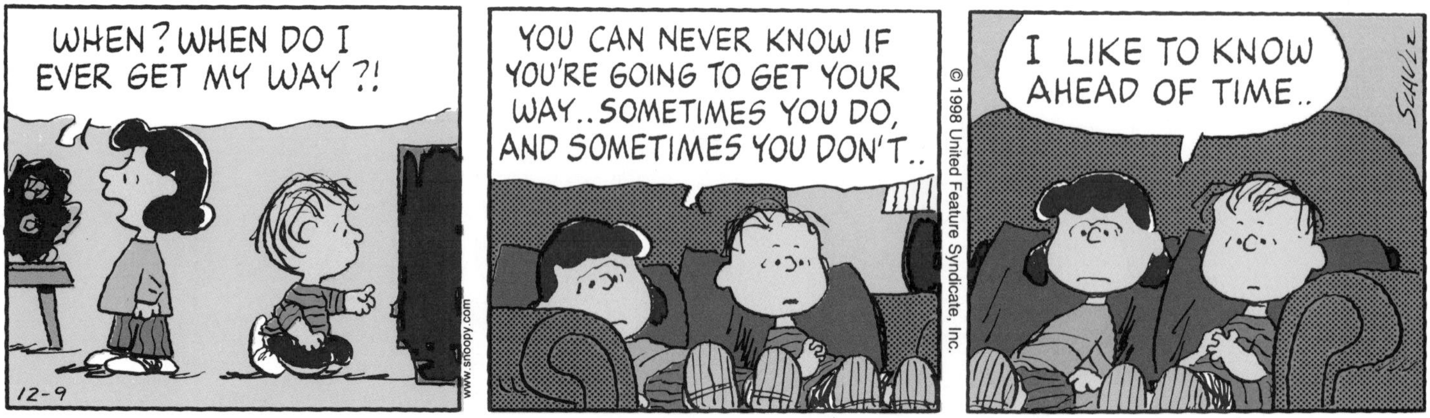
WHEN? WHEN DO I EVER GET MY WAY?!
12-9
www.snoopy.com
YOU CAN NEVER KNOW IF YOU'RE GOING TO GET YOUR WAY..SOMETIMES YOU DO, AND SOMETIMES YOU DON'T..
© 1998 United Feature Syndicate, Inc.
I LIKE TO KNOW AHEAD OF TIME..
SCHULZ

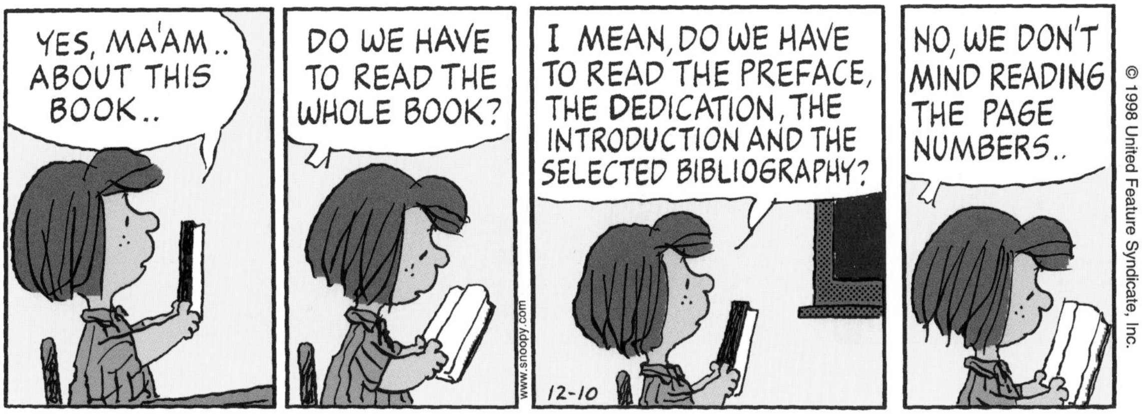
YES, MA'AM.. ABOUT THIS BOOK..
DO WE HAVE TO READ THE WHOLE BOOK?
I MEAN, DO WE HAVE TO READ THE PREFACE, THE DEDICATION, THE INTRODUCTION AND THE SELECTED BIBLIOGRAPHY?
NO, WE DON'T MIND READING THE PAGE NUMBERS..
A LITTLE SARCASM THERE, HUH, MA'AM?
www.snoopy.com
12-10
© 1998 United Feature Syndicate, Inc.
SCHULZ

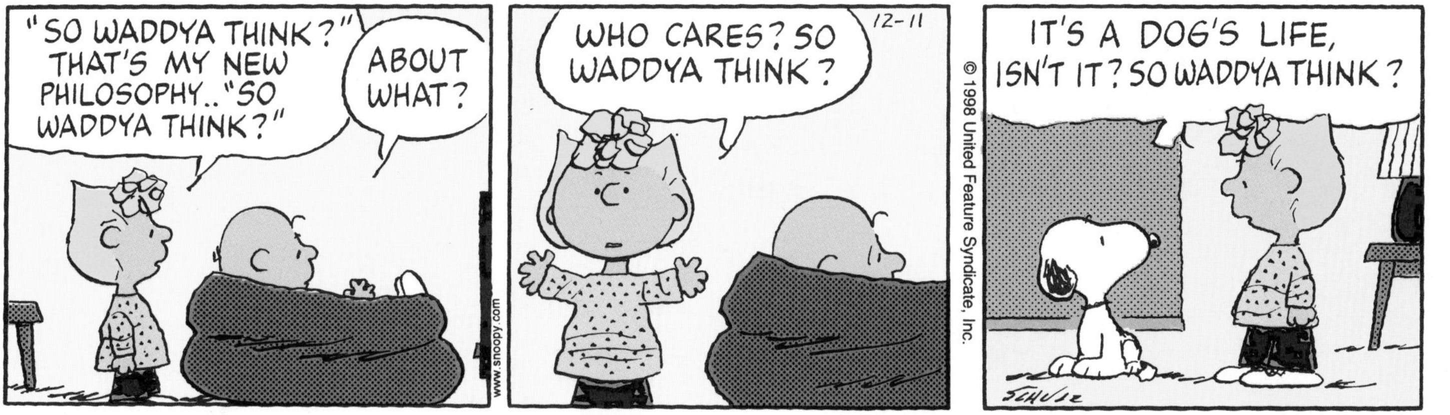
"SO WADDYA THINK?" THAT'S MY NEW PHILOSOPHY.."SO WADDYA THINK?"
ABOUT WHAT?
WHO CARES? SO WADDYA THINK?
IT'S A DOG'S LIFE, ISN'T IT? SO WADDYA THINK?
www.snoopy.com
12-11
© 1998 United Feature Syndicate, Inc.
SCHULZ

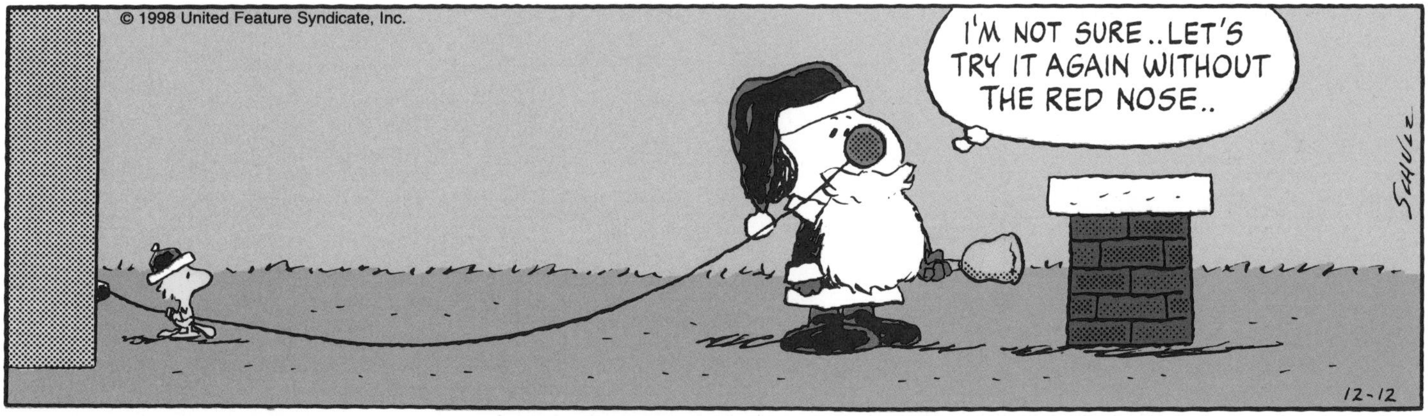
© 1998 United Feature Syndicate, Inc.
I'M NOT SURE..LET'S TRY IT AGAIN WITHOUT THE RED NOSE..
SCHULZ
12-12

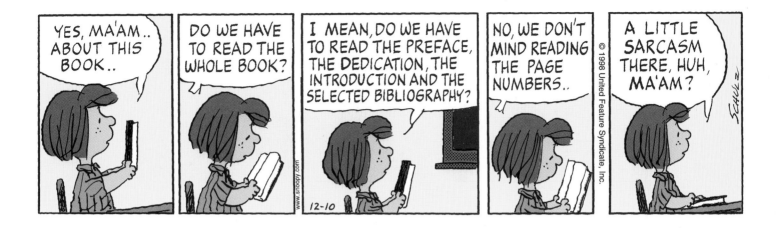

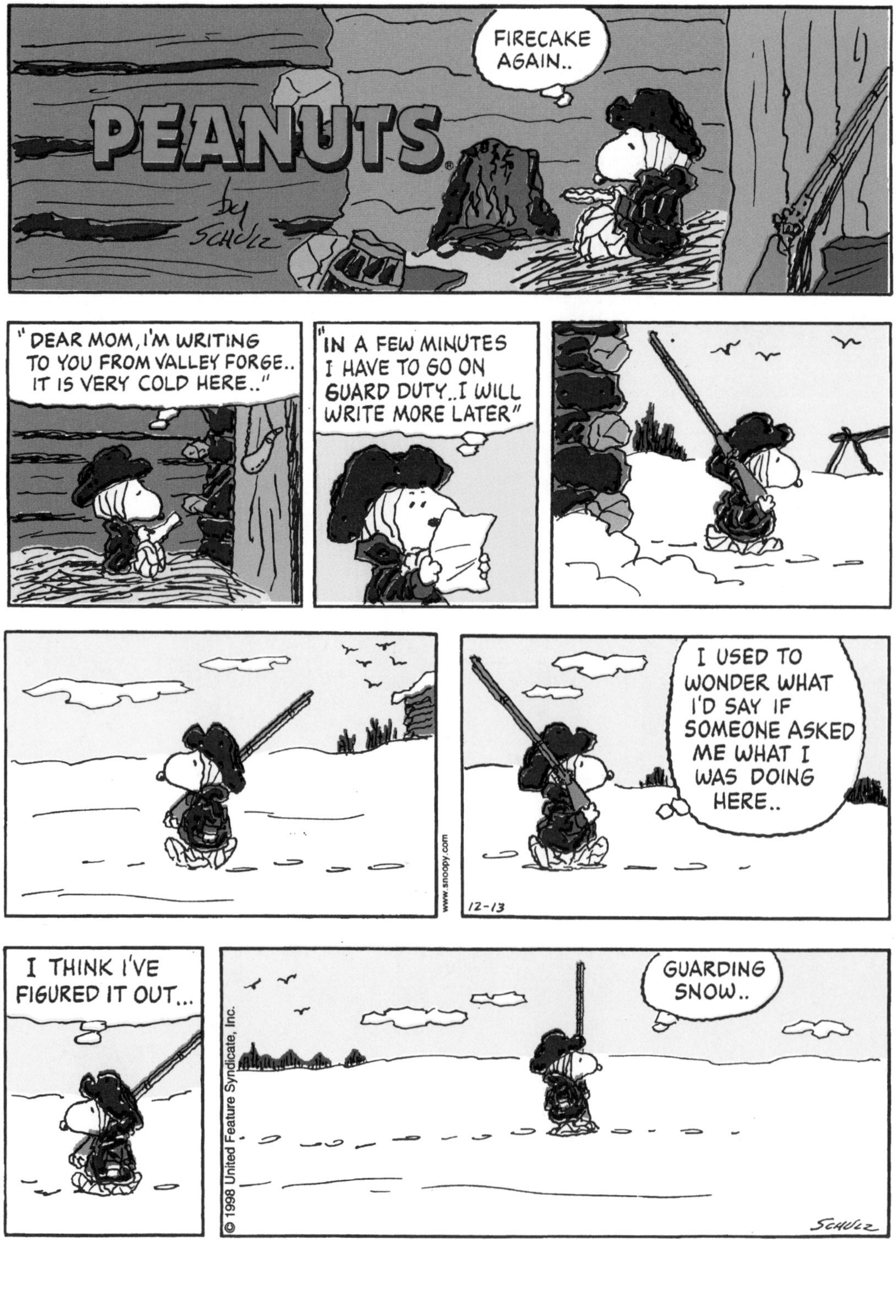
PEANUTS®
by SCHULZ
FIRECAKE AGAIN..
"DEAR MOM, I'M WRITING TO YOU FROM VALLEY FORGE.. IT IS VERY COLD HERE.."
"IN A FEW MINUTES I HAVE TO GO ON GUARD DUTY..I WILL WRITE MORE LATER"
www.snoopy.com
I USED TO WONDER WHAT I'D SAY IF SOMEONE ASKED ME WHAT I WAS DOING HERE..
12-13
I THINK I'VE FIGURED IT OUT...
© 1998 United Feature Syndicate, Inc.
GUARDING SNOW..
SCHULZ

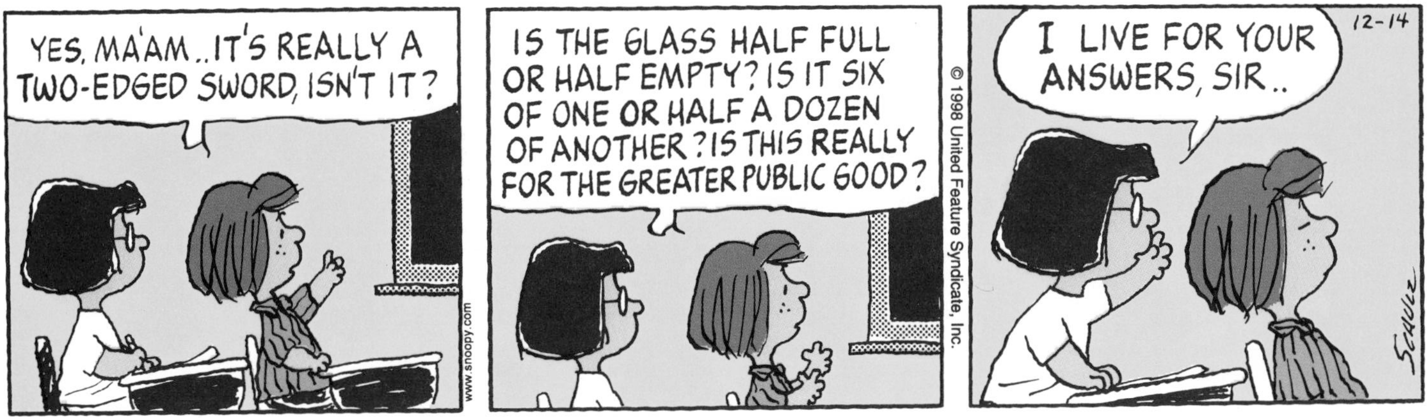
YES, MA'AM..IT'S REALLY A TWO-EDGED SWORD, ISN'T IT?
www.snoopy.com
IS THE GLASS HALF FULL OR HALF EMPTY? IS IT SIX OF ONE OR HALF A DOZEN OF ANOTHER? IS THIS REALLY FOR THE GREATER PUBLIC GOOD?
© 1998 United Feature Syndicate, Inc.
12-14
I LIVE FOR YOUR ANSWERS, SIR..
SCHULZ

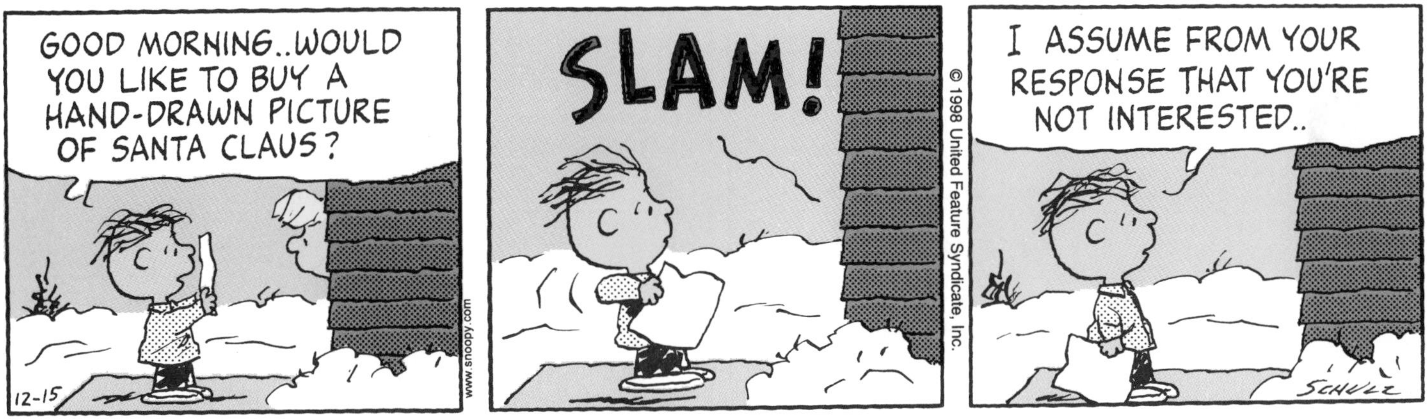
GOOD MORNING..WOULD YOU LIKE TO BUY A HAND-DRAWN PICTURE OF SANTA CLAUS?
12-15
www.snoopy.com
SLAM!
© 1998 United Feature Syndicate, Inc.
I ASSUME FROM YOUR RESPONSE THAT YOU'RE NOT INTERESTED..
SCHULZ

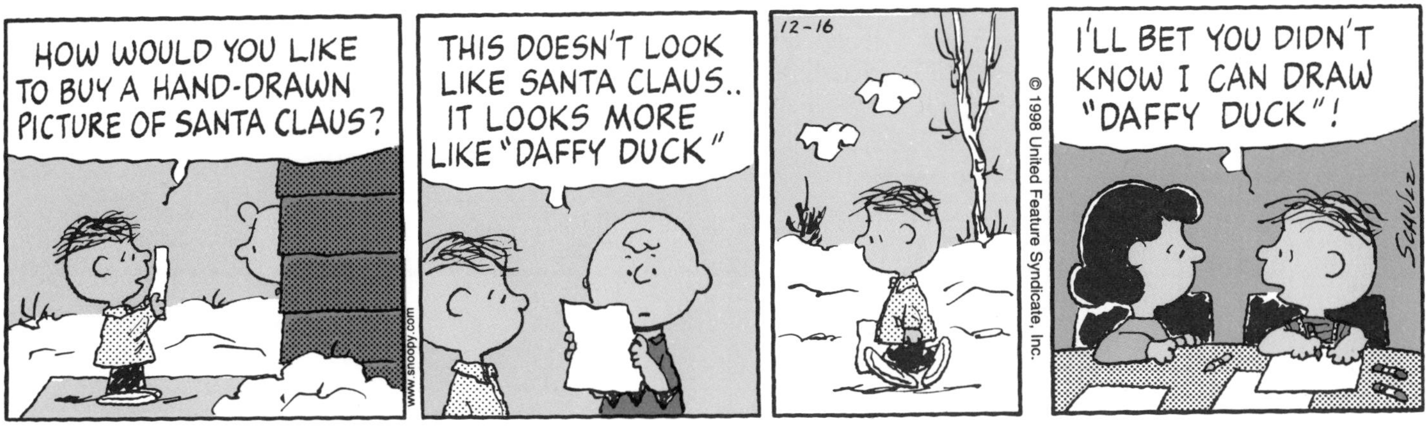
HOW WOULD YOU LIKE TO BUY A HAND-DRAWN PICTURE OF SANTA CLAUS?
www.snoopy.com
THIS DOESN'T LOOK LIKE SANTA CLAUS.. IT LOOKS MORE LIKE "DAFFY DUCK"
12-16
© 1998 United Feature Syndicate, Inc.
I'LL BET YOU DIDN'T KNOW I CAN DRAW "DAFFY DUCK"!
SCHULZ

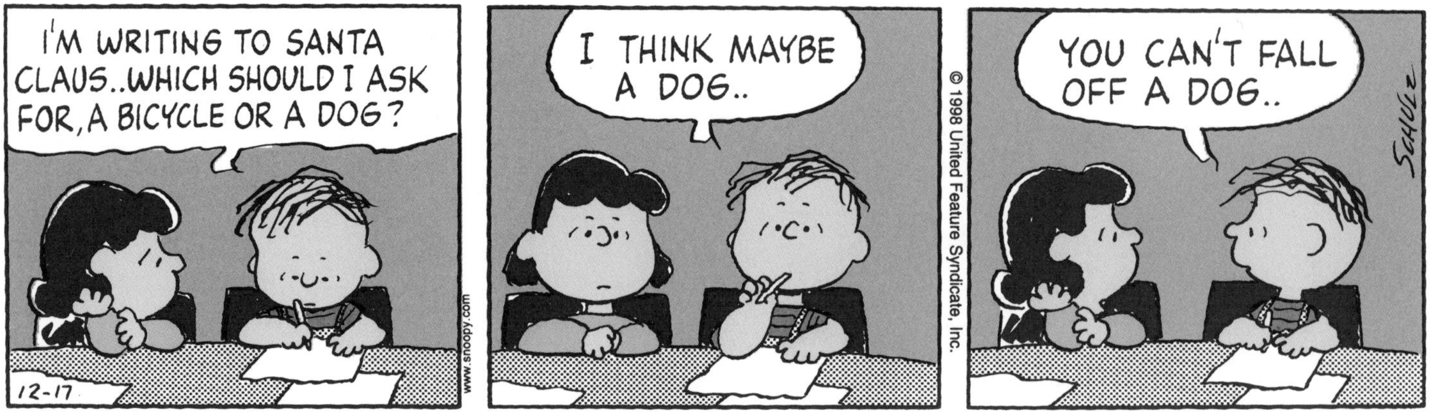
I'M WRITING TO SANTA CLAUS..WHICH SHOULD I ASK FOR, A BICYCLE OR A DOG?
I THINK MAYBE A DOG..
YOU CAN'T FALL OFF A DOG..
12-17
www.snoopy.com
© 1998 United Feature Syndicate, Inc.
SCHULZ

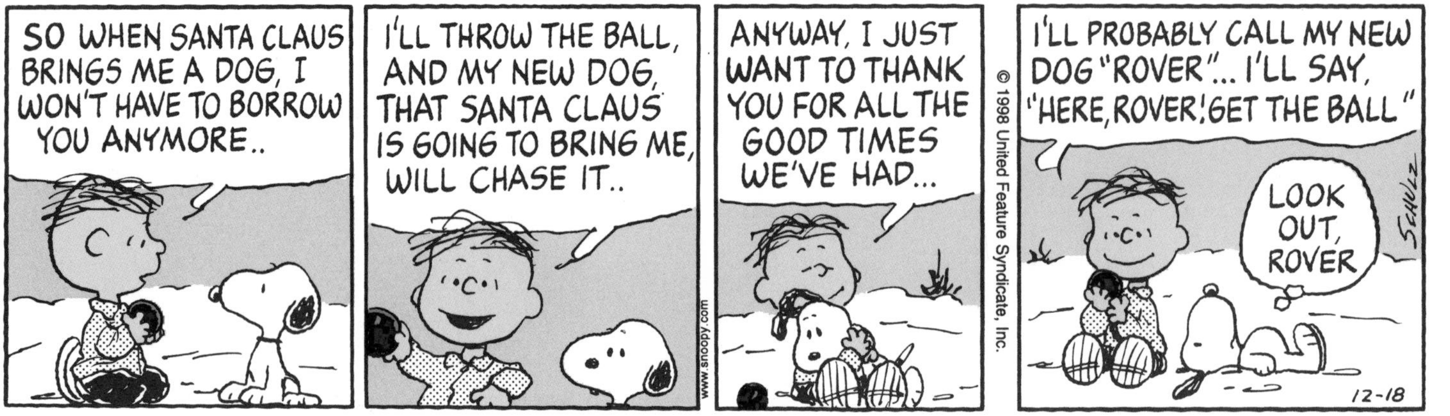
SO WHEN SANTA CLAUS BRINGS ME A DOG, I WON'T HAVE TO BORROW YOU ANYMORE..
I'LL THROW THE BALL, AND MY NEW DOG, THAT SANTA CLAUS IS GOING TO BRING ME, WILL CHASE IT..
ANYWAY, I JUST WANT TO THANK YOU FOR ALL THE GOOD TIMES WE'VE HAD...
I'LL PROBABLY CALL MY NEW DOG "ROVER"... I'LL SAY, "HERE, ROVER! GET THE BALL"
LOOK OUT, ROVER
12-18
www.snoopy.com
© 1998 United Feature Syndicate, Inc.
SCHULZ

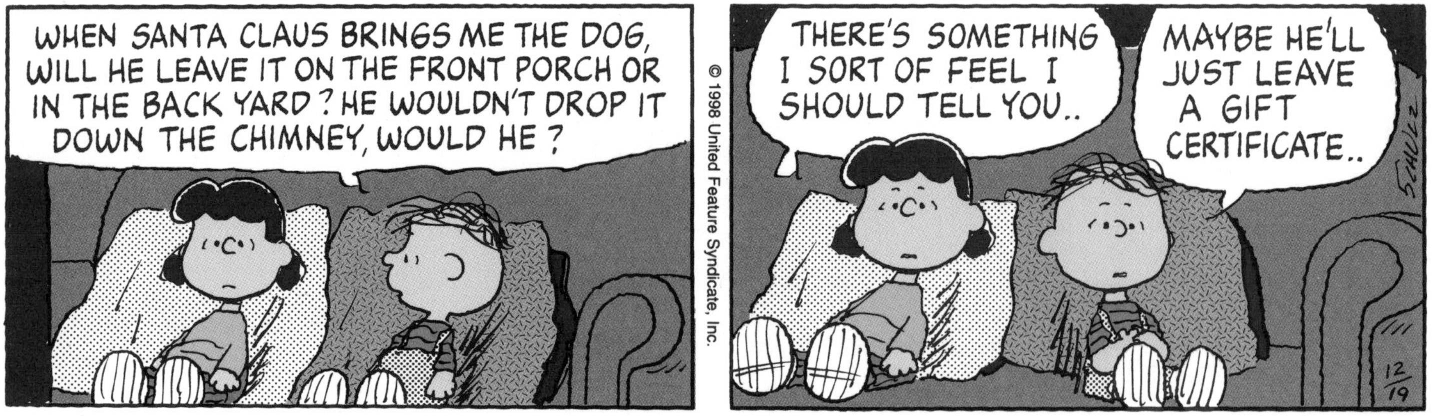
WHEN SANTA CLAUS BRINGS ME THE DOG, WILL HE LEAVE IT ON THE FRONT PORCH OR IN THE BACK YARD? HE WOULDN'T DROP IT DOWN THE CHIMNEY, WOULD HE?
THERE'S SOMETHING I SORT OF FEEL I SHOULD TELL YOU..
MAYBE HE'LL JUST LEAVE A GIFT CERTIFICATE..
12/19
© 1998 United Feature Syndicate, Inc.
SCHULZ

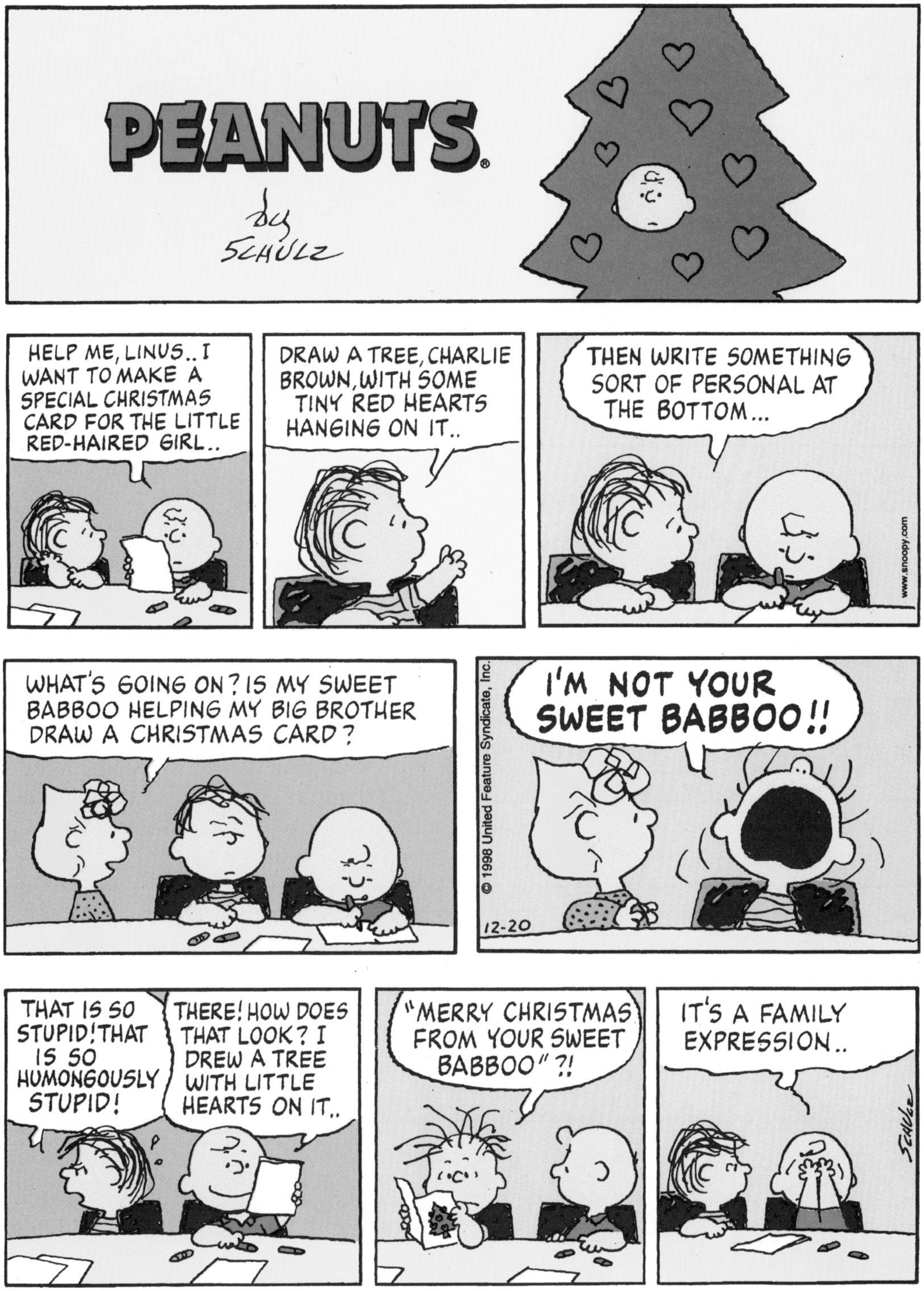
PEANUTS
by SCHULZ
HELP ME, LINUS.. I WANT TO MAKE A SPECIAL CHRISTMAS CARD FOR THE LITTLE RED-HAIRED GIRL..
DRAW A TREE, CHARLIE BROWN, WITH SOME TINY RED HEARTS HANGING ON IT..
THEN WRITE SOMETHING SORT OF PERSONAL AT THE BOTTOM...
www.snoopy.com
WHAT'S GOING ON? IS MY SWEET BABBOO HELPING MY BIG BROTHER DRAW A CHRISTMAS CARD?
© 1998 United Feature Syndicate, Inc.
I'M NOT YOUR SWEET BABBOO!!
12-20
THAT IS SO STUPID! THAT IS SO HUMONGOUSLY STUPID!
THERE! HOW DOES THAT LOOK? I DREW A TREE WITH LITTLE HEARTS ON IT..
"MERRY CHRISTMAS FROM YOUR SWEET BABBOO"?!
IT'S A FAMILY EXPRESSION..
SCHULZ

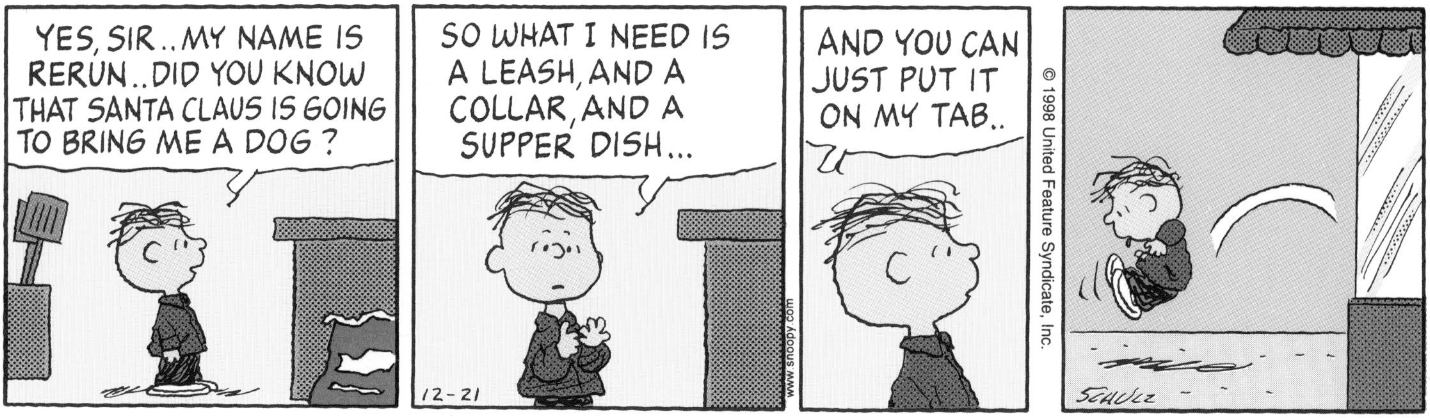
YES, SIR..MY NAME IS RERUN..DID YOU KNOW THAT SANTA CLAUS IS GOING TO BRING ME A DOG?
SO WHAT I NEED IS A LEASH, AND A COLLAR, AND A SUPPER DISH...
12-21
www.snoopy.com
AND YOU CAN JUST PUT IT ON MY TAB..
© 1998 United Feature Syndicate, Inc.
SCHULZ

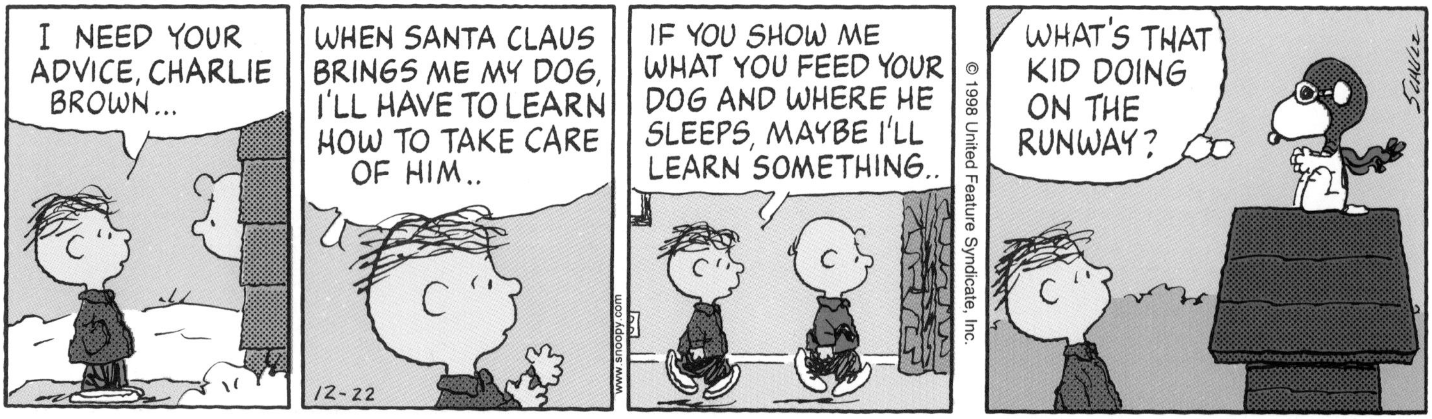
I NEED YOUR ADVICE, CHARLIE BROWN...
WHEN SANTA CLAUS BRINGS ME MY DOG, I'LL HAVE TO LEARN HOW TO TAKE CARE OF HIM..
12-22
www.snoopy.com
IF YOU SHOW ME WHAT YOU FEED YOUR DOG AND WHERE HE SLEEPS, MAYBE I'LL LEARN SOMETHING..
© 1998 United Feature Syndicate, Inc.
WHAT'S THAT KID DOING ON THE RUNWAY?
SCHULZ

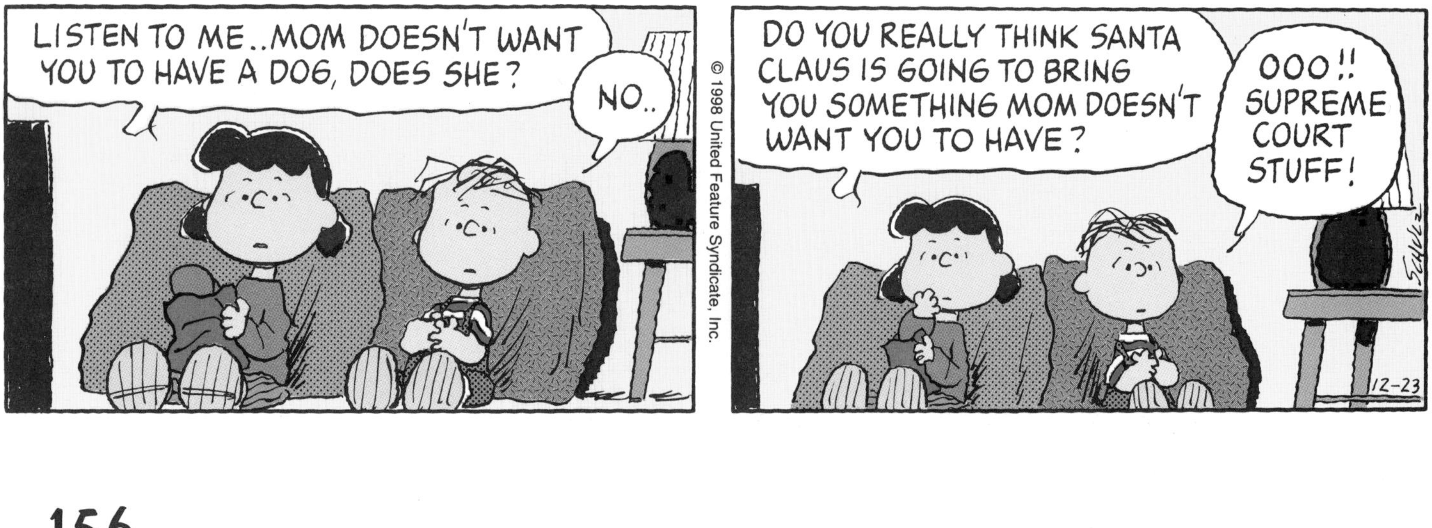
LISTEN TO ME..MOM DOESN'T WANT YOU TO HAVE A DOG, DOES SHE?
NO..
© 1998 United Feature Syndicate, Inc.
DO YOU REALLY THINK SANTA CLAUS IS GOING TO BRING YOU SOMETHING MOM DOESN'T WANT YOU TO HAVE?
OOO!! SUPREME COURT STUFF!
SCHULZ
12-23

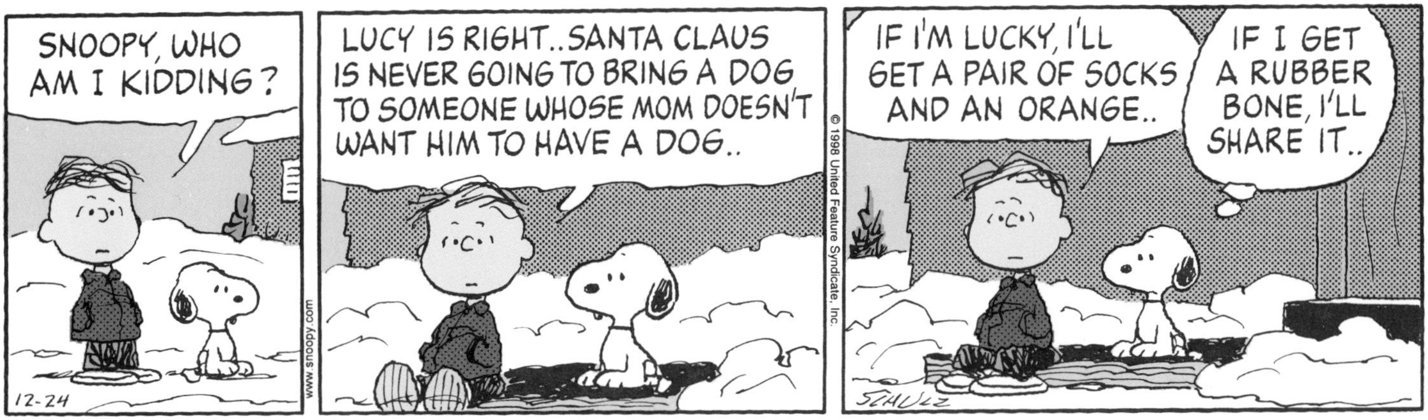
SNOOPY, WHO AM I KIDDING?
LUCY IS RIGHT..SANTA CLAUS IS NEVER GOING TO BRING A DOG TO SOMEONE WHOSE MOM DOESN'T WANT HIM TO HAVE A DOG..
IF I'M LUCKY, I'LL GET A PAIR OF SOCKS AND AN ORANGE..
IF I GET A RUBBER BONE, I'LL SHARE IT..
12-24
www.snoopy.com
© 1998 United Feature Syndicate, Inc.
SCHULZ

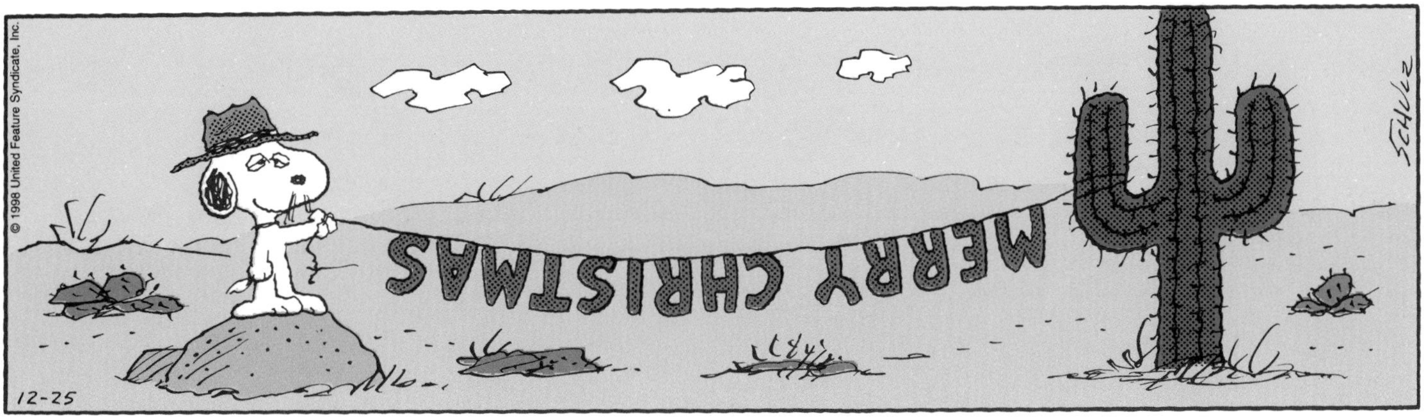
MERRY CHRISTMAS
12-25
© 1998 United Feature Syndicate, Inc.
SCHULZ

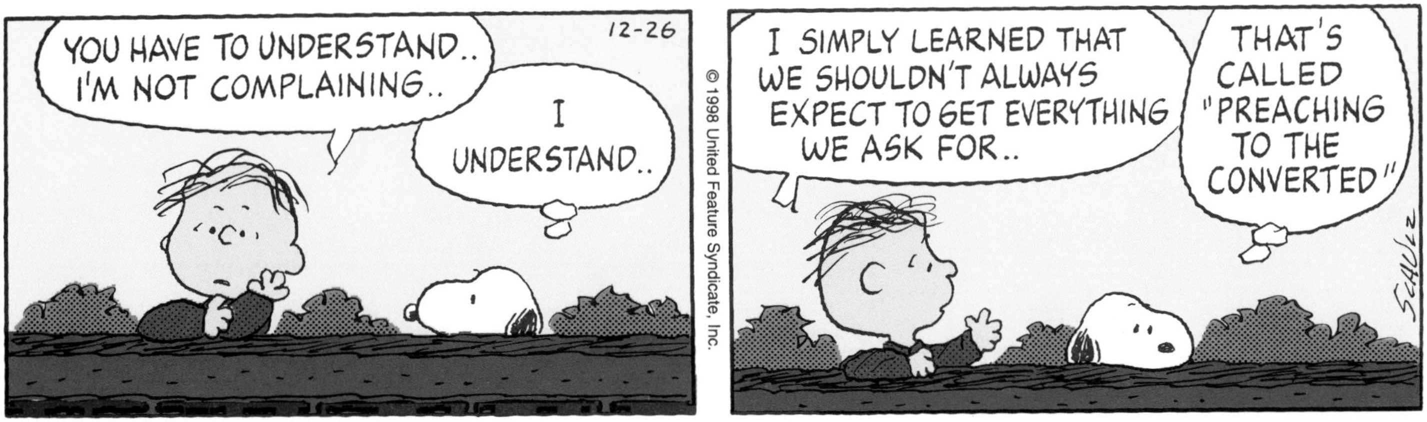
12-26
YOU HAVE TO UNDERSTAND.. I'M NOT COMPLAINING..
I UNDERSTAND..
I SIMPLY LEARNED THAT WE SHOULDN'T ALWAYS EXPECT TO GET EVERYTHING WE ASK FOR..
THAT'S CALLED "PREACHING TO THE CONVERTED"
© 1998 United Feature Syndicate, Inc.
SCHULZ

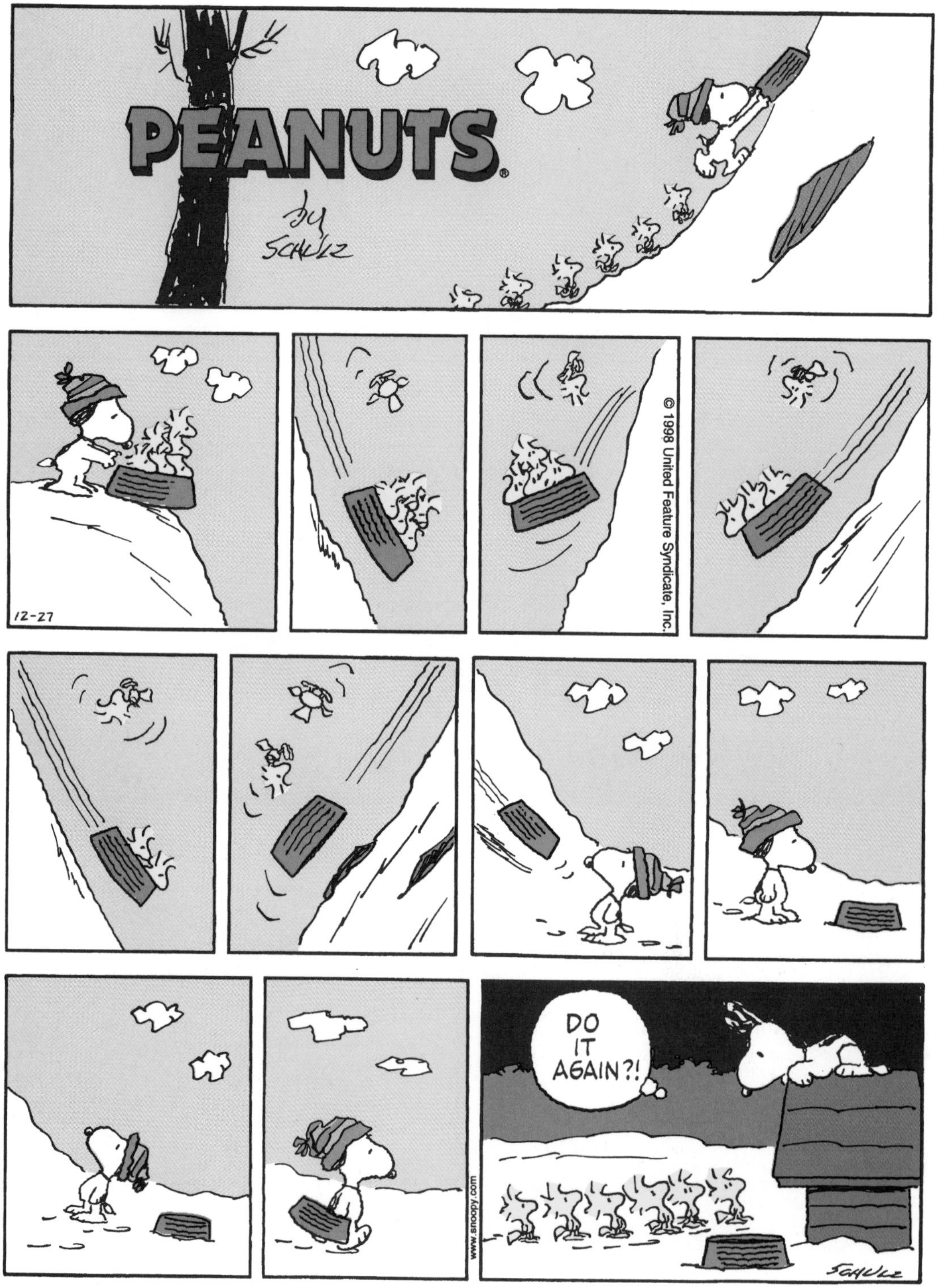
PEANUTS®
by SCHULZ
12-27
© 1998 United Feature Syndicate, Inc.
www.snoopy.com
DO IT AGAIN?!
SCHULZ

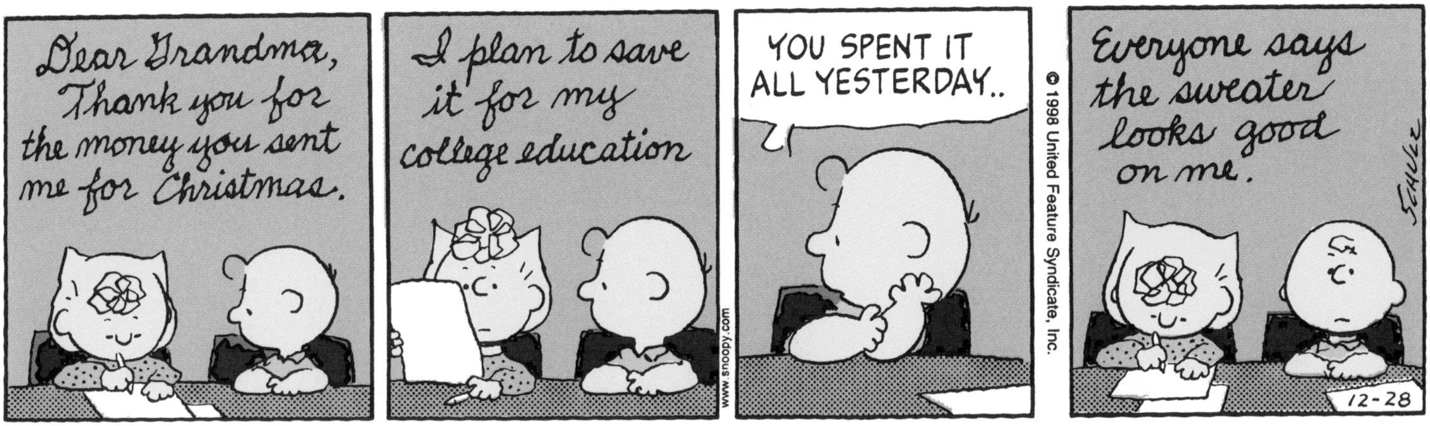
Dear Grandma, Thank you for the money you sent me for Christmas.
I plan to save it for my college education
YOU SPENT IT ALL YESTERDAY..
Everyone says the sweater looks good on me.
© 1998 United Feature Syndicate, Inc.
www.snoopy.com
12-28

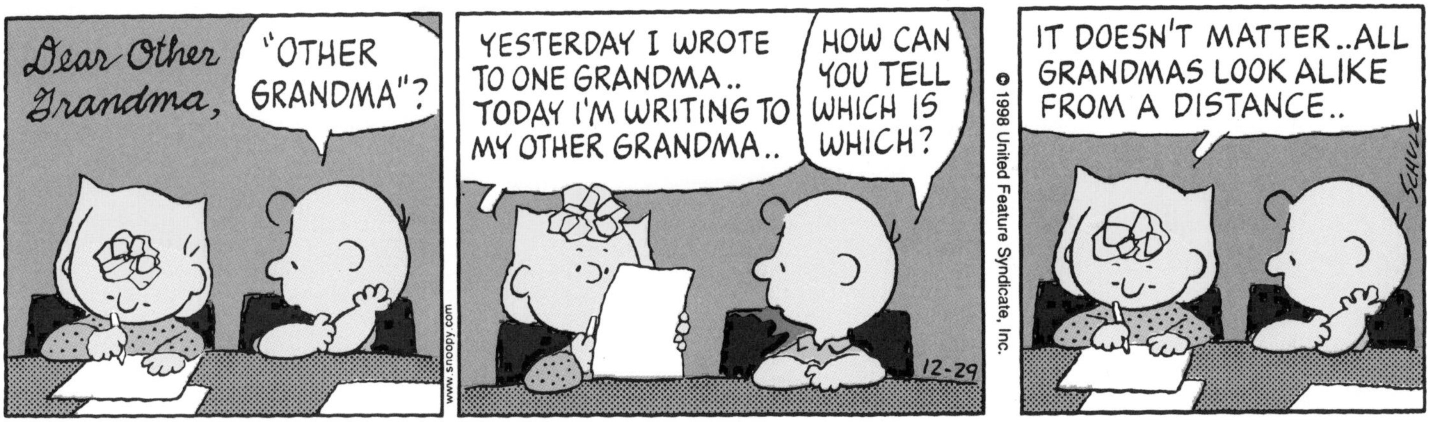
Dear Other Grandma,
"OTHER GRANDMA"?
YESTERDAY I WROTE TO ONE GRANDMA.. TODAY I'M WRITING TO MY OTHER GRANDMA..
HOW CAN YOU TELL WHICH IS WHICH?
IT DOESN'T MATTER..ALL GRANDMAS LOOK ALIKE FROM A DISTANCE..
© 1998 United Feature Syndicate, Inc.
www.snoopy.com
12-29

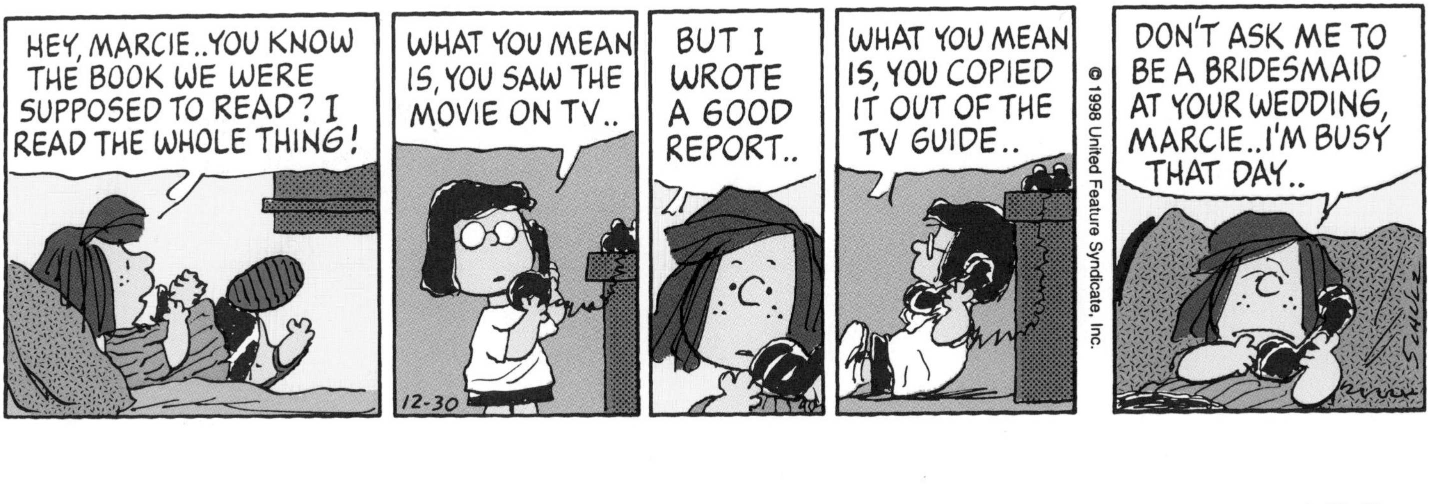
HEY, MARCIE..YOU KNOW THE BOOK WE WERE SUPPOSED TO READ? I READ THE WHOLE THING!
WHAT YOU MEAN IS, YOU SAW THE MOVIE ON TV..
BUT I WROTE A GOOD REPORT..
WHAT YOU MEAN IS, YOU COPIED IT OUT OF THE TV GUIDE..
DON'T ASK ME TO BE A BRIDESMAID AT YOUR WEDDING, MARCIE..I'M BUSY THAT DAY..
© 1998 United Feature Syndicate, Inc.
12-30

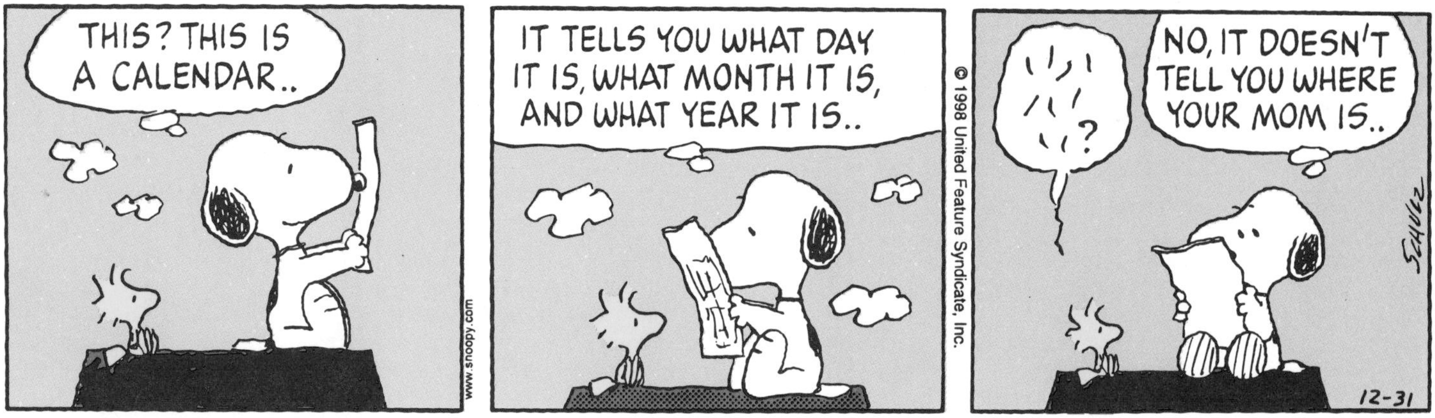
THIS? THIS IS A CALENDAR..
www.snoopy.com
IT TELLS YOU WHAT DAY IT IS, WHAT MONTH IT IS, AND WHAT YEAR IT IS..
© 1998 United Feature Syndicate, Inc.
?
NO, IT DOESN'T TELL YOU WHERE YOUR MOM IS..
SCHULZ
12-31

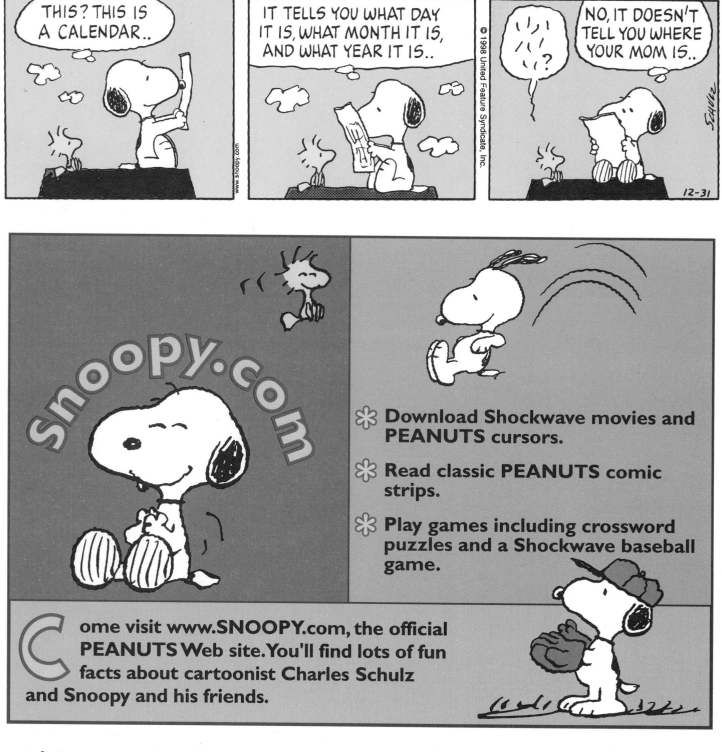